FRAMED!

Bad Guy Turns Good Guy

Thank You! And, may you Always Shine Brightly!
Talbert Jennings

Talbert Jennings

NEWMAN SPRINGS PUBLISHING
320 Broad Street
Red Bank, NJ 07701

First originally published by Newman Springs Publishing 2018

ISBN 978-1-64096-392-4 (Paperback)
ISBN 978-1-64096-393-1 (Digital)

Printed in the United States of America

TO MY GOOD FRIEND THE Honorable Carl B. Stokes. But not for being the first black to hold elective offices in all three branches of government—the legislative, administrative, and judicial during his long, distinguished, and brilliant career of public service for which he has received ample accolades. It is, however, dedicated to him for his "fighting spirit," and for always being a "man" in holding firm to his convictions.

To reference cases cited in the book, see Index on page 431 of the book.

Prologue

THE AUTHOR WISHES TO STATE at the outset that the dialogue in the book is not construed to be verbatim. But was only used in that manner to be semblable to the setting of actual events that, in fact, did take place; and the characters involved used such dialogue that I recall, in essence, to express themselves during those events that actually happened.

Part I

The Truth Shall Set You Free

Chapter 1

I T WAS AN UNUSUALLY BEAUTIFUL and mild prespring Sunday morning on March 16, 1980, when I arrived at the Southgate shopping center to open our store. I never realized at that time that this day was going to be the beginning of a new nightmare in my life.

Southgate was located in Maple Heights, Ohio, an eastern Cleveland suburb. The shop I was entering was a small boutique called Zodiac World that specialized in selling zodiac giftware, books dealing with astrology, and other occult subjects such as mind reading, palmistry, numerology, tarot, extraterrestrialism, etc.

As I placed my key in the door, I was mindful as usual that I had forty-five seconds to reach the rear of the showroom and turn off the burglar alarm system before it would become activated. Having done that, I turned on the store lights in the showroom and also in the rear of the store that was used as an office, study room, and storage area.

Almost instantly, a very faint aroma of smoke permeated my nostrils. I became immediately concerned and made a thorough search of the shop for any indication of fire. The search proved negative. My concern now at rest, I gathered up Saturday's sales slips, sat down at my desk, and started adding them up. It was about 10:15 a.m., which left me more than ample time to do my paperwork and clean up the shop before opening for business at 12:30 p.m.

As I busied myself with these tasks, the time went by quickly. Still, that puzzling aroma of smoke persisted, although nothing seemed amiss in the store itself. This caused me to ascribe the source of the odor as coming from some condition elsewhere.

Shortly before noon, I discovered that there was no instant coffee left. Delores O'Bryant, my associate, had held her astrology class as usual on Saturday afternoon in the rear study area of the store. She had evidently served herself and her students the last of the coffee.

I locked the shop up and hurried down to the K-Mart store that was located several stores from Zodiac World. There I purchased an eight-ounce jar of Taster's Choice instant coffee. K-Mart, a discount store, opened at 11:00 a.m., on Sunday, and already at noon, it was teeming with customers. Some of the customers lined the checkout counters.

Having only the one item, I produced the exact change for the coffee and got permission from a few customers ahead of me to pass through the line ahead of them, explaining that I had a store to open at twelve thirty. Showing the cashier the price on the coffee, I placed the exact change on the counter and hurried out of the store without waiting for a receipt.

It was a few minutes after twelve when I arrived back at the shop. Placing the coffee on the front counter, I gathered up my window-washing material and went back outside to take advantage of the nice weather to give the show windows a much-needed cleaning before opening the shop for business.

I was pleased as any merchant would be to notice the parking lots beginning to fill with potential customers. With its 150 stores, Southgate was reputed to be one of the world's largest strip shopping centers.

Next door to the right of our shop was an empty boarded-up store in the process of being remodeled for a new bedding shop, due to open in the very near future. The store had previously been a women's apparel shop called Calvins that had gone out of business about the same time that we opened Zodiac World in April of 1979. Now, the prospect of a new store opening next door to us was a propitious sign that we could expect to draw trade from some of their customers brought into the shopping center. Because Zodiac World, being a small store with a very limited advertising budget, depended heavily on the customers that traded at the larger stores.

Shortly before the twelve thirty opening time, the beginning of the incubus that would plague me for the next two years occurred. As I stood outside wiping the windows off, my eyes suddenly noticed swirls of dark smoke emanating from cracks at the edges of the plywood that boarded up the front of the empty store.

"Holy shit!" I exclaimed to myself. "This place must be on fire!"

I rushed into our store to call the fire department. There was a telephone on the wall at the front of the store behind the cash register. While reaching for it, I noticed smoke seeping over the door that led to the rear of the store. Without any more hesitation, I rushed to the rear of the showroom and pushed open the partially closed door. A sudden gust of dark smoke followed almost instantly by heat met me flush in the face.

The rear room was thick with the acrid smoke. To the right of the door, I observed flames burning through the wall near the ceiling that separated our store from the empty store next door. There were also some flames on the floor where some paper had apparently caught fire.

Instinctively, I groped for the fire extinguisher that was on the wall about a foot from the door. Seizing the fire extinguisher, I got off a couple of quick shots directed at the flames before being overcome by the thick pungent smoke that smarted my eyes and suffocated my nostrils. Quickly, I withdrew outside the store. Gulping for air, I set the fire extinguisher on the sidewalk.

Spectators had begun to gather and gape at the now extremely heavy smoke coming out of the empty store. The airtight front door and windows of our store did not emit the smoke that was now circulating from the rear office area into the showroom.

There was a pay telephone outside near the empty store where I intended to call the fire department. But before I could call, I noticed a uniformed officer, and I assumed him to be one of the Southgate security guards. He was standing in front of the empty store, talking on his portable radio.

"Get some equipment at Southgate right away! There's an empty store on fire on the Libby Road side," he was saying.

When the officer finished his conversation, I said, "There's fire in my store too."

The officer peered momentarily through the window of Zodiac World before shouting to the on lookers, "Any of you people with cars parked in the lot in front of these stores that are on fire should move them immediately to the adjacent lots so you won't obstruct the fire equipment that'll be coming in here."

My 1978 Chrysler Newport was parked in the lot several feet away. I drove it into the adjacent lot and parked it in a position where I could observe our store. Within a few minutes, the first Maple Heights fire truck arrived from its station located less than a half mile away. Immediately, the firemen set about getting out their hoses in preparation to fight the blaze.

Excitement was beginning to mount as spectators rushed forth from all directions to get as close to the fire scene as possible. Several police cars arrived. Officers immediately took steps to control traffic and the huge crowd. Several minutes had now ensued since the first fire truck arrived and smoke was making its way through the roofs of the stores.

Yet no water was being discharged from the fire hoses. A second Maple Heights fire truck arrived, and several more minutes elapsed before the firemen finally had water in sufficient force spouting from their hoses. In the meantime, flames and smoke were licking upward through the roofs. A gut feeling that somehow this fire might resurrect gray areas in my past that I would prefer be left buried in limbo.

Having been trained as a legal investigator, I realized that a fire of this magnitude would be thoroughly investigated by the fire authorities as well as by our insurance company and any other insurance companies that might become involved as a result of the fire. This greatly bothered me as I continued to sink into an even deeper mood of depression.

Suddenly, I became conscious of the fact that I just couldn't sit here idly doing nothing. I felt the urge to take a drink, although I had been on the wagon for fifteen months because of a drinking problem that had gotten out of hand, I considered for a moment or two my responsibility as a member of Alcoholic Anonymous; but still, the urge for a drink blanked out all thoughts of adhering to any additional effort of maintaining my sobriety. I needed a drink! And I needed it now!

There was a lounge bar called a Touch of Glass located in the shopping center only a short distance away. I would drive there. But first, let me call home and break the bad news to my wife. I drove to a pay telephone near the bar. When I tried to call my wife, there was no answer. She was probably attending one o'clock mass, as was her wont on Sunday afternoons. My son, Leonard, a sixteen-year-old, was not home either.

Next, I tried calling Delores O'Bryant as I observed that the stores were forming billowing dark clouds and orange heated flames that shot high into the atmosphere.

It was quite evident that the firemen were fighting a losing battle in gaining quick control over the fire. As other fire trucks arrived from Maple Heights and other eastern suburbs, the fire had spread to Jo Ann Fabrics, a store on the other side of Zodiac World. It was not long thereafter when the roofs suddenly collapsed while fireman standing high above the ground on ladders directed water on the fire and on other stores nearby to prevent further spreading of the fire.

While observing this calamitous spectacle, a great feeling of depression and despondency seemingly overwhelmed me as I recollected all the planning and the work that we had put into the store, which had only been in business one year. It was such a beautiful store with its colorful wall murals of enlarged color photos taken of the earth, moon, and stars by astronauts in American spacecrafts. There were murals of billowy white clouds that blended in harmoniously with the planets and stars that gave the shop a unique motif of celestial grace and beauty. This first Zodiac World shop was the model and showcase to launch our dreams and plans to sell franchises all across the nation. That is why we made this particular store so beautiful. When I say we, I include my wife and her godchild who had formed a corporation in the furtherance of our ambitions.

The thing that troubled me most though was a deep-down feeling this would be a great disappointment to Delores personally because she and I were in the process of negotiating the sale of Zodiac World to her as the first franchise of the corporation. Her line was busy, so I gave up temporarily of trying to reach anyone in favor of going into the Touch of Glass for that much-needed drink. It was a little after one o'clock. The fire had been in progress about forty-five minutes.

Inside the bar, I found only a few people. Taking a seat on one of the vacant stools. I was almost immediately approached by the bartender. "What'll it be, sir?" he asked.

"Double vodka and grapefruit juice," was my anxious reply.

I downed my first drink almost instantly. The bartender seemed surprised when I summoned him back for a refill no sooner than he had turned his back to walk away.

"Gee! That was real fast!" he exclaimed.

"Well I'm damn well upset since one of those stores out there burning belongs to me."

"You don't say!" he ejaculated, then added, "Which one is your store? I saw some of the fire before opening up. It was burning like hell out there when I arrived at work today."

"Zodiac World, the little store between Jo Ann Fabrics and the empty store where Calvins used to be."

"Oh yeah. I've seen your store. It's the astrology shop, right?"

"That's right," I said while sipping at my drink.

The bartender's youthful face reflected genuine sympathy as he addressed a couple seated a few stools down the bar from me. "Did you hear that? This gentleman's shop is one of the stores on fire out there."

"My! We're sorry to hear that," the young lady said.

"Yes indeed! That is too bad!" her companion added as he set his glass on the bar.

"Got any idea what caused the fire?" the bartender asked.

"Not really," I replied. "I first noticed smoke coming out through the boarded-up front of the empty store. Shortly afterwards I discovered fire in my place. You see, I was outside washing my windows when it happened."

I sat at the bar long enough to consume another drink before paying my tab and leaving. Outside, huge spirals of smoke still filled the sky as a TV-5 helicopter circled the perimeter of the shopping center, presumably taking pictures for the evening newscast.

I decided to once again try to reach Delores. Driving to one of the parking lots facing the stores on fire, I got out and dialed Delores at a pay telephone. This time I got her.

"Hello, Delores," I returned her greeting eagerly. "Got some bad news. The shop's on fire." I said almost in one breath.

"Come on! You're kidding me," she replied.

"No way! I'm for real! The store is just about completely wiped out along with Jo Ann Fabrics and the empty store next door. I think the fire started in the empty store."

"Oh my God! This is awful!" she exclaimed. "Can't believe it, Bert!"

"Well, it's burning like hell! The whole goddamned place is seething with excitement. It's just burning, burning, burning!" I reiterated, almost hysterically as the full realization of my loss descended once again over me while I watched the firemen vainly trying to bring the conflagration under control.

"Look, Bert, where are you going to be in the next hour or so? I'm coming out there," Delores said.

"I'll be around here by the store someplace, Delores, because I'll want to talk to the police and firemen when they get this thing under control."

"All right. I'll try to find you, Bert. Good-bye," she concluded, hanging up abruptly.

I knew she was excited and upset just as I was. We both had a lot to lose because of the fire.

The odor of smoke was on my sweater, and I was becoming more conscious of it. My almost new leather trench coat that I wore that morning was hanging in the shop—probably destroyed by now. *That's over two hundred bucks down the drain*, I thought. And it was at that moment that I decided to take a quick ride home to change into something else. It would only take me about fifteen minutes to drive to my home in Shaker Heights, another eastern Cleveland suburb about seven miles from the shopping center.

When I arrived home, I was greeted by my son, Leonard, who informed me that his mother had not arrived home from mass.

I quickly explained to him about the fire before going upstairs to take off my sweater and don a sport coat. I could sure use another drink, but there wasn't a drop in the house. When I stopped drinking, I had ceased to keep any liquor on hand. Part of my drinking problem was fighting the temptation to drink when something went wrong. Even a family dispute could trigger my urge to take a drink, and I never stopped at one drink once I got going on the stuff. No, one drink was always too little and a thousand not enough as I kept up the battle with the bottle one day into the next, never really getting dead drunk but simply floating on one mellow high day in and day out.

What the hell! There was a neighborhood bar called the Casa Blanca a few blocks away. I decided to stop in there for a drink before returning to the shopping center. I used to be a steady customer there before I went on the wagon. Most of the regular customers there knew me as Big Fun because of my jovial mood during my drinking sprees. But today, Big Fun was not in a jovial mood, and those that knew me could sense that something was wrong.

Everyone in the bar appeared sympathetic when I told about the fire. Several of the bar's patrons wanted to buy me consoling drinks. And I managed to down a couple of vodkas in grapefruit juice before moving on. The vodka acted as a tranquilizer. It also buoyed up my spirits, temporarily chasing away my depression.

I drove down Lee Road to South Miles and headed back to the shopping center. When I stopped for a traffic light a few miles from Southgate, I could see great clouds of smoke still hovering over the shopping center. In a few minutes, I was parked back in the same lot I had been in before. I stared at the ruins that had once been our beautiful store. My spirits, lifted somewhat by the alcohol, made me think optimistically about starting over again. We had built up a substantial following in the past year. The sensible thing to do was to get back in business as soon as possible to preserve these customers. One thing in our favor was that we were unique. No other store in the Cleveland metropolitan area could boast anywhere near the large stock of zodiac gifts and books on occult subjects that we stocked.

Only a specialty shop could carry zodiac gift items in sufficient quantities. There were twelve zodiac signs that represented the birthdays of all people born during the eminence of any given zodiac sign divided into the twelve constellations. We sold pendants, earrings, tie clasps, rings made of gold and silver—all bearing the signs of the zodiac on each item. There were a great variety of other gifts, cigarette lighters, brass ashtrays, letter openers, key chains and holders, wallets, bracelets, pocketbooks, sunglasses, coasters, candle sticks, book ends, vanity boxes, decals, plaques, stoneware and china mugs, dishes, belts, phonograph records, and many, many others all inscribed or relative to the signs of the zodiac. We also carried a complete line of fortune-telling cards, zodiac greeting cards, bio calculators, astro calculators, biorhythm kits, puzzles, games, pyramid power kits, aura pendulum kits, and an almost endless selection of books on various occult subjects. That is what Zodiac World was all about. And emblazoned on a dazzling sign displayed in the showroom was our motto: *a true birthday gift is a zodiac gift.*

It was after 3:00 p.m. The firemen had the fire pretty much under control. I waited several more minutes before deciding to approach a fireman. I identified myself to him as one of the owners of Zodiac World. The fireman took me over to a huge man dressed in firefighting garb. "This is Mr. Joe Scharfenberg, our fire prevention officer," the fireman said to me. "He'll be in charge of investigating the cause of this fire."

"How do you do, Mr. Scharfenberg. My name is Talbert Jennings. I'm one of the owners of Zodiac World."

"Yes, Mr. Jennings, we have been trying to get in touch with you. I had our fire department call your home. We had your number listed in our emergency index. Come with me. I'll introduce you to Mr. Pete Petronis, the deputy state fire marshal assisting me with this investigation," Scharfenberg said.

I followed the big clean-shaven man who dwarfed my six-foot, 170-pound frame by several inches and many more pounds. He appeared to be in his late forties or early fifties, and he took long strides as he led me to another man wearing a thin mustache who was almost about the same size as myself. He too was dressed in helmet and firefighting clothes.

Also, like myself, he was probably in his late fifties judging from his graying temples and finely lined countenance.

"Pete, this is Mr. Jennings, one of the owners of the Zodiac World store," Scharfenberg said. Turning to face me, he continued, "Mr. Jennings, this is Mr. Petronis, the deputy state fire marshal."

Petronis nodded his head in acknowledgment of the introduction, and I nodded mine in return. We did not shake hands.

"Mr. Jennings, we would like to get a statement from you, if you don't mind," Petronis said.

"Oh, I don't mind at all," I replied.

"All right then, let's go over here someplace where we can talk," Petronis said, leading the way toward a Dr. Scholl's store located several doors down from Zodiac World. The Dr. Scholl's store was open and had sustained some minor fire and smoke damage.

Inside Dr. Scholl's, Petronis took his coat and helmet off and placed them on a chair. I noticed a holstered snub-nosed revolver on his belt as he pulled out a wallet with a badge and ID card bearing his photo. Showing it to me, he commented: "This is a formality, Mr. Jennings. I have to properly identify myself to you and advise you that, as a deputy state fire marshal, I have police powers." Next, he laid a tape recorder on a table, saying, "You don't mind if we tape your statement, do you, Mr. Jennings?"

He struck me as being officially pompous in his demeanor. But I replied cooperatively, "No, I don't mind."

"Okay. Let's all just take seats here at this little table and get started," Petronis said as he turned on the tape recorder.

Petronis asked me to relate what I did from the time I arrived at Zodiac World until I first became aware of the fire, and also what I did thereafter up until the time I came in contact with Scharfenberg. This I did truthfully, with the exception of telling him about the drinks I had at the two bars. I wasn't proud of falling off the wagon, and being an alcoholic, it was not unusual for me to try to conceal my drinking from my family or from people in authority such as law enforcement officials. Besides, I thought, it wasn't any of their damn business if I had a nip or two.

The vodka I consumed couldn't be detected on my breath; and even though I was somewhat high, my level of intoxication was apparently not too obvious if they overlooked a few errors I made in calling the fire extinguisher a "fire hydrant" and stating that "I went home at about 3:00 p.m.," when in fact, I was sitting there in the presence of Scharfenberg and Petronis at that time. My sense of time was always poor after several drinks, and my memory was oftentimes inaccurate, leading me to inadvertently confuse what I might truthfully be trying to say. Yet these two fire investigators either pretended to ignore these discrepancies in my statements, or they did not want to question my sobriety because it would be illegal to take a statement from me if I were intoxicated.

The interrogation continued in essence: "Mr. Jennings, what do you keep in the backroom of the store?" Petronis inquired.

"Some of my stock, office goods, and things like that, including some spray paint and stuff left over from decorating the shop."

"Where was that stored at, you remember?"

"It was all stored between the bathroom and some shelves and racks for holding merchandise. There was some aerosol cans and some other paint, regular paint."

"Could you draw me a plan basically of what the store looked like in there?" Petronis asked. Whereby I drew a rough sketch of the rear of the store for him. He continued to question me further until it was brought out about the electrical problem I had with my calculator the night before the fire. He then asked me to draw on the sketch where the electrical outlets were located.

"Well, it was against this wall," I said, drawing a little circle where the outlet was located where I had plugged in the calculator.

"Then it was not working last night?" Petronis asked.

"No, that didn't work last night."

"Did you notice anything over in this corner? Where your electrical junction boxes are?" Petronis went on.

"There's one thing I always noticed over there, sir, and I told the sign people about it. Every time I pulled that switch for the sign, I'd always see sparks," I told him.

"Okay. This would be . . . there's a lot of boxes there . . ."

"Right."

"Would it be the smaller box?" Petronis inquired further.

"It would be the sign box, yes, sir. I told Buddy Simon, the sign people, that every time I pulled that switch for the sign, I would always see sparks."

Scharfenberg interjected. "I want to come back to something else here. You said a guard was with, a Southgate—"

"I said a guard came along when we noticed smoke coming out."

"What did he look like, the guard, the security?" Scharfenberg pressed on.

"He was a security guard for Southgate," I said a little uncertain. Because some of the Southgate security guards are off-duty Maple Heights policemen working part-time for the shopping center in their police uniforms.

"You think he called the fire department?"

"I know he did. He was right there on his radio."

"Let's go back to the guard, okay? I'm gonna come back to him because he's going to be in court personally," Scharfenberg said as he eyed me suspiciously.

I paused momentarily to ponder what he had just said about the officer going to be in court personally. *What the hell is he thinking about "court" for?* I asked myself. *Is this guy trying to make a case against me?* At that moment, I ceased to trust my interrogators, as once again, that deep-down gut feeling of a pending crisis gripped me.

Petronis broke the silence. "How much insurance did you have, sir?"

"About twenty thousand dollars, that's what we're insured for."

"When was that taken out?"

"When we first opened, last year."

"Is this insurance renewed every year?"

"I think I had a three-year policy," I said hesitantly because I wasn't quite sure.

"Well, we'll check it out," Petronis said matter-of-factly.

I caught Scharfenberg staring at me introspectively as though he were trying to decide whether I was telling them the truth. He quickly diverted his glance and held his head down thoughtfully. Taking off his helmet, he ran his hand over his bald pate a couple times with that quiet introspective look on his face. There was something about that look on his face that made me think of an inner cunningness about him that almost appeared innocent on the surface of his calm expression that was almost benign in appearance.

After getting my address and telephone number, the interrogation ended, and I was permitted to leave. As I walked out of the Dr. Scholl's store, I took another look at our store. The fire had been put out, and all that remained was the blackened fire-gutted structure. A poster with a color photo of Delores O'Bryant that was used to advertise her Saturday appearances and classes hung precariously out of the space where one of the show windows used to be. The photo was not even scorched. That's miraculous! I thought. Well, at least Delores survived the fire. The witch must have some supernatural powers, I laughed to myself. I often teasingly called her a witch, and being an extremely pleasant person, with a great sense of humor, she never seemed to resent my calling her that.

Delores was the staff astrologer on TV-5, a Cleveland channel. She also had her own radio programs that she hosted in Cleveland and Akron. Appearing at our shop on Saturdays and teaching astrology was a mutual promotional agreement that we had between us. She would promote Zodiac World, and we in turn would promote her by soliciting students and clients for her. Her presence in our store helped increase business. She had even put on her TV show in our shop, and it went over real big! We also advertised on her radio programs, and sometimes she would give us free plugs. It was soon after she had her TV program at the store that she got around to bringing up the subject of buying a franchise and taking over Zodiac World in Southgate. She was a very busy person advising her many clients, teaching astrology as a community college instructor, being a faculty member of the American Federation of Astrologers and vice president on the board of directors of the Ohio Astrological Association. If that was not enough to keep her busy, she still found time to lecture and write numerous articles for journals and periodicals.

Before going home, I decided to stop at Bill White's apartment. He and I were good friends, and he was also a close friend of my insurance agent with the Nationwide Insurance Company. It was in fact Bill who had put me in touch with the agent when I was shopping for insurance for the store. Bill only lived a couple miles from the shopping center. And I arrived at his neatly appointed apartment within a few minutes to find him home in the company of his girlfriend, Gloria. They were both surprised and shocked to hear that my store had been destroyed by the fire when I told them the facts.

"You know, Bert, there's the fire and police stations down the street. Well, I heard sirens and a hell of lot of commotion earlier this afternoon as the vehicles sped down Lee Road. But I never dreamed that a fire was at Southgate or that your store was involved," Bill said. He shook his head incredulously, adding, "Boy! That's a goddamned shame! You were just beginning to make progress with the business, and now this!"

"I just don't want to believe this, Bert," Gloria said, also shaking her head with a show of doubt.

"Well, it's true! It's over! It's gone!" I exclaimed. Noticing the fifth of gin and fifth of scotch on the cocktail table, I continued, "Don't suppose you got any vodka, Bill? Well, I'll just have some of this gin and a little tonic. Boy! Do I need this drink."

"Thought you were off the sauce for good?" Bill said with a look of surprise on his thin countenance.

"Shit, man! After what I've just been through, a shot or two is just what the doctor would order." In a few moments, I held a tall frosty glass of gin and tonic garnished with a piece of lime. "Here's to better luck!" I toasted before sipping the drink.

"To better luck!" Bill and Gloria said in unison. They were a friendly couple, both in their early fifties. Gloria was a widow, and Bill was divorced. There might be the possibility of a matrimonial match between them if Bill settled down to serious courtship. But he was infected with a roving and ogling eye for the ladies, which often kept him in hot water with Gloria, who was a pretty bedimpled, dark-brown-skinned woman on the plumpish side, but still attractive.

"Bill, why don't you give my insurance agent a call for me so we can tell him about the fire?" I suggested before adding, "He's your main man who can advise me what to do in a situation like this."

"Good idea, Bert. I'll get right on Jimmy," Bill said as he picked up his telephone and dialed. He waited a moment before speaking. "Hello, is Jimmy home? No. Well, this is Bill. Yeah, Wild Bill. Have Jimmy call me when he comes in. I got Bert Jennings here. He's one of Jimmy's clients. His store just burned down at Southgate, and he wants to get in touch with Jimmy. Good-bye now," Bill concluded, hanging up. Turning to me he said, "You heard that, Bert. Jimmy's not home right now. That was his wife I had on the phone. Jimmy will call us when he gets home."

I hung around Bill's apartment drinking, eating and talking for several hours. I called my wife and talked with her too. She could tell I was drinking and was quite disappointed with me. I even took a nap when the gin got the best of my alertness.

Shortly after midnight, Jimmy, my insurance agent, finally called. He gave me a number to call where I could report my fire claim. After that, I got up and went home.

Chapter 2

I DIDN'T HAVE A HANGOVER WHEN I awoke the next morning at six o'clock. But I did have that uneasy feeling that told me that I could use an eye-opener. I sat on the side of the bed in the guest room, thinking, *Man, you're a real first-class ass to be back in the old rut drinking around the clock. How in the hell are you going to square this with Juanita?* I knew better than to enter the master bedroom that my wife and I usually occupied when I had been drinking because it would only prompt her to go into the guest room. I had a tendency to snore loudly when I was drinking, and if I reeked of alcohol, that only disgusted my wife that much more. I cursed the fact that there was no liquor in the house. The state liquor store did not open until eleven o'clock, and the thought of waiting five hours to buy a bottle chagrined me greatly. I got up, shaved, showered, and dressed before preparing myself a quick breakfast of dry cereal, toast, instant coffee, and orange juice. I usually left home for work at the automotive warehouse about seven thirty and arrived shortly before the eight o'clock starting time. It was now only seven o'clock when I completed my breakfast.

I went to the front door for the morning newspaper and returned to the kitchen to look through it while having a second cup of black coffee. My wife came into the kitchen, displaying a concerned expression as she greeted me, "Good morning, dear. Are you all right?"

"Yeah, I'm okay. How are you this morning?" I replied with my eyes focused on the newspaper.

"I had sort of a restless night thinking about the fire and how it must have worried you," she said as she moved her buxom frame quietly about the kitchen, preparing breakfast for our son and herself.

She evidently was not going to bring up the subject of my drinking. She had joined Alanon and had learned to cope with the problems of a husband suffering from alcoholism. She therefore was not apt to nag me about the relapse I suffered because of the fire. The thing to do was to let me convince myself of the need to return to the alcoholic recovery program as soon as possible. A little patience and encouragement would work far more wonders than nagging me to stop drinking.

"There's a piece in the *Plain Dealer* about the fire," I said.

"What does it say, dear?"

"Oh, not much, just that fire damaged at Southgate Jo Ann Fabrics, Calvin's, which was vacant, and Zodiac World. Fireman were unable to estimate damage or pinpoint the source of the fire. It took forty firemen from Maple Heights and neighboring communities three hours to control flames. Cause of that blaze is under further investigation." I finished reading before commenting, "Most of the article is devoted to two other fires that took the lives of two people, which of course is more important than damage done to property only."

"Did you see the late news last night on channel 5? They had the Southgate fire on their program with lots of aerial pictures. The devastation was really awful!"

"No. I dozed off at Bill's and didn't catch the late news. I saw it all live and firsthand, so I know all about the devastation. As I told you over the phone last night, Zodiac World was completely destroyed."

"We are going to reopen the business somewhere, aren't we? We can't let this defeat our purpose. There's so much work we've put into this venture, and it still has great potential," Juanita said with determination written all over her winsome dark-brown visage.

"Yeah. We'll have to keep going somehow," I reassured her. Getting up from the table, I asked, "Is Leonard up yet? Don't let him be late for school again. It's getting to be a habit with that boy to be tardy."

"Yes, I awakened him just before I came downstairs. He's in the shower," she replied before adding, "You know he had a run-in with one of the fire officials yesterday evening."

"What was that all about?"

"He and his friend David rode out to Southgate on Leonard's moped, and Leonard wanted to take some of the gold and silver zodiac jewelry out of the broken show window so nobody would take anything. When the fire officials refused to let him do that, Leonard got into an altercation with one of the fireman, and Leonard was almost arrested. The poor boy was only trying to protect our property," she concluded defensively.

"That boy has got to try to curb his temper. The authorities can't just let anyone come along and claim a right to any property in these matters. The firemen and the police are responsible for protecting the property out there. Anyway, they are going to board the place up today. I'll run out there this evening to see how everything is."

The clock on the kitchen wall showed 7:25 a.m. I got up to leave for work. Leonard almost bumped into me as he came into the dining room just before I reached the hallway. He was headed for the kitchen.

"Hi, Dad!" he greeted me without stopping.

"Good morning, son."

"Too bad about the store, huh, Dad. David and me went out there. I tried to protect some of the stuff that was in the window, but one of those dumb, jerk-ass fireman wouldn't let me. I almost punched him out." Leonard said pugnaciously before taking a seat at the kitchen table.

He was a scrappy kid with a temper that easily flared at the slightest provocation. He had had a few run-ins with the law over traffic violations and mischief. His temper always came into play in these instances, which always gave me cause to worry that one day, he might hurt someone or get hurt himself.

"Son, you've got to learn to control that damn temper of yours. I've told you time and time again to be civil to the authorities. You're becoming too goddamned antiestablishment!" I blurted out angrily.

"Ah, Dad, go stow it!" he exclaimed. Then turning his tall well-proportioned frame toward his mother, he demanded, "Come on, Mom, let's get some food on the table."

"Wait a minute!" I cut in angrily. "What the hell did you say about 'stow it,' boy? You fuck around with me, and I'll knock the holy shit out of you!"

"Now, dear, let Leonard alone. Can't you see that he's upset? You'll be late for work, and he'll be late for school if you stand here fussing," Juanita remonstrated. "Besides," she added, "I wanted to be at school a little early today to work on my lesson plan before the children arrive for class."

Juanita had been teaching in the Cleveland school system for over twenty years, and prior to that, she had taught for several years in the Catholic parochial school system. It therefore always astounded me that with her background and experience in handling thousands of children down through the years, why was she so lax in disciplining her own son? At least she could back me up when I tried to discipline him. *Now here she is again, taking up for the smart ass*, I thought irritably. More than half the arguments in our home were about how to raise and discipline our spoiled son.

We both loved Leonard very much in our own ways, but for some reason, we weren't reaching through to him in a vital parental way to command his respect for us, his teachers, and other people in authority. I certainly had my own good reasons for wanting this kid to grow up and amount to something and to steer clear of trouble. Because when I was his age, I had started to make a complete mess out of my own life with a lifetime of regrets to pursue me. It was only after I married his mother eighteen years ago that I commenced to lead anything resembling an honest and normal life. It was therefore important to me that my kid stay out of trouble and grow up to amount to something decent.

Still ruffled, I left for work, feeling the urge for a drink to get me through this already hectic morning. I stopped at a neighborhood grocery and beverage store to purchase a pint of 42 proof vodka. This was as strong as state law would allow liquor to be sold in Ohio by beverage stores. Only the state liquor stores carried the regular brands of high-powered liquor. Although I disliked this watered-down booze, it was the best I could do until lunchtime, when I could go out and get a fifth of the 90-proof stuff. I sat in my car and downed well over half the pint before continuing on to work with a warm glow inside of me to ease the tension of my mind and body.

My coworkers teased me all day about the fire. They called me pyro—short for pyromaniac. They implied that I had gasoline in the fire extinguisher that I used to try to put out the flames, and they jokingly accused me of trying to bilk the insurance company. I pretended to take their perverted humor good-naturedly. But to the contrary, I wasn't pleased at all. It gave me reason for thought that perhaps they really believed that I may have torched my business.

On second thought, however, I concluded that they were only kidding me as I shrugged off a feeling of paranoia.

I was glad when the work day ended at 5:00 p.m. so that I could get the hell out of there and away from the ribbing they were giving me. Outside in the car was a fifth of 90-proof vodka that I had purchased during my lunch period. I sure wanted to get back into that bottle.

I drove around the corner to the next street from where I worked and parked at the curb to pour a good three fingers of vodka into a paper cup. The liquor felt hot going down without a mix. But what the hell! It felt good too. And it did the job of lifting my low spirits up to a pleasant mood.

Earlier at work, a Mr. Ward had called me. He said that he was a representative of the Alex N. Sill Adjustment Company and that he wanted to talk to me about his company representing our fire insurance claim. I agreed to meet with him at 6:00 p.m. at Maxson's, a bar, restaurant, and delicatessen located a few doors from what was left of our Zodiac World Shop.

When I arrived at Southgate about 5:30 p.m., I found the fronts of Jo Ann Fabrics, Zodiac World, and the vacant store all boarded up with plywood. The plywood door to Zodiac World was open. I peered in to see what was going on. Petronis and two other firemen were examining the debris. Scharfenberg was taking photographs.

"Just the person I want to see," Petronis said when he spotted me.

"What about?" I inquired politely.

"There's a little technicality to be taken care of, Mr. Jennings. You see, the law requires that we must have a warrant to enter your store to make our investigation after the fire has been extinguished. We can get a warrant from the court, or you may waive having us do so, thus saving us time and trouble."

"I see," I said, pausing thoughtfully. What the hell did they need a warrant for? They were already in the store investigating. Suddenly, my legal mind flashed the thought that they needed the warrant to preserve any evidence they might find to base a charge of arson against me. They wanted to be able to stand up in court and say that they legally entered and searched my premise or store. I decided to waive the warrant knowing that nothing incriminating could possibly be on the grounds. "I certainly don't wish to put you people to any unnecessary trouble. I'll be happy to sign the waiver."

"Very good, sir. I'll go over to my car and get the form."

Petronis left and came back shortly with several papers in his hand. Scharfenberg came out of the burned-out shop and greeted me in his usual calm manner. "Hello, Mr. Jennings. We have been going over these stores practically all day long trying to determine the point of origin of the fire and its cause."

I returned his greeting courteously then inquired, "Have you come up with anything specific?"

"At this time, we haven't made up our minds completely. The investigation is still open." The big man seemingly hedged on disclosing more conclusive information to me.

"Here we are, Mr. Jennings. Just sign this waiver right there near the bottom," Petronis offered.

After first perusing the document, I signed and returned it to him saying: "I would like to enter the store to see if anything is salvageable."

"I am sorry, Mr. Jennings, but no one but the investigators are permitted in there until we are done with the investigation. If anything is salvageable, we'll protect and preserve it. The fire sites will be under guard until we are done," Petronis advised. Then he offered me another legal form to read.

"What's this for?" I inquired before accepting the form.

"This is a document to permit us to examine your business bank records, Mr. Jennings," he informed me with a tight smile that stretched his thin mustache into a fine line under his nose.

I was taken back momentarily surprised. "My bank records, you say? And may I ask what purpose do you want access to my bank records for?"

"Just to assist us in our investigation," he pointed out.

"Investigating my store is one thing I can understand, but my business bank records, no. I don't understand that unless I'm some kind of suspect. But in any case, I would consult with my attorney before turning any of my business records over to anybody voluntarily," I told him with firm determination.

"Well, sir, I have subpoena powers if you don't wish to cooperate," he said in a threatening manner.

"Then use your powers, Mr. Petronis," I replied indignantly. "Because you are not going to get me to volunteer any of our records to you or anyone other than my insurance company."

"Suit yourself, Mr. Jennings," he commented.

Petronis and Scharfenberg walked several feet away from where we were all standing, and they held a sotto voce conversation.

A few minutes later, Scharfenberg returned and said, "Mr. Jennings, we located your cash register in the rubble last night. It had about fifty dollars in it. You can pick the money up at the fire station on Lee Road by signing a receipt.

"Well, thank you," I said gratefully.

"When you come to the station, ask for the captain if I'm not there. He will give you the money."

"Fine! I'll stop over at the station tomorrow about five thirty." With that, I walked to Maxson's where Mr. Ward was waiting for me out front.

"Are you Mr. Jennings?" he asked.

"Yes. And bet you're Mr. Ward."

"Yes, sir," he replied, extending his hand. As we shook hands, he went on, "I saw you over there talking to the fire investigators before you walked over here. I talked to them earlier, and they described you to me, that's how I sort of figured it was you. Well, shall we go inside and talk? Perhaps you would care to have something to eat or a libation, or perhaps both?"

"A libation sounds real good," I commented as we walked inside and took seats at a table.

Ward was a handsome, friendly, and persuasive man in his midforties. Over drinks, he convinced me that the Alex N. Sill Adjustment Company could efficiently handle the intricate negotiations of adjusting my claim with the Nationwide Insurance Company for a 10 percent fee of what they recovered for us.

I signed an agreement with the Sill company and promised to mail my insurance policy to his office the next day. We shook hands and parted in the parking lot.

En route home, I decided to stop at Pat's Lounge on Lee Road to have a nightcap. The owner, Bill Woodridge, was a good friend of mine. I used to frequent his bar almost every night before I stopped drinking fifteen months ago. But during the period of my abstention from alcohol. I only occasionally dropped by the bar for a Coke and friendly chat.

Many of the regular habitués were present. They greeted me warmly when I took a seat at the bar. Some of them seemed genuinely sincere when they expressed their sympathy over the loss of our store. One patron, Big Ray, began to tease me much as my coworkers had done.

Big Ray sauntered up to me, his huge hand wrapped around a beer glass. His enormous protruding belly seemed about ready to burst out of his jacket as it brushed against me. "Hey, Bert, how come you ain't in jail? Nigger, you done burned down those white folks' shoppin' center. and I know they's out to cream your yella ass," he said, laughing uproariously. His big belly heaving up and down and his fully round black face a mask of humor.

"Naw, Big Fun, didn't burn that place down, Ray," a patron called Don cut in. "Those white folks got tired of having a token black out there that they didn't want in the first place, so they lit a fire right under Fun's ass to send him steaming back from whence he came—the dark side of town."

"Just cause his skin's light don't make him white. The nigger's still a darkie to them white folks out there," Big Ray chimed in facetiously.

More laughter broke out. I pretended to accept all of the jocosity in good spirits.

My friend, Bill Woodridge, who was my contemporary, walked up and shook hands with me as he flashed a sparkling smile that revealed a sound set of even white teeth that were accentuated by his dark-brown complexion. "Don't pay any attention to these bar rats, Bert. They are all full of shit and booze as ever," Bill said as he took the bar stool next to mine. Calling to the barmaid, he ordered, "Bring Bert a Coke and me a brandy."

"Hold the Coke and bring me a double vodka with grapefruit and lime," I shouted over the blare of the jukebox and chattering of the customers.

"Hey, buddy, you're back on the hard stuff, I see."

"Yeah, Bill. After what I've gone through the last two days, it's a wonder I'm not on dope."

"Sure, sure, I understand. It's rough to build a business, put everything you got into it, only to have it wiped out right before your very eyes," Bill said sympathetically before asking, "Did the fire investigators come up with how the fire started in your store?"

"In my store, you say?"

"Yes. That's what was said on the six o'clock news. The TV commentator said that the investigation showed that the fire started on the floor of Zodiac World."

"I didn't see the newscast, Bill. But I was just out there talking to the investigators. They didn't say anything to me about the fire starting in our store. Hell! I just saw signs of fire first coming out of that empty store and thought the fire had started in there. Something fishy is going on. I can smell it," I said bewilderedly.

"Oh, don't let it get you down, buddy. I'm sure there's a logical explanation for the whole thing."

"Maybe. But those two investigators didn't mention anything to me about it starting in my store. And I was just out there with them. That's what has me puzzled. The more I think about those two guys investigating the fire, the more I distrust them. They seem determined to try to build a case of some kind against me."

"Don't put anything past whitey. You know they never wanted a black out there, and even you had to threaten to call in the NAACP and the black press before you could get a lease out there. That tells me that they weren't thrilled to have a black out there. Besides, Maple Heights is just as prejudiced as the Western suburbs. No blacks on the police or fire departments, and if it weren't for the fair housing laws, blacks would still be relegated to that little ghetto section across Broadway in Maple Heights. I know. Being a real estate broker, I come in contact with all kinds of flagrant as well as subtle discrimination in Cleveland and its suburbs."

"Yeah. I guess you would know better from a professional point of view than most folks about the discrimination in housing and business," I commented before ordering another round of drinks for Bill and me.

"You and your family are fortunate to have chosen Shaker Heights to buy a home," Bill went on. "Shaker is progressive. I wish the rest of the Cleveland area was like Shaker. There you have blacks on your police force and in council. You also have voluntary school busing and organized efforts to encourage whites not to flee once blacks buy in their communities. Now that's democratic progress! That's as it should be. All of Cleveland and the suburbs should follow the example set by Shaker. Blacks are on the school board and Shaker has the twelfth best high school in the nation. Now who says that black and white folks can't live in peace and go to school in a progressive community fashion?" Bill concluded before taking a sip from his glass of brandy.

"Maybe I should have opened the store in Shaker. But we wanted to open it in a large shopping center, and Shaker didn't have one."

"Well, keep your chin up, old buddy. I hope things will work out okay for you and Juanita," Bill said encouragingly as we continued to drink and talk for another hour.

*   *   *   *   *

The next day, Mr. James Morman, the adjuster for the Nationwide Insurance Company, called me at my job and asked could I meet with him at Southgate about 4:30 p.m. I assured him I could.

I left work a couple hours early because I wanted to stop at the Maple Heights fire station located on Lee Road.

At the fire station, I signed a receipt and received the $50 that was taken from my cash register. I was told by the captain at the fire station that Scharfenberg was at Southgate pursuing the investigation. The captain asked me to fill out a form for their records giving my eyewitness account of what occurred the day of the fire.

Having completed the statement, I inquired whether any of my records were salvageable that were contained in the two steel file cabinets that had been taken from our store. Because I noticed them standing in the hallway of the fire station.

The captain told me that the file cabinets had been impounded by Petronis, the deputy state fire marshal, and that I could not examine them until he released the file cabinets to me after they were done with their investigation. The file cabinets I insisted might contain records of my purchases, sales, invoices, and other vital correspondence that might be valuable in reconstructing my business operations and inventory if the records were legible. I wanted to examine the files to see if anything in there was legible. But the captain, nevertheless, was adamant in refusing to let me take a look inside the file cabinets.

When I left the fire station, I proceeded straight out to Southgate to find Mr. James Morman taking extensive photographs of the burned-out interior of Zodiac World.

Also present was Petronis and Scharfenberg, who were directing Mr. Morman where to take pictures.

Assuring me that he would be with me shortly, Mr. Morman continued to make more photographs of the shop, or what was left of it. And while waiting outside the store, I noticed a badly burned forklift truck parked in the lot in front of the empty store next door. There was a large crane, mechanical shovel, and two dump trucks in the lot. They were being used by several workmen to load debris taken from the empty store into the dump trucks. Workmen were also dismantling the steel beams that supported the roof over the empty store.

I recognized the forklift truck as the one that had been used by the workmen remodeling the empty store before the fire, but I had no idea that they had parked it in the store overnight and that it was in there when the fire occurred. It was a gasoline-fuel-burning vehicle, and I noticed the cap was missing from the gas tank.

I addressed one of the workmen nearby, "Are you going to remove the steel beams from over all of the burned-out stores?"

"No," he replied, "just over the one store there. The beams are badly damaged, and the wall supporting them may collapse at any time. Probably the worst part of the fire was in this empty store."

"What are you going to do with this forklift truck?" I inquired.

"I don't rightly know. We were just told to put it out here on the lot. Some company that rents these trucks will come out and pick it up, I guess."

"It's sure burned pretty bad," I remarked.

"Sure is. Probably was a can of gasoline in that store somewhere that went up to cause this place to burn like this because you don't take forklift trucks to a filling station when they need refueling on a construction site," the workman speculated.

I agreed. "You sure don't." Then I inquired, "By the way, you or your coworkers didn't happen to find any evidence of a gas can in there, did you?"

"No. None at all that I know of. Could have been one though. But if it was in there, it would have been blown all to hell! And with the roof caving in, covering up the floor with rubble—well, our big shovel could have picked up what was left of the gas can along with some of the other junk and dumped it all in one of those trucks over there," he theorized.

This conversation gave me food for thought. There could be a link between the forklift truck and why the place burned so rapidly in the empty store. When Mr. Morman came out to talk with me, I pointed all of this out to him. But he at first tried to convince me that the forklift truck was run on propane gas. I quickly pointed out that the open gas tank was quite obvious that the vehicle did not run on propane gas. Besides, there was no mounting on the truck for securing a propane gas cylinder. Still, Morman was not impressed that the forklift truck had anything to do with either starting the fire or fueling the fire. I also told him that I had not been permitted to enter my store. He then offered to take me back inside the store with him.

Inside the burned-out structure, for the first time since the fire occurred, I poked around aimlessly in the rubble. The almost total destruction of the place satisfied me that nothing much of salvage value could be recovered. There were only studs left standing where plasterboard walls used to be attached, leaving a complete view into the other two burned-out stores. I noticed too that there was no evidence of any of the metal giftware that would not have burned, and I commented about it.

Scharfenberg assured me that all salvageable merchandise had already been gathered up and taken to the fire station for safekeeping. When I left, I had the feeling that Morman, my insurance company's adjuster, was partial to Scharfenberg and Petronis's investigation, and that he did not intend to make any extensive investigation of his own. Morman appeared to me to be one of those soft-spoken individuals who were always willing to take the easy way out of a difficult situation.

Chapter 3

ABOUT A WEEK AFTER THE fire at Southgate my optician, Dick Howell, called me to say that he had heard about Zodiac World being destroyed by fire and that if I were looking for a place to reopen my business, he had a vacant store for rent. I was grateful for his interest because my wife and I had discussed with Delores O'Bryant the possibility of getting back into business as soon as possible—especially since Delores was keen on purchasing the franchise. This of course would hinge on how soon the Nationwide Insurance Company would settle our claim. Still, it wouldn't hurt to look into Dick's offer.

Having set up an appointment, Delores and I arrived at the optical shop located in Shaker Heights only a quarter mile from where I lived. There was only a clerk and two customers besides Dick in the shop when we entered. Dick, a handsome brown-skinned man in his midforties, was as gracious as ever when I introduced him to Delores, who as usual became the cynosure of all eyes when she entered a room. There was the ever-present charming smile on her pretty dark-complexioned face. The comely and elegant way she moved her petite body and gestured with her hands and arms while expressing herself gave enchantment to her presence.

Delores's attire was always chic, and she glittered with adornments of diamond rings, platinum and gold jewelry in forms of bracelets, pendants and amulets, most having some significance to astrology. Even her platinum wristwatch was shaped like a pyramid, symbolizing her belief in the ancient and mystic powers of the pyramids.

Delores's speech was rapidly syllablized by distinct enunciation, almost in a staccato fashion that oftentimes was punctuated with mirthful laughter. She became instantly excited as Dick gave us a quick tour of the vacant store.

"Here is the showroom that you will have," he said as we walked into the adjacent store. "You see, when we leased this space for the optical business, it had more room than we really needed. We've been using this extra store as a storage room, although there is ample space in the basement for storing things."

"You have a basement. Oh, I must see that! We may have it done into a classroom and office. You must let us see that, Dick. You don't mind me calling you Dick, do you? I really don't like being formal when I can get away with it. I can get away with it with you, can't I, Dick?" She uttered the sentences in rapid succession as was her customary speech pattern.

Dick rolled his eyes, apparently marveling at her mode of speech and instant informality. "Of course you can call me Dick, if I can call you Delores." He smiled.

I could see that these two were going to get on famously together. We took a quick tour of the basement and returned upstairs to the optical shop to talk business.

"Okay, Dick, let's have it. What's the leasing agreement like?" I inquired.

"Reasonable and simple," he began. "We'll sublease the store to you with use of the basement for two hundred fifty dollars a month. This will include heat and lights. And since we are responsible for insuring the building against casualties, you don't even have to insure anything other than the contents of your shop."

"All for just two fifty! Why! that is reasonable!" Delores exclaimed.

Considering that we had to pay $600 a month plus another $134 for assessment at Southgate, this was indeed a good deal, I thought before speaking aloud. "Sounds good to me too, Dick. Guess we'll take it if you agree, Delores, that this is what you want."

"Oh, I definitely agree! We will fix this place up so cute, just you wait and see, Dick," she said excitedly.

"When do you think that you will be able to move in? I would like to talk this deal over with my partner who runs our other store

40

on the west side. Then too we'll want to talk to our landlord before we can sublease, but I don't anticipate any problems there," Dick assured us.

"We can't do anything definite until we receive a settlement of our claim from the insurance company because we don't have the money available to open this store at this time. But if you like, we could give you an earnest money deposit, and you can have a tentative lease agreement drawn up," I suggested.

"A deposit won't be necessary, Bert. I just hope your claim is adjusted promptly. In the meantime, I'll hold the store vacant a reasonable period until you can move in," Dick said as we headed toward the door to his shop.

"This may not be a shopping center, but it is an ideal location with lots of parking space in the rear of the shop," Delores commented as we said farewell and left.

While driving Delores home, she told me about a visit she received from Scharfenberg and Petronis, who recorded her statement that she had every intention to purchase the Zodiac World store before the fire. And this told me that the two fire investigators were checking everything I had told them in my statement that was recorded on the day of the fire.

*   *   *   *   *

I received a letter under date of April 3, 1980, from Mr. Harold H. Reader of the law firm of Ulmer, Berne, Laronge, Glickman & Surtis. The letter requested that I bring all my business records pertaining to Zodiac World to his office on April 17, 1980, at 1:30 p.m. for the purpose of taking a statement from me under oath.

On April 10, 1980, Scharfenberg wrote me a letter advising me that I could pick up my file cabinets and four boxes of what turned out to be merchandise that had been removed from the store and impounded by Petronis, the deputy state fire marshal.

I had the material picked up and stored in a friend's basement who lived only a short distance from the Maple Heights fire station. And when I went by my friend's house to examine the file cabinets,

I found some badly burned papers, most of which were only ashes. Some of the papers that were packed tightly in the cabinets were legible, and I retained those papers along with the smoke-damaged merchandise consisting of metal ashtrays, letter openers, vanity boxes, belt buckles, candlestick holders and jewelry items.

Promptly at 1:30 p.m. on April 17, 1980, I showed up at Mr. Reader's office, carrying what bank records and other business records not destroyed by the fire that were pertinent to the operation of Zodiac World Incorporated. The law firm's suite of offices was very well appointed and located in the heart of downtown Cleveland.

I was ushered into Mr. Reader's private office where I found Mr. James Morman, the Nationwide Insurance Company's adjuster. A lovely blond stenotypist was waiting to record my statement. Mr. Reader was all business for a youthful-looking lawyer who stood tall and erect. "Please take a seat over here, Mr. Jennings, and we'll get underway. You have met Mr. Morman and know who he represents. This young lady will be recording what is said here today. Her name is Terri Evans."

"How do you do," I said, nodding in the lady's direction. She smiled and nodded back as I greeted Mr. Morman, who politely returned my greeting.

Reader took a seat behind his desk, leaned back in the comfortably upholstered chair and began. "This will be the statement under oath of Mr. Talbert Jennings, on behalf of Zodiac World Incorporated, taken pursuant to the terms and provisions in a policy of insurance issued by the Nationwide Insurance Company to Zodiac World Incorporated relative to a store operation at the Southgate shopping center in the City of Maple Heights, Ohio. The statement will specifically relate to a claim, which has been and is being submitted by Zodiac World Incorporated to Nationwide Insurance Company as a result of a fire occurring on or about March 16, 1980, at the aforementioned premises." He paused momentarily before continuing.

"Mr. Jennings, please understand as we take your statement here this afternoon that everything you tell me should be accurate, truthful, and correct for the reason that what you tell me is being conveyed to Nationwide Insurance Company, and Nationwide is going to consider what you tell me, and it will rely upon the truth of what you tell me in reaching some resolution of the insurance claim that you have submitted. Is that understood?"

"Yes, understood," I replied.

During the questioning that followed, I in general gave much the same version of what occurred during the fire that I had given to Scharfenberg and Petronis. But Mr. Reader asked me a wide variety of pertinent questions, and some impertinent to the fire or my business operations with Zodiac World.

Reader was a vigorous, probing, thorough, and shrewd interrogator. The examination went on with relentless perseverance. I felt the need for a shot of liquor on several occasions during the questioning, although I had fortified myself with a few drinks before I arrived. On and on it went:

Q: Mr. Jennings, where did you go to get this coffee you talked about?

A: K-Mart.

Q: Where is the K-Mart located?

A: Just a few doors down from my store.

Q: How long did it take you to go to the K-Mart store to buy the coffee and return?

A: Five or ten minutes at the most, because I just walked in, picked the coffee up, and walked through the cashier.

Q: What sort of container of coffee did you actually buy?

A: I bought Taster's Choice, eight-ounce jar.

Q: You had no petroleum products such as kerosene or fuel oil or gasoline or anything of that sort that was in the store?

A: No, none whatsoever was in our store.

Q: You never used any such products?

A: No. My son brought his moped in and parked it in the back, because he worked in the shop, but I told him, "Don't do that. Get that thing out of there." It has gasoline in it, and it was a fire hazard.

Q: So the moped wasn't there at the time of the fire?

A: No, his moped is at home now, but I was conscious of that sort of thing, and I told him, "Don't bring it back to the store, because it was a gasoline vehicle." And he was saying, "What could it do?" And I said, "Well, it leaks. It could leak gas back there, and besides, I don't like to smell the odor of it." But he didn't want it stolen or anything, so I told him to chain it up and lock it up outside.

Q: Do you smoke?

A: No.

Q: You weren't smoking on the day of the fire then?

A: No, I haven't smoked in thirteen years or more.

Q: Have you ever been indicted or convicted of a felony?

A: That's irrelevant, and that's got nothing to do with this hearing, and if I did, I resent the implication. I am not in court.

Q: It is a simple question.

A: It is not a simple question. It has nothing to do with this hearing. It is irrelevant. My lawyer said if I answer that question, you would dig deeper. You would want to go here, you would want to go there. You are supposed to confine your questions to Zodiac World, and that's according to the insurance policy. It is also according—you are not to ask me if I was ever arrested for drunken driving or something like that because I am not even going to bother to dignify that question with an answer because it is irrelevant. It has nothing to do with this hearing.

Q: You are refusing to answer, is that correct?

A: It is irrelevant. It has got nothing to do with this hearing.

Q: Are you refusing to answer the question? I am not withdrawing the question.

A: Well, I don't care what you do with it. I say it is irrelevant, and I resent the implication.

Q: Are you refusing to answer, that's all I want to know.

A: I am not saying anything. You should know better than to even ask a question like that. My lawyer told me to beware of any type of thing that you try to dig into my personal life.

Q: Have you filed for bankruptcy at any time within the past seven years?

A: No, never in my life. I haven't filed for bankruptcy ever in my life.

Q: Did anybody have a lien or security interest or encumbrances on the fixtures or contents in the store?

A: No, they were completely paid for.

Q: Did you borrow money from anybody or any person or any place to finance this business or any portion of it?

A: No, the only time that I put some money, additional money—I took some money out of my Visa account and put it in there.

Q: How much money?

A: I would say, approximately, $1,500.

Q: Were you having any personal financial difficulties at the time of the fire?

A: No, I didn't have any personal—when you say "financial difficulties," do you mean when you are deep in debt and you can't get out? I owed some people money, sure, but I am current. You can get my credit rating downtown, and you can see that I have got A-1 credit, so evidently, I was paying my bills.

Q: Do you own your own home?

A: Yes.

Q: And are you current on your mortgage payments on the house?

A: Everything is caught up.

I was sure happy to hear Mr. Reader say, "I have no further questions for you." Because the long grueling interrogation had its moments of taxation as well as aggravation. But I thought that I had held my own ground and given a true account as possible of the events concerning the fire. The thing that teed me off the most was his asking me had I ever been indicted or convicted of a felony. That was of course irrelevant. But the fact that he asked it was tantamount to saying, "If this guy's got a past criminal record, it's a sure bet he set his store on fire to collect the insurance money." Why, I thought, can't an investigation proceed on the line of evidence available to make a determination without trying to bring up a past conviction that has absolutely no bearing on the issue at hand other than to create prejudice against the party submitting himself to interrogation? But time and time again, this procedure is used by police, investigators of all kinds, to try and raise a question of guilt. I carried an abiding hatred in my heart and mind for this prejudicial type of investigation. And I had my reasons—good reasons too. Because I knew firsthand of many innocent men who had been made to suffer for something they did not do, all because they had past criminal records and not because they committed the crime for which they had to suffer.

Petronis, Scharfenberg, Morman, Reader—yes, I could see the handwriting on the wall. They were out to build a case at any cost to point the finger of guilt at me for being the culprit who started the fire, and now they would go all out to investigate my past to see if I actually had a criminal record. But whatever they came up with, they would find at the proper time that they had greatly underestimated me as being an easy victim for a frame-up.

I hurried into the nearest bar for a couple of drinks, furious at the prospect of being considered a prime suspect for something I was not guilty of. "Holy shit!" I exclaimed to myself. "Those damn devils are out to get your ass. But what do they really expect to use as evidence that will stand up in a court of law?" That is what puzzled me the most, unless—unless, I thought again—unless they intended to use manufactured evidence. The thought appalled me!

*   *   *   *   *

When I received a certified letter from the clerk of the Court of Common Pleas in July of 1980 to come down to the Justice Center, located in downtown Cleveland, to pick up my indictment. I was neither surprised nor shocked. Because the one-sided direction that the investigation of the fire had been headed by Petronis, Scharfenberg, Morman, and Reader left me no alternative but to expect the worst.

I went downtown to the Clerk of Court's office and picked up my indictment, which charged me with three counts: (1) aggravated arson, (2) attempted grand theft, and (3) possession of criminal tools, namely, gasoline.

I was also presented with a summons to appear in the arraignment courtroom at 8:30 a.m. on the thirtieth day of July 1980, for arraignment to answer to the charges as set forth in the indictment. It also stated, "Failure to appear at the time and place in this summons may result in a warrant being issued for your arrest."

Well, the shit has sure hit the fan, I thought, incensed at the prospect of facing trial for something I did not do. To me, this was just another clear example of persecution instead of prosecution because of my vulnerability as a logical suspect by being black, having stepped out of my place, and, of course, having a past criminal record, which they probably had discovered by this time. Even though the past offense was committed in 1948 over thirty years ago, and the fact that I had paid dearly for my offense by serving twelve years in prison, would not in itself ever wash the slate clean. No. For the rest of my life, it would have to be the weakest part in my character for people to pick on. It would always be there no matter how honestly I lived and no matter how long I stayed out of trouble; the record could never be lived down. Even though I had resided in the State of Ohio for eighteen years without a single blemish on my record—not even a single arrest for a traffic violation—I, nevertheless, would not be treated like a normal citizen in a criminal investigation to those who would see me convicted on the barest thread of circumstantial evidence.

But what about this criminal tool thing "gasoline" that I was charged with? Were they going to say that I "used gasoline to burn our store"? Somehow, at first, I just could not relate to them deeming me to be that stupid. The charge, nevertheless, was there in the indictment.

I was halfway through a bottle of gin when my wife got home early that same afternoon from a World Book sales call. Selling World Books was a sideline that she was especially active at during the summer vacation period, away from teaching.

The indictment was spread out on the dining room table, and I was seated on a chair staring at it with my hands cupping the sides of my face.

"Hi, dear," Juanita greeted. "How did your day go?"

"Terrible!" I growled.

"Oh! What happened?"

"I've been indicted for arson and attempted grand theft. Can you imagine that?"

"My God! You can't be serious!"

"Absolutely! This morning, the mailman delivered a certified letter from the clerk of the Court of Common Pleas, ordering me to come down and pick up my indictment. I went down and got it along with a summons to appear for arraignment on July 30 to enter a plea to the indictment. I—"

Before I could continue, Juanita blurted out, "Are they crazy? We know you didn't burn the shop. It doesn't make sense that they would accuse you. What do they expect to use for evidence, I wonder?"

"I really don't know. The indictment mentioned possession of criminal tools and names that as gasoline, so I guess they are going to try and say that I burned the place down with gasoline."

"That's utterly ridiculous! They are out to try to frame you for something you didn't do," Juanita uttered angrily before adding, "And how come it took them so long to indict you? Here it is, July, and the fire happened in March."

"The grand jury was evidently sufficiently convinced by whatever evidence the prosecution produced because they did return the indictment. Even though grand jury proceedings are one-sided, there still has to be sufficient evidence to make what the law terms a prima facie case that a crime has been committed and that there is reason to believe that a person or persons committed it before the grand jury can return what they call a true bill or indictment. And the grand jury can return an indictment at any time within what is known as the statute of limitations, which is a fixed period of time by law—say three years or seven years for some offenses—that a person must be apprehended and charged from the date a crime is committed. Of course some crimes, like murder, do not have a limitation, as far as I know." As I concluded, I poured myself another gin and tonic.

Juanita gave me a disapproving glance, saying, "Man, you had better get your head together and lay off that stuff. You know how it affects your memory, and you are going to need all of your wits to cope with this situation." Having said that, she went on, "Now what about a lawyer? Are you going to have Mr. Snowberger represent you?"

"No, of course not, Snowberger is a civil lawyer. He's okay as our attorney for Zodiac World, but I'm going to need a damn good criminal lawyer for this case."

"What about Stanley Tolliver? He is a good criminal lawyer. Besides, his wife and I are friends. She's a teacher too, you know," Juanita said, as if that made a big difference.

Why in the hell wasn't she a friend of the wife of the judge who was going to try my case? That might have been helpful, I thought before telling her, "Of course I have heard of Mr. Tolliver's reputation of being one of the ten best criminal lawyers in Cleveland." I was thoughtful momentarily before agreeing to see Tolliver.

"Now, for God's sake, dear, don't go into see him drinking. It is not my intention to nag, but you simply must get yourself together and stay sober. This is too serious a matter to work out under the influence of alcohol."

I knew what she was saying was true. Right now, though, I was powerless to resist the urge to drown the full impact of the reality of the situation in a glass of gin or vodka. Gulping my drink down in one swallow, I rubbed my hand across my mouth and chin to catch the little bit I spilled out over my lips. Then I blurted out in a fit of wrath, "Who in the hell do those devils think they are? They picked on the wrong nigger this time. Shit! I'll make an ass out of them in a courtroom. They don't know who they're fuckin' with. This is Blacky Jennings they're fuckin with!

"And who in the fuck is Blacky Jennings? Well, they'll find out. I took on the whole State of Illinois and won three big ones before the highest court in this Country. Now do you think Blacky Jennings is going to let some little hick shits like the Maple Heights fire department and that deputy state fire marshal hang a bum beef on him? I tell you, they don't know who they're fuckin' with. Ha! Ha! Ha! Ha! Ha! Ha!"

I laughed, as my head began to feel the impact of the last drink. "I'm going to fuck them good when this case comes up for trial. They don't know who they're fuckin' with."

"Now, Talbert, that's enough! Cut out the profanity. Every time you get drunk and upset, your mouth becomes a cesspool," Juanita almost screamed at me.

"Go sit your butt down, woman, and get the hell out of my face if you don't believe that I'm going to make asses out of those dirty devils for trying to frame me."

I went on cursing in a tirade of condemnation. "Shit! They'll never live to see the day of me spending a day in jail on these god-damned trumped-up charges. It's bullshit! Pure bullshit! This is Blacky Jennings they're fuckin' with, and they aren't hep to him. They think they're fuckin' with some dumb nigger named Talbert Jennings. But I got news for them! Boy have I got news for them.

"Sure. Sure, you got news for them," Juanita said in an attempt to pacify me. "Now how about going upstairs and take a nap before supper is ready. It'll do you good."

"Hell! I'm not sleepy, woman," I said, getting up from the table with the bottle of gin in my hand. "But I'll get the hell out of your face 'cause you don't believe I'm going to make asses out of those goddamned, no-good devils for fuckin with me in the first fuckin' place. Goddamn 'em all!"

"Oh yes, I do, dear. You get yourself sobered up, and you can lick the world," Juanita cried out as I made my way upstairs to the guest room. Falling heavily back on the bed, my mind suddenly faded into retrospection.

Part II

With Egg on Their Faces, Let Them Eat Crow

Chapter 4

EVE MURMURED ECSTATICALLY IN HER throaty voice as she rolled her warm naked body on top of me and pressed her voluptuous form firmly against mine. Her tongue began to pick eagerly about my face until it slid its moist tip between my lips. My hands began to wander aimlessly over her curvaceous body, sweeping along her symmetrical thighs and creeping between them until my fingers lingered in her crotch. The pubescence between her legs was moist, and I could feel her body quiver with anticipation as she guided the penetration she desired slowly into herself, gradually filling herself with the full rapturous delight that gave her so much thrilling pleasure.

Eve's body began to undulate and writhe almost mechanically. My fingers began to expand and close her well-rounded rump in rhythmical motions until she could no longer resist the urge to give vent to her heated emotions. With several gurgling cries of sheer ecstasy, she released her passion, just as I, fully in tune with her own body, released mine in perfect synchronization. Our timing was always beautiful! How sweet it is to make love with such perfect harmony, I thought, lolling into a state of complete relaxation after toweling myself.

A few moments later, Eve rolled over on her back to towel her own body, her breathing returning to normal. She lay quietly relaxing alongside of me. When she finally spoke, her voice was husky and subdued. "Blacky, baby, when you go out of town again, you're not going to leave me here to yearn for your return like I did for the past several days, are you, honey? That's why I'm so greedy for you tonight. You've neglected me for a whole week."

"Couldn't be helped, Eve. I had some business in Detroit to take care of, and as much as I wanted to be near you, I just couldn't take you with me, you understand, don't you?"

She turned her pretty beige face toward mine and pursed her full sensuous lips, pouting, "No, I don't understand. When you leave again, I'm going too. You never take me anywhere on trips."

I slipped my arm under her shoulders, pulling her close to me. "All right, all right, sweetheart, next time, I'll take you when I go out of town."

"Promise?"

"Yes, I promise, honey. You can make book on it," I reassured her with a kiss on the cheek.

It was nearing midnight. Having made love three times that evening, I began to feel drowsy. I had just arrived back in Chicago from Detroit, Michigan, that same afternoon, and I did not get much rest during the several days that I had been away, so it was very restful to be comfortably relaxed in Eve's bed.

I couldn't have been asleep over ten or fifteen minutes before I was suddenly awakened by Eve's excited voice, calling, "Blacky! Blacky! Get up! Get up, Blacky! The police are downstairs."

I thought for a moment that I was dreaming. I shook my head and rubbed my eyes bewilderedly.

"What must I do, Blacky?" Joan asked fearfully while standing in the doorway to Eve's bedroom. She and Eve shared the apartment together.

Hearing loud knocking at the front door, I jumped to my feet. Eve was slipping on her housecoat as I rushed to the front window and peeped out cautiously. Sure enough, there were two cars out front with spotlights on the building.

"Don't open the door or turn on the lights," I said, rushing back into the bedroom to hastily don my clothes.

With my revolver in my hand, I headed for the back door. I didn't know what the police wanted with me because I had been involved in so many illegal things that it could be anyone of them for all I knew. I heard the front door downstairs snap as it was forced open, because Joan was standing upstairs with the door to the apartment ajar. I rushed to her side and locked the door, just as footsteps could be heard running up the stairs. Suddenly, there came a pounding on the door to the apartment.

"Open up! We're police officers! This building is surrounded. Open up or we'll break the door down!" bellowed a voice on the outside. Eve snatched the revolver out of my hand. "Go into the bathroom, baby. We'll try to make them believe that you are not here," she whispered.

I hesitated momentarily to reach for the revolver in Eve's hand. "Give me that piece."

"No, no," she said softly. "Don't try anything crazy. They might kill you. Go into the bathroom."

I followed her advice and locked myself in the bathroom. Eve let the police in, and I could hear her voice saying, "What's the meaning of this intrusion?"

"Lady, we're looking for Blacky Jennings," a loud voice said.

"Well, he's not here. Now will you please leave," Eve told him.

"Not so fast, lady. You don't mind if we look around, do you?" the same voice inquired.

"Yes, I do. It is late. I have to be at work early tomorrow morning, and I need my rest. I've already told you that he isn't here. Now will all of you please leave," Eve insisted.

I quietly raised the bathroom window and contemplated the two-story drop to the gangway below. Someone tried the doorknob, and I froze.

"What's in here?" a voice inquired.

Joan's voice replied. "That's the bathroom."

"How come it's locked?" the same voice asked, at the same time, he kicked open the door.

Standing there in the darkness of the bathroom, I stared at a tall detective pointing a long-barreled .38 revolver at me. "All right, Blacky Jennings, come on out of there with your hands up," he ordered.

I walked out as ordered. There were four police officers all together in the apartment, two detectives in plainclothes and two

Chicago patrolmen in uniform. I was later to learn that the two detectives were from Oak Park, Illinois, a Chicago, suburb.

I was searched by the tall detective, who took my wristwatch and a diamond ring off my fingers. He then handcuffed me. Addressing the other detective, he said, "Better see if these ladies have any jewelry that might not belong to them."

I just stood there silently while the other detective, a large heavyset man, asked Eve and Joan to remove rings from their fingers. They refused, and the officers removed their rings forcefully, but not before they experienced some resistance.

Joan, being a diminutive brown-skinned woman, nevertheless, had a scrappy disposition. She cursed her tormentors bitterly as they twisted at her fingers. "Those are my wedding rings, you fat bastard!" she cried out. "Get your goddamned hands off me this minute!" She tried unsuccessfully to bite the heavyset detective, who managed to wrestle her wedding set from her finger.

Eve did not put up much resistance as the tall detective grabbed her by the wrist and slipped a diamond ring off her finger.

The two Chicago patrolmen searched the women's bedrooms and returned with some more jewelry belonging to Eve and Joan.

"What the hell are you going to do with my jewelry?" Joan asked angrily.

"Look, ladies, all we are going to do is see if this jewelry came out of the jewelry store heist in Oak Park a couple weeks ago that Blacky Jennings and his gang held up. If this jewelry did not come from that robbery, you ladies can have it back," the heavyset detective explained.

"Okay, let's get out of here," the tall detective said.

They led me downstairs where they were met by two other uniformed Chicago patrolmen who had been staking out the rear of the building. I was placed in an unmarked police car with another detective behind the wheel, who did not come upstairs. The Oak Park detectives thanked the Chicago patrolmen for their assistance in arresting me. About a half hour later I was sitting in an office in the Oak Park Police Station.

The heavyset detective, who appeared to be in his midfifties, stared at me across his desk, not saying a word, just staring thoughtfully, as though he were making up his mind how to commence his interrogation. The tall detective, somewhere in his early forties, stood behind me with an unpleasant look on his face as I glanced back at him. In fact, he looked downright mean. Another detective was seated to the right of me. He was younger looking than the other two, probably in his early thirties.

"All right, Blacky," the heavyset officer opened up. "I'm Lieutenant Fremont Nester. The officer standing behind you is Edward Piotter, and this other officer to your right is Larry Vodvarka. Now that you know who we are, we want to know a lot about you, Blacky. To begin with, what is your full name?"

"Talbert Hendricks Jennings," I said.

"And your date of birth?" Lieutenant Nester asked.

"December 31, 1922," I replied as he wrote the information on a sheet of paper.

"Let's see, this is June 6, 1948, so that would make you twenty-six, right?"

"Yes, that's right."

"Do you live at the Dearborn street address where we picked you up? I mean is that your permanent address?" The lieutenant wanted to know.

"No, I live five eleven east forty-eighth street."

"Why do they call you Blacky? You're lighter than some Caucasians" Lieutenant Nester asked curiously.

"It's just a nickname I got as a kid because I was the black sheep in the family," I lied, not wanting to tell him that when I was fourteen, a neighborhood kid called Bobo started calling me Blacky because I had a penchant for fighting and getting into trouble.

At first, I had disliked the appellation, but it nevertheless stuck because the other kids in the neighborhood found a pleasure in provoking my ire by calling me Blacky. After a while though, I got used to the nickname and even began to like it when I later found out that it went well with my gang leadership and tough-guy attitude.

"Now, Blacky, or Talbert, let's get down to cases. We want to know all you know about the Barr Jewelry Store heist that occurred on May 24th of this year," Lieutenant Nester said in a calm manner.

I shrugged uneasily. "Really, sir, I don't know anything about it. I can't imagine what you are talking about or why you picked me up in the first place," I protested.

"Why, you lying son of a bitch!" Piotter shouted. Stepping around in front of me, he continued, "I ought to knock your god-damned teeth out," he threatened.

"Now, now, Ed, let's give Blacky a chance to think this over sensibly first," Lieutenant Nester cut in.

"These goddamned jigs got a lot of nerve coming out here to rob a jewelry store in broad daylight down the street from this police station and cause us all these sleepless nights tracking them down," Piotter complained angrily. "Why, if this half-breed bastard don't cooperate, he'll get the same thing his pal Morgan got. And before I'm done with him, he'll tell us everything, including how many times he played hooky from school."

Morgan? Have they got Buddy Morgan? I asked myself.

"Now, tell us you don't know Edgar Morgan or Buddy Morgan as he is usually called?" Lieutenant Nester inquired.

"The name does sound familiar," I hedged.

"Familiar my ass!" Piotter cut in. "I'm sick of fucking around with you already," he added, snatching me up out of the chair.

I struggled to pull away from him, and the other detective, Larry Vodvarka, pinned my arms behind my back. I felt Piotter's fist plow hard into my stomach, and I sunk to my knees in pain.

"Hold on, Ed," Lieutenant Nester cautioned. "Give him a chance to talk."

I was shoved roughly back into the chair holding my stomach and grimacing in great agony as I tried to catch my breath.

"Come on, Blacky, make it easy on yourself. You can't gain a thing by being contrary. We got you, Arthur Smith, and Edgar Morgan dead to right as the guys who robbed the Barr Jewelry Store. Morgan has given us a complete confession, and he implicated you as the ringleader," Lieutenant Nester said. Pulling open his desk drawer, he pulled out several typewritten sheets of paper that were stapled together. "Here read this. It's Morgan's confession. He even told us that we could find you at Eve Johnson's apartment. Here, read it, Blacky. The whole story is all on these pieces of paper signed by Morgan."

I accepted the statement and perused its contents. Sure enough, it was a confession made by Morgan, implicating me in the robbery and that he and Arthur Smith, who drove the getaway vehicle, which was Arthur's cab, acted as my accomplices. He went on to confess that we disposed of the stolen jewelry and divided up the proceeds from the sale.

Laying the confession back on the desk, I shook my head negatively, saying, "I still wasn't involved. I can't imagine why Buddy would tell you this unless you beat this lie out of him."

"Why, you goddamned son of a bitch!" Piotter screamed, punching me in the jaw at the same time. I was able to throw my hands up defensively, warding off most of the force of the blow as it glanced off my cheek. Then he kicked me on the shin and slapped me across the face. "Let's kill this lying bastard!" he shouted menacingly as I rolled out of the chair onto the floor.

Lieutenant Nester got up and collared me with his huge hands. "Okay, Blacky, you asked for it. Now you're going to get it good if you don't talk. I'm done being Mr. Nice Guy." He backhanded me across the face several times before pulling me to my feet and shoving me back into the chair.

I was dazed and in great fear of receiving even greater punishment. My mind was racing thought after thought through my head in a desperate effort to find a solution to stave off more beatings. I decided to feign an epileptic attack to stall for time. Quietly working up a mouth full of saliva, I collapsed on the floor, frothing at the mouth in a convulsive fit of thrashing and jerking movements.

"What's wrong with you?" Lieutenant Nester shouted.

I remained silent and rolled my eyes wildly while continuing to thrash and jerk my body about the floor.

Vodvarka felt my pulse. "I believe this bastard's faking. Ain't nothing wrong with him that a good ass kicking won't cure," he ended menacingly.

"He may really be having an epileptic seizure," Lieutenant Nester said with some concern in his voice. "Pick him up and put him back in the chair. He seems to be quieting down somewhat." Going to a water cooler, he got a cup of water and offered it to me as I slowly began to calm down with a dazed look on my face. Turning to Piotter, he ordered, "Bring Morgan up here. Maybe he can convince Blacky to talk before he gets his brains beat out." Turning his attention back to me, he held out the cup of water. "Here, sip some of this. It'll make you feel better." I pushed the cup away and hung my head weakly, almost falling out of the chair again. Nester grabbed me and held me in the chair. "Maybe he isn't faking, Larry," he said to the other detective. Then he asked me, "Hey, Blacky, are you an epileptic?"

I held back the urge to smile over having this big baboon baffled with the act I was putting on. I nodded my head slowly in reply to his question before dropping my chin on my chest as though I were still suffering from the seizure.

A short time, later Morgan was brought into the office. His face was swollen, and he had a defeated look on his light-brown face. Usually a dapper dresser, his clothes and hair were unkempt and disheveled. His eyes averted mine as he stood before Lieutenant Nester looking down at the floor.

"Well, Morgan, do you know this guy sitting here?" Nester asked, nodding in my direction.

"Yeah, that's Blacky Jennings," Morgan said in almost a whisper.

"And everything you said in your confession concerning Blacky is true and correct, is it not?" Nester went on.

"Yeah, it's correct," Morgan murmured.

Facing me, Nester said, "You heard that, didn't you, Blacky? What have you got to say now?"

"Nothing," I said.

"He means is it true or not?" Piotter bellowed.

I remained silent, and Piotter grabbed me by the throat. "Nigger, didn't you hear me talking to you?"

I still remained silent.

"Tell this guy the game is up, Morgan, before we give him the water treatment. Go on, tell him," Nester said.

"You may as well admit it, Blacky. They've got the goods on us," Morgan pleaded.

I still remained silent.

"All right, let's take this bastard in the john and flush his god-damned head in the crapper. That's the treatment that'll make him admit it," Piotter suggested angrily.

'*Holy shit! Can these assholes be for real?* I asked myself.

"Don't let 'em do that to you, Blacky. It's not worth it 'cause it's no use. You may as well fess up to it. They've got us, man!" Morgan pleaded earnestly.

"All right! All right!" I exclaimed. "Whatever Buddy said in his confession, I'll agree to," I capitulated.

"Fine!" Nester said, pushing himself back from his desk. "Now you're being smart."

Piotter typed on the last page a paragraph stating that I had read the statement and that it was true and correct and made on my own freewill. After that, I signed my name on Morgan's confession, thinking, *Freewill shit! Why these rotten, no-good sons of bitches don't give a fuck if they murder a prisoner to try and make him talk.*

"Now, we can all go get some sleep," Lieutenant Nester said, pleased with the fact that they had apparently wrapped up the case. "Take Morgan down to the lockup, and let's go home, boys. You better send Jennings over to River Forest so these two don't get their heads together until we're done with them," he concluded.

Morgan was led away to the lockup, and I was handcuffed before being transported to the River Forest Police Station located in an adjoining suburb where I was held in custody incommunicado. It was now early morning, about two o'clock.

Later that evening, I was taken back to Oak Park where the detectives took a joint statement from Morgan and me. Then I was taken back to River Forest for the night. The next day, June 7, 1948,

I was brought back to Oak Park where Morgan and I were given a hearing before a magistrate. We were bound over to the Cook County grand jury for armed robbery.

The first time Morgan and I got a chance to talk in private together was down in the Oak Park lockup after our court hearing. We were placed in cells next to each other. When we were alone, Morgan said, "I'm really sorry I got you busted, Blacky."

He sounded remorseful "Come on, Buddy, it's done now. Let's just forget it ever happened. I'm tired as hell. Didn't sleep good last night," I concluded before becoming quiet. But how could I forget it? It looked like I was headed back to the penitentiary.

"You sure you aren't pissed off at me, Blacky? You don't want to kill me or somethin'?" Buddy spoke up after several minutes. He sounded suspicious of the nonchalant manner in which I accepted his perfidy.

"Hell no! I don't want to do you no harm. Now let's forget it," I replied irritably. Then all became quiet again.

Several minutes later, Morgan spoke up again: "Really, Blacky, I'm sorry, but they forced me to rat on you. I took a lot of punishment before I talked. I couldn't take having my head and face doused in the toilet bowl. Those bastards were serious about holding my head down and flushing the toilet. I tell you, it was awful! It makes me ill to think about it. But I'll remember to laugh every time I read in the paper that a cop gets killed, and one day I hope to even the score.

I felt sorry for the guy. "It's okay, Buddy. I couldn't have taken that either," I said reassuringly.

"I just want you to know that I didn't give 'em your home address. I was hoping you were still in Detroit and that you wouldn't be at Eve's when they got by there and that Eve or Joan would warn you that the cops were looking for you so you could go on the lam. Too bad you had to be there when those motherfuckers arrived," Buddy said with genuine regret.

"Yeah, too bad," I said before inquiring, "But tell me, Buddy, how did they get a line on you to bust you?"

"Li'l Arthur fingered me," Buddy began. "You see, Blacky, after the heist, the Oak Park Police canvassed the area of the robbery to see if anyone saw anything suspicious or any Negroes in the area about the time of the robbery. Oak Park, being an all-lily-white community, you don't see many colored people out here except those that have jobs in this suburb. Well, this nigger working in the gas station down the street from the jewelry store told the police that there was a colored guy in a black limited Buick jitney cab who came in the filling station about the time of the robbery to check the air on one of his tires. He also told the cops that the cab had blue tinted windows. This information evidently made the cops suspicious because they know that jitney cabs like that run up and down certain streets on the south side of Chicago in the colored neighborhoods, so they got with the Chicago police and investigate all of the jitney cabs with blue tinted windows. Besides Li'l Arthur's cab, there are only a few others with blue tinted windows, and I think his is the only black limited Buick with 'em. Anyway, they stopped his cab, and Markus was driving it. Well, Markus tells the cops that Li'l Arthur was driving the cab the day of the robbery. The cops picked up Li'l Arthur and worked him over, I guess, until he fingered me. I don't know why he didn't finger you. Maybe he was more afraid of you. Anyway, the cops came out to my place and busted me," he concluded.

"Where is Li'l Arthur now?" I asked.

"He's in the county jail."

"Holy shit! What a mess!" I exclaimed. Then I asked, "In your confession, you told them that the loot was sold to a fence in Ohio, didn't you? Well, what in the hell did you have to tell those bastards that for?"

"Nester said they would go easier on me in court if they recovered the loot. They busted the fence on the information I gave them, but the police didn't recover any of the jewelry, and the fence has denied everything from what Nester told me. So now I may have to go to Ohio with these dicks when the fence appears in court for a hearing," Buddy explained.

"When did they bust you, Buddy?"

"Three days ago, I was picked up."

"And when did they bust Li'l Arthur?"

"Two days before I was busted."

"I wish to hell I had kept my ass in Detroit. Why in the fuck did I have the bad luck to return to Chicago with all this heat on me?"

"How long was you over there?"

"About a week. I was setting up a score with an old pal of mine that I served time with," I said before asking, "Hey, man, you got any smokes. I'm out."

"Sure, hold your hand out through the bars and I'll slip you a pack and some matches. I got a half-dozen packs. It's amazing how nice those motherfuckers will get once they get you cooperating with them."

I reached out and took the pack. Lighting up a cigarette, I inhaled deeply and let the smoke slowly drift up and out of my lungs.

"Was you going to cut me in on the Detroit caper if this hadn't happened?" Buddy asked.

"Sure. You'd have been cut in. In fact, I came back to get you and Li'l Arthur. He was always a damn good wheel man. I just can't figure why he would go into the gas station to get air and expose himself that way. He was supposed to have remained stationary until you came out with the loot."

"But he didn't, and that's what fucked up the show," Buddy said.

"It sure did," I agreed dejectedly as I contemplated our predicament.

Chapter 5

THE COOK COUNTY JAIL WAS a huge and complex edifice comprised of numerous cellblocks with several tiers to each block. Each tier had a large dayroom where the inmates were allowed to congregate for eating and recreation purposes. In the front of the tier outside of the dayroom was a barred cage where the guard watched and operated the doors by levers to the cells at the rear of the dayroom where the inmates slept at night.

The cells were small, consisting of a steel bed with mattress, pillow, and covering. When an inmate wanted to go to the toilet at night, he would have to wait until the guard made his rounds, usually every hour, and then ask the guard to let him out of his cell so he could go to the toilet and washroom adjacent to the dayroom.

Each tier had anywhere from thirty to forty inmates that had to live together in whatever harmony they could during their stay in the jail that was integrated with all nationalities and races mingled together. There was a tier boss inmate appointed to see that the food that was sent up to the tier on a dumbwaiter was shared equally by all the inmates. And the tier boss was responsible for assigning other inmates jobs in helping to serve the food and keep the tier clean. If the tier boss was smart, he could use his influence to turn favors for extra food and light jobs to those inmates who could afford to pay him for favors. Some tier bosses had access to alcohol and narcotics through bribe-accepting guards, so it wasn't unusual to smell the aroma of marijuana on the tier or the odor of alcohol on the breath of an inmate who could afford to pay for such pleasures.

At times, tempers would flare between the inmates, and fights would break out. Most of the times when this happened, the tier boss and his assistants could quell the disturbances. If not, guards would be sent in to break up the fights and hustle the offenders off to punishment cells.

Gambling went on daily among the inmates who were allowed to keep money on their persons for trading with the jail commissary, which was a large mobile cart containing tobacco, sandwiches, rolls, candy, cookies, coffee, soft drinks, toilet articles, postage-stamped envelopes, and writing paper. The commissary cart usually came to each tier three times a day during the morning, afternoon, and evening hours.

As a rule, the tier boss controlled the gambling games of stud or draw poker and blackjack by having himself or one of his assistants cut the pot of winnings to a nominal sum. The games were against the rules of the jail, but nevertheless, the games flourished because the rule against them was not vigorously enforced.

Tier bosses were usually inmates serving six months or a year in the jail, but not always. Sometimes, inmates awaiting trial with influence with the guards could get themselves appointed tier boss. The next best thing to being tier boss was to be the number one assistant to the tier boss.

I had been in the county jail before, so I was no stranger to the place. I knew the ropes, and it was only a matter of time before I would maneuver myself into an advantageous position to hold some sway over either the tier or the gambling games.

The tier boss was named Benny. He was a big black and brawny good-natured fellow serving a one-year sentence for larceny. His lumbering gait with big hands on long primatial dangling arms gave Benny a chimpish mien, and his constantly grinning face made him a likeable person to the inmates—especially since he was not a scheming or malevolent type of person.

When I arrived on tier B-3, I went about quietly sizing up inmates by holding friendly chats with each one of them. I recognized a few of the inmates with whom I had served time in the penitentiary. They, like myself, were awaiting trial for new crimes that they had been accused of committing.

Joe Smith, an inmate I was acquainted with on the outside as a local pimp, was on the tier serving one year for assault with a deadly weapon. He shot a man for not paying one of his prostitutes. Joe and I immediately formed an alliance with the primary purpose of taking over the tier and gambling games from the likeable but slow-witted Benny.

It was said by those who knew Joe Smith well that this handsome and glib panderer of female flesh had never worked a day in his life because his mother had raised him specially to become a pimp and thrive on the weaknesses of the ladies of the evenings. And Joe did not let his mother's ambitions for him go unrewarded, it was rumored. For he used women as whores, shoplifters, con women, and in any capacity possible where they could make money for him. His star had been rising rapidly until the shooting incident landed him in the county jail on tier B-3.

I had gotten in touch with Eve by writing her a letter the same day I arrived in the county jail. Visiting days were once a week, and I knew that she would visit me on the very next visiting day. I also contacted my lawyer, Howard Geter, who came to see me at the jail the day after my arrival. When I told him about the coerced confession that was extracted from me by severe police brutality, he seemed to give me encouragement that if all of us stuck together and recanted our coerced confessions, he might be able to get the confessions thrown out of court as inadmissible evidence since they had been obtained through force and violence.

Geter also thought that he might be able to have the ring taken from me suppressed as evidence on grounds of illegal search and seizure since the police did not have a warrant for my arrest or a warrant to search the premises where I was arrested. My wristwatch had been returned to me as not having been identified as loot taken from the robbery. The ring, however, was identified as having on it the same brand name as merchandise taken from Barr's Jewelry Store. Geter convinced me that this, per se, did not necessarily prove that the ring came from Barr's store since hundreds of other jewelry stores carried the same brand of rings.

I asked Geter about the so-called positive identification Mr. Barr made of me as a participant in the robbery after being told first by the Oak Park police that I was one of the robbers identified in

Morgan's confession. Actually, Barr had never seen my face in his store because Morgan entered the store first, held him up, and took him into the rear of his store where he was bound and gagged. I had entered a few seconds later and proceeded to clean out the place while Morgan stood outside, cleaning the windows and acting as the "lookout" once Barr was secured in the rear of the store.

Geter advised me that since I wasn't picked out of a lineup of several persons, he could challenge the propriety of the identification when the trial came up. The more Geter talked of building a defense, the more my hopes rose of beating the rap. I told him that I had a witness who would testify that I was in Detroit when the robbery occurred, and Geter became elated over the possibility of having an alibi witness.

Before parting, Geter told me that he would try to have my bail reduced so that I could get out on bond; but first, I would have to give him a thousand dollars retainer fee. I only had a few hundred dollars cash that I could put my hands on, but I assured the attorney that his fee would be forthcoming.

When I saw Eve a few days later, she told me how she had hidden my revolver under the sofa cushion in the living room of her apartment, and I told her to sell it to raise money for my defense. She also told me that the Oak Park police had returned most of the jewelry taken from her and Joan with the exception of a diamond ring that Joan owned, because it, like my ring, had the same brand name as rings included in the loot taken in the heist.

Before Eve left, she promised me that she would do all that she could to try and help me raise money to pay my lawyer and also money to get me out on bond. I gave her the names and addresses of several friends to contact with a view to obtaining funds from them to assist me in my defense. We were both more optimistic now that the situation did not seem as dismal as it did earlier.

I discovered that Li'l Arthur was on tier A-3, directly across the hall that divided his tier from B-3, the tier that I was on. Soon, we were able to exchange messages to one another by sending notes that the inmates called kites. The kites were carried by trusties or inmates going to court who would meet in a common holding cell and exchange gossip and kites for delivery on their tiers. This was a common courtesy among some of the prisoners, even though they could get punished if caught carrying the kites to other inmates.

Li'l Arthur agreed to recant the statement he had given the police. He also agreed to retain Geter as his attorney. And When Buddy Morgan returned from Ohio, he was placed in the Cook County Jail on tier D-1. I soon contacted him with a kite and got his agreement that he too would accept Geter as his attorney and that he would also recant his confession as untrue.

It was now agreed by all three of us that we would fight the case rather than cop out to the charges. We were all very incensed over the brutal treatment that we had received at the hands of the Oak Park police, who violated our constitutional rights on several occasions. We never raised our hands to swear to God on a Bible that we would not break His laws or man's laws. But those dirty, no-good cops had raised their hands to swear before God to uphold the law and constitution and protect the rights of all citizens. They not only violated their oaths to God, but they violated the law and constitution as well, we reasoned. Because the police had committed criminal acts against us in the course of their investigation, so they were just as much criminals as we were, if not, in fact, worst criminals than we were.

Joe and I had agreed to become partners in the stud poker games played on our tier. We arranged signals to stay or pass when one of us got a good hand, and this was done by simply tapping each other's foot under the table. Consequently, we won more often than the other players in the games, and we divided our winnings between ourselves. We were just biding our time to the day when one of us would take over the tier boss job and the games.

Playing cards all day made the time go fast. My second week in jail found me receiving my indictment for armed robbery that had been handed down by the grand jury. A few days later, Buddy Morgan, Li'l Arthur, and myself were taken before the chief justice of the criminal court of Cook County for arraignment. We pleaded not guilty, and Attorney Geter requested a jury trial.

Judge Alan E. Ashcraft Jr. was assigned as our trial judge. Our bail was set at $10,000 each, and the judge refused to reduce the bail when Geter complained that it was too high. Not having money for bond release after paying Geter his fee, we were remanded to the custody of the sheriff of Cook County to be returned to the county jail to await further proceedings in our case.

While waiting in the holding cell adjacent to the courtroom, the three of us had time for further conversation before being taken back to the jail. Li'l Arthur was the first to speak after the bailiff locked the door to the bull pen and left us alone.

"You know, I've been thinkin' hard about how to screw up the cops' case against us," he said in his raspy and gruff voice. "There's nothin' in the statement I made implicatin' Blacky. I never mentioned him. And I wouldn't have mentioned you, Buddy, if Fred Anderson didn't give the cops your name when we got to your apartment and he let us in."

"Well, what I want to know is how in the hell did those fuckin' cops get my address in the first place if you didn't tell them and take them there?" Buddy asked accusingly.

"The hell I did!" Li'l Arthur blurted out. "Markus told 'em. Remember after we pulled the job," he whispered, "and I called Markus from your place to come pick up the cab 'cause I wasn't goin' to use it no more that day? Well, when the cops stopped Markus on South Parkway and asked him who was drivin' the cab on the day of the heist, Markus told 'em that he was drivin' the afternoon and evenin' but I had the cab that mornin. Later he told the dicks where he picked up the cab at your place. That's how the dicks knew to come to your place. They took me over there when they busted me, and your good pal Fred Anderson told 'em that we were together the day of the heist. And I never ratted on you, Buddy," he concluded in earnest.

"If I buy your story," Buddy said with a frown on his tan face, "why in the hell did you have to go into the goddamned gas station? You gassed up and checked out the fuckin' cab before we left to make the score, didn't you? So you are in fact responsible for us getting busted."

"Lower your fuckin' voice," I cautioned Buddy.

He went on in a whisper, "How come you went into the fuckin' gas station, I asked you? You were supposed to stay put until we came out with the loot."

Li'l Arthur shifted his feet uneasily with a scowl on his tough-looking brown countenance. He was only about five feet five inches tall and weighed about 140 pounds. Morgan was about five ten and weighed around 160 pounds. I stood six even and scaled just under 170 pounds. But what Li'l Arthur lacked in stature he made up for it in wild animal-like aggressiveness.

We all were guilty of frequent profanity. Arthur, however, was extremely profane and often voiced foul epithets and profanities without caring who was in listening range, that included man, woman, child, priest, or nun. When he let go with curse words, he let go regardless!

"One of the rear tires on the fuckin' cab needed some air. I noticed it drivin' funny goin' out to Oak Park that day, so I figured it wouldn't do no harm to go into the gas station almost across the street from where I was parked for a minute or two to put some air in the tire. How in the goddamned hell did I know those asshole, cock-suckin' cops would go in there askin' questions after the heist?"

"'Cause you're a dumb-ass motherfucker, that's how come you didn't know, you sorry son of a bitch!" Buddy cursed him angrily.

"Nigger, kiss my ass until you get shitty drunk!" Li'l Arthur shouted, flaring up aggressively.

"Okay, both you bastards knock it off!" I said, getting angry too. Then I went on in a calmer tone, "If we expect to beat this rap, we got to let bygones be bygones and stick together. Now you started to say something, Li'l Arthur, about how to screw up the dicks' case against us. What you got in mind?"

"Just this, Blacky, I can testify in court that I picked up two passengers, a black guy and white guy. They told me to drive 'em to Oak Park and wait on 'em for a return ride to the South Side. I can say I didn't know they robbed anybody, that they were just two passengers, see what I mean?"

"Yeah, but how about you going out to my apartment with the cops?" Buddy wanted to know.

"I already told you, Marcus led the police to your place. I'll testify to that in court, and also that they beat my ass to get me to agree with Fred Anderson that we were together on the day of the heist. I'll say that was not true. Most of my statement was ex—expulsary or somethin' like that Geter called it."

"Exculpatory," I corrected him.

"Yeah, yeah, that's what Geter called it, exculpatory. It means he told me that I wasn't takin' no direct blame for nothin' because I—"

"No, motherfucker, 'cause you was too goddamned busy trying to put all of the fuckin' blame on me," Buddy interjected.

"Now didn't I tell you guys to lay off the personal hostilities?" I reminded them.

"But Nester said you spilled your fuckin' guts when they hauled your black ass in," Buddy persisted.

"Then that fuckin' son of a bitch Nester is a lie and a sissy, and his breath smells pissy! What's more, his mother fucks gorillas," Li'l Arthur cursed heatedly.

"Cool down, fella," I said in a soft tone. Then I asked both of them, "Did either one of you guys give Joan a ring taken in the score? The cops are holding one of her rings as evidence."

Both of them shook their heads negatively.

"Come on, don't you guys lie to me. I know for a fact that both of you have screwed Joan one time or another. Now which one of you gave her the rock?"

"Honest, Blacky, I swear on my mother, I never gave her anything from the caper," Buddy avowed.

"Me neither, Blacky and I ain't bullshitin' ya either 'cause the only thing I ever gave Joan was a good fuckin' and a damn few dollars—but never, never no jewelry," Li'l Arthur assured me.

"Oh well, maybe she came by it elsewhere. Hell, the same wholesalers who sold Barr jewelry could have sold the same brand of jewelry to hundreds of jewelers across the country, so it doesn't necessarily follow that because we're accused of the heist that Joan's ring came from Barr's store."

"Yeah, that's true, Blacky," Buddy agreed.

"Fuckin' well right!" Li'l Arthur added as two deputy sheriffs showed up to return us to the county jail.

Back on tier B-3, I thought about the possibility of raising money for bond. The more I thought about it, the more the possibility appeared to be unfeasible. I was lucky to have scraped together the grand to pay Geter his retainer. That was all the money that Eve and I were able to raise. Many of my so-called friends on the outside were not cooperative in making any contributions. Had I been smarter instead of so extravagant in lavishing much of my ill-gotten gains on these fair-weather friends, I would have been a lot better off financially; and had I laid away a cash reserve for just such a contingency that confronted me now, I would be out of jail on bond. But paradoxically, most malefactors do not believe that they are going to be caught when they decide to commit a crime. And if the person planning a crime dwelled long enough on the consequences of his act, he probably wouldn't commit the crime in the first place.

Now here I was, locked up in jail with no one to turn to for means with a sympathetic propensity to assist me in this hour of dire need. Because if I could get released on bond, I could make some fast money in no time at all, which of course meant that I would end up compounding my chances of creating even further grief for myself if I were caught.

Two brothers and one sister were the only propinquity I had left. My mother died when I was seven, and my father had died a few years ago, although I never could depend on him for anything. When my mother died, my brothers and I were placed in a foster home. My sister, the youngest in the family, was adopted by one of my mother's cousins and her husband. This was necessary because my natural father was an alcoholic and a ne'er-do-well, incapable of providing a home for his children.

My brothers and I were fortunate in being placed in a good Christian foster home and parented by a loving and devoted couple who had one daughter of their own. These foster parents treated us as well as they did their own daughter and provided us with a good home. But alas! The beginning of the Great Depression occurred in 1929, shortly after we were placed in our foster home. Soon thereafter, the hardships of the 1930s descended upon the family and eventually brought about poverty, loss of jobs, and eventually, the home we lived in was foreclosed.

During this era of poverty and deprivation, I soon became a delinquent in my quest to provide myself with the material things that neither I nor my foster parents could afford. Although I possessed a good mind, I did not pattern myself after my older brother, who was an outstanding student steering clear of delinquency. To the contrary, I was an indifferent student who often was truant and intractable.

Step by step, I graduated from the juvenile detention home to parental school, an institution run by the city of Chicago for truants and delinquent boys and girls under seventeen. I did not finish at St. Charles, the Illinois State Training School for Boys, where I was sent for riding in a stolen automobile, because I escaped from there a few weeks after my arrival with two other inmates after we assaulted a guard and stole a car to make good our escape.

But I eventually got my degree in crime from the Illinois State Penitentiary at Pontiac. Upon my release from there, I was well educated in crime and ready to practice my profession with daring abandon.

I took a postgraduate course in crime at Western State Penitentiary in Pittsburg, Pennsylvania, having earned the right to matriculate there by assisting in robbing a local jewelry store. Later, I took refresher courses in criminal activities at Stateville Penitentiary in Illinois where I did a short stint for parole violation of my Pontiac release agreement.

Now facing the possibility of becoming a three-time felony loser, I had no friends or relatives that I could rely on for the help I needed. My foster father had died, and my foster mother was elderly and chronically ill. My younger brother and sister, as well as my foster sister, also lacked the means to be of any financial help. All that they could offer me was support for my morale in letters, visits, and a few dollars' spending money.

My older brother was in the process of getting married and buying a home. He disapproved greatly of my proclivity for constantly getting into trouble with the law and bringing shame upon myself and the family. He was an honest, hardworking individual seeking advancement through honorable means. I could not therefore depend upon him to be supportive of my present plight.

Eve and Jimmy Marshall, a very close and dear friend of many years, going back to my early childhood, were the most supportive people in my corner, although my foster mother never failed to make her love known to me in her caring letters.

She would write to me often and visit with me when she could.

*   *   *   *   *

The morning after my court appearance, I was seated at a table, sharing the morning newspaper with Joe Smith. We had just finished our breakfast of oatmeal, plain rolls, and weak coffee. This was the daily breakfast fare day in and day out—fed to us with such regular monotony that it was a blessing to have money to purchase sweet rolls, good coffee, and sandwiches from the commissary cart.

Finishing the front-page section of the *Chicago Tribune*, I laid it aside. Lighting a cigarette, I idly observed the scene before my eyes. Joe was preoccupied with the sports section of the paper and was oblivious to what was going on around him. It was too early for the poker game to start. Besides, Benny was supervising several of the inmates assigned to cleanup duty that were sweeping and mopping the floors of the dayroom and washroom.

Other inmates were reading or chatting with one another as the beginning of another day in jail got underway. What a potpourri of humanity, I thought as I studied my fellow miscreants with amusement. A couple of inmates were doing sit-up exercises on the bench across from me. Several Mexican illegal aliens smuggled into the country from Mexico and driven all the way to Chicago in a melon truck with a false bottom had been placed on our tier a couple days ago, and they were seated together at the table across from where I was seated. Including women, children, and men, there were over twenty of the Mexican aliens scattered throughout the jail and in the

Juvenile Detention Home. The ride from the West Coast to Chicago must have been almost unbearable, I thought.

The several aliens on our tier could not speak any English and were without funds of any kind. They were just waiting deportation proceedings and were trying to make the best of their predicament in a foreign country. Usually, we had a homegrown Mexican or two on the tier. Unfortunately, at this time, there were none among us to interpret for the aliens and the rest of us.

I felt a sense of compassion for these broke and helpless people, and I endeavored to befriend them as best I could with tobacco and occasional candy bars. Most of the other inmates on the tier made fun of the Mexicans, calling them wetbacks and greasers. I tried, however, to encourage the other inmates to chip in on a collection to keep the Mexicans supplied with tobacco; a few sacks of Bull Durham or Dukes Mixure didn't cost that much. But only a few inmates like myself made contributions.

I spoke a little Spanish that I had learned in prison, and although it was difficult, I could communicate with the Mexicans and understand some of their basic needs better than any of the other American inmates on the tier. The Mexicans consequently accepted me as a person who championed their plight and looked up to me for assistance.

One of the group named Juan approached me with a wide grin and greeted me politely, "Buenos dias, senor. Me muero por flunar."

"Buenos dias, Juan," I returned his greeting, at the same time extending my pack of cigarettes to him.

His grin expanded over his bronze features with great pleasure as he withdrew one cigarette from the pack, saying, "Gracias, senor, gracias!"

The commissary cart had not arrived on our tier as yet, and the Mexicans had apparently smoked their yesterday rations. The other aliens stared at me longingly. Knowing they too were craving for a smoke, I took my pack of cigarettes arid placed it in Juan's hand with a motion for him to share the smokes with his amigos.

Juan nodded his head gratefully and asked, "Tiene ud. un fosforo?"

"Si," I said, handing him a book of matches.

"Gracias, senor," he thanked me again and hurried over to the table with his friends to share his good fortune with them. The other Mexicans waved to me appreciatively as they lit up their smokes.

Joe looked up from his paper, saying, "Man, you're spoiling those wetbacks. What Benny ought to do is work those greasy bastards' asses off and free some of the poker players from cleanup duty so we can get the game started earlier."

"That's all you think about is poker. Where is your sense of humanity and charity? Didn't you ever hear of the Golden Rule, 'Do unto others as you would have them do unto you'?" I chided him.

"Yeah, I live by my own golden rule, 'Do unto others before they get a chance to do unto you.' And those goddamned greasers would cut your throat for a fuckin' centavo if they had your benevolent ass in Mexico."

"I could get my throat cut just as fast on the South Side of Chicago if I'm not wary," I countered, then added, "Now fork over a buck or two so I can buy our Mexican friends a few sacks of tobacco when the store gets here."

"Are you kidding or bullshitting? All I got is my poker stake," Joe complained.

"A little charity will make you lucky," I coaxed.

Joe was thoughtful for a moment. "You might be right, Blacky." Digging into his pocket, he pulled out a small wad of bills and peeled off a dollar. "Here," he said, handing me the bill. "I once gave that old blind man selling pencils under the Ell on Fifty-fifth Street a buck, and I'll be damned if I didn't win over a grand playing blackjack in Russel's joint."

That was typical of Joe to give with the expectation of a material return, as though he were making an investment. I knew that if he did not win today at poker, the Mexicans could kiss him good-bye as one of their benefactors.

"I used to have a Mexican whore named Conchita," Joe went on. "But she wasn't worth shit when it comes to turning tricks. The bitch was downright lazy, and I hate a lazy, trifling whore like God hates sin. When I got tired of kicking the bitch's ass, I put her down."

He turned his attention to poker and called out to Benny, the tier boss. "Hey, man, tell your stickman to start the game."

Benny lumbered over to the table, displaying his broad smile. "In a few minutes, Bill will be over to git things goin'. What's a matter, Joe, you can't wait to lose your money?"

"Never mind all the bullshit, nigger, just get Bill's ass over here and get the fuckin' game going," Joe grumbled peevishly.

Benny walked off, still grinning good-naturedly. Joe turned his attention back to me. "Look, Blacky, I know it's not much to be had out of these small stake games. But every little bit counts. Besides, the games help to pass the time, and that matters more than anything else—just passing the time, you know what I mean?" I nodded and he was thoughtful for a moment before going on. "Somehow we got to get control. These dumb, square-ass niggers don't know how to run this fuckin' tier."

Again, I nodded, agreeing, just as Bill Johnson, Benny's number one assistant who ran the poker game, came over and laid a blanket on the end of the long table. The players quickly assembled, and the cards were dealt by the dark-skinned stickman who was about my age. The five-card stud poker game was underway. And the small talk that went on during the games was always amusing.

Kevin Conery, a redheaded young Irishman, sitting in the game across from an elderly Italian named Gino Bagliana, was telling the dago about his court-appointed lawyer.

"After the judge found me guilty, this jackoff lawyer jumps up and cops a plea to the judge that I ain't got no bad criminal record, and this was my first felony conviction, and I shouldn't get over one to five years for burglary. But the judge says, 'Hold on, counselor, I was thinking about maybe we should have this lad investigated for probation.'" Kevin's face was flush with anger as he went on, "Can you imagine that jerk lawyer asking for a light sentence before trying to get me probation?"

Gino, an old-timer with a long criminal record, chuckled. "There's an old saying, 'You get just what you pay for.' If you don't pay nothing, you don't get nothing. And that's exactly what you got for a lawyer—nothing!"

Everyone around the table laughed at Gino's remark.

"Anyway, it was nice of the judge to protect my rights, or I'd be on my way to the joint with a nickle max instead of a chance for probation if it was left up to my shyster lawyer," Kevin said.

"Think you'll get pro, Kev?" Bill asked, picking up the cards to deal a new hand.

The players anted up.

"My mom said an investigator from the probation department came by the house a few days ago and he told her that my chances for pro were very good, so I'll probably be released when I go back to court this Friday."

Joe was king high and opened the pot for 50 cents. There were six players in the game. Everyone called but Bill, the stickman who always played his cards close to his chest, meaning that he only called when he had a potentially good hand at the start of the deal because his primary aim was to cut the pots and play only good hands. Everyone paid attention as Bill dealt the third card to the players.

"Most of those court-appointed lawyers in private practice aren't any better than the public defender. They don't give a shit. All they want to do is get you to cop a plea of guilty," Gino commented, peeping again at his hole card.

Tom Blackman, the sixth man in the game, was a middle-aged Negro awaiting trial for allegedly having intercourse with his thirteen-year-old stepdaughter. He said, "Well, I got a PD, and he ain't so bad. In fact, he's good. He beat a murder rap for a guy last week before a jury. Not all of those PD guys are bad lawyers. Some of 'em care and bust their rumps to put up a good defense."

Joe, still high with the king, was dealt a jack. He tapped my foot under the table. He evidently had a jack in the hole. Gino made a pair of trays with his third card and bet a dollar. His was the only pair showing. Kevin and I folded. Blackman and Joe called Gino's bet.

"Sure, they win a case now and then, but take it from me—a guy who has been around jails and courts' almost all of his life—the pen is full of cons because they never had a decent lawyer to represent them," Gino said.

"Most of the motherfuckers that come in here are guilty anyway, so what do you expect, miracles?" Joe asked sarcastically.

"No, Joe, just a good defense for the guys, that's all. Because I've served time with too many innocent men that got to the joint by having lawyers that were incompetent," Gino answered in defense of his remarks.

Bill dealt the fourth cards, saying, "I got a PD, and he just beat a rape case."

Knowing that Bill was being held on a charge of statutory rape involving a fifteen-year-old girl too young to consent, Joe ridiculed him, "And that PD will probably end up screwing you harder than you screwed that young girl when your case comes up for trial."

Joe's remarks provoked laughter around the table before Gino bet another dollar on his pair of trays. Joe raised him a dollar. Blackman, who was showing a queen high card, also called and raised Joe a dollar. Joe deliberated the hands before him before he called Blackman's bet and raised the pot another dollar. Gino passed, and Blackman called.

Bill replied to Joe as he dealt the fifth and last cards to the two remaining players, "You were able to hire a good lawyer, Joe, 'cause you got money behind you, or your ass would be in the penitentiary instead of sittin' here in the county, playin' poker. But it don't mean your lawyer gets all his clients off free or with light sentences."

Joe caught a king. He now evidently had two pairs, kings and jacks. He contemplated his hand momentarily before betting three dollars. Then he answered Bill. "Maybe my lawyer can't win all his cases. But he gets results, and that's what I pay him for. He is capable of either winning the case or fixing the case, or at the very least, he is capable of paying off to get the lowest possible sentence or probation. A PD can't fix a case. He can only try it or plea bargain for a cop out. Like Gino said, you get just what you pay for," he ended with arrogance and complacency written all over his good- looking light-brown countenance.

Gino nodded his head in agreement. Blackman folded up his hand, not calling Joe's bet, and Joe pulled in the pot after Bill took out his cut. The cards were shuffled for the next deal, and we all anted up again.

We played on until the commissary cart arrived. I bought a few sacks of tobacco and some candy bars for the Mexicans, and we gave them an old deck of playing cards to amuse themselves with.

Our poker game continued until it was time to take a break for lunch. Joe and I were ahead in the game as usual.

The day moved on swiftly into evening, and we were locked up for the night. Some of the inmates amused themselves with light banter and song. Others, like myself, relaxed with a book or magazine to read.

Soon thereafter, the guard walked by, making his first round since taking the count of inmates locked in their cells.

Finally, there was silence, and I turned my attention back to the book I had been reading by the light that filtered into my cell from the lamps on the gallery wall.

Chapter 6

I STOOD IN THE WASHROOM CAREFULLY shaving and grooming myself for my first court appearance since we were arraigned before the chief justice of the criminal court of Cook County. Our attorney, Howard Geter, had filed motions to suppress evidence that was taken during the time of our arrests. One motion even included suppression of the rings seized from Joan at the time of my arrest.

All inmates were allowed to wear their own clothing in jail and to court. And most prisoners kept their best clothing, brought in by their friends and relatives, neat and clean until time for their court appearances. I was no exception. Fashionably attired to sartorial perfection in an expensive silk suit and imported leather shoes from Italy, I adjusted my necktie and stepped out into the dayroom to await being escorted to the courthouse.

"Hey now! Look at Blacky styling like a model out of *Esquire*," Fingers McBride commented. He was a pickpocket who had served time with me in Stateville. He had arrived on the tier a few days ago to await trial for grand larceny.

Joe, dapper dresser himself on the outside, came to give me his eye of approval. "Nice, man. Real nice. Your outfit's together. I like that."

"Thanks," I said simply. Because if this natty pimp liked my attire, it was like getting the seal of approval of the National Tailors Association.

"Blacky, you ought to be like Joe and start macking if you beat this rap you're facing. That stick candy bit ain't your shot," Fingers remarked.

"Yeah. He ought to give that pipe up before he ends up with a murder beef fuckin' 'round with his trigger-happy rap partners. Buddy Morgan will kill a dead house brick, and that loudmouth little mother fucker—Li'L Arthur I'm talking about—well, he's a cold-blooded nigger if I've ever seen one," Joe said disparagingly.

I smiled while listening to their comments. "So you think I'd make a good pimp, eh, Fingers?"

"Shonuff, man! You're a clever cat and a cool dude, Blacky. You could pull some choice broads into a nice stable and let them take care of you," Fingers assured me seriously. He stood watching Joe light a cigarette before going on, "Ain't that right, Joe?"

Joe laughed. "Blacky wouldn't make a pimple on a good pimp's ass. The nigger hasn't got it in him to mack. He's a thief. He'll steal the stink off of shit and sell the smell before God can tell," he concluded, laughing at his own hyperbole.

Fingers let out one of his famous belly laughs. He was tall, thin and semi bald with grayish temples. His wrinkled brown features placed him in the late sixtyish age bracket. He had been around a long time and knew most of the crooks and hustlers around Chicago's South Side, and many other parts of the country where he had plied his deft profession were aware of his light-fingered reputation. He rubbed his chin thoughtfully with his long thinly tapered fingers that still showed a neat manicure. Finally, he said, "I could turn Blacky out to be a dip in a few easy lessons. All it takes is sure fingers and heart. Anything beats putting a pipe in somebody's face and taking their money."

The con men, pickpockets, and pimps always thought that they were the elite among thieves and hustlers, and they viewed robbery with a form of arrogant condemnation that they did not bother to hide with subtleties of expression.

"Don't you cats worry about me. They got your asses in here just like they got mine," I rejoined. "Besides, the only reason a whore has a pimp is so she can wake up every morning and look down on him and say, 'There's one dirty motherfucker lower than me.'" I paused to look at Joe and laughed. Then I added, "I don't want to be a whore's man because I like my pussy without traffic. And none of you will ever see me put my hands in someone else's pocket. Because, brothers, that really takes nerve."

Joe grinned good-naturedly. "Let Blacky keep fuckin' around with those rods and they'll throw the key away on him. Then the only pussy he'll see is round eye on a punk in the joint."

We all laughed together amiably. A few moments later, I was led off the tier to court.

Buddy Morgan, Li'l Arthur, and myself discussed our case in the bull pen adjacent to Judge Ashcraft's courtroom until his bailiff came and led us into the courtroom. We stood before the judge's bench alongside of our attorney. James Brown, the prosecuting attorney, stood off to the side of the bench.

The judge was already seated, and he announced, "For the record, this is a hearing on motions of defense counsel to suppress evidence in the case of *people of the state of Illinois versus Edgar Morgan, Talbert Jennings, and Arthur Smith*." He paused for a moment to spread the typewritten motions out before him. "All right, gentlemen, you may be seated, and the ladies may be seated also. We will now proceed with the hearing. Call your first witness, Mr. Geter."

"Thank you, Your Honor," Geter said before telling Morgan to take the witness stand.

Morgan took the stand and was administered an oath by the clerk who occupied a desk to the right of the judge's bench. Morgan testified under direct examination by Geter how he was arrested and how the jewelry he was wearing, which was a watch and diamond ring, were seized from him by the police. The prosecuting attorney cross-examined him briefly before he was dismissed from the stand.

Next, Li'l Arthur was called to the witness stand. The same procedure followed. I took the stand next followed by Eve and Joan.

After we had all testified, James Brown called Nester, Piotter, and a few other police officers to testify concerning our arrests and the seizure of our property. All the police officers testified that they knew a crime had been committed and that they had reasonable grounds under the circumstances to suspect each of us as being involved in the commission of the crime, that they did not therefore need an arrest or search warrant in apprehending us.

One thing of particular note that developed during Brown's direct examination of Piotter was that Piotter denied, for some inexplicable reason, having seized a ring from me at the time of my arrest.

Judge Ashcraft recessed court for a short period before returning to the bench to make his ruling on the motions. He was a tall, well-proportioned man with a smooth complexion. He seemed almost impassive as he spoke softly in a very distinct voice.

"It is the court's ruling, based on the testimony and arguments I have heard, that the Oak Park police had reasonable grounds to suspect the defendants of having committed crimes—namely, robbery of the Barr Jewelry Store in Oak Park, Illinois. And it is the further ruling of this court that the police did not therefore require a warrant to make the arrests or to search the defendants, the person, or persons in their company or the premises where the defendants were arrested. The motions to suppress the jewelry seized from Edgar Morgan, Arthur Smith, and Joan Wilson are hereby overruled." He paused to glance at his trial notes before he continued. "Since the officer Edward Piotter testified that he did not take a diamond ring from the defendant Talbert Jennings, there is nothing to suppress with regard to him. Therefore it is the ruling of this court that the motion as to him be dismissed."

"Thank you, Your Honor," the prosecutor said, displaying a smile of satisfaction.

The judge set a trial date and remanded us to the custody of the sheriff to be returned to jail. We were led out of the courtroom and returned to the county jail.

The hearing had only taken a couple of hours, and I was back on tier B-3 in time for lunch. The poker game had been temporarily terminated. Benny and Bill were both locked inside the kitchen making preparations to feed the noontime meal. I got permission from the guard to go to my cell and change into my casual clothes before taking my place at the table alongside Joe and Fingers, where I related to them what had happened in court that day.

"You're lucky not to have any evidence they can use that was taken from you connected with that heist, Blacky," Fingers said.

"But I can't figure out for the life of me why that dick denied taking the ring from me, because he sure as hell did take it," I said, still flabbergasted over the situation.

"I wouldn't let it bother me, Blacky. The main thing now is that it won't be used against you," Joe reasoned.

"I guess you guys are right. Why worry about it," I agreed.

We had been confined a little over four months in the county jail without trial. On two occasions, when we were set for trial, the prosecution moved the court for continuances. Judge Ashcraft granted both the continuances over the objections of our counsel. On another occasion, the court continued the case on its own motion because the judge was trying a case before a jury and could not try our case as scheduled. As a result of these delays, our attorney was having us brought into court on a motion he filed to discharge us because the Illinois speedy trial provision, holding that a person committed to jail, must be tried within four terms of court or four months from the date of his commitment if there was no delay on his part. Geter was therefore trying to effectuate our release under the provisions of the speedy trial statute.

When we appeared before Judge Ashcraft, Geter argued his motion predicated upon the court's journal entries, clearly showing that we had not requested any delays in being brought to trial within the four-month statutory period.

James Brown, the prosecuting attorney, argued that we had filed for and had been given a hearing on our motions to suppress evidence, and that in itself was a delay on our part in being brought to trial within the statutory period mandated by law.

Geter further argued that both the state and federal constitutions protected our right to a speedy trial and that the prosecution was trying to use a technicality to have us denied the right to be discharged under the speedy trial provision. The hearing held on our motions to suppress evidence was not a delaying factor per se within the purview of the statute in that we were ready to stand trial that same day after the court ruled against our motions to suppress evidence, that the continuance that followed must thereby be construed as having been done on the court's own motion.

Judge Ashcraft nevertheless ruled against our motion for discharge, thus upholding the prosecution's argument. This made me feel strongly, as Geter did, that the judge made a bad ruling, and I was seething with resentment. Because it seemed quite evident, even to a layman, that the trial record clearly showed that we were not tried within four months from the estate of our commitment in the county jail, and the delay was not caused by us.

Geter too was quite upset over this recent ruling coming after what he believed was a very bad ruling on the motions to suppress evidence. But there was nothing he could do about it.

I liked the way Geter kept his cool. He was a rather smallish brown-skinned man in his late forties who was very astute in the practice of criminal law, and he was very eager to make use of every legal tactic possible to defend the rights of his clients. But I was nevertheless developing a feeling that our attorney was going to be ineffective no matter what, because Judge Ashcraft was a biased and indifferent judge not given to judicial fairness to Geter or to us. And before the case was over, I would be thoroughly convinced beyond an infinitesimal fraction of a doubt that my early opinion of Judge Ashcraft's unfairness was indeed correct.

Again, the prosecuting attorney, James Brown, was pleased over the judge's ruling. He grinned slyly at us like a fox eyeing a flock of chickens. Inwardly, I despised him—not so much because he was prosecuting us but rather because there was something else about him that I found repulsive, like the way he parted his slicked-down hair that had dandruff caking on the nape of his neck in the lower end of the hairline. Or it could have been his yellow teeth that were large and slightly protrusive that made me dislike him so much. But if there was one thing I would learn to respect him for, it was his knowledge of the law and his extraordinary ability to use it to the state's best advantage along with a little chicanery in winning a case. Yet I would also come to deplore his lack of ethics and fairness. In short, James Brown was the kind of lawyer that would try to get away with anything in the interest of winning a case, and I would perhaps be hypocritical if I didn't say that I would rather have him fighting for me any day than fighting against me.

I received my first inkling of wanting to study law when William Donavan came on tier B-3 carrying a box with several law books in it. He had been brought to the county jail from Joliet Penitentiary for a hearing on a petition for writ of habeas corpus that he had composed and filed in the criminal court of Cook County, alleging that he was being held in prison in violation of his state and federal constitutional rights.

Donavan was an elderly man that had a scholarly appearance that reminded me of a college professor. He was soft-spoken and precise in his diction. His clear-blue eyes seemed to mirror a depth of wisdom and patience for a man serving a life sentence for murder. We became friendly almost immediately, and I asked him a lot of legal questions about my case. He seemed to intelligently answer with ease most of my inquiries—sometimes referring to one of his law books to substantiate a point of law.

When I discussed the recent speedy trial hearing that Judge Ashcraft presided over before overruling our motion for discharge, Donavan too was of the opinion that the judge erred in his ruling. He opened a law book titled *Chapter 38: Illinois Revised Statutes - Annotated*. It was the Illinois Criminal Code. He let me read the statute providing for a speedy trial, and I became instantly fascinated with the book! I asked to borrow it to read in my cell at night. Donavan made me welcome to all his law books, and from that day on, I became an avid reader of the law and the cases rendered in written opinions by the state and federal appeals courts.

I wanted to know everything I could find out about illegal arrests, searches and seizure of property, coerced confessions, the knowing presentation of perjured testimony to obtain convictions, and the legal procedures necessary to file appeals. Card games no longer appealed to me as a source of recreation or means to financial gain. Because I became so absorbed in law books that I soon became oblivious to all else.

I sat in a corner and perused Donavan's law books. This was, indeed, a new experience for me, which I enjoyed immensely. I asked Donavan many questions, and I looked up all the legal terms in Black's Law Dictionary that I did not understand.

With time off for good behavior, Joe was scheduled to go home in a few days at the expiration of his one-year sentence. I would miss him and his sardonic wit, unbelievable arrogance, conceit, and scheming disposition. Notwithstanding the quirks in his character and personality that made most people disdainful of him, I found Joe amusing and likeable, but for what particular reason I could not specifically discern because his effect on most people was ambivalent to say the least.

The Mexicans had been deported back to their homeland, and many of the other prisoners who were on the tier when I arrived had either been released or sent to the state penitentiary. But there were always some new prisoners to take their places like a nonending procession of troubled humanity making a transient entrance into this citadel of deprivation before being admitted back into society or into an even greater stronghold for longer periods. Then there were those who entered the county jail to find that it was their final living place on earth. For these were the few that committed suicide, died natural deaths, or were doomed to perish in the electric chair that waited grimly in the execution chamber to claim its victims with mortal efficiency.

While reading the newspaper one morning, I read about a case that the United States Supreme Court had held was a violation of a man's constitutional rights because he was arrested without a warrant, and certain property was seized from him that was later used as evidence against him during his trial. I called the case to the attention of Donavan, and he too read it. When he was done reading, he said, "We can get this complete opinion of the case by simply writing to the clerk of the United States Supreme Court."

"Really!" I cried excitedly. "How much will it cost?"

"It's free. I'll show you how to write for the opinion so that when you want cases in the future ruled on by the US Supreme Court, you will know how to get them. The clerk of the court will also send you copies of the briefs filed by lawyers after the cases have been decided. These are printed in booklet form and will help you to get a better insight into how the lawyers prepared and argued the pros and cons of a case."

"Do you think we can get the briefs in this Upshaw case?" I asked.

"I don't see why not if the clerk has some copies left. At least we can include the request for them along with the request for the Hight Court's opinion."

The more I talked to Donavan, the more I learned, and the more I enjoyed studying the law. I don't know whether it was innate talent or what, but I do know that what so many people found difficult in understanding about the way the law worked did not seem difficult to me. I seemed to enjoy a facility for picking up legal knowledge with extraordinary comprehension. And Donavan, who was a self-taught legal scholar himself, was quick to perceive my ability and therefore encouraged me all the more to keep studying.

Donavan related to me how several years earlier prisoners were not permitted to send out petitions to the courts to contest the legality of their confinement. They had to have lawyers do it for them. If they could not afford lawyers, they were out of luck. And only because of a ruling by a federal judge, the Honorable John P. Barns, chief judge of the federal district court for the Northern District of Illinois, in a case titled United States exrel Bongiorno v. Ragen, Warden, Illinois State Penitentiary, Joliet, Illinois, could it be possible today that inmates could prepare their own petitions and file them in the state and federal courts to seek redress for their grievances. The good judge had threatened to put the warden in jail unless he stopped badgering the prisoners and preventing them from exercising their constitutional rights. The warden, Joseph E. Ragen, who had been acting under the advice of the Illinois attorney general, had to reluctantly permit the prisoners to have access to the courts.

If there was any good I gained from serving time, it could perhaps be ascribed to the education I received that was, for the greater part, self-taught. Having been an indifferent student in school, my education only extended to first year high school before I started my rounds of the penal institutions. But once I was caged and unable to squander my time on lesser enlightening pursuits, I became an eager scholar, thirsty for knowledge in almost every category. My thirst was universal and unquenchable. Reading became my favorite pastime in all the institutions I entered, if there was anything worthwhile reading; and usually, there was plenty of reading material available.

At Western Penitentiary in Pittsburg Pennsylvania, during a twenty-one-month sojourn, I browsed the complete set of the World Book Encyclopedias well as many volumes of philosophy, world history, science, and the classics of fiction and nonfiction literature that filled the shelves of the prison library. I took courses in typing, English grammar, and creative writing to prepare myself for a literary career that never materialized because of my lack of stick-to-itiveness once I was liberated from my confinement.

I loved to read poetry and biographies. Almost no particular subject failed to fascinate me and captivate my mind, even if I only gained a smattering insight into the subject. My thirst for an all-embracing background of knowledge was insatiable! And the thirst for more knowledge followed me into each place of confinement that I found myself. But strangely enough, it would leave me no sooner than I returned to free society where the thrill of freedom gave me the illusion that I could make up for the loss time spent in confinement by the constant pursuit of the pleasures of life that I had sorely missed.

My attitude, however, inevitably led to my own undoing. Because in order for me to pursue the pleasures of life, I first had to obtain the wherewithal with which to purchase these amenities. And as usual, this was done by illegal activities. Activities that only ended up compounding my errors and misdeeds that left me vulnerable to further prosecution and confinement.

Thankfully, the time spent in prison and my self-education was to prove a valuable asset in the days, weeks, months, and years ahead. The seeds of ingenuity had been planted and cultivated almost without me being aware of my potential scholastic ability. What to me was a pastime would soon turn out to be the greatest weapon I had in my mental arsenal with which to fight the tyranny of the judicial system as it presently existed in the lower courts of Illinois, and with which to also challenge the almost crass indifference of the state's appeal courts that failed to properly address themselves to the blatant injustices prevalent in the legal system.

The trial courts in the state of Illinois, in many cases, were making a mockery of justice in dealing with the poor, the uneducated, and the oppressed prisoners that passed through them daily without hope of receiving the due process of law and protection of the law guaranteed to them by the state and federal constitutions. And Illinois was not the only state guilty of these inequities. Although most of the attention would be focused on Illinois, many of the other states were equally as guilty of treating their prisoners just as badly or worse than Illinois when it came to redressing their grievances.

Little did I know at the time that I was being groomed as the catalyst to one day initiate proceedings that would put an end to some of these inequities in the judicial system that effectively denied appeal rights to indigent prisoners.

I felt a great loss when Donavan was returned to the Joliet Penitentiary following the denial of his freedom after the court held the hearing on his habeas corpus petition. Donavan accepted the denial of his freedom philosophically and calmly said that he would appeal the decision. But the loss of my tutor did not, in the least way, deter me from the pursuit that I had undertaken to learn as much about the science of law as I possibly could.

*　　*　　*　　*　　*

Finally, after several months, our case came on for trial before Judge Alan E. Ashcraft Jr. in 1949 A jury was selected, and the trial got underway with James Brown's presentation of the state's case against us. As to be expected, he used all his cunning and skill to convince the court and jury of our guilt.

Our attorney, Geter, fought valiantly to see that we were given a fair trial. He resisted having the incriminating statements that we had made admitted into evidence on the grounds of police brutality and coercion. A hearing was held out of the presence of the jury in which Buddy Morgan, Arthur Smith, and I were allowed to testify to the brutal beatings and coercion used by the Oak Park police to illicit confessions from us.

The Oak Park police, of course, denied any brutality or force was used, and Judge Ashcraft, of course, purported to believe their testimony over our testimony. He therefore admitted the damaging confessions into evidence.

The trial before the jury continued, and we were given a chance to rehash the issue of coerced confessions before the jury for their determination as the triers of the facts of the case so that they might decide in their own minds whether under the circumstances the confessions were the products of having been made on our own volition and were therefore free and voluntary statements.

The all-white jury either apparently believed apathetically that the confessions were made voluntarily, or they, like Judge Ashcraft, were not going to be swayed by the fact that the confessions were involuntary because other incriminating evidence in the case convinced them of our guilt.

One crucial thing of grave consequence did develop with respect to me at the trial. The ring taken from me at the time of my arrest was introduced by the prosecution and admitted into evidence by Judge Ashcraft as part of the loot taken from the jewelry store robbery. This was done over the vigorous objections of Geter. But Judge Ashcraft allowed the ring to be used against me, knowing full well that Piotter had lied at the hearing to suppress the ring illegally seized, and the judge had to know also that the prosecutor, Mr. Brown, was aware of this travesty of justice.

Geter could not believe what he was seeing unfolding before his very eyes as he muttered, while sitting at the defense table, "This is incredible beyond anything I have ever witnessed in all the days of my trial experience."

I too was flabbergasted! It was so difficult to believe that this standard of justice could exist in a courtroom in a supposedly liberal city like Chicago that was far removed from the Deep South where blacks could expect this type of treatment from the judiciary. I sat next to Geter, momentarily mortified. Then suddenly, I became alive with resentment that surged through my mind with such caustic bitterness that it threatened to make me vent to an outburst of profanity in the courtroom. Rallying my reasoning powers, I contained the

93

urge; and instead I manifested my hatred for Judge Ashcraft, James Brown, and the Oak Park police by cursing them silently with every foul epithet and curse word that I could think of. I cursed their mothers for giving birth to them and wished that they had all drowned in their mothers' afterbirth.

The inward eruption of wrath soon subsided, and I felt better for having vented my outrage in the manner I had done. But it would have served to my disadvantage had I made a spectacle of myself by verbally cursing all of them out in open court.

When the jury returned a verdict of guilty against all three of us, I vowed to fight Judge Ashcraft's unfair rulings until somehow, I obtained redress for those wrongs. It was no longer to me a question of guilt or innocence. Certainly, I was aware that I had taken part in the robbery of the Barr Jewelry Store, but at no time had Mr. Barr been physically abused or harmed. True, we had tried to beat the rap to avoid punishment. After all, we were thieves. We were not expected to have ethics or moral values conducive to upholding law and order. We were true to our code to lie, cheat, steal, and try to get away with it. And we did not violate that code. But these stinking bastards, having taken oaths and glorified themselves in being servants of justice and law and order, were a bunch of hypocrites! They were perpetrators of one of the most flagrant violations possible: they all aided and abetted in the knowing use of perjured testimony to obtain the conviction of a defendant.

It was bad enough that Piotter, a police officer, had committed the perjury and that the prosecuting attorney was aware of it in using the ring against me at the trial. But for the trial court to be aware of it too was not just a travesty of justice, it was the epitome of judicial misconduct—at its worst. Because it was all there in the record for everyone to see. Yet it was going to take me over three years—three long years—to get this outrageous miscarriage of justice redressed.

There was no wonder in the fact that I left the courtroom that day in utter bitterness, believing that the judge, the prosecuting attorney, and the police were all lower than the whale shit that lies on the bottom of the oceans.

Geter filed the usual motion for new trial and motion in arrest of judgment in which he listed numerous procedural and constitutional errors made during the course of the almost weeklong trial. Judge Ashcraft, as expected, denied the motions and sentenced Morgan and me to from ten to twenty-five years in the state penitentiary. Li'l Arthur, not having a prior felony conviction, was given a five- to fifteen-year sentence.

There was no way that we could appeal the case through regular judicial channels because we lacked the funds to hire counsel, to purchase the trial transcript, which cost fifty cents per page, or to have abstracts of the trial record and briefs prepared for presentation to the Illinois Supreme Court. To do all this was out of the question. We were indigent, and all these costs incurred in filing an appeal were prohibitive.

Our only hope to seek redress for the violations of our state and federal constitutional rights would have to be done through some type of postconviction proceedings, which at that time in Illinois, we were soon to discover, was simply a farce in trying to determine what if any remedy really did exist.

Shortly, we would join the other prisoners in Illinois for a merry-go-round ride on the so-called existing postconviction remedies that the state made a mockery of to frustrate attempts by prisoners to seek redress for alleged constitutional errors that occurred at their trials.

I had my work cut out for me. But my courage and determination were all the driving force I needed. Maybe Judge Ashcraft, James Brown, and the Oak Park police didn't know it at the time of my conviction, but they had made a crusader for justice out of me with an unswerving determination to litigate my grievances through the state and federal courts.

There was no way that I could possibly know at the time how effective my crusade would be. Because I was obsessed with my own selfish desire to redress my own personal grievances and the thought of helping anyone else, other than perhaps my two rap partners, never entered my mind.

Chapter 7

STATEVILLE PENITENTIARY, KNOWN AS ONE of the toughest prisons in America, was a sprawling maximum-security institution that spread out over several acres of beautifully well-attended landscaped lawns, flower gardens, recreation yards, and modernly constructed buildings and workshops were enclosed inside a tall thirty-two-foot concrete wall on top of which guard towers were strategically stationed.

The inmates wore uniforms of vertical-striped blue shirts, blue denim trousers, and blue caps. Each inmate was also issued a dark-blue light denim jacket and a heavier hip-length coat for cold weather. The state issued a pair of black oxfords to each inmate and a pair of work shoes if he worked on the coal detail or performed heavy labor outdoors. An inmate could purchase another pair of black oxfords through the commissary.

The guards wore khaki shirts, brown uniforms, and brown caps. In the fall and winter, they wore long brown overcoats over their uniforms. The brass-hats were the lieutenants and captains; they wore the same type of uniforms as the guards, only they had extra brass and braid on their caps and coat sleeves. Only tower guards had guns, and only the captains and lieutenants carried blackjacks concealed in their hip pockets.

Four of the five cellblocks were cylindrical in structure; they were called panopticans. There were four tiers to each cellblock called galleries. In the middle of the four cellblocks stood a huge cylindrical-shaped panoptic building that contained the inmates' kitchen, dining room, bakery, and vegetable room where fruits and vegetables were cleaned and processed for cooking or for salads. Leading from the building to the four cellblocks were ground-level tunnels that provided walkways for the inmates to get to and from the dining room without going outdoors.

The four panoptic cellblocks were known as C, D, E, and F houses. And inside each cellblock there were panel-glassed-enclosed cells. The panels of thick glass were small, and each panel had wire enclosed inside the panel to make it shatter proof. Only the windows inside the cells were covered with steel bars.

In the center of the cellblocks was an open round-shaped guard tower from where the doors to the cells were operated and from where constant vigilance could be maintained over the inmates.

Most cells contained three bunk beds and housed that many prisoners. There was a sink with hot and cold running water, toilet, and three radio headphones in each unit for the inmates' listening pleasure. A table desk and stools were all the other furniture in the cells.

A short distance from the panoptic cellblocks stood a long rect-angular-shaped cellblock containing five tiers called galleries on each side of the building. The steel-barred doors to the cells were operated by keyed locks and also by levers at the end of each gallery, which permitted all the cell doors to be opened at the same time. This cell-block was known as B-House. The cells housed two inmates and had a toilet bowl and sink with cold running water only. Headphones were also available to the inmates who had a choice of three radio stations to listen to.

B-House was mostly occupied by inmates assigned to undesir-able jobs such as the coal-hauling detail. Other inmates were held in isolation security cells because of escapes, attempted escapes, or because they refused to conform to prison regulations. These inmates held no jobs and remained alone almost constantly locked up in their cells.

Homosexual inmates, passive and aggressive alike, were held in security cells alone much as the nonconformist inmates were held. Most of the homosexual inmates isolated in these cells were either caught in flagrante delicto participating in acts of anal sodomy or fellatio.

Each prisoner had his name and number painted on a wooden shingle that hung outside his cell. Conventional prisoners had white shingles with black lettering. Prisoners who escaped or attempted to escape from the Joliet Stateville Penitentiaries or the honor farm had red shingles with black lettering. An inmate isolated for attacking a guard had a blue shingle with black lettering. Homosexual prisoners had yellow shingles with black lettering. If an inmate had a combination of offenses, such as attempting an escape and assaulting a guard, his shingle would be painted half red and half blue with black lettering. There was one inmate who had been caught committing all three of the prisons most serious offenses: escaping, assaulting a guard, and homosexuality. Since those offenses entitled him to a red, blue, and yellow shingle, the inmates aptly nicknamed the prisoner Rainbow. And these shingles followed the inmates to each cellblock that they were transferred to and served to single them out to the guards for caution and extra vigilance.

The length of time a prisoner stayed in isolation was determined by the warden or assistant warden based on recommendations of the disciplinarian officer who was usually a captain of the guards.

For infractions of a prison rule, a guard would write up a discipline report stating what the inmate had done. This was called a ticket. The inmate would be summoned to court the next day, except on weekends, and he would be given a hearing before the disciplinarian officer. The officer would read the information on the ticket and allow the inmate to briefly explain his side of the incident. In most cases, the guard writing the ticket was upheld and the prisoner punished. But in a few cases, a glib inmate with a logical explanation for some alleged rule infraction could talk himself out of being punished.

Punishment consisted of deprivation of privileges, such as denial of access to the recreation yard or movie theater for a short period or confinement in a cell called the hole for anywhere from one day to fifteen days. In more serious offenses, an inmate could lose some or all the merit time or so-called good time off his sentence.

The hole was in a small cellblock building that contained the death house and electric chair. Inmates awaiting execution or very

98

desperate and intractable prisoners were kept in the death house cells. On the opposite side of the death house was the hole.

Several inmates could be placed in one cell in the hole because they were roomy with one toilet and no bunks. The inmates in the hole were given two blankets, and they slept on the hard surface of the concrete floor. Prisoners in the hole were given one meal a day at lunchtime, and they were denied reading material and tobacco or any privileges whatsoever.

New prisoners, called fish, were usually isolated in a building annexing the old Joliet Penitentiary, which was located several miles from Stateville. This building was called the diagnostic depot. And that is where I entered prison on March 31, 1949. Here, the new prisoners were held for three to four weeks in quarantine where they were given inoculations against diseases and had the hair sheared off their heads and bodies with electric clippers. Blue Ointment to kill any pediculosis hitchhikers was applied to the prisoners pubic and armpits areas. This was done immediately upon arrival of the new inmates right after they had taken showers. Later, the inmates were given medical, psychological, and sociological examinations.

On the basis of the psychological and sociological examinations given an inmate, the staff at the diagnostic depot would determine to which institution in Illinois would be best suited for the inmate's confinement and possible rehabilitation. Mostly, youthful inmates with no prior felony convictions were sent to the Pontiac penitentiary located in Central Illinois. Inmates with special mental problems were sent to Menard penitentiary in Southern Illinois, where there was also a division for the criminally insane. And mostly middle-aged, elderly, and inmates with past criminal records were sent to the Joliet Stateville penitentiaries, because these were maximum security institutions. Both prisons, however, were run by Warden Joseph E. Ragen, who had built his reputation as a no-nonsense penologist in favor of strict discipline, which he exacted from guards and inmates alike. Infractions of rules by either called for the administration of swift punishment or, in the guards' case, possible suspension or dismissal.

Warden Ragen was a tall, paunchy individual with an Irish ruddy complexion and sparsely graying light-brown hair, which he kept covered most of the time under a wide-brimmed felt hat. There was no doubt about this man in his late fifties being a tough customer if anyone crossed him. Yet he was an apparently religious man, often appearing at the Catholic services with the inmates to worship. He also apparently thought of himself as being a fair and just man. In a lot of ways, he was. But in some other ways, because of his autocratic way of administrating the prisons that he was in charge of and his eagerness to carry out unfair legal restrictions on the prisoners upon the advice of the Illinois Attorney General's Office, many of the inmates deemed him to be a tyrant.

Some of the prisoners thought that the warden was too strict and too set on punishment for the slightest liberty that they might take with his rules. Each inmate, upon arrival, was given a rule book pamphlet with a host of rules between its covers. The inmate was urged to read the booklet immediately, and he was presumed to therefore know each and every rule governing his conduct in the institution. There was no such thing as "I didn't know" or "I didn't understand" tolerated. You read the rule book, and if you couldn't read, you got someone to read it to you. But an inmate never could make use of ignorance of the rules and expect to be excused from punishment.

Warden Ragen had acquired the nickname Meatball from the inmates, probably because they were fed meatballs more frequently than cuts of meat. But it was foolhardy to be caught referring to him by that demeaning sobriquet. Because he prided himself on feeding the inmates a well-balanced diet, and he had a large sign posted in the middle of the dining room: ALL YOU CAN EAT BUT NO WASTE.

Still, the inmates, among themselves, referred to Warden Ragen as Meatball and often made disparaging remarks about his intelligence because he had a limited formal education and was reared in a hick town in Illinois. To illustrate the warden's strict attitude on discipline and punishment, together with his provincialism, old-timers around the prisons were fond of telling new prisoners the following anecdote Meatball was summoned to the honor farm where a tractor cultivating machine was on fire.

"Who done it?" the warden cried out angrily.

"It was started by spontaneous combustion," the guard replied.

"Well, damnit, man, don't just stand there! Throw him in the hole!"

With due deference to Warden Ragen, he was a self-made man and quite intelligent, with a spark of good old Irish humor when he wanted to turn on a bit of charm and temporarily drop his stern mien. A biography of him titled *Warden Ragen of Joliet* by Gladys Erickson contains many humorous incidents of his relations with the prisoners during his tenure as the warden of the Joliet-Stateville Penitentiaries and the Menard penitentiary in Southern Illinois where he first broke in as a warden.

Warden Ragen's approach to penology was to keep each inmate, who conformed to the prison rules, busy with a job or learning one of the many vocational trades offered at the prison or in elementary school furthering his education. Educational programs in the prison were many and varied if an inmate wanted to take advantage of them. They ranged from completing grammar school and high school also through general educational development testing sponsored by the American Council on Education and an official agency of the veterans testing service. A two-year college course was offered at the prison and administered by Wilson Junior College located in Chicago. Upon graduation, an inmate would receive his degree from the college with no evidence of it having been earned in prison.

Religious services were encouraged. There were Catholic, Protestant, and Jewish services and chaplains available to the inmates. The black Muslim religion was not permitted, and this was because of their radical and so-called racist background. This prohibition, however, was later to create such a controversy among those prisoners wanting to practice their faith that it eventually led to possible court litigation that got me involved in the background, although I attended the Episcopalian services and on occasions participated as an acolyte. Still, I felt that the Muslim inmates had a right to enjoy the same equal treatment of worship that was accorded the other denominations.

It was back into the foregoing prison atmosphere that I found myself. Prison-wise from past experience made my first thoughts concerned with getting the hell out of B-House where new prisoners were domiciled until given a job or school assignment that would transfer them into one of the more comfortable panoptic cellblocks.

Having completed the apprentice barber course while serving time in Pontiac several years ago, I planned to seek a transfer to the inmates' barbershop in Stateville, under the pretext of obtaining my registered or master barber license. With additional practice and study, I of course obtained the registered license, but my main objective was to be in a position where I could make contacts with practically all of the inmates in the institution.

Twice a week, an inmate was permitted a shave in the barbershop; and once a month, he got a haircut. Because no safety or electric razors were allowed the inmates in their cells. In the barbershop, I could easily contact the best prison lawyers for advice and acquire loans of law books while at the same time build my own law library. This was highly essential since the prison library did not have many law books; and what few law books there were, they were usually always out on loan.

I had been temporarily assigned to the coal detail working the morning shift until there was an opening available in the inmates' barbershop. I knew several of the inmates working in the barbershop whom I had served time with at Pontiac and the prior stint I served in Stateville. These acquaintances would put in a good word for me with the barber instructor, Mr. Harry Wenger, and it wasn't long before I was assigned to the barbershop and to C-House where the barbers were domiciled.

My first day on the coal detail was not very pleasant. I had not done any exercise during my confinement in the county jail or in the diagnostic depot. My muscles were not accustomed to the hard work of shoveling coal.

The coal was hauled to the prison in railroad cars and dumped outside the wall. A detail of trusties would shovel the coal through a chute, and it would fall inside the prison where it would be loaded into wheelbarrows and hauled to storage piles inside the yard. My assignment was to shovel the coal to the top of a storage pile as it was unloaded in my work area.

My first day on work duty was not a total loss because I met an inmate named Bill Trigg who was studying law. He was in the process of litigating his case through the Illinois courts. Trigg had been assigned to the coal detail several months ago because he had been discovered preparing a petition for a writ of habeas corpus for another prisoner. Prison rules forbade any inmate from helping another inmate to prepare his case for litigation. This rule, at best, was based on the flimsy grounds that it was illegally practicing law to help an inmate with a legal matter. A prisoner therefore was allowed to work on his own case, but no one else's case; and if caught doing so, punishment usually ranged from ten to fifteen days in the hole and a transfer to the coal detail until the officials saw fit to reassign the offending prisoner to another job. Most prisoners deemed the rule oppressive and an attempt to repress their access to the courts. Because most of the prisoners lacked the education, self-confidence, and ability to understand the complexities of the science of law to the degree required to petition the courts or file appeals.

Some prisoners with legal knowledge, known as writ writers, preyed on other naive prisoners for fees of cigarettes and other commissary items to prepare petitions and appeals for their unlearned fellow inmates. Some of these writ writers deliberately convinced other inmates that they had meritorious appealable errors in their cases, when in truth, these con artists knew perfectly well that there was no merit in the victimized inmates' cases. These same writ writers even went as far as encouraging their clients to have their friends and relatives send money to them in payment for their services. This practice had become so prevalent in the institution that it only served to convince the officials that they were right in their regulation to prohibit inmates from assisting other inmates in the preparation of their cases for appeals.

Notwithstanding the prison rule, many inmates, acting undercover, continued to write petitions called writs for other inmates, either for a fee or simply to help another inmate who was not capable to prepare his own writ. In the latter situation, the inmate assisting gratis usually firmly believed that his client had a meritorious cause of action. But these charitable writ writers were in the minority in this large dual-prison system with a population of about 4,700 inmates in the Joliet-Stateville penitentiaries.

The seemingly endless coal-bearing wheelbarrows continued dumping load after load of coal, and every muscle in my body seemed to ache at the same time as I tossed shovelful after shovelful of coal on to the pile. I paused to wipe my heavily perspiring brow and wondered how Buddy Morgan and Li'l Arthur were faring. Buddy was assigned to the coal detail working on the afternoon shift, and Li'l Arthur had been assigned to work in the dining room as a waiter.

Bill Trigg wheeled a load of coal to my area and dumped it in front of me, saying, "Blacky, you look a little pooped out there, boy. What do you say we take a break and walk over to the water cooler for a drink?"

"I say it sounds good to me, Trigg," I responded, breathing rather heavily.

I dropped my shovel and strolled over to the water cooler with Trigg. Everyone called him by his last name, he had told me earlier, so I refrained from calling him Bill.

"Of course, you know, it'll take a couple weeks to get your muscles used to this grind, Blacky. The best thing is to switch from shovel to wheelbarrow and vice versa. That way, you rest your shoveling muscles. Then when your wheelbarrow muscles get tired, you can switch back to the shovel," Trigg suggested amusingly.

"And how do I make the switch?" I asked before drinking down a cool cup of water.

"Pick out another newcomer hauling coal, and he'll be glad to switch with you, because his wheelbarrow muscles are just as tired as your shoveling muscles."

I laughed at his remark and said, "Sounds like sense to me."

"I would switch with you, Blacky. But since I want to continue our discussion, perhaps I can find one of the guys on this detail to make the switch with you."

"Fine! See what you can do, Trigg. I can sure use the relief."

One of the guards spotted us lingering about the water cooler and shouted, "Trigg, you and the new inmate get back to work."

"Yes, sir," Trigg acknowledged politely. Then he whispered hastily, "I'll try to find someone to spell you."

"Thanks. See you later," I replied before walking back to my work area.

The guard walked over to me, took notice of the number on my back, and growled, "Hey, 28051, when you go to get a drink of water, get it and get back to work. You don't stand around the cooler chewin' the fat. If I catch you doing that again, I'll have to write you up."

"Yes, sir," I replied courteously and added, "And I wantta thank you too, Officer." Inside my mind, however, I was thinking, "Aw, go fuck yourself, screw!"

Trigg returned shortly with a load of coal. Another inmate followed closely behind him. When he too dumped his load, Trigg introduced us. "Blacky, this is Frisco, he's a pal of mine. Frisco, meet Blacky Jennings, he's no fish. He's been down before."

Frisco and I greeted each other. Then Trigg continued, "Frisco came to spell you on the shovel. You can take his wheelbarrow now."

"Is it okay with that guard? The screw just hassled me about hanging around the water cooler."

"Sure, it's okay. The screws don't give a shit what you do so long as you're working. Now let's get moving before that son of a bitch looks over here and accuses us all of loafing," Trigg remarked.

I rolled the wheelbarrow back toward the coal chute with Trigg alongside of me. "Blacky, you have to watch out for that screw that jumped on you. His name's Allen, and he's bucking for a promotion. He writes a lot of tickets, and some under the slightest provocation."

"Yeah, I know the type. I'll keep my eye on him though."

We stopped for loading at the coal chute before slowly pushing our wheelbarrows back to the storage pile. "Tell me, Trigg, what law books do you have that maybe I can borrow? I'll take good care of them. I'll be purchasing some law books shortly, and I'll be more than glad to share them with you."

"I can let you have the Illinois Revised Statutes, some volumes of *Corpus Juris Secundum, Illinois Criminal Procedure*, and *Illinois Civil Procedure*. Also, I have copies of a lot of Northeastern Reports containing Illinois Supreme Court decisions and some federal reports containing opinions of the US Supreme Court, and a bunch of other stuff. You're welcome to any of it."

"Thanks, pal. Loan me everything you got on coerced confessions, illegal search and seizure, and the knowing use of perjured testimony to obtain a conviction; that'll do it for starters."

"You got it, Blacky. I'll go over my stuff when I get back to my cell, and I'll send it to you this evening by the runner. But be careful! Put your name and number on the material when you get it, so if a screw is nosing around in your cell, he'll think the books belong to you."

"You mean inmates can't loan law books to one another?"

"Hell no! The runner is only allowed to carry newspapers and magazines. You've been here before. You ought to know that. The runner can even get busted for putting law books in cells. But John will take a chance carrying anything for a pack or two of butts."

"I see. I just didn't know about the law books because when I was here before, all this law business didn't interest me. Anyway, I'll give the runner a couple packs of cigarettes when he delivers the books."

"Okay."

"And, Trigg, I've got a few bucks on the commissary books, so if you need anything when I go to the store, I'll be more than glad to get it for you."

"Knock it off, Blacky. You don't owe me a thing. You seem to be an all right dude, and I'm glad to help out any way I can."

"Thanks again, pal. I really appreciate it."

"And by the way, Blacky, I'll try to set you up in good standing with some of the other guys who have law books. Maybe you can arrange to borrow books from them also—especially after you start accumulating some books of your own to lend."

"Very good, Trigg! You're a real pal!"

At eleven o'clock, we ended our shift and lined up to march to the shower room where we would shower and change into clean uniforms of blue denim pants and blue-striped shirts. The shower room was adjacent to the prison laundry; and, thankfully, another plus for the warden was his being a stickler for cleanliness.

After showering, we returned to B-House for a short period before being let out of our cells for lunch. Trigg celled on seventh gallery, and I celled on fifth gallery, one tier below. There were ten galleries in B-House, an even side and an odd-numbered side; so on our side of the cellblock the numbers ran 1, 3, 5, 7, and 9 galleries. On the other even side of the cellblock, the numbers ran 2, 4, 6, 8, and 10 galleries.

Following lunch, we returned to our cells for another period of relaxation before being permitted the privilege of recreation outdoors in one of the large yards provided for that purpose. Some of the inmates played baseball, basketball, and checkers or chess. Some other inmates lifted weights, pitched horseshoes, or just walked about, chatting idly.

Being too tired to play anything, I joined Trigg in strolling around the yard, discussing law. Occasionally, Trigg would stop and introduce me to other inmates interested in law or who had cases pending before the courts, and we would stand and chat with these inmates. We all had the same thing in common—a desire to litigate our cases.

Sometimes in discussing a case with an inmate, Trigg and the other prisoner would get into a difference over a point of law, and there would be a debate on the spot with promises to look up the law and the decisions governing the particular issue being discussed to prove who was right. They would stand confronting one another, citing cases like lawyers in a courtroom, and this fascinated me. I enjoyed watching and listening to these yard-court arguments.

Trigg, like myself, being a light-skinned Negro, would become flush-faced in stressing his point of view. He had red hair to blend with the tinge of redness in his complexion. His body was firm, with broad shoulders, and he stood just under six feet tall, weighing I would think just a shade under 180 pounds. He was in his early thirties and was serving a sentence of five to ten years for armed robbery. His conviction, he claimed, was obtained by reversible procedural errors and constitutional errors that denied him due process of law.

Sometimes in the not too distant future, I knew that I too would be participating in these yard-court debates because I had become obsessed with the study of law. And my number one mission in life at the time was to get that unscrupulous bastard, Judge Ashcraft, overruled and my conviction reversed on the basis of the unthinkable errors he made in his rulings during our trial. Somehow and someway, this just had to be done because I knew that he was wrong in his rulings—especially in permitting perjury to be used by the prosecution at the trial.

Right and justice was on my side all right. But to make myself heard in a court of competent jurisdiction was my immediate problem, and I realized that it was not going to be easy solving that problem.

Chapter 8

I HAD BEEN WORKING IN THE prison barbershop for about two months, having been transferred there after spending about six weeks on the coal detail. Work in the barbershop was heaven compared to working on my prior assignment. I was always neat, clean, and well-groomed. Most of all, I was having all kinds of success in meeting the best writ writers in the joint and obtaining access to a wealth of legal information and legal material with which to further my studies.

Being considered a good barber with past experience, I was immediately assigned a barber chair instead of working as a barber's helper as the student barbers did. About thirty barber chairs lined the walls of this large shop, and there was a large waiting room adjacent to the barbershop. An inmate assigned to the barbershop would stand in the middle of the floor, directing inmates to barber chairs by calling out the number on the wall behind each chair as a vacancy became available. There would be one inmate in the chair being worked on and another inmate standing in front of the chair to be worked on next.

The inmate doing the directing was the key to making contacts for a slight payoff in cigarettes, which was the inmates' form of currency in the institution. Because no inmate was permitted to have cash money on his person or in his cell, that is not to say that some inmates did not have cash money, which they used to bribe some guards with for special favors.

The chair caller knew the special customers of the barbers and directed their customers to them. Although there was no charge for shaves or haircuts, some inmates preferred to be worked on by the same barber each time they visited the shop, and they were willing to put out a pack of cigarettes for a shave and two packs for a haircut. The barber in turn would pay the chair caller a few packs each week for sending him his customers. Needless to say, this was all in violation of the prison rules against "contacting" and "accepting remuneration for tonsorial services.

Cigarettes were confiscated as contraband by the guards if they caught a barber accepting them from an inmate. The guard would also write the barber and his customer a ticket. And the barber would not only be punished by a stint in the hole, but he might also be transferred to the coal detail. Inmates, however, were rarely caught in these transactions. They were usually much smarter than the guards in finding means of violating prison rules with impunity than the guards were at catching them in the act of violating the rules.

Since commissary day fell on one of the same days an inmate went to the barbershop, most of the barbers would have their customers leave cigarettes in the commissary adjacent to the barbershop waiting room. The inmate who clerks in the commissary would hold the cigarettes until the barber or one of his C-House contacts would pick them up and deliver them to him or his gallery boy. Gallery boys were inmates who were assigned one of the tiers to sweep and mop a couple times each day as well as joining together with the other gallery boys to sweep and mop the spacious cellblock floor area. Inmates, however, were responsible for keeping their own cells clean. And their cells must pass the inspection of the cellblock keeper, or the inmates occupying an untidy cell would be given tickets and subjected to punishment for uncleanliness.

The barbershop chair caller worked closely with the inmate working in the adjoining waiting room in charge of seating the inmates brought in for barber service and for shopping at the commissary. The waiting room attendant, for a slight fee, would set up contacts between inmates and barbers for all kinds of transactions that broke prison rules. Pills for getting high on, alcoholic beverages made from raisins and other fruit that was secretly fermented in the prison, while not in common supply, were, nevertheless, available to those inmates with the wherewithal to negotiate for these contraband items. Marijuana and a host of other contraband was cleverly smuggled about the institution as well, a great deal of which passed through the barbershop and was passed on to inmates, who passed it elsewhere.

In spite of prison security shaking down the inmates at various checkpoints, the inmates, nevertheless, concealed items with little chance of being discovered in a routine frisk. Kites, pills, marijuana, knives, and other small items were difficult to detect. Larger items were snugly stashed in the inmate's crotch where guards were reluctant to feel. Only a strip search threatened the security of an inmate carrying contraband on his person. But strip searches occurred rarely and only when a guard had reasonable grounds to suspect that an inmate was carrying concealed contraband on his person, or in the case of a tool of some kind being unaccounted for. Sometimes, an entire shop of inmates might be ordered to strip naked for a thorough clothing and body search if a steel cutting tool was missing or some other object that could be fashioned into a weapon.

Obtaining loans of law books from inmates in other cellblocks was quite simple with the proper connections. Since each cellblock had an inmate librarian assigned to it, who returned and picked up books from the prison library each day, an inmate, paying a slight fee, could get the cellblock librarian to either transfer or pick up law books from other cellblock librarians when they met in the prison main library to pick up regular library books.

The guards never inspected the many books taken out of the cellblock or brought into it by the cellblock librarian. They only frisked his person going out and coming in, and the guards only made a cursory examination of his library cart for other forms of contraband, such as food, liquor, tools, and things of that kind. I therefore encountered no difficulty in getting all the law books available once I selected some of the prison's best writ writers as my barber customers.

Prison regulations limited each inmate to possesing only eight law books. Needless to say, that was wholly insufficient for one seriously undertaking the study of law as I was. To circumvent this rule, I had each of my cell mates acquire permits for eight law books as well as other friends not studying law. The books were held for me by these inmates until I needed them.

There was always the never-ending game between inmates and the guards to see who could outfox who—and I played the game damn well. One clever inmate had made a replica of the rubber stamp used by the officials to imprint the law book permit on books owned by the inmates. For a nominal fee, an inmate could get all the permits he needed made on a sheet of paper that could be cut down to the size of any law book and glued inside the cover.

Trigg, being one of my regular patrons, kept me informed of everything going on in B-House with respect to legal matters and legal material that might be of interest to me. When an inmate went to court on a writ or was paroled or discharged, they all came to the barbershop for a shave and a haircut. This afforded me an excellent opportunity for contacting friends not on my correspondence or visiting list.

The rules of communication were so strict that an inmate could only write one censored letter each week to a relative or friend on his authorized correspondence list. And he had to select the relatives and friends to whom he desired to communicate with when he first arrived in prison. After that any changes in his correspondence list would have to be approved by the warden, captain, or officer in charge of the mail office.

A qualified friend or relative could visit an inmate for one hour every two weeks in a visiting room across a table with a guard watching the whole time the visit takes place. Visitors were not permitted to bring an inmate any foodstuffs or beverages. They were, however, permitted to purchase ice cream, candy, fruit, and cigarettes at a commissary stand in the administration building before they left the prison. These items purchased would later be delivered to the inmate's cell.

Prison life was a whole network of scheming, concealing, spying, stealing, lying, and trying to outwit the prison administration in every way possible. Stool pigeons were therefore dealt with harshly if discovered. Serious harm or even death could befall an inmate snitch.

Because a traitor could upset the network of subterfuge carried on by the inmate body.

Once a snitch was discovered, it was a race between the administration and the inmates to see who could get to him first. If the snitch was lucky, the administration got to him first and transferred him to another prison. If the inmates got to him first, the snitch might be transferred to the cemetery. I have known of cases where stoolies met fatal vengeance after their release from prison. Because once a stool pigeon was discovered, his reputation followed him by the "grapevine," no matter where he went. As a result, Stateville, being one of the toughest prisons in the country, was not overpopulated with informers as the paranoia of some inmates would erroneously lead some people to believe.

Because of the strict manner by which this maximum-security prison was run, it was necessary for the inmates to band together against the administration. Most of the inmates disliked Warden Ragen and his staff because they kept a tight lid on the prison and inmates alike. But there were always some members of the staff that enjoyed popularity with the inmates for demonstrating commendable fairness in their treatment of the prisoners. Assistant Warden Joseph Dort, an elderly, smooth-talking, kindly appearing gentleman who had risen from the ranks to become assistant warden, was generally regarded by the convicts as a fair person. And inmates reluctant to take their problems directly to Warden Ragen would seek out Warden Dort or a chaplain for advice, or for a special letter or visit when there was serious illness or death in the family, or when some other personal problem existed.

Father Weir, the Catholic chaplain, was another very popular person in the prison that inmates of all faiths could turn to for help in solving personal problems. What a prisoner said to Father Weir was like a confession if the prisoner wanted the conversation held in the strictest confidence. The Catholic priest held great influence in the prison and saved many an inmate from a trip to the mental ward by intervening at the right time to help solve a problem that less sympathetic and indifferent prison staff member could not solve.

His successor, Father Brinkman, was equally effective as the inmates' priest.

Although Father Brinkman was sympathetic to black inmates' claims of prison biasness, he could not sway Warden Ragen to change the prison's unfair job assignment policy in which blacks were not given equal opportunities. This troubled the Catholic chaplain greatly, because he felt that all the prisoners should be treated in a like manner. And this too was another thing that I would address myself to in the future when my legal talents became recognized and my influence considered a viable and effective force in extracting compromises from the administration.

Neither Joliet nor Stateville were integrated racially. Although white and black inmates shared the same cellblocks and the same galleries, they did not share the same cells. Like many places on the outside, blacks found themselves shut out from certain jobs in the prison such as clerical, teaching, and instructor positions, as well as nursing and hospital lab technicians. Most of the menial jobs around the prison were assigned to blacks, such as portering and janitorial jobs. The prison administration's attitude, therefore, instilled blacks with bitterness over the prejudicial treatment being accorded them. Making up over 30 percent of the prison population at that time, it was not easy for black inmates to swallow the old bullshit cliché that the white inmates were better qualified for some jobs more so than black inmates.

Blacks, however, were given an equal opportunity for vocational training jobs. And although most of the blacks deemed Warden Ragen a racial bigot, a more liberal analysis would not seem to place him in that exact category. He usually employed a black inmate as his personal barber and showed a preference for blacks as domestics in the spacious and luxurious apartment that he and his family occupied in the administration building. But some black inmates would argue, "Didn't whites do that in Southern households?" Others argued, "Warden Ragen is so escape-conscious that he thinks it's too risky to place too much trust in white inmates that are regarded a far greater menace when it came to plotting and carrying out escapes." But these were both fallacious arguments, because many white inmates were given responsible trusty jobs in and outside the prison without incident. And wasn't it a black who aided Roger Touhy and his band of inmates in their daring escape from Stateville by smuggling guns into the prison while a trusty working outside the prison walls.

The truth of the matter was that Warden Ragen based his black-and-white inmate job policy on trying to avert trouble between the races. True, he showed favoritism in his policy in favor of the white inmates, because it was the attitude of many white inmates and guards alike—especially the ones from Southern Illinois—that they felt more comfortable working closely with their own kind and being administered to or instructed by their own kind rather than by or with a black inmate. The same policy applied to hiring guards. Not a single black officer was on the prison staff inside the wall when I arrived at Stateville. Warden Ragen's attitude, therefore, left no room for doubt that he was biased and, in that sense, to be a racist. This belief was formulated by my own thinking and personal analysis of the warden gleaned from confidential talks with my own chaplain and the Catholic chaplain who both left no room for doubt that they did not approve of the unfair situation in job assignments with respect to white and black inmates.

Being short of funds was a handicap, but through the generosity of Eve and Jimmy Marshall, who both wrote to me often and visited me several times a year, I was able to obtain the common-law record of my trial proceedings, which included the rulings of the court on continuances, pretrial motions, motions during the trial on some law matters and other orders of the court including sentencing and final judgment. I also was able to obtain certified copies of excerpts of the testimony taken at the trial by paying fifty cents per page for the portions I needed to support my allegations. Because it was impossible, under my existing financial condition, to obtain the complete transcript that ran well over one thousand pages, I therefore decided to obtain just those portions of the transcript that dealt with the following claims upon which I intended to petition the court for relief:

1. Denial of a speedy trial.
2. Conviction with the use of illegally obtained evidence.

3. Perjury known to the trial court and prosecution.
4. Use of a coerced confession to obtain my conviction.

These would be my four cardinal allegations in raising constitutional questions of violations of my state and federal constitutional rights.

I could not file an appeal directly to the Illinois Supreme Court because I lacked the funds to file a bill of exceptions, which included the entire transcript of the trial proceedings. I therefore decided to start exhausting my state remedies and see if I could maneuver my case into the federal district court for a habeas corpus hearing.

My first attempt at preparing a petition was perhaps more than a trifle amateurish, but I could only gain experience by doing it myself. I therefore drew up my own petition for writ of habeas corpus and filed it in the Will County Courthouse after first having Trigg go over the petition for any constructive criticism that he might care to offer. He thought that I had done a fairly good job with a few exceptions, and he helped me improve my petition in accordance with his critical advice.

The reason I filed my first petition in the Will County Courthouse was because I was being held in Will County where Stateville was located. Then too I was naming Warden Ragen as the respondent and alleging that he was holding me in prison illegally, contrary to due process of law based on the four cardinal allegations alleged in my petition.

I did not have much confidence of receiving either a hearing or a discharge from confinement in the Will County Court. But before I could reach the federal court with my complaints, I had to first give the state courts every possible opportunity to redress my grievances. This was known as "exhausting state remedies," which was usually done by filing habeas corpus or coram nobis petitions.

The attorney general of Illinois, along with the local prosecuting attorneys, was resisting my efforts by making use of the same technicalities and stratagems that they used to circumvent all prisoners' attempts to find a remedy with which to redress their grievances; namely, that habeas corpus was not the proper remedy to redress constitutional violations, that the questions raised by the prisoners had been adjudicated by the trial courts, and that res judicata precluded another hearing on these issues in that habeas corpus could not take the place of a direct appeal from the prisoners' convictions.

When I was denied relief in the Will County Court, I filed a similar petition for habeas corpus in the trial court in Cook County while appealing the decision of the Will County Court to the Illinois Supreme Court. Later when my petition was dismissed in the trial court, I appealed that too. And whatever legal move I made for myself, I also made the same move for Buddy Morgan and Li'l Arthur by preparing their legal documents so that they could personally file them with the courts.

When my appeal was denied by the Illinois Supreme Court, I filed a petition for writ of certiorari in the United States Supreme Court; and when that court denied certiorari, I filed a petition for writ of habeas corpus in the United States District Court for the Northern District of Illinois that was located in Chicago, only to have it, too, denied; mainly on the grounds that I had not exhausted all of my available state remedies. The attorney general of Illinois had contended in his reply to my petition, as he did in most cases, that the prisoners should allow the trial courts an opportunity to redress the allegations. This of course was contrary to the res judicata theory he had raised in the state courts as a basis for denial of relief. Another favorite reply was that "the petitioner's petition did not state a cause of action upon which relief could be granted." Then to top that off, opposing counsel from the Office of the Illinois Attorney General went even a step further by contending that the Illinois Pardon Board was an adequate state remedy that should be exhausted before a prisoner could seek a hearing in the federal district court. That, of course, was just a bunch of legal bullshit to keep prisoners on the Illinois legal merry-go-round.

The runaround in my case had started, and I wondered what the state of Illinois would do next to deny prisoners a chance to be heard in court on their grievances. The state's lawyers simply continued to grease the gears of the merry-go-round, and the vertiginous ride seemed to be endless for the inmates filing their petitions. And like all merry-go-round rides, the prisoners always ended up right back where they started from—in prison.

Through constant reading of the law and preparing petitions and appeals, I was fast becoming learned and proficient in its practice and procedure. I had gained a lot of knowledge because of my genuine interest in the subject, and my obsession with the purpose of proving Judge Ashcraft wrong that I wanted to do more than anything else no matter how long it took to do so. Yes, I wanted him to eat crow, and then maybe later see the attorney general of Illinois eat a bit of crow too for being a stumbling block in the path of justice.

But for the nonce, I must face the fact that even though I had learned firsthand how to prepare and file appeals to the Illinois Supreme Court and the United States Supreme Court, nowhere was I getting a hearing on my allegations as the weeks turned into months and the months into years.

* * * * *

Because of much criticism by the federal district courts and the United States Supreme Court that were being inundated with petitions for relief filed by prisoners (riding on the Illinois legal merry-go-round) to have their complaints aired in court, the Illinois legislature enacted into law in 1951 what has come to be known as the Illinois Postconviction Hearing Act. The new act was intended to provide a clear-cut remedy for any person who is imprisoned in the penitentiary in violation of his constitutional rights.

With the enactment of the new law, excitement swept through the prison like a charge of electricity. At last! It appeared that there now existed an appropriate remedy for prisoners seeking judicial hearings on their allegations of constitutional violations occurring at the trials in which they were convicted.

Almost before the print was dry on the new law, the Illinois legislature was flooded with requests for copies of the law.

I received a copy and studied it carefully before preparing and filing my petition and petitions for Morgan and Li'l Arthur. The new postconviction law seemed to rectify defects in the other so-called remedies of habeas corpus and coram nobis proceedings.

The new act also made provision for appointment of counsel in the trial court if a hearing was allowed. And the act also made provisions for the court to refer to a transcript or so much of those proceedings culminating in defendants' convictions as relevant, if such transcript was in fact available, and the court could give such measure of credence to all evidence adduced as it deemed proper.

Having gone over the law very carefully, I could only detect at the time one possible flaw—that was that the petition had to be filed in the trial court and might end up back before the judge who tried the case. I did not have long to wait before my foreboding thought was proven correct. The chief justice of the criminal court of Cook County and his colleagues decided that common comity dictated that if a judge was still sitting on the bench, then cases he tried should properly be assigned to him for hearing and disposition on all postconviction proceedings filed under the new act.

Needless to say, when Judge Ashcraft received our petitions, he treated them with the same unfairness that characterized his conduct at our trial. He did not grant a hearing but instead dismissed the petitions on the Cook County State's attorney's motion that our claims were foreclosed by the doctrine of res judicata and that the petitioners failed to state a cause of action.

Yes, sir! Here we were again back on the Illinois legal merry-go-round, I thought. That old hackneyed legal stratagem was put into play again—*res judicata*, meaning the trial court had previously ruled on our allegations during the trial. But where and when would we ever find a remedy to test the correctness and propriety of Judge Ashcraft's rulings?

Undaunted by this latest setback, I appealed to the Illinois Supreme Court under the appeal provisions of the Illinois Postconviction Hearing Act, and I waited on that court's decision with high hopes. Surely, I thought, any layman or uneducated person with not an iota of legal understanding but capable of interpreting "fair play" could readily perceive by reading Detective Plotter's testimony that he had indeed lied, and that this fact in the record was clearly known by the trial judge and prosecutor. But law and legal pleadings have never lent themselves to such simplicity, and therefore, law interpretation was and always will be something of a mystery in America to laymen. Because there must always be grounds for complications, artifice, and a lawyer's most staunch ally in opposing a case—"technicalities." For without the use of oftentimes meaningless and irrelevant technicalities, the law might make a whole lot more sense to lawyers as well as to lay people.

How else could lawyers make a living if everyone could easily fathom their world of legal hocus-pocus. Why! Had not lawyers invented their own language—"legalese?" Was not this done to befog and befuddle the laypeople whom the lawyers made their living from? Did you ever notice how lawyers can almost vent their spleens of anger and vituperation upon one another in the courtroom and walk away palsy-walsy like two prize fighters after having battered each other to a pulp? Well, to lawyers, it is all a sport too—just an exercise in legal gymnastics. This point can no better be illustrated than in the cause celebre murder case in which the great criminal lawyer Clarence Darrow defended Nathan Leopold and Richard Loeb. He and the state's attorney, Robert Crowe, berated one another for days during the trial, as pointed out in Irving Stone's biography, *Clarence Darrow for the Defense*. Yet Darrow and Crowe were to remain friends after the trial just as Darrow remained friends with most of the prosecutors he had faced in his long career.

What is "due process of law"? Due process of law is simple to understand when viewed from a basic standpoint. It simply means "fair play." If a football player gets clipped by another player on the field, or a boxer hits his opponent with a blow below the belt, the crowd screams, "Hey! That's not fair!" Well, in court, there are rules to be played by; and when you see a judge and a prosecutor look the other way when a policeman commits perjury to convict a defendant, the cry of, "Hey! That's not fair!" should be in order. But so far, the only one crying out, "Hey! That's not fair!" was voiced by me, and I didn't have the key to the prison gate to redress my own illegal confinement. Someone with jurisdiction and judicial authority had to cry out with me, "Hey! That's not fair!"

I discovered that although law is a vast complex of divisions and subdivisions of legal functions necessary in our society, the fundamentals of law, nevertheless, can readily be understood and even practiced by anyone with average intelligence who has a positive attitude and genuine interest in it. The positive attitude is most important. This I base on the fact that I have observed countless prisoners with limited educations do a fairly good job of preparing and filing their own petitions, seeking redress for what they believe to have been violations of their constitutional rights. But those inmates with the same limited education who approached law with a negative attitude that law was too hard for them to understand; they were the ones always dependent upon someone else's assistance in preparing their cases. But the positive-minded prisoners only required a form to follow, and they did quite well in presenting their claims to the court with sufficient clarity to raise a claim, which if true, would be a violation of a substantial constitutional right. Once the postconviction petition reached the court, it was incumbent upon the judge hearing the case to appoint the petitioner counsel if he requested counsel. From there on, an experienced attorney would be in charge of pleading the case further.

Better-educated prisoners have done commendably well in opposing learned lawyers for the state. At times, these well- trained lawyers ended up eating a lot of crow when decisions were handed down by appellate courts. To be defeated by one's peers is not a disgrace in the practice of law. But to be defeated by a comparatively uneducated layman in prison, with no formal legal training, I have been told, can have a devastating effect upon some lawyers' egos. And the prisoner who emerges victorious becomes an instant hero to his peers. The crow is probably more difficult for a lawyer to swallow than the ordinary person because most lawyers, whether true or not, pride themselves on being smarter than most other professional people, when in truth, the lawyers believing themselves smarter are confusing being smart with being crafty.

The only defense to stave off embarrassment when a prisoner files an airtight case is for the opposing lawyer to confess error for the state. Such a confession of error on the part of counsel has no derogatory implication on him as an individual because he is not responsible for the error under most circumstances. But only rarely, under extremely exceptional circumstances, will the attorney general or a state's attorney resort to that measure to save face.

*   *   *   *   *

Most of my legal practice had concerned myself and my rap partners. But on several occasions, I had assisted other inmates in preparing their cases, and this was a clear violation of prison rules. But these were uneducated prisoners unable to prepare their own petitions. At first, I only prepared petitions under the Illinois Postconviction Hearing Act, and the inmates received the same result that I and the other inmates received; their petitions were all denied on the very same technicalities—res judicata and failure to state a cause of action.

I had made up my mind from the first case I accepted that I would adhere to the strict principles of being governed by two things. One, that I would not take a case unless I honestly felt that it had merit; and two, I would not charge an inmate anything whatsoever except the cost of the paper upon which the petition was prepared.

Legal paper was rather expensive to inmates with limited funds. Most of the time, paper was pilfered from the prison office supplies, but so much of the prison's 8½ × 13 inch paper disappeared from the various prison offices that Warden Ragen added another rule to his book. All petitions pertaining to legal matters going out of the prison had to be written or typed on pink paper, which was placed on sale in the inmates' commissary.

The beginning of my first successful case materialized one day during my recreation period. I had started a regimen of exercise to firm up my muscles and keep my weight down. Too much inactivity from working in the barbershop and standing around talking law on the yard had caused me to become paunchy and overweight. By playing basketball and lifting weights, I had strengthened and improved my physique back to its normal trimness.

While waiting to participate in a game of basketball, I stood listening to one of the courtyard legal discussions. Two inmates were discussing another prisoner's case. I knew both of the inmates and did not feel that my presence was an intrusion if I listened to what they were saying.

Bob Banks, a short, fulvous-complexioned individual who also worked in the barbershop, was saying, "I can't find any case law on the subject of Saint's case. It's a somewhat unfair situation. Still, I have known other inmates to be treated in the same manner by the parole board. No one, to my knowledge, has ever tested the legality of the situation."

"From what you've told me, Bob, there is something about the situation that just doesn't seem kosher," Art Freeman, a Jewish inmate in his late twenties, responded with a perplexed expression.

"That's why I'm asking around to see if I can locate anybody studying law who may have some knowledge on this particular type of situation." Facing me, Banks continued, "Blacky, have you ever heard of a case similar to this? A person on parole commits another crime and receives a sentence. After serving the new sentence, the parole board then wants the prisoner to serve the balance of his sentence on his prior conviction for violation of his parole when he committed the new crime, although the parole board had declared him a violator when he returned to prison to start serving his new sentence."

I rubbed my chin thoughtfully before replying. "I think recall though reading something like that in one of the report, but I can't remember offhand what report I read it in or whether the circumstances that you just hypothesized. But I'll give further thought to it and maybe I can recall something relevant."

"Hey, Blacky!" Gene Ross, one of my cell mates, called out from the basketball court. "Come on, man, we got the court now! The games about to start."

"Look, guys, I got a game to play the winners. I'll talk to you later," I told them before hurrying off to the basketball court. The discuss I had just had, however, was still very much on my mind.

A couple days later, Bob Banks called me over to his barber chair, pointed to an inmate in the chair, and said, "Blacky, meet Saint."

"Hi, Saint," I said.

"Whatta ya know, man," Saint returned my greeting. He was a tall, handsome, brown-skinned man in his late twenties. His smile was enhanced by the whitest teeth I had ever seen. I was almost tempted to ask him if they were real, but I was almost sure that they were.

"You recall the discussion that Art and I had on the yard the other day? Well, Saint is the guy in the case," Bob said.

"Sure, I remember. But what's his beef? I mean what did he get sent down for besides parole violation?"

"Larceny," Saint said. "I got one to three years for grand larceny. When I served the max on the larceny beef, the parole board gave me the balance on what was left of my first sentence for violating my parole when I caught the other beef. I was talking to Gary Howard over in D-House. He's a half-ass writ writer, and he told me that the board did that to lots of cons."

Suddenly it hit me! "Hold it!" I exclaimed. The name *Gary* had stimulated my recollection. The case I had read that was somewhat similar to Saint's case was contained in one of the Indiana case reports. Banks and Saint gazed at me expectantly, and I continued, "Now tell me one more thing. When did the parole board declare you a parole violator, before you finished the new sentence or after you finished it?"

"Before I finished it. The board gave me a parole hearing and continued my case until after I finished my new sentence."

"What do you think, Blacky? Has he got anything or not?" Banks asked as he lathered Saint's face for a shave.

"Sounds like he may have something. But let me try to locate the case I believe is in point with his," I replied before returning to my barber chair, very much interested in Saint's case.

That evening in my cell, while going over some of my case reports, I found the case I had in mind that was similar to Saint's case. Sure enough, the case was adjudged in an Indiana court where a prisoner was released on a petition for writ of habeas corpus under practically the same set of circumstances.

"I found it!" I shouted elatedly.

Gene Ross, one of my cell mates lying on the middle bunk, removed his radio headphone and inquired. "Now what? You found what?"

"The precedent I've been searching for that may free a guy."

"What guy? Do I know him?"

"I don't know. They call him Saint."

"You mean Ladies' Man Saint?"

"I don't know about Ladies' Man. His name or nickname is Saint. He works in the tailor shop."

"That's Ladies' Man. Good-lookin' guy, right?"

"Yeah. That's him. But what's with the Ladies' Man crap?" I wanted to know.

"The broads all go for the dude. I know him from hangin' 'round the Mocambo. The cat's got all the makings to be a mackman."

"Then why in the hell is he down here for grand larceny? You guys kill me with that bullshit that just because a guy's nice looking and dresses well has got the makings of a pimp. Why, some of the ugliest guys I know are pimps," I argued.

"Well, I never said that you would make a pimp," Gene retorted. "'Cause you ain't got it, boy. It's niggers like you that spoil bitches, givin' 'em everything you rip off."

"Look, Gene, I don't want to hear that shit. I'm trying to concentrate on helping this dude."

My other cell mate on the top bunk was Li'l Arthur. He had been transferred to the barber shop as a student barber a few months ago. Buddy Morgan, my other rap partner, had been given a job in the prison furniture factory. Leaning over and looking down at Gene, he cursed, "You red-faced, maroon-baboon-ass motherfucker, why don't you let the man concentrate on his law work?"

"I wasn't talkin' to you, you little asshole. Stay outta my conversation, you ignorant son of a bitch!" Gene retorted.

These two bickered all the time about anything and everything just for the hell of it. They argued about how much the window should be opened, making too much noise when getting up at night to use the toilet or farting without sitting on the toilet and flushing at the time gas was expelled. On and on it went, all day and through the night; they grumbled and cursed about something incessantly. Both of them could not complete a sentence most of the time without using profanity. They were a strange contrast in physical appearance. Li'l Arthur—short, brown and given to wearing almost a constant scowl on his countenance.

Gene was large, well built, and muscular. His dark-brown hair was silky, and he had the appearance of being Caucasian. His voice was loud and raucous, his mannerisms vulgar and brusque, much like Li'l Arthur's. He was serving time for the sale of narcotics. I had known him a long time, both on the streets and in prison. We had served time in Pontiac together. He had managed a notorious nightclub on the South Side called the Mocambo in a neighborhood around Oakwood Boulevard that had notoriously earned the name of Dopeville, USA. Gene used to be an amateur heavyweight fighter and a bouncer in South Side taverns before getting into the narcotics business.

Gene hid a kind heart behind a tough-guy facade that those who knew him well were aware of. Hard outside but soft as a boiled grape inside was the way I sized him up.

One anecdote I liked particularly was that when Gene was running the Mocambo nightclub, a Hollywood movie actress, who along with her husband, had been hooked on the use of heroin and morphine, and they had settled in Chicago and were down on their luck. Gene befriended them. The movie actress, a beautiful blonde, supplied Gene with sexual favors in return for narcotics. Her husband, a talented pianist, later ended up in Stateville for armed robbery growing out of his desperation to supply his enormous drug habit. Gene, squiring the movie actress around town to all the best bars and restaurants, would run into acquaintances and immediately ask them did they recognize the actress. Before they could answer, he would blurt out the actress's name, adding, "You ignorant, motherfucker, this a great Hollywood actress! Ain't you gonna ask her for her autograph?" A moment's hesitation to ask for an autograph brought a belligerent scowl to Gene's face, and the request was immediately made for an autograph, although the actress was never rated more than a B-grade performer.

Li'l Arthur asked in typical fashion, "Blacky, do you think one of these asshole judges in Illinois will uphold an Indiana judge's ruling and free Saint?"

Seated at the small table in front of my typewriter, I shrugged. "Hell, I don't know. All we can do is try and see. A fair-minded judge could follow that decision. And who knows, there may be some precedent rendered by an Illinois judge on the same point of law," I told him before addressing Gene.

"When Saint comes in the shop again, send him to my chair. I want to talk over his case with him."

"Whatta you mean your chair! That's our chair," Li'l Arthur cried out.

"Well, our chair," I replied. True, he worked with me. I was his barber instructor. He had proven more than an apt student and was about due to have a chair of his own before long.

Gene was the chair caller in the shop. He acknowledged that he would send Saint to me before lying back on his bunk to listen to his radio. I returned to reading my law reports, and Li'l Arthur went back to listening to his radio. Thankfully, everything was quiet now. I could concentrate. Rarely did I listen to the radio until after the lights went out because I was usually always preoccupied with my law books and writ writing. I also had gotten into the habit, out of sheer enjoyment, of reading biographies and autobiographies—especially those about some of the nation's best-known judges and criminal lawyers. Biographies and articles about judges like John Marshall, Charles Evans Hughes, Oliver Wendell Holmes, all late justices of the United States Supreme Court—and Judge Learned Hand of the United States Court of Appeals as well as those of criminal lawyers like Clarence Darrow, William Fallon, Moman Pruit and Jerry Geiser to name a few—all intrigued and fascinated me.

A few weeks after I had prepared Saint's petition for writ of habeas corpus, he was sitting on my barber chair getting a haircut and shave. We could hardly believe it. He had been granted a hearing in court on the petition. This was too good to be true! All I had left to do was give him his shave before he would go to the clothing room and dress in a prison-made suit for his court appearance. When I was done, Saint got out of the chair and shook my hand. Then he said, "You know, for a barber and a lawyer, you're all right. If I make it, man, I owe you everything."

"You don't owe me anything. Even the haircut and the shave are on the state. If you win your freedom today, I'll derive such great hunks of joy that it'll be almost like getting my rocks off in some fine babe," I cracked. "Now get the hell out of here, Saint. Don't keep the judge waiting. And good luck!"

"I won't forget you, man, that's a promise," he said.

Saint also said good-byes to many of the other inmates in the shop as though he knew that he was going to be released that day. Maybe he had a premonition or something that morning because the judge did free him. And a few days later, I received a money order for one hundred dollars from Saint's brother with a little note expressing gratitude for what I had done and suggesting that I use the money to purchase law books or records for my own case.

Later, I succeeded in getting a copy of the release order in Saint's case and freed another inmate incarcerated under the same circumstances as Saint had been.

When the word got out around the prison that I had prepared Saint's petition for writ of habeas corpus, my popularity soared among the prisoners. Every day, I was solicited by one or more inmates to review their cases for errors. But this was a natural phenomenon with the prisoners when a writ writer won a case. Given a short period of time with no new successes and my popularity like the other writ writers would fade into oblivion.

It should perhaps be pointed out that neither Saint's case nor the other inmate's case was decided on any constitutional question but decided strictly on a question of law, whereas habeas corpus, the great writ, was a proper remedy to redress the claim of illegal detention.

Chapter 9

THE ILLINOIS SUPREME COURT, WITHOUT argument and without opinion, dismissed my petition for writ of error. In doing so, the court used a form order that it also used in dismissing other prisoners' petitions for writs of error. The Illinois Supreme Court, in their order, simply stated that "after having examined and reviewed the petition and record in the postconviction hearing, the same is found to disclose no violation or denial of any substantial constitutional rights of the petitioner under the constitution of the United States or the constitution of the State of Illinois."

I was furious with disappointment! How could the highest court in the state of Illinois say that there was "no violation or denial of any substantial constitutional rights of the petitioner"? Was not the evidence of the perjury known to the trial court and the prosecuting attorney clearly manifested in the record before them? How then could they be so indifferent to the undeniable fact that there existed an unmistakable flagrant violation of my rights—substantiated by that very same record before the court?

What the dismissal order amounted to was the fact that the highest court in the state of Illinois was attempting to sweep the trial court's dirt under the rug. The Illinois judicial system was worried, knowing perhaps that the despicable brand of justice that it had meted out to many of the indigent defendants in cases over the years would not stand scrutiny if given a fair hearing. As it now stood, the Illinois Postconviction Hearing Act, having been tested in both the trial court and the Illinois Supreme Court, was worthless as a remedy—just as the other remedies had been worthless if my case was any criterion.

The Illinois Supreme Court was grinding out the perfunctory form orders of dismissal as fast as the prisoners' petitions for writs of error were filed.

I as well as other writ writers in the prisons were being overwhelmed with requests from inmates to appeal their dismissals to the United States Supreme Court. I had already very carefully prepared and filed my own petition for writ of certiorari, knowing full well that the Nation's Highest Tribunal was one of the busiest courts in the land. It was now extremely important that either my petition or some other prisoner's petition for writ of certiorari would have to be favorably received and reviewed by the US Supreme Court if we were ever to have a definitive ruling on what if any remedy was available either in the state or federal courts to resolve our allegations.

I knew too that the odds of having a petition for writ of certiorari granted by such a busy court, that was reviewing cases that came up from all of the federal courts of appeals as well as from all of the state courts in the union, was heavily weighted against my petition succeeding. I also realized that no less than four justices of the United States Supreme Court had to agree to hear a case before the court would grant a petition for writ of certiorari. Still, with all these great odds staring me in the face I previewed every opinion I could get my hands on rendered by the US Supreme Court concerning the rights of prisoners to an adequate postconviction remedy to review alleged violations of substantial constitutional questions. Now my petition was filed for the High Tribunal's consideration.

I also selected a few cases from other inmates that I regarded as having real merit, such as my own case, and I prepared petitions for writs of certiorari for these inmates so that the US Supreme Court would have several cases to consider and select from with the hope that one or more of these cases would impress at least four members of the court as being worthy of being reviewed to set a precedent for the state courts to be guided by, and it was my fervent hope that a majority of the nine justices would agree with us to overrule the Illinois Supreme Court's decision.

I relied heavily on a recent case titled *Young v. Ragen* in which the US Supreme Court had said in its opinions, "Of course we do not review state decisions which rest upon adequate nonfederal grounds, and of course Illinois may choose the procedure it deems appropriate for the vindication of federal rights. But it is not simply a question of state procedure when a state court "of last resort" closes the door to any consideration of a claim of denial of a federal right. And that is the effect of the denials of habeas corpus in a number of cases now before this court, for in none of the cases does the attorney general suggest that either of the other two Illinois post trial remedies, writ of error and coram nobis, is appropriate. Unless habeas corpus is available, therefore we are led to believe that Illinois offers no post-trial remedy in cases of this kind. The doctrine of exhaustion of state remedies, to which this court has required the scrupulous adherence of all federal courts presupposes that some adequate state remedy exists. We recognize the difficulties with which the Illinois Supreme Court is faced in adapting available state procedures to the requirement that prisoners be given some clearly defined method by which they may raise claims of denial of federal rights. Nevertheless, that requirement must be met. If there is now no post-trial procedure by which federal rights may be vindicated in Illinois, we wish to be advised of that fact upon remand of this case."

The *Young v. Ragen* case was decided by the High Tribunal in 1949, and now in 1951, the state of Illinois still had failed to provide an adequate remedy. Therefore the time appeared ripe for the US Supreme Court to come down hard on the defiant state. Because reading these opinions of the US Supreme Court emanating out of appeals from the Illinois Supreme Court, I sensed a feeling that the nation's Highest Tribunal—and especially its Mr. Chief Justice Vinson—was gradually losing patience with the Illinois courts and the Illinois attorney general in their use of petty technicalities to circumvent the prisoners' efforts to obtain review of their claims. I also sensed a feeling that the US Supreme Court did not want the federal district courts to be totally burdened with the state court's duty to provide an adequate remedy and hearing on state prisoners' allegations. It also had to be taken into consideration that whatever action the US Supreme Court took in the Illinois cases would have national significance on every other state in the union with regard to postconviction proceedings affecting prisoners in those jurisdictions.

Therefore, in spite of the odds, I felt a spark of hope. I prevailed upon the prisoners to be patient that were pleading with me to help them file appeals in the US Supreme Court from their dismissals by the Illinois Supreme Court. I advised them that we had adequate test cases prepared and filed in the US Supreme Court and that a ruling would be forthcoming in the very near future whether that august judicial body would review the Illinois Supreme Court's decision.

Several weeks later, when the guard passing out the mail handed me a letter from the clerk of the United States Supreme Court, my heart pounded with nervous excitement. Never before had I received a letter that could mean so much or at the same time could mean so little if its message destroyed all the hope and faith I placed in the nation's highest court. I was actually afraid to read what was inside the envelope for fear that it would be unbearably disappointing. I had not received any good news concerning my own case since I had been in prison. Why should I expect the news in this envelope to be any different?

Slowly, I drew the letter out of its enclosure that had already been opened and censored by the prison mail department. When I finally focused my eyes on the contents of the Court's order I sat down heavily and let out a great sigh of relief. "Wheeew!" I uttered audibly. "Thank God!"

Gene and Li'l Arthur were relaxing on their bunks. They stirred almost simultaneously. Li'l Arthur was first to speak. "What's happenin', Blacky? Sounds like you got some good news."

"We have," I said, rising and handing him the letter.

Gene, sensing a big moment, said, "Well, let me in on it, too. What's it all about?"

"Gene," I said, still in a state of supreme elation. "The highest court in this country had granted my petition for writ of certiorari. This means that a full review will be made of the Illinois Supreme Court's decision! And before long, we will know whether there is any justice left in this nation for the poor little guys dumped in these joints like us by cold and indifferent trial judges and unscrupulous prosecutors without an adequate means of redressing any grievances we may have over the manner in which they placed us here."

"Blacky, you done it, man! You got Washington on these dirty motherfucker's asses in this state," Li'l Arthur blurted out excitedly after he read the court's order.

"Hold on, pal! This doesn't mean that the US Supreme Court is on our side yet. They could hear the case and uphold the Illinois Supreme Court," I cautioned him.

"Yeah, you're right. I don't trust none of these goddamned courts. From what I seen, most of 'em don't give a shit about a poor-ass nigger anyway, and the federal courts ain't no fuckin' different than the state courts when it comes to fuckin' you around."

"Li'l Arthur, shut up! You don't know crab apples from sheep shit! The federal courts can't be compared to these political-dominated state courts. Tell this fool-ass nigger, Blacky, that the federal judges got lifetime jobs and damn near as much power as God Almighty! They don't give a shit about the state courts. They can overrule the president of this country. Tell this fool, Blacky, that he's a goddamned idiot!"

"You're the one that don't know shit, you half-breed bastard!" Li'l Arthur retorted angrily.

"Here you guys go again," I laughed. "Let's let it ride and see how the US Supreme Court rules. I got a strong feeling that they'll rule in favor of the cons and not the state this time. I don't want to sound overoptimistic, but I think at long last, we got the Illinois Supreme Court and the attorney general on the killing floor, and the United States Supreme Court is about ready to butcher the old goats."

When the grapevine spread the news around the prison that Blacky Jennings was granted a writ of certiorari by the US Supreme Court, I was more popular than ever among the prisoners. Now the elite among the prison population would look over and nod at me when they came into the barbershop. Roger Touhy, Basil "the Owl" Banghart, Peter "Gloomy Gus" Stevens, Willy Niemoth all smiled in my direction and made such remarks as, "Nice goin', kid. Keep pitching it at 'em. Attaboy, Blacky!" Even Nathan Leopold heartily congratulated me when I ran into him in the prison hospital where he worked in the malaria experimental program.

The US Supreme Court appointed Nathaniel L. Nathanson, professor of constitutional law at Northwestern University to represent me. I requested that Attorney Calvin P. Sawyier—a young lawyer who had been appointed to represent me on my postconviction proceedings before Judge Ashcraft—be appointed now by the US Supreme Court to act as co-counsel with Mr. Nathanson in filing briefs and arguing my case before that august body.

Mr. Sawyer, a member of one of Chicago's largest and very prestigious law firms, impressed me very much during our correspondence as being a very sincere and interested person in my behalf. He had thoroughly studied my case and agreed that my rights had been flagrantly violated—especially by the knowing presentation and use of perjured testimony to obtain my conviction.

If there was one single redeeming factor in what Judge Ashcraft did in my case, I would unhesitatingly say that it was in appointing Mr. Sawyer to represent me at the postconviction proceedings in the trial court. For I had implicit faith in Mr. Sawyer's sincerity of purpose and legal competency.

Both Mr. Nathanson and Mr. Sawyer visited me at the same time in the prison, and they complimented me on my tremendous effort in getting my petition for writ of certiorari granted. Mr. Nathanson, a Harvard Law School graduate and honor student, served as a law clerk to the late Justice Louis Brandeis. He therefore was very familiar with the workings of the US Supreme Court from inside and out. "What a valuable attorney," I thought. "There's certainly nothing cheap about the US Supreme Court. They give a poor person a first-class deal like the rich folks can get." That made me feel real good.

Mr. Nathanson cautioned me not to be overly optimistic, although he conceded that I had a very good cause of action. The State of Illinois, he emphasized, would oppose us with all of the forces at their command before final judgment would be rendered. This tall, slender, scholarly gentleman with an aquiline nose and Lincolnesque bearing instilled my confidence considerably regardless of how much he cautioned me about being too optimistic.

"The die is cast!" I thought. "With the help of these two lawyers, the dragon of injustice would be slain."

While awaiting further developments in the US Supreme Court on the momentous ruling that we anticipated, I never slowed down in my legal practice in the prison. I was pressured almost constantly by inmates for legal aid, and I found myself spending almost all of my spare time reading transcripts of trials to determine in my own mind whether the prisoner who submitted his trial records to me had any substantial questions of constitutional violations that occurred during his trial. In the great majority of these cases, I could find no merit, and I returned the records to the inmate with a note explaining why I deemed his case to be without merit. The few cases in which I thought presented issues of merit with supporting prima facie evidence, I accepted these cases for preparation with a view to having the prisoner file for relief under the Illinois Postconviction Hearing Act. This method of handling cases for the prisoners not only made me look good but prevented many unworthy cases from cluttering up the court dockets in the state when the prisoners accepted my advice as final. And because I only handled cases with merit, it improved my track record for assisting in victories more often than any other writ writer in the prison.

For those inmates who would not heed my advice to put aside filing their cases presenting unsupportable and frivolous claims—well, they found themselves victims of the writ writers who accepted their cases for fees. Since the word was out around the prison that I did not charge for my services, it was sometimes difficult to comprehend whether my popularity as a writ writer was based more on my charitable disposition than on my legal talent. Although I liked to feel that both traits played an equal role in gaining me the respect of the prisoners.

Both Gene and Li'l Arthur told me that I was a goddamn fool to take on all that work for nothing, and that if I charged a fee, a lot of my potential clientele would disappear. Perhaps that was true, but I strongly suspected that a lot of the prisoners pestering me to assist them were really only curiosity seekers bent on seeing what if anything I could discover that might be wrong in their cases.

Many of the prisoners who would not heed my advice to give up their useless efforts to file their cases in court ended up being bilked by a notorious writ writer called the Gooch. The Gooch, a fat, pimply faced individual with shrewd gray eyes and a pallid complexion, gouged his foolish clients not only for commissary items and money from their relatives and friends on the outside but being a homosexual, he also preyed on them to satiate his lust if they would engage in sex acts with him. I couldn't imagine many convicts enjoying themselves with this fat and ugly epicene. But the Gooch evidently settled some accounts on the flesh side of his ledger in bilking and milking some of the dupes that fell victim to his "con artistry" and his carnal lust.

The Gooch was fond of sweets and was constantly nibbling on candy and cookies all day long. Tickets could be purchased at the commissary for pies and ice cream that would be delivered to a prisoner's cell on Sunday evenings. It was not unusual for the Gooch to have two or three pies and a couple pints of ice cream delivered to his cell where he would consume a whole pie and the ice cream in one sitting while sometimes starting on the second pie. Because of this habit of his, the prisoners had a saying about him and his clients. The saying went, "The Gooch will eat up their ice cream and eat up their pies. Then he'll eat them up too, to their surprise!"

As a prison lawyer, I soon found out that I was open to all kinds of propositions by inmates seeking my services. One inmate named John Henry, who was serving a life sentence for a murder committed during a robbery, offered to share his prison paramour with me if I would handle his case. I told him that I did not charge fees of any kind, but I would go over his court records to determine if there was anything worthwhile contesting. John Henry got his records over to me, and I couldn't find any merit whatsoever in his case. I told him so, and he did not press the issue any further.

John Henry's paramour, called Mellow Baby, encountered me one day in the auditorium building that housed the movie theater and chapels. I had gone there on a pass for a chat with Father James Jones, the Episcopal chaplain.

While waiting in the lobby, Mellow Baby, a nice-looking tan-faced gay, who always appeared neatly pressed in prison garb that had been altered for a snug fit, came up to me and said in a decidedly feminine voice, "Hi, Blacky! If you have a minute, baby, I'd like a word or two with you."

I returned the greeting. "What's on your mind?"

Poised with one hand on his hip, Mellow Baby murmured, "I got a proposition for you, honey."

"Hold on now! I've already told John Henry that I couldn't find anything wrong in his case——"

"You're jumpin' the gun, baby. This isn't hardly about John Henry," he interjected.

"Oh yeah? Well, what's it about?"

With an effeminate gesture of his hand, he went on in a low tone of voice. "Don't breathe a word of this to my old man John Henry 'cause you know how damn crazy the bastard is—promise?"

I hesitated, because John Henry had a rep around the prison as being a tough old con that it did not pay to cross. He had long been a troublemaker. But he had tapered off his misconduct somewhat after tasting every conceivable punishment that Warden Ragen's staff could mete out, including a stint at the Menard Penitentiary for psychiatric treatment. Still, he was considered to be dangerous and capable of flying off the handle at any time if provoked sufficiently.

"Well, okay, Mellow Baby. It's confidential. Let me have it."

Mellow Baby smiled sweetly. "Nothing like a lawyer-client relationship, huh, baby?"

"Whatever you say."

"I want you to help this friend of mine. He's a young dude that hasn't been in the joint too long, and he's a real cutie-pie. I'm having a secret affair with him, and he wants to appeal his case. Now, don't you go telling him he hasn't got a case, Blacky. I know you can find something to fight his case on. He believes that he was railroaded."

"Where is your dude now?" I asked.

"He's in B-House on the coal pile. But I'm going to get him in the laundry with me. My officer and I are tight. He'll say a word to the cap'n. If you see my dude, you'll really like him, Blacky. He's so cute!" Mellow Baby giggled girlishly and went on, "He'll be over here shortly. We are having choir practice this afternoon."

It was no secret that the auditorium building was one of the trysting places for inmates who engaged in homosexual relationships. It seemed everyone but the guards and clergymen knew what was going on in the auditorium. Inmates could meet in the building under the pretext of seeing a chaplain or to attend Bible classes and choir practice, and with a lookout stationed to keep an eye out for the guard, a couple could slip off in privacy for a few minutes. There were usually only one or two guards at the most on duty, and they certainly weren't ubiquitous.

"Look, Mellow Baby, I don't make any pretenses about anyone's case. I'm too busy to waste time on bullshit, you dig?"

Mellow Baby moved so close to me that his body brushed against me. "I'm going to take care of you, honey, if you take care of my dude. You can get it all, baby—hips, lips, and fingertips," he whispered seductively as his hand reached out to touch my genital region.

I jumped back quickly as his fingers made contact. "Hold on, Mellow Baby. We can talk without you being so damn demonstrative. Now here's what I'll do. Have your dude write me a kite outlining what he thinks his problem is and what proof he has to substantiate his claim that he was railroaded. Tell him to get the kite passed to me in the barbershop by Gene."

Mellow Baby gave me his most engaging smile. "All right, honey. I'll tell my dude. Now about us, Blacky, do you want a down payment on your fee today? I can give you a lick and a promise before my dude gets here."

"No! Not this dude, you won't!" I laughed good-naturedly before adding, "I don't work for pay or play."

"You've got to be kiddin', Blacky. You don't know what you're missin'. Better let me turn you on now."

"Thanks, but no thanks," I responded. "I can't chance it. But have your dude contact me anyway, okay? Now I'll talk to you later," I concluded as I walked into Father Jones's office. Hell, I wasn't about to front myself off and get caught in that tender trap with a "punk" like Mellow Baby, her crazy shiv-wielding old man, and that young dude. Besides, my profound and constant interest in studying and practicing law afforded me more than sufficient sublimation for my libido.

Father Jones was a youthful-faced priest intensely interested in helping prisoners rehabilitate themselves. One of his primary concerns was to sponsor a halfway house where prisoners without homes or jobs awaiting them upon their release could stay until they found work and got adjusted to living in the outside world.

Father Jones and I had become friends, and through his counseling, I had renewed my interest in the church. I was also especially interested in his theories of rehabilitation, although my personal belief is that there is no way to decriminalize a person convicted and sent to prison. The person can, however, be changed for the better—thus arresting his criminal tendencies. Because how can something be restored that always existed in the first place? I base my premise on the fact that all men and women are potential criminals. Criminality is inherent in mankind's nature. Most adults, if not all, have committed some form of crime in their lifetimes that was prohibited by a criminal statute, whether it be petty theft, sexual, or criminal trespass. But the great majority of lawbreakers have not been caught or punished. Stop right now! Think, reader, when you last committed a crime for which you were not caught or punished. Gotcha! didn't I?

Father Jones was well aware of the legal battle I was involved in while approving wholeheartedly of my desire to help the other prisoners with their cases. Knowing that I was breaking prison regulations in helping the inmates, the priest, nevertheless, justified the righteousness of my deeds as conforming to the teachings of the Lord "to help thy neighbor" instead of the mandate of Warden Ragen not to help them.

There was a lot of satisfaction to be derived from helping my fellow inmates, and in so doing, I could feel a change in my perspectives and values. There was a feeling of emotional maturity that wasn't evident before. It came with doing something constructive. When I looked back into the past on the folly in my life, I shuddered at the unforgivable wastefulness. Maybe there was some hope for me yet. Because for the first time in my life, I had a genuine good feeling about myself. I liked me in my present role—hurting no one and helping everyone I could that needed my legal assistance. Being a force for good was, indeed, a new experience in my life.

I used to think a lot about men like Clarence Darrow, Thurgood Marshall, Louis Brandeis, and Eugene Debs, who fought all their lives for the protection of the little man's rights when people were the victims of oppression under the law or under the mores or our socioeconomic society in all of its geographical areas. If I had my life to live all over again, I would like to have modeled it after those men. Because in their own individual and unpretentious way, a mark of greatness, much like a bright star, lit up their paths for other champions of the disinherited of our society to follow. And many have come before them in whose paths these four great Americans walked, because there have always been champions of the underdogs to curb the tide of repression and tyranny that flows at times from the very embodiment of our Democracy—the legislative, the executive, and the judiciary branches.

*　　*　　*　　*　　*

After riding the Illinois legal merry-go-round for two years, it suddenly came to a screeching stop for the prisoners on December 3, 1951, when the United States Supreme Court handed down its opinion in *Jennings v. Illinois*. The high court, in so doing, said in part,

> Under the Illinois Post-Conviction Hearing Act, petitioner in an Illinois penitentiary, filed in the state court in which he had been convicted a petition alleging facts sufficient to establish a prima facie violation of his rights under the Federal Constitution through the admission of a coerced confession in evidence at his trial. The State's Attorney did not deny these allegations but moved to dismiss the petition on grounds of res judicata and failure to state a cause of action.

140

The court dismissed the petition without a hearing or otherwise determining the factual issue presented. The State Supreme Court, without argument and without opinion, "dismissed a writ of error by a form order reciting that it had examined and reviewed the petition and record in the post-conviction hearing and found the same to disclose no violation or denial of petitioner's constitutional rights. Held: Judgment vacated and cause remanded for further proceedings.

1. If his allegations are true and if his claim has not been waived at or after trial, petitioner is held in custody in violation of federal constitutional rights: and he is entitled to his day in court for resolution of these issues.

2. On remand, petitioner should be advised whether his claim that his constitutional rights were infringed at his trial may be determined under the Postconviction Hearing Act, or whether that Act does not provide an appropriate state remedy in this case.

3. If petitioner's claim may be resolved in a proceeding under that Act, either by an inquiry into the verity of his factual allegations or a finding that his federal rights were waived during or after his trial, such resolution may proceed without further action by this Court.

4. If Illinois does not provide an appropriate remedy for such a determination, petitioner may "proceed without more to apply to the United States District Court for a writ of habeas corpus."

We had won a clear-cut victory in the highest court in the land. We could get off the Illinois legal merry-go-round at last and carry our cases into the courts for hearings on our claims without having the door slammed in our faces by petty technicalities. Because if the state courts in Illinois did not comply with the US Supreme Court's mandate, the doors to the federal district court would now be standing wide open to welcome us. I laughed to think of the State of Illinois letting this happen. No, the state judiciary would lose all jurisdiction over the cases, and especially the opportunity to apply whatever sly and subtle impediments that they could come up with to keep the prisoners locked up in their control. Because the state officials knew that if they could stall deliverance of prisoners by the courts long enough, most of the prisoners fighting their cases would either be released on parole or released after having served out their sentences before ever getting a hearing in court. And once the prisoners were released from prison, under most circumstances, their cases would be moot and no longer open to judicial review.

The Illinois Supreme Court now had to "defecate or get off the old proverbial pot." Because the court had no further evasive action that it could take to keep the merry-go-round turning.

The State's Highest Court was compelled to follow the United States Supreme Court's decision in my case in which the dictum applied to the rest of the Illinois prisoners filing cases under the Illinois Postconviction Hearing Act, or we could wave good-bye to them, pack up our petitions, and head straight for the federal district court for a hearing on a petition for writ of habeas corpus. For at last, the prisoners had something to crow about while the Illinois Supreme Court, and the attorney general, had some crow to eat.

On January 25, 1952, the Illinois Supreme Court, in compliance with the US Supreme Court's opinion in my case handed down its own per curiam opinion in *People v. Jennings et al.* The court's opinion said in part,

> On remandment from the United States Supreme Court.

142

Talbert Jennings, Arthur LaFrana and Julius Bernard Sherman filed separate petitions against the State of Illinois under the Post-Conviction Hearing Act alleging that petitioners were held in custody in violation of the Federal Constitution in that coerced confessions and officially sub-orned perjury had been used to obtain their convictions. The petitions were dismissed by the Criminal Court of Cook County. Judge Alan E. Ashcraft, Jr. (Jennings case). Judge Thomas J. Lynch (LaFrana case) and Judge John F. Haas (Sherman case). Each of the petitioners brought "error. After the Illinois Supreme Court had dis-missed the writ of error in each case, the United States Supreme Court granted certiorari, vacated the Illinois Supreme Court's dismissal orders, and remanded the causes to that court for further proceedings. On remand the Illinois Supreme Court, Per Curiam, held that the Post-Conviction Hearing Act afforded an appropriate remedy for the assertion of the petitioners' claims.

"Reversed and remanded with directions." Pursuant to the Illinois Supreme Court's opinion and remandment of my case to Judge Ashcraft for further proceedings, I felt confident that at long last, I would have my day in court. My confidence, however, was shaken considerably when I received a letter from my court-ap-pointed attorney, Mr. Calvin P. Sawyer, several weeks after the Illinois Supreme Court remanded my case to the trial court.

Mr. Sawyer advised me that Judge Ashcraft had held a so-called hearing—but in the secrecy of his chambers with only himself, the assistant state's attorney and the court reporter present—that the case was discussed briefly, and the judge entered an order reversing my conviction and remanded me back to the criminal court of Cook County for a new trial on the basis of Detective Piotter's conflicting testimony at the first trial.

To me, however, this was a bitter victory. Because I had wanted to be there at the hearing to see their honorable faces looking me in the face. I wanted to ask the judge and the state's attorney, did they intend to prosecute Piotter? I wanted to ask Judge Ashcraft, did he intend to censure himself and the prosecutor for permitting this outrage against justice to happen in the first place since they all had knowledge of it happening during the trial?

Later I obtained a copy of the transcript of proceedings had in Judge Ashcraft's chambers. I was appalled at the cover-up that this so-called honorable judge had seen fit to employ in making his ruling with respect to Piotter's perjured testimony.

Trapped like a fox with the hounds baying close at his heels, Judge Ashcraft abandoned his open courtroom and sought refuge in the privacy of his chambers to eat his crow. But not without making one more mockery of justice by ruling, "Detective Piotter testified at the hearing on the Motion To Suppress Evidence that he did not take a ring from the Defendant Jennings. During the trial, however, a ring was introduced into evidence against Jennings, and Piotter testified at that time that he did take a ring from Jennings. Therefore it is quite possible that Piotter was *mistaken* [italics my own] in his testimony one time or another."

"A mistake! He called it a mistake!" I cried out in wrath. "Why! The son of a bitch is guilty as hell of perjury!"

A mistake is no substantial violation of a state or federal constitutional right within the amendments of the state or federal constitutions, or within the purview of the Illinois Postconviction Hearing Act. It must be the "knowing use of perjured testimony" or nothing. If it wasn't that, I did not deserve a new trial under the act or the constitution.

I was furious! Yet I was helpless to make Judge Ashcraft rule in accordance with truth and justice. Because I could see now that this judicial misfit was not even capable of upholding the letter and the spirit of the law. Perhaps in his viewpoint, the judge thought that he could erase the stigma of perjury known to the court and prosecution of the record with semantics. But the record will be there forever to impeach that viewpoint.

If Judge Alan E. Ashcraft Jr. could have been removed by a time machine to Texas, west of the Pecos, in the 1890s, he would have made Judge Roy Bean look good when it came to making judicial decisions.

The terrible irony of the judicial handling of my case can readily be recognized when we stop to consider that we have here the outrageous and unique situation of a lower court overruling its own decision that originally held that there was no violation of my constitutional rights at my trial, while at the same time the disputing the Illinois Supreme Court's finding on appeal that held that a review of the trial records did not show any violation of my constitutional rights. These judges, for the most part, were all learned men in their profession who had one thing in common: they were all hell-bent on depriving the Illinois prisoners of not only free access to the courts but justice as well if they could get away with it.

Chapter 10

THE RECENT OPINIONS BY THE United States Supreme Court (*Jennings v. Illinois*) and the Illinois Supreme Court (*People v. Jennings*) soon became jailhouse and courthouse watchwords that were cited by prisoners and lawyers alike in monotonous regularity in petitions, briefs, and in oral arguments before the courts. To many of the prisoners, I was a hero; and almost overnight, my popularity spread throughout not just Statesville but all of the state's penal institutions. And stories of my so-called legal prowess were propagated about the state institutions with great exaggerations of false exploits that were accredited to me. These stories only tended to heighten my popularity no matter how much I disclaimed being responsible for freeing all these prisoners that were being fictionalized by some inmates as the rumors ran rampant. I had actually only been instrumental at the time of directly gaining the freedom of three inmates. But now, these three had been multiplied tenfold by exaggerating fans who always seemed to overlook the fact that I had excellent representation by my attorneys, Mr. Nathanson and Mr. Sawyer, who prepared outstanding briefs and journeyed to Washington DC to argue my case before the US Supreme Court to greatly assist me in winning my case.

No one can stop a legend from being born once the momentum is started in that direction. And although I deserved the credit for being instrumental in initiating the final "straw that broke the camel's back" when the US Supreme Court ruled in our favor, the fact nevertheless remained that it all began with a prisoner in Joliet Penitentiary named John Bongiorno. His case is titled *United States ex rel Bongiorno v. Joseph Ragen.*

Were it not for Bongiorno in 1942, a very courageous inmate that risked the surefire wrath and punishment of Warden Ragen, the prisoners in Illinois perhaps today would still be unable to send petitions out of the prisons to the courts to question the legality of their convictions.

It was fair and commendable, indeed, for the late Honorable John P. Barnes, chief judge of the United States District Court for the Northern District of Illinois, to have made it possible for the prisoners in Illinois to have access to the courts through his ruling in the *Bongiorno* case, because hell would have probably frozen over before a state judge would have made such a ruling. Judge Barnes, however, had this to say in part in writing his memorandum opinion:

> In October 1942, the writer of this memorandum received through the mails a letter from one Sam Bongiorno, stating, "My father (John Bongiorno) is an inmate of the Illinois State Penitentiary at Joliet, I'll. He has a petition for a writ of habeas corpus which he has been trying to send to you for the past two years, but the authorities will not let it out. If there is any way "in which you can obtain, or aid us in obtaining the release of this petition, it will be very much appreciated." Believing MS that this communication made it the duty of this court to determine whether John Bongiorno was being denied access to the courts, in violation of his constitutional and statutory rights, the court caused an order to be made on November 27, 1942, reading in part, as follows:
>
> It having been represented to the court that John Bongiorno, who is an inmate of the Illinois State Penitentiary at Joliet, Illinois, has sought to file in the office of the clerk of this court a petition for writ of habeas corpus but that the

authorities at such penitentiary will not permit the filing of the same:

It is Ordered that the Warden of the Illinois State Penitentiary at Joliet, Illinois be, and he is hereby, commanded and directed to show cause, if any he has, in writing, on or before the opening of court on December 7, 1942, why the said John Bongiorno should not be permitted to file, in the office of the clerk of this court, a petition for writ of habeas corpus.

Thereafter, prisoners in the Illinois penitentiaries had access to the courts in the state as well as in the federal district court. But Warden Ragen still, at times, showed a reluctance to fully comply with Judge Barnes's mandate to let the prisoners have free and unobstructed access to the courts. As a consequence, the warden was ordered before the court, and Judge Barnes threatened Warden Ragen with imprisonment if all harassment did not cease in badgering the prisoners who sought free access to the courts. Needless to say, the warden from that day on took Judge Barnes very seriously and refrained from blocking in any way an inmate from petitioning the courts.

The Honorable John P. Barnes became a living hero to the prisoners until the day he died at a ripe old age. And the fiery old jurist will always be remembered by ex-convicts like me for his clenched-fist pounding on the bench whenever he became upset over state authorities violating the rights of the prisoners. To the State of Illinois attorney general, he probably appeared to be a pragmatic interloper of state's rights. But to the prisoners, Judge Barnes symbolized "firmness" and "fairness" in the truest sense of the words; and the prisoners categorized Warden Ragen, who strived for the same recognition, as being nothing more than a fourflusher.

The fight against the State of Illinois's injustice in trying to frustrate prisoners in their right to challenge the legality of their convictions in postconviction proceedings did not begin with Talbert Jennings. Almost a decade before *Jennings v. Illinois* was decided, prisoners hammered away diligently at the Illinois barricade to the courthouse. And with each case ruled on by the United States Supreme Court, the barricade was weakened. There was *White v. Ragen, Woods v. Nierstheimer, Carter v. Illinois, Foster v. Illinois, Marino v. Ragen, Loftus v. Illinois,* and *Young v. Ragen.* All these prisoners and their cases were the gallant forerunners that chipped away at Illinois's barricade until it collapsed before the onslaught of *Jennings v. Illinois* into a rubble of disintegrated judicial subterfuge.

When I was returned to the Cook County Jail on June 20, 1952, to await my second trial, I found several prisoners from Joliet and Stateville there either awaiting postconviction hearings or new trials growing out of such hearings. The decision rendered by the Illinois Supreme Court in my case made it almost mandatory that petitioners alleging substantial violations of constitutional rights be given a hearing, and the trial courts in Illinois had started showing deference to the Illinois Supreme Court's mandate.

No sooner had I been placed on tier D-l than I was greeted warmly by Patty Joyce and Frank Hains, two Stateville prisoners awaiting postconviction hearings. I also recognized other inmates among the county jail prisoners with whom I had served time. They all treated me like I was a celebrity of some sort, to my great embarrassment Why couldn't they understand that just because my name was on two crucial judicial precedents and that I helped to free a few prisoners, that per se did not make me a legal wizard? But as fate would have it, I soon discovered that this latest display of adulation was brought on by one of my clients being freed following a postconviction hearing after he was granted a new trial and the state's principal witnesses had died. This victory of course did not help to detract from my popularity.

The door to the courthouse was wide open. Getting away from the doldrums of penitentiary life to the county jail for a hearing was like taking a vacation, and the prisoners in the county jail awaiting postconviction hearings were hopeful, happy, and heartened by the fact that they too might get lucky and walk.

I had brought several volumes of law books with me, and chief among them was my trusty old copy of *Black's Law Dictionary* as well as my copy of *Webster's Collegiate Dictionary*. I was a firm believer in that if you don't understand thoroughly what you read or hear, you can't make anyone else understand thoroughly what you are trying to express orally or in script.

I had therefore formed a habit long ago of looking up the definitions of every word I did not understand. As a result, I had gleaned an expansive vocabulary. Since man thinks with silent words flowing swiftly through his brain, it follows that the more words he understands, the better he can think to produce a comprehensive conscious flow of ideas for transference into the minds of others in such a convincing manner as to sway them toward his point of view.

I was told repeatedly by my peers and by lawyers that I expressed myself clearly and well. This then was the secret, if any, of what little success I had achieved at this point of my jailhouse law career; and this trait of clarity of thought and expression would stand me in good stead of achieving even greater accomplishments in the study and practice of law that I, at this particular time, did not dare entertain the thought of achieving. Because my number one aim was to win an acquittal at my upcoming trial and walk away a freeman. After that, I would retire from my short law career since it was impossible for me to practice law legally on the outside. Even if I were to finish law school and pass the bar examination, my past felony convictions would preclude me from being admitted to the bar to practice law. Why! I hadn't even graduated from high school.

Frank Hains and Patty Joyce had sidled out a corner in the dayroom where they asked me to join them. We pooled our law books and declared this section of the tier to be our law office. From here we discussed cases with the prisoners and dispensed legal advice.

I would guess that many lawyers considered us to be a bunch of pragmatic bastards for interfering in their cases. Although questions of coerced confessions and the knowing use of perjury to obtain a conviction was the more frequent claims raised in postconviction proceedings, there still was an alarming number of petitions alleging that the petitioners were represented at their trials by incompetent counsel who failed to protect all the rights of their clients. This kind of claim was very difficult to sustain. Nevertheless, there were many cases that showed a lack of legal talent as well as a lack of interest in protecting a client's constitutional rights. The trial judges, however, were invariably on the trial attorney's side in these matters and would lean over backward to absolve the attorneys of being incompetent.

As will be developed in a future chapter, to this writer's knowledge, not once has any lawyer in Illinois "properly raised" the constitutional question of affording appeals to those with money but not to indigent defendants who could not afford to appeal their cases. The state only allowed appeals without cost to those defendants sentenced to die in the electric chair. And no lawyer or lawyers ever made a concerted effort to test on appeal this flagrant inequality in the law. Perhaps they did not do so because they could not make any money on an indigent defendant. Be that as it may, thousands of penurious prisoners, some innocent no doubt, were doomed to spend years in jail, having been sent there by judges and prosecutors who took every unfair advantage of these prisoners just as Judge Ashcraft did in my case, knowing full well that the defendants could not afford an appeal, and they—the judges and prosecutors—would have to answer to no one for their unfair conduct during the trials of these poor defendants. And many shameless defense attorneys have stood by in ignorance or indifference without lifting a single finger through proper legal channels to redress this great inequity in the law.

I personally became aware of this blatant lack of equality in the state's appeals system when I began to study law. My prescience of mind and a hint I detected in the opinion handed down in my case by the United States Supreme Court alerted me to the fact that if this inequality of justice was "properly" brought before the High Tribunal, there was a possibility that the issue could be redressed. The court had said, "We do not consider here any independent question that might be raised by a state's failure to provide to an indigent defendant the transcript of his trial (*Jennings v. Illinois*)" (italics my own). Therefore, in the back of my mind lurked the intention to test this constitutional question either in my case, if I was convicted again, or in some other prisoner's case. Because I sensed something big here! Yes! Even bigger than what the US Supreme Court had already done in my case if we could get them to rule that the state had to supply every convicted pauper with a transcript of his trial proceedings if he requested it.

Having been exposed to many cases in which defendants were the victims of a poor defense, we jailhouse lawyers were very critical of the defenses and trial conduct of some practicing attorneys. Because from our experience in reading trial transcripts or portions of transcripts, we were well aware of the inadequacies that occurred all too often in some prisoners' cases where the defense attorney either waived substantial rights or was remiss in his duty to observe, protect, persevere, and practice law in accordance with correct legal procedures—all to the detriment of his client. So, when we asked prisoners, "Did your lawyer do this? Did your lawyer do that?" we were only making the prisoner aware that doing those things to fully protect the client's rights. In most instances the lawyers had done the things or intended to do the things we suggested on their own initiative. And in few cases, they had not fully protected their clients' rights.

The critical interference by jailhouse lawyers was often taken by many lawyers to be an affront to their capabilities when in truth, it was a signal to them to become sticklers for seeking justice in the interest of their clients.

I recall one instance in particular when an indigent defendant with a court-appointed attorney was found guilty of robbery. I advised him to have his attorney make a motion for the transcript of his trial proceedings in forma pauperis to preserve in the record that he wanted to appeal his case on writ of error but had no funds with which to purchase the transcript. His lawyer told him that it was useless to make the motion because Illinois law only provided a free transcript to defendants under sentence of death.

When the defendant insisted on the motion being filed and told his lawyer that I had advised him to have the motion entered in the record, the lawyer told his client, "You go tell that jailhouse lawyer to make the motion, and while you're at it, tell him for me to go to hell!"

Well, I did write the motion in longhand, as no typewriters were permitted in the county jail for the use of the inmates. The inmate mailed the motion to the trial judge and was called into court, whereby the judge denied the motion, as expected. The motion nevertheless was made a part of the trial record. A substantial constitutional question was "properly" preserved for review for a subsequent postconviction hearing.

Far be it for me to intimate that jailhouse lawyers are legally smarter than formally educated and highly trained trial lawyers. To do so would not only be a fallacy but a disservice to the legal profession as a whole. But I can say with complete veracity and confidence that I have met some jailhouse lawyers with extraordinary intellects; and equipped with their highly developed mentalities, diligence, and aggressiveness, these men accomplished legal feats that were fantastic! Because they were dauntless in the face of the judiciary and their opposition. The jailhouse lawyers could say what they wanted to say in any way they wanted to say it. They were not afraid to experiment, suffered no embarrassment at failure, and, in most cases, had nothing to lose with everything to gain. Tell me what lawyer could approach the bar with that attitude and survive the scorn and criticism of the courts and his peers?

Whatever disparaging remarks are made about jailhouse lawyers, they are a breed apart and deserve a respected niche in American jurisprudence for some very outstanding contributions that they have made for the betterment of justice in this country. The statute books and case law reports are replete with laws, decisions, and precedents attesting to the jailhouse lawyers' prowess and influence that revolutionized some aspects of criminal law and procedure.

Moman Pruiett, perhaps one of the most successful criminal trial lawyers of all times, who came out of the penitentiary, apprenticed as a law clerk, and was admitted to practice law by a district judge in Oklahoma back during the turn of the century, never went to law school—something that cannot be done today. Not only did Moman Pruiett go on to become one of the most outstanding criminal lawyers in the country, he could boast a record of having tried 343 murder cases without ever losing a single defendant to the gallows. His autobiography, titled *Moman Pruiett: Criminal Lawyer*, records 303 acquittals out of the 343 murder cases he tried, which only goes to prove that you don't have to be a law school graduate to be a damn good lawyer.

In the book *Doing Life* by Stephen Bello, the protagonist, Jerry Rosenberg, is touted in this true life story as "the world's greatest jailhouse lawyer." Rosenberg serving life in prison in New York State actually finished a law course and successfully passed the New York State bar examination and has practiced law in the penitentiary. Amazing!

Cecil Wright, a convict who served time in several state and federal penitentiaries including Alcatraz was considered by many lawyers to be an expert on the habeas corpus writ. He was instrumental in freeing dozens of prisoners.

The following three paragraphs were borrowed with permission from page 121 of the book titled *Warden Ragen of Joliet* by Gladys Erickson:

> The most successful cell house lawyer ever to hang out his shingle in Stateville was Maurice Meyer, who is serving a ninety-year sentence for murder. Meyer never saw a law book before enrolling at Joliet, yet he wrote a treatise on jurisprudence entitled "Exhaustion of State Court Remedies," which was used as a basis of a lecture one Chicago lawyer delivered before the Yale University Law School.
>
> During the course of his legal career, Meyer prepared one case that was taken to the United States Supreme Court and won the release of four men who were serving life terms for murder. After that, an inmate who could get Meyer to prepare his writ wouldn't have traded his attorney for Clarence Darrow. Another time, Meyer was able to prepare a petition that resulted in the release of a man imprisoned for life on a conviction of rape.

Ragen stopped Meyer and he has retired from active practice, but the rest of the cell house lawyers are hard at it. The odds are decidedly against them, but every once in a while, someone, hits the jackpot, and that is all the encouragement needed.

I knew Maury Meyer well. He was indeed an exceptional legal scholar from whom I gained some knowledge to assist me in my own legal studies. Meyer, however, did not actually stop helping other inmates. He went underground like the rest of us and continued his law practice. His legal reputation was established long before I entered prison and started establishing a reputation of my own with the help and assistance of Meyer and other jailhouse lawyers.

Nathan Leopold, either a genius or near-genius-type person, who was a member of the celebrated *Leopold-Lobe* case in which they were defended and saved from execution by the late Clarence Darrow, also studied law in prison. And Leopold had the potential to become a great legal talent and jailhouse lawyer. But he elected to remain passive and not offend the prison authorities by assisting the other inmates in their legal endeavors on a regular basis. It was a fact though that on occasions, for sexual favors, he would accept some inmates' cases. Since Leopold, the scion of a wealthy family, had no money problems, anything he did to help another inmate with his legal services was either an act of charity or an act of sex. No one questioned Leopold's epicenism, not even the officials, because it was all brought out in his notorious trial. Then too all during his incarceration, he had good rapport with the prison administrations that regarded him as a celebrity prisoner who remained aloof of the riffraff and run-of-the-mill prisoners. Because Leopold enjoyed mingling with the intellectual and studious inmates.

On a number of occasions, I had opportunities to talk with this awesomely "brainy person" who seemingly could touch brilliantly on any topic imaginable. I watched him type dictation with rapid-fire accuracy from a medical specialist who used sesquipedalian medical terms that I couldn't even pronounce much less spell. Leopold finished the paper, snatched it out of the typewriter, and proffered it to the specialist who read it before saying, "Excellent, Nathan. Simply excellent!"

I marveled at such precision and intellect. All I had ever heard and read about Leopold's brilliance could not impress me as much as this single feat of excellence, because I saw it with my very own eyes.

*   *   *   *   *

Judge Wendell E. Green was a frail-looking man in his late sixties with a bald pate that made his oblong head seen larger than it really was. He was a scholarly-appearing person with a courteous disposition that was unmistakably sincere. He had been assigned by the chief justice of the criminal court of Cook County to be the trial judge at my new trial. Today, he had me appear before him to appoint counsel to represent me. I had made a formal motion for court-appointed counsel other than from the Cook County Public Defender's Office. Because at that time, there were too many palsy-walsy relationships going on between the state's attorney's office and the public defender's office. One of the assistant state's attorneys, Mr. James McGovern, only recently had been considered one of the best public defenders in the county. He now had switched over to the state's attorney's office and ended up prosecuting me along with Mr. Robert McDonald, another assistant state's attorney. This had happened on several recent occasions whereby the best lawyers were coaxed away from the public defender's office by the state's attorney who was siphoning off all the best legal brains and talent for his staff—taking the wheat and leaving the chaff.

When I was a young lad in 1934, I lived across the street from Judge Green who also resided on the 6800 block of Langley Avenue in a community in Chicago called Woodlawn. I knew the judge couldn't remember me over eighteen years later, and I was glad that he couldn't. Because if he had, he would have remembered me in a bad light as that bad kid across the street who was always fighting and raising hell in the neighborhood.

The judge himself had reprimanded me, as well as his wife, on several occasions for running across his lawn, using foul language and creating disturbances. He had even complained to my foster parents, Mr. and Mrs. James, about my mischievous conduct. I therefore felt secure in my secret, and that the name *Jennings* would not stir his memory to associate me as being that mean little kid that lived across the street from him when I was twelve years old.

Back in 1934, Judge Green was a civic-minded practicing attorney who was highly respected by everyone in the community. He had the reputation of being a scholarly lawyer, and this small of stature, brown-skinned man brought that attribute to the bench with him when he was elected a judge of the Circuit Court of Cook County and ex-officio judge of the criminal court.

The judge gazed through his gold-rimmed spectacles at me and said pleasantly, "Mr. Jennings, I have an excellent attorney who has agreed to accept the court's appointment to represent you pursuant to your request in these proceedings. Perhaps you have heard of him. His name is George N. Leighton. And Mr. Leighton is what we in the profession call a constitutional lawyer! So I feel certain that since he excels in that field of law, as well as being an excellent criminal lawyer and civil attorney, you too will find him very satisfactory."

"Thank you, Your Honor. I'm sure I'll find a man with his credentials very satisfactory."

"Mr. Leighton will be here shortly, Mr. Jennings. You may be seated at the defense table," the judge concluded.

I seated myself in front of my guard, a deputy sheriff, and I watched and listened as the judge heard a motion in another case.

Several minutes later a tall, middle-aged brown-skinned man with a military erect bearing approached the judge's bench and stood off to the side until Judge Green concluded the business before him. Then the judge said to me, "Mr. Jennings, will you please approach the bench." When I stood there before him, the judge went on, "This gentleman here is Mr. George N. Leighton. He is appointed as your attorney."

I turned, facing the attorney, and we exchanged greetings while shaking hands. Mr. McGovern and Mr. McDonald looked on in silence.

"I will now set a date for trial, Mr. Leighton. Then you and your client may want to go to the back for a conference in the bull pen."

"Very good, Your honor. Please set the date down, and I would appreciate an ooportunity to confer with my client," Mr. Leighton responded in a very articulate voice.

The judge studied his docket book for a few seconds before writing down a notation. Looking up, he said, "The only date I have open for a jury trial is sixty days from now. Is that all right with you and Mr. Jennings, Mr. Leighton? And the state?"

"Fine. I have no objections, Your Honor," my attorney said.

"I have none either," I commented.

"The state has no objections, Your Honor," McDonald said.

"Then it is settled," Judge Green responded.

The bailiff and deputy sheriff led me to the bull pen followed by Mr. Leighton, who stepped up to the bars after I was locked inside. Leighton took a yellow legal pad out of his briefcase, saying, "Mr. Jennings, I want to get as much background information about this case as you can give me. I understand from having read the opinions in your case handed down by the US Supreme Court and the Illinois Supreme Court that there is some question of a coerced confession."

"That is true, sir."

"Well, we certainly will challenge the admissibility of that at the trial. Now fill me in on your arrest and what led up to the confession."

We talked for about an hour. When Mr. Leighton left, he had a good history of the case. He did not believe, nor did I, that the state would bring up the ring again because that would lead to the impeachment of Detective Piotter's testimony. I was very much impressed with Mr. Leighton's methodical professionalism after having confided in him. He was very astute and serious-minded. And I felt fortunate to have an attorney of his caliber defending me, although at the time, I had no way of knowing just how great, dedicated, and endowed in jurisprudence this man was, who was later to be elected a judge of the superior court of Cook County and thereafter be appointed to the federal bench as a United States District Court Judge for the Northern District of Illinois where he carried his deeply rooted dislike for coercion of any kind to the bench with him, and which followed him all through his tenure as a judge.

Sitting as a judge of the federal district court in Chicago, Illinois, on August 13, 1982, thirty years after he defended me, Judge Leighton acquitted a defendant, Erma Roberts, who had been charged with her husband for failing to report $73,000 in her income on their tax returns for 1975 through 1978. The judge said that "there was a presumption of coercion because Erma Roberts signed the tax return in the presence of her husband," and he ruled that "when a woman who is married commits a crime in the presence of her husband, the mere presence of the husband gives rise to a presumption of coercion." Judge Leighton's ruling was based on a very old concept of law that many law scholars believed was antiquated. The ruling, nevertheless, is demonstrative of Judge George N. Leighton's willingness to uphold the law against coercion in any form whatsoever.

When I returned to my tier in the county jail, Patty Joyce and Frank Hains were seated at the end of the table in one corner of the dayroom that we called our law office. They were in a heated discussion raking Warden Ragen over the coals. Frank hated the warden's guts. He would often say that whenever the warden's name was mentioned. Although Hains had a brilliant mind, his psychopathic personality sometimes made him obnoxious.

In his quest for freedom, Hains had become embroiled with the prison administration long ago over petitioning the courts for himself and for other inmates. He was known as an instigator and agitator to the prison officials. Consequently, his embroilment with them led to numerous punishments being imposed upon him—confinement in the "hole," deprivation of privileges, isolation cells, and finally, transfer to Menard Penitentiary for psychiatric treatment.

It was a frequently practiced procedure under Warden Ragen's administration that when an inmate became too intractable, he was transferred to Menard as a mentally ill person, and Hains had been no exception. At Menard, he was given electrical shock treatments to the extent that he probably suffered some brain damage. And while at Menard, he had made such a nuisance of himself that the warden there got tired of him and transferred him back to Ragen's prison at Stateville where Hains got busy preparing civil suits for compensatory and punitive damages against Ragen and other members of the Illinois Department of Public Safety.

Hains always represented himself in court and argued his case with a fiery vehemence in condemning the prison officials, the courts. and the prosecuting attorneys. One day in court, his language became so intemperate as to irritate the judge hearing his case.

The judge declared, "Mr. Hains, if you persist in your deplorable conduct, I shall have to hold you in contempt of court."

Hains replied in an equally irritable fashion, "I don't give a shit, your dishonor, because I have already held you in contempt of justice!"

The judge was so frustrated, infuriated, and flabbergasted that he shouted, "Get this maniac out of my courtroom!"

The judge apparently realized that he was powerless to inflict any realistic contempt of court punishment on Hains, who was already under a life sentence.

That day, Frank Hains confided in Patty Joyce and me that he had turned Warden Ragen in to the Criminal Investigation Division of the Internal Revenue Service. The mailman had just delivered him a letter from Internal Revenue acknowledging Hains's claim against Ragen and assuring Hains that an investigation would be undertaken to determine whether his charges against the warden could be sustained. If they could be sustained, criminal action would be taken against the warden, and Hains would be paid a percentage of the tax money recovered from Ragen to reward Hains for turning in the warden.

I thought the whole thing sounded ridiculous! How could this convict be intimate enough with the warden's financial affairs to make such charges? I told Hains what I thought, and he immediately flashed a show of temper. He began to cite all the perquisites that came with the job of being warden.

By painstaking and cunning research, Frank Hains had gathered information from other prisoners concerning approximately how much meat, produce, and other foodstuffs was requisitioned by the warden annually from the prison larder, including such household items as toilet paper. Hains had even garnered information about how much gasoline the warden used that came from the prison gas pump. The warden, he claimed, had everything at no cost—eleven-room apartment rent-free, laundry, maintenance, and much, much more. Yet Ragen only had a basic annual salary of $9,600.

"I tell you, the goddamned son of a bitch is living like a king!" Hains said heatedly. His heavy jowls giving him a bulldoggish look.

"True, the warden gets all of that and a lot more that you or no one else but him knows about. But how in the hell do you expect the government to make a case against Ragen on the basis of the information you gave them?" Patty Joyce wanted to know.

Hains, getting impatient, threw his arms out widely. "Well, goddamnit, Patty, you know the son of a bitch isn't going to report all those perks he gets. He's stealing the joint blind, I tell you!"

"But everything you've said is based on pure supposition. You've never seen his tax returns," Patty insisted.

"You don't get the idea at all, Patty. Now I'll run it down to you this way. I gathered all that information about Meatball from cons I know to be 'stand-up guys'—guys that hate old Meatball as much or more than I do. These cons trust me and want to see Meatball get his fat ass kicked in the slammer and out of their hair forever! So, these cons know what I'm up to, and they want to help me fuck Meatball. They trust me, get it? There's nothing hardly that Ragen does in that place that some con don't know about, right? They can even tell when he fucks his wife by looking at the sheets on his bed. Anyway, I got all this info, and I turned it over to the government tax people. I smuggled it out of the joint with my legal papers, using codes and fictitious names. Now the government has got copies of Meatball's tax returns, right? So all they got to do is examine the returns and put two and two together. Bam! They got him dirty!" Looking at me, Hains concluded, "Right, Blacky?"

"Hell, Frank, I don't know a damn thing about income taxes.

"Just the same, you guys watch and you'll see this asshole go on trial and get convicted," Hains remarked.

I didn't comment any further on Hains's wishful thinking because the whole scheme sounded ridiculous. But by doing what he did might serve to vent some of the enmity he felt toward the warden.

Patty Joyce, however, was getting a kick out of riling Hains. "They'll never nail Meatball. He'll say he uses all of that stuff for business purposes, entertaining guests at the prison and travel expenses. Shit, Hains, Internal Revenue will never nail the son of a bitch. You're wasting your fuckin' time."

"Goddamn you, Patty! Don't you want to see Meatball put away like us?" Hains's face was flush with wrath. Saliva was oozing at one corner of his lips. He looked like a mad bulldog.

He was all steamed up. "Look what the dirty bastard did to me and to you. Think about all the punishment you suffered when you attempted to go over the wall. Think about that, Patty!"

Patty, in his late forties, a small, baby-faced Irishman with a soft-spoken voice that sounded almost boyish, responded, "Hey now, buddy! I don't like the prick any better'n you do. I'd love to see him get nailed. But it ain't going to happen like you want it to."

Hains was furious now. He ran his fingers through his thick mane and walked around the floor in a fit of exasperation, reiterating, "I'm going to get that son of a bitch! I'm going to get that son of a bitch!"

The other men on the tier and the guard stopped what they were doing to stare at Hains while he wore off his rage. I smiled at his antics. Knowing how much he hated the warden, Hains would try anything to assuage his bitterness and lust for vengeance against Ragen.

Patty shook his head in amusement. These two old-timers had both been serving long sentences. Patty was doing life, and Hains also had a life sentence. They had been incarcerated a long time. Patty and some other inmates at Stateville did try an escape once by drugging the tower guards' coffee in 1939.

The guards on the towers, high on the concrete walls, would use a rope with a hook on the end to pull up lunch baskets that had been prepared in the officers' kitchen because they could not leave the watchtowers to go to the officers' dining room. The escape plot failed, however, and Patty Joyce and his henchmen were caught and punished severely.

When Hains finally cooled down he returned to our makeshift law office and lit a cigarette. We stared at one another bemusedly for about a minute. Then for no apparent reason we all suddenly and spontaneously started laughing together—probably to relieve the tension. We laughed at least for a minute more while the other inmates stared at us in astonishment.

Many of the inmates called Hains a "bug" because they thought of him as being "stir-crazy" since he frequently had temper eruptions and other peculiarities of a paranoiac nature. Yet Hains was a soft touch for a hard-luck story and thereby became generous to a fault.

Hains had inherited some money and property from his family. It was placed in trust because at the time, the family estate was probated, Hains had already been probated as noncompos mentis while he was in the Menard Penitentiary. His court-appointed trustee who administrated Hains's inheritance would mail him a small allowance every month for commissary items. When Hains would want additional funds for law books, typewriter, or other things, he would have to apply to the trustee. And this angered the hell out of Hains. He almost hated his trustee as much as he hated Warden Ragen. Try as he may, he could not get the court's order lifted that declared him mentally unsound. He believed that the trustee was in league with Warden Ragen and the prison psychiatrist. The trustee would not release money to pay for a private psychiatrist to examine Hains with a view to having him restored to normal mentality, nor would the trustee approve money to be paid to a lawyer requested by Hains to represent him at a sanity hearing.

Hains having resources could not declare himself a pauper and seek a court-appointed lawyer to represent him in any court proceedings, and the probate court would not grant him a hearing on his mental condition unless the trustee approved. Because under the circumstances, the probate court did regard Hains as a person of unsound mind and therefore would only show interest upon the recommendation of the trustee or the prison psychiatrist. Hains had a real problem on his hands, and he knew it. To make matters worst, he did not have any propinquity on the outside to come to his rescue. All this only added to his rancor against Warden Ragen, the trustee, and the probate court that had jurisdiction over him and his inheritance.

While Hains did a beautiful job of preparing his own petitions seeking to overturn his conviction and even though he was well-versed in criminal law and appellate procedure, he nevertheless had not been successful in the many years he had been fighting his case. But he had successfully helped other inmates without any charge whatsoever, and that I respected him for.

It was not long after we discussed Hains's tax claim against Ragen that the prisoner's petition for relief under the postconviction act was denied following a hearing that was held on his allegations seeking his freedom. Hains was subsequently shipped back to the prison to continue service on his life sentence imposed under the Illinois Habitual Criminal Act. To my knowledge, nothing ever came of his complaint against Warden Ragen that he filed with the Internal Revenue Service.

Patty Joyce was lucky. The little Irishman won his freedom after his postconviction hearing, and I will never forget the happy look on his face when he came back to the tier to get his belongings. I felt proud too. There goes a lifer back into the free world—not because I helped him directly because he had been fighting his conviction for allegedly killing a Chicago policeman in 1929, for years without any results. But the decisions handed down in my cases, mandating hearings under the Illinois Postconviction Hearing Act, did, indirectly help to get him a hearing—just as those decisions would help many more prisoners gain a day in court that would spell freedom for them.

LeRoy Lindsay and I had been close friends during our early teens into our young adulthood. We both lived in the Sixty-first Street area on the Southside of Chicago when I met him. I lived on the Sixtieth and Calumet block, and LeRoy lived on the Fifty-ninth and Prairie block, just around the corner from me. He had a lovely twin sister named Margie that I used to have a terrible crush on. We dated on several occasions, but I never was able to score big with her.

LeRoy was a member of my gang, the Thirteen Phantoms. We were a hell-raising bunch of teenagers engaging in all kinds of delinquency from gang fights, to gambling and thievery. I and other members of my gang had been arrested on several occasions for these offenses. And once a few of us were arrested in a stolen car as far away from Chicago as Cedar Rapids, Iowa. Most of us were fifteen and sixteen years old at the time. We were on our way to St. Paul, Minnesota to get into some more mischief when the cops stopped us and locked us up in one of the Cedar Rapid police stations. A few days later, we were returned to Chicago by the Chicago police and placed in the juvenile detention home.

We were all later released under court supervision and immediately resumed our youthful crime careers no sooner than we hit the streets. LeRoy and I later ended up in Pontiac Penitentiary for separate offenses involving auto thefts. We both came out of prison apprentice barbers and master thieves.

We worked only briefly at our barber trade while on parole before going our separate ways to get into even more trouble with the law.

Now my good pal LeRoy was downstairs in one of the death cells. He had been sentenced to die in the electric chair for participating in the killing of a policeman in a tavern on April 24, 1950, at Fifty-ninth and State Street that he and three other members of his gang held up.

Most of the Phantoms who had been in our gang were fated to end up serving time or becoming the victims of untimely deaths. Two gang members were slain, one in a bad fight and another one in a robbery attempt. But LeRoy was the first and only one to have the hard luck to face "Old Smokey," the electric chair, in the basement of the Cook County Jail. And the fact that he was going to die shook me up pretty badly. We had been close buddies, and I knew what this was doing to his mother and the rest of his family who had tried her best to raise here children in a Christian home without a husband or father for the greater part of their existence. Then too Margie, his twin sister, had died suddenly only a short time ago from a fatal illness. LeRoy's pending date with death coming so close behind his sister's passing made this dual tragedy an extreme burden to bear.

My compassion for the Lindsay family was heartrending as I sat upstairs in the county jail, awaiting my second trial with the realization that if there was not some judicial, executive, or divine intervention, my old buddy was going to be cooked.

And that is literally what happens when a person is strapped down in the electric chair and the switched is pulled. The blood actually boils and the flesh is seared. The electric chair in the Ohio State Penitentiary once caught fire during an execution and the victim was almost cremated before his body was retrieved from what turned out to be a cruel pyre. The thought of this happening to LeRoy all but nauseated me.

I never gave capital punishment too much thought before I became personally involved with LeRoy's plight. Now I could certainly empathize with him and his family. This was 1952, and the celebrated *Caryl Chessman* case was in the limelight focused on Chessman's fight to escape execution in the California gas chamber. The case was beginning to make national news and would later become a worldwide cause célèbre. To me the *Chessman* case demonstrated the utter futility of using capital punishment as a deterrent to crime or a moral justification for punishing any kind of criminal act. Capital punishment, in my opinion, is simply legalized murder. The men who do it do it in the name of God contrary to the Christian teachings in a civilized society, and most of the people involved in obtaining and carrying out the death sentences in this country profess to believing in God. But let someone close to them receive a death sentence and these proponents of capital punishment would doubtlessly change their beliefs in it faster than a chameleon lizard can change its colors.

Before I am tempted to use this vehicle as a diatribe against capital punishment, let me say, simply and quite clearly, that I utterly detest especially any law that will take a life where a life has not been taken. In Chessman's case, he did not take a life. Therefore the California officials responsible for his death ought to be damned by God someway, somehow and sometime . . . Because if these barbarians predicated their actions on the old biblical theory of an "eye for an eye," then there still cannot be any parity between rape and murder.

All crimes should be made punishable, and the punishment should be swift, fair, and appropriate with the crime committed—not commensurate. What makes capital punishment such a failure, in my opinion, is that it is the only law on the books that tries to exact a true equation for the crime of taking a life; and when capital punishment is diverted into other areas of crime, such as kidnapping and rape, the equation is diverted into an inequity. Then the reality of capital punishment's purpose becomes confused and distorted.

The world would best be better off without the use of capital punishment for any offense. From experience, I can truthfully say that the prospect of life imprisonment or a long term in servitude is the worst so-called humane punishment that anyone could suffer. Because in a sense, it is not humane at all to subject a person to a lifetime of mental torture and deprivation of freedom that brings with it perpetual regret of ever having committed a crime. Sparing a person from such imprisonment by death is merciful in comparison.

Many other prisoners like LeRoy have preferred death to life behind bars? LeRoy had been in prison. He knew what prison was like just from spending several years in confinement. Death is not the worst thing that can happen to mankind. People take their lives every day for various reasons. My own grandfather committed suicide in 1932 during the Great Depression, and I have thought about suicide several times myself when life seemed almost unbearable. So why in the name of heaven or hell do the proponents of capital punishment make such a big thing of death? People who listen to their unrealistic theories are being swindled by these death advocates if it is real justice and punishment they want to see inflicted on murderers and other malefactors. Believe me! Imprisonment is the only realistic answer; and it is the best suited answer to protect the rights and interests of all concerned.

I say this in all sincerity. Assuming that Chessman was guilty and my very own beloved sister or wife was the victim, I would have felt cheated if he went to the gas chamber instead of to prison for life or for a long, long stretch. For that is the only way I honestly and very truly feel that I would be getting the most for my lust for vengeance or cries for justice. I know. I've been there!

LeRoy and I had exchanged a few kites that were carried by the trusties and jail barber. I tried to encourage my old friend as much as possible that if his appeal failed, the governor could commute his death sentence to life imprisonment. But LeRoy evidently had a premonition of doom. Because in his kites, he always wrote of "getting it over with" and that he didn't want to spend the rest of his life locked up. He even hinted of suicide rather than spending the balance of his life in that "hellhole" he knew as prison.

When LeRoy's final appeal was turned down and the governor refused to grant him clemency, LeRoy prepared himself very bravely to die. One of his last requests was to see me before they pulled the switch, and I think that my visit with a soon-to-die buddy and the *Caryl Chessman* case did more to demonstrate to me not only the futility of capital punishment but also the futility of leading a life of crime than anything else, not because of the fear of death per se but because it made me realize the true significance of the terrible waste that crime exacts from life, time, and property—three precious things indeed! But the fact that a close friend was about to die in the electric chair had no lasting deterrent effect upon my way of thinking at that particular time. Although I would have preferred to live outside the circle of criminal conduct, it still would remain my last option to live within it if all else failed to keep me outside that circle.

The law has always had a streak of tyranny and vengeance in it as administrated by some seemingly heartless and callous men. How in the hell can the law—a supposedly intelligent network of fairness and impartiality—expect a prisoner to forego vengeance against society upon his release when the law itself is not tempered with mercy or forgiveness and is oftentimes symbolical of gross retaliation? The sword of justice has two edges, one to cut with and one to backlash with. It is therefore possible to destroy the damned and the damner at the same time. Because over 95 percent of these previously damned prisoners are going to one day return to what we call society and, in accordance with the rate of recidivism existing at the time, will punish and damn that society with a new wave of crime; and on goes the vicious cycle. Now I realize that many readers have heard the foregoing tireless argument time and time again expostulated by penologist and criminologist. But what I do not understand is why society is so apathetic to its own safety by not heeding the warnings of these learned professionals who know whereof they speak.

LeRoy looked thin, almost frail in comparison to when I had seen him several years ago. His fulvous complexion seemed almost colorless, and his light-red almost blondish-looking hair was sparse and flecked with gray. His shortness of stature caused him to look up into my face since I was several inches taller. His voice always had a stutter, so it was not easy to detect whether his speech was faltering because of the anxiety of the ordeal he faced or whether it was his customary mode of delivery. It could have been both. But his light-brown eyes were steady, and his grip dry and firm as he took my handshake.

The guard that had brought me down to death row stood back against the wall as far away as possible to give LeRoy and me some privacy in our conversation, and I thought that was nice of him to do so although I had been searched thoroughly before being allowed to enter death row. The time was short. It was October 16, 1952, the day before LeRoy's execution date.

I was hesitant and nervous. I didn't know what to say. LeRoy evidently sensed my uneasiness, and he said, smiling broadly, "Come on, man, don't let this thing upset you. I'm not afraid. I've conditioned myself for this ordeal. I mean it, Blacky. I'm not afraid to die. And I'd rather it be this way than go back to prison. Now, come on, man, tell me what's been happening with you. Win any more big cases? I've been hearing all kinds of good things about you making law in the joint." He paused to light a cigarette, and he offered me one.

"No thanks. I quit," I said, shaking my head.

Leroy laughed. "That's great! Smoking's bad for your health. I ought to quit 'cause you'll live a long time if you don't smoke."

I knew he was being facetious about quitting smoking and was only attempting to put me at ease. Still, I shuddered inside. One minute he's talking about dying and the next minute he's talking of living a long time. I still didn't know what to say. How do you comfort someone or say anything encouraging at a moment of doom? It would sound artificial if I tried to talk religiously because LeRoy and I never talked religion before, even though he was reared a Roman Catholic. No, let the priest handle that. There was no future for LeRoy now, so talking about religion would, in his case, be delving into the hereafter—something I professed to knowing nothing about. I cursed myself for being so reticent when I was usually so glib. Well, I thought, there was a past. Why not talk about that?

I brightened up. "Say, man, you remember Little Red, don't you? Well, he's up on my tier on a larceny beef. He told me to tell you hello."

"You know I remember Little Red, man. That's one of my old partners. We sure used to have a lot of fun together in the old days," LeRoy stammered. "Is that joker still pulling his pranks on people? Hey, Blacky, how about when we were kids and Little Red gave you the shitty end of the stick. Boy did I bust my side on that one. And you wanted to kill him but couldn't catch him." LeRoy broke out laughing at his recollection.

Sure, I remembered. I'll never forget it. One of the neighborhood kids nicknamed Lips, because of his prominent mouth and gabby nature, was pretending to fight with Little Red, who had a stick in his hand, which he was holding down by the side of his leg in a threatening manner. Lips offered that if Little Red would put down the stick, or better still let me hold it so Red couldn't get it during the "scrap," that he would fight him fairly. Thinking that I was going to see a good fistfight, I didn't object when Little Red offered me the stick to hold. When I grabbed the stick, it had dog shit on it, and Little Red and Lips ran off laughing like hell at me standing there momentarily occupied scraping the crap off my fingers before giving chase to the two pranksters. And it was a good thing that I didn't catch them before cooling off, or I would have rubbed that filthy stick right under their noses.

Now the old memory of that prank brought forth a big chuckle as I said, "How can I ever forget getting the shitty end of the stick. Little Red and Lips seemed to have started something back then that has been following me around for the most of my life."

"And how about our boy Fat Phillips, Blacky? Remember when we were kids and that big turkey got stuck in the hole we knocked open on the roof of Sam's grocery store when we burglarized the joint. I can still see Fat Phillips dangling from the ceiling like a fuckin' chandelier," LeRoy let out a big raucous round of laughter and I joined in with him.

Wiping tears of mirth from my eyes as I recalled the incident, I responded, "And do you recall that after we got back up on the roof and ripped away at it to make the hole bigger so we could get the fat bastard out, he could not hold on, and his big ass fell through and hit the floor with a thunderous thump!"

"Do I!" LeRoy started laughing again until he could control himself long enough to add, "And the first thing that fat fucker did when he got to his feet was to get a quart of chocolate milk and a coconut cake to stuff his fat gut with—not giving a fuckin' damn about the money or nothing."

More laughter from both of us, and I was beginning to feel very much at ease.

"Say, remember my sister Margie in that white rubber swimming suit that busted in her crotch and she jumped into the pool in Washington Park to hide herself from the crowd?"

"Yeah! Yeah! Yeah! Boy do I remember that! She couldn't even swim," I recalled.

"But I jumped in to save her before realizing that I couldn't swim either," LeRoy resumed.

"And I got the lifeguards to save both of you. And although Margie was damn near drowned when they pulled her out of the pool, she hadn't lost her vanity, because she cupped her hands over her crotch until they threw a jacket around her!"

"Man! Those were the days, weren't they?" LeRoy reminisced.

"They sure were! And I miss those happy, carefree times."

"Me too. Boy! It sure is good to see you, Blacky," LeRoy cut in with a happy expression on his face.

We talked on for several minutes in the same carefree fashion until the guard told us that it was time to take me back to my tier.

But we pleaded with him for a little more time, and he was understanding in allowing us several more minutes together.

Before I left, LeRoy was feeling sorry for me. He was apologetic that his pending execution was causing so much sorrow among his friends and relatives.

"So help me, Blacky, I would rather it be this way than going back to prison for life. Don't feel bad about it. It is something that's got to be, I guess. I sure didn't want my life to end this way, but neither did that cop, Murphy, want to go out with eight bullets in his body the way he died. I am sorry about what we did to him. He had loved ones to mourn him too. I never wanted to kill anybody— he . . . he just got in our way during the heist . . ." his voice stammered and then trailed off.

Facts in the case show that LeRoy Lindsay, Earlie Burton, Emanuel Scott, Emil Washington, and James Picket were jointly indicted and convicted for the murder of William Murphy, a Chicago police officer. Emil Washington died before trial of a gunshot wound received during the holdup. Lindsay, Burton, and Scott were each sentenced to death in the electric chair, and Picket was sentenced to fourteen years imprisonment because he supplied some of the guns used in the robbery and murder, although he was not present when the holdup and murder occurred. Earlie Burton died a natural death on June 12, 1952, while in a county jail cell, he had been suffering with tuberculosis. Scott received several stays of executions and did not die in the electric chair until March 19, 1953.

At 12:05 a.m. October 17, 1952, the day after my visit with Lindsay, he was strapped in the electric chair, and he was pronounced dead at 12:14 a.m. He died as courageously as he could without breaking down under the ordeal of facing the chair. I had been hoping until the very end that some miracle might save him, and I had asked the guard on my tier to please let me know when it was over. About a half hour after midnight, the guard came to my cell and gave me the fatal details of LeRoy's execution. After the guard left, I closed my eyes to hold back the tears of sadness that moistened them by refusing to be repressed.

Chapter 11

THE DAYS AND WEEKS HAD passed swiftly and my trial date was fast approaching. My girlfriend, Eve, and my best friend Jimmy Marshall were still loyal. They wrote letters and visited with me regularly. My foster mother also wrote to me often, and in spite of her infirm condition, she managed to visit with me as often as she could since I had been confined in the county jail.

Mom always reminded me that I was eternally in her prayers, and she hoped that I would be freed soon. She also prayed that I would continue to strive for self-betterment through God, Christ. and the church so that I would be prepared to lead a good Christian life when I came out of prison. She herself was a sincere Christian believer who devoted her life completely to God and Christ by making an extraordinary effort to live in accordance with the tenets of the Scripture beyond any question—something that I had never been able to do and perhaps would never be able to do.

Although I believed in God and attended the Episcopal church in prison—finding hardly no time for church on the outside—I had innate reservations about the virgin birth tenet and the Genesis version of creation. I could not force myself to believe anything that I did not feel deeply inside of me was the truth or at least possible, notwithstanding the dogma in the Scripture that declared in essence: all things are possible with God. These are mere words of man placed between the covers of a book easily refutable by other words of men. For instance, if all things are possible with God, can he build a rock so big that he can't pick it up? The foregoing question semantically says that God cannot do everything, just as the saying that all things are possible with God semantically says that God can do everything. But which question is the most logical, the one that merely states a blind trust or belief or the one that clearly and logically demonstrates that God cannot do everything?

I did not raise the above questions to make a mockery of the Holy Scripture. I did raise them solely to demonstrate the rationale that when one accepts a belief on blind trust or faith, one also sacrifices his God-given power to reason for himself.

A story comes to my mind that further illustrates the concept of blind faith as opposed to rationality. The story goes that a philosopher giving a lecture on religion at a Baptist convention, before a huge audience, told his listeners in the course of his talk: "I know something that God Himself doesn't know, and all of you too know something that God doesn't know." He paused to let his words sink in as frowns of disapproval showed on the faces in the audience and murmurs of displeasure with the speaker's remarks pervaded the auditorium. Several ministers and deacons on the dais stood up as though in preparation to eject the speaker from the premises. But at that moment, the speaker shouted, "God doesn't know no man, woman, or child who knows as much as he knows!" And immediately, the tension disappeared amidst the cries of "Amen!" and "Hallelujah!"

Personally, I felt comfortable believing Darwin's version of creation because to me, God in his mysterious ways seemed to always create things naturally and not so much by miracles like a magician producing a rabbit out of a hat. I firmly believe that God created nature to function in an evolutionary manner. And God did not write the Bible; man, an imperfect being, wrote it. Just as Darwin, an imperfect being, authored his theory of evolution. Darwin, however, neglected to state in his works that God told him that the theory of evolution was how the universe and its inhabitants were created. Had Darwin done so, he probably would have found his theories more widely accepted among Christian believers, some of whom will accept anything on blind faith; and certainly, Darwin had put a lot of reasoning into his theories to go along with any blind faith that one wanted to apply credence to.

The Darwin version of the creation of mankind is pure reasoning based on scientific research. God no doubt expects man to unravel many secrets of the universe. I could therefore never be a fundamentalist-type believer. Too often I questioned the truth and authenticity of things in the Bible. Yet I could rationalize to the point of believing many, many things in the Bible, which made my beliefs all the firmer. In trying to interpret some stories in the Bible caused me to waver toward agnosticism. I found it exceedingly difficult to be a true Christian believer. Yet I wanted very much to identify with God and be a part of Him in the universe. But somehow, I could not place blind credence in the divinity bestowed by man on other men and women among the living and the dead who supposedly received sainthood.

I was an avid reader of Voltaire's philosophy. But like the tenets in the Bible, I could not accept the teachings of Voltaire wholeheart-edly. I was caught in between two extremes—to believe a part of both teachings without accepting the whole loaf from either source. I could of course comfort myself with the prudent sayings. "A half of loaf is better than none." But perhaps by putting the two half-loaves together, I could make a whole loaf of religious philosophy that would serve my individual needs. I therefore sought a compromise between the teachings of Christ and the teachings of Voltaire and Darwin and other writers and scientist—something that the New Testament would never do, because it taught that one should never compromise Christ the Lord. But it is my firm belief that my personal religious philosophy does not compromise God the Father Almighty. Because my belief in him is beyond an atom of a doubt. It was easy for me to reconcile my belief without the principle of blind faith becoming involved. For I had learned to believe in the effects of God. Yes, the effects of God in all his creative wonderwork, his ubiquitous control over the whole universe and all living things and matter.

Just as I have seen people and have never seen their parents, I know beyond all doubt that they had to have parents before they could be created. One does not always have to see a person or thing to believe that it exists. One can see the effects of an unseen force and know that the force exists that created the effect. I have never seen God, and I sincerely doubt if any mortal has ever seen Him. But the effects of His existence cannot be denied. The world, universe, and everything in it had to be created by some force or great power.

Whatever that creative force or great power is becomes my God with unmistakable certainty. For I can see with my own eyes and feel with my own senses the awesome presence of an Almighty Creative Force.

To me, it was a fact that all religions were created by man to fashion out a mode of moral ethics or taboos by which to live and be guided by. And every religion is purported to be the correct or perfect answer to how man should live in conformity with God's laws. But I would be a fool to believe that any man has created a perfect religion or that God, in His final judgment, will single out any one of the multitudinous religions now practiced throughout the world and say: "This is the true religion. The others are frauds." No one or no religion is ever going to make me believe that a just God is going to do that.

Man, not being perfect in mind, body, or spirit, how then can he create anything perfect when God did not create man perfect? Man is a fraud when he claims to have created the perfect religion, and he is presumptuous at best when he says that God created the religion of his choice. God has given all mankind a free will to create whatever is necessary for his comfort of mind, body and spirit. And it is man who infringes upon man's free will—not God. Man will always have a kindred spirit with God. But let no man ever walk this earth and die like the rest of us claim that he is a god. For there is only one God, and there will always be one God who will ever remain a mystery to mankind.

I can accept Christ as the son of God just as I can accept all men as his sons and all women as his daughters. God is our evolutionary creator. Some men and women that have graced this earth have been endowed with a higher degree of moral and spiritual values than others. They have endeavored to impart the teachings of these values to others in the hope that mankind could live in peace, love, and harmony with one another. Voltaire expressed the mystery of man in the universe very aptly and very beautifully in his poem "The Lisbon Earthquake," from which I now quote a few lines:

> Mysteries like these can no man penetrate,
> Hid from his view remains the book of fate. Man

his own nature never yet could sound He knows not whether he is, nor whither bound. Atoms tormented on this earthly ball, The sport of fate, by death soon swallowed all, But thinking atoms, who with piercing eyes Have measured the whole circuit of the skies; We rise in thought up to the heavenly throne, But our own nature still remains unknown. (Quoted from page 568. *The Portable Voltaire*, edited by Ben Ray Redman. Published January 1949, The Viking Press Inc.)

While Jesus Christ is widely revered as he should be, he is no more revered than the prophet Muhammad or Buddha by their religious worshipers. I therefore respect all these great teachers for their religious philosophies. Because they all predicate their teachings on good things that are not evil. But to me, none of them are gods. A person's religion, in most cases, is based on his culture and rearing. My culture and rearing happened to be Christianity, and I can accept that with some modifications, even though the modifications may be in conflict with other believers of the same faith. But has not there always been a tendency to modify Christianity to serve the individual needs of its followers? If this were not so, how then does this one religion (Christianity) have so many widely conflicting and divergent denominations?

I enjoy being a latitudinarian. And I do believe that someday, someone will form a church of another denomination of Christianity and find ample followers to question the virgin birth theory, but at the same time, they will accept Christ and his teachings as a basic philosophy of what is good and what is evil. Because today, we live in an age of reasoning where man has gone beyond the earth in his quest for knowledge, and more and more people are seeking answers with reason rather than legend or myth. Even the Roman Catholic church is changing its dogma gradually to conform with the times and morals of its modern parishioners. But it would be foolish indeed to ever expect the Catholic church to change its belief in the immaculate conception.

Too often man as an individual forgets to think and permits others to do his thinking for him, and that is when he gets into trouble. I personally believe that blind faith can be extremely dangerous when one places total trust and confidence in any person or in anything. Because he will become vulnerable to the point of self-destruction. Blind faith reduces a human being to a vegetable state—like a head of cabbage, without a brain, lying in the garden waiting to be harvested. And where does the head of cabbage end? As a feast for man or beast. If the head of cabbage had a brain like man, it might figure out some way of getting out of the garden before the farmer got there with his harvesting tool. Even with a brain though, that would be a very difficult feat for a cabbage. It has (down through history) been a very difficult feat for millions of gullible people that have accepted blind faith as their religious philosophy. And many religious leaders have grown fat on these human sheep or cabbage.

Father Jones, the Episcopal priest, taught us to interpret the Bible in three ways—literally, figuratively, and historically. When an inmate once questioned the biblical story of Jonah and the great fish as being literally true, Father Jones told the inmate to interpret the story figuratively. That it was only a story to symbolize that if one refuses to do God's bidding he will be punished. Then Father Jones told the inmate to think of Stateville as the belly of a great fish that had swallowed him up from the outside world because he did not do God's bidding, and that when God determined that he had been punished enough he would have the great "prison fish" regurgitate him back into the outside world.

I thought that the priest's interpretation of the story about Jonah was beautifully explained in an acceptable way that would insult no reasonable person's intelligence. But try convincing a fundamentalist that that great fish didn't literally swallow Jonah and he lived there in his belly three days and three nights.

Father Jones probably realized that I was an irreformable heretic. But he nevertheless accepted me without bringing pressure upon me to mend my ways or withdraw my presence from the church. For he too realized that all things in the Bible were not to be accepted literally. After all, that is what he taught us, so why shouldn't he too believe it. What difference did it make if I felt as comfortable with Voltaire, Darwin, Will Durant and other philosophers as I did with Christ. The main thing Father Jones evidently felt about me was that the church had half my attention, and someday, by some miracle, it might get my whole attention. He used to say, "We will all keep praying for you, Talbert. Prayer does change things, you know." This meant I supposed that he never intended to banish me or abandon me. And I have always regarded him as one of the most decent people that I have ever met.

I certainly believe in prayer as a form of meditation. And if God helps those who help themselves, then I'm certain the corollary to that is nothing can take the place of hard work and reasoning to achieve a goal.

My foster mother had raised all of us to believe without reservation what was printed in the Bible. "Do not question God's word," she used to admonish us. We all attended the Methodist church services every Sunday, going to Sunday school and then to church service when I was growing up. But today, I could not find the courage to tell my mother my religious philosophy for fear of hurting her very deeply. So completely devoted to her own blind faith in the Bible and trust in the Lord Jesus Christ, she could not be expected to understand my heretic acceptance of the Bible.

I truly loved and respected this benign, devout, and devoted mother who had provided my brothers and me with a good home, sustenance, and love. Mom and her husband had made many sacrifices for us as though we were the issue from her own womb. Yet in subtle ways, I did not lie to her. If she asked me was I going to church? The answer, of course, was yes. If she asked me if I was praying to God? The truthful answer was always, yes. She never probed any deeper than that and accepted my affirmative answers as expressing a true and complete faith in all of the Holy Scripture.

Sometimes, I felt a little guilty though and wished that I could interpret my true religious philosophy to her. But I knew that she would never understand or accept me believing any less than she believed without hurting her very deeply.

*   *   *   *   *

The day my new trial started before Judge Green found me in an optimistic frame of mind. Buddy Morgan and Li'l Arthur had been subpoenaed from Stateville to testify for me at my trial. Eve and Joan were also available to testify at the trial. My alibi witness from Detroit, Michigan, who had testified at my first trial had died, and I was left without that part of my fraudulent defense. Still, I was hopeful that if the confessions were ruled inadmissible I would have a good chance of being acquitted by the jury.

A jury was selected, and the trial before Judge Green got underway. And out of the presence of the jury, the judge held a hearing on the admissibility of the confessions when time came for the prosecution to seek permission to place them in evidence. All the witnesses were called who were present at the time the confessions were made. As to be expected, the state's witnesses all denied that any force or violence was used to extract the confessions from Buddy Morgan and me. We of course had testified truthfully that force and violence was used. It was now left up to the judge to believe who he wanted to believe. If he believed us, he would throw out the confessions; if he believed the police, he would admit the confessions into evidence.

Without having heard any new evidence on either side that was not presented at the first trial, Judge Green was placed in an unenviable dilemma. If he ruled out the confessions as being inadmissible because of coercion, he would be offending the concept of "common comity," in a sense, by going contrary to a colleague's ruling (in this case, the colleague being Judge Alan E. Ashcraft Jr.) who was currently seated as an ex-officio judge of the criminal court. On the other hand, if Judge Green believed that the confessions were made involuntarily and let them go into evidence because he did not want to breach the "common comity" that existed between judges sitting at the same trial level, he would then be violating his legal obligation to rule fairly and impartially.

I could not conceive of any experienced judge being satisfied under the circumstances of my case that the police got a voluntary confession from Morgan and myself. The evidence showed that after I signed Morgan's confession, I was shuttled back and forth from the Oak Park Police Station to the River Forest Police Station in another suburban municipality. If I were in such a cooperative and voluntary mood, why was I hidden out in another suburb's police station? This has long been a practice of police to hold a prisoner incommunicado so his friends and attorney cannot locate him while the police extract information of an incriminating nature from the prisoner by force and violence.

The confession that I signed that Morgan had made before I was arrested was not introduced at the new trial because it was inconsistent with the joint confession that Morgan and I had made together later on the same day. In Morgan's original confession that I allegedly signed voluntarily, it was stated therein that I actually committed the robbery, brandishing a gun at the owner of the jewelry store. The joint confession stated that Morgan announced the "stick-up" and was the bandit who actually perpetrated the robbery with the gun.

Why would I voluntarily sign another person's statement taking blame for something I did not do if the signing of the confession was voluntary? This is certainly unnatural, to say the least, that a person allegedly giving a true and voluntary confession will take blame for something he did not do. This fact alone should have given the court greater insight into the credibility of whether either of the two confessions was voluntary. In any event, the court should have at least admitted both confessions into evidence after ruling that there was no coercion so the jury could determine in their own minds what weight to ascribe to the voluntariness of the confessions when that evidence came before them for consideration as triers of the facts in the case. Judge Green, however, only admitted the joint confession into evidence over the objections of my attorney, Mr. Leighton, who later commented to me in privacy, "Sometimes, a lot of politics are played in the course of a criminal trial. I'm surprised and disappointed in Judge Green's ruling. Yours is a clearly sustained case of coercion."

After all of the evidence was in and final arguments were heard by counsel on both sides, the jury went out to deliberate, and I was locked up in the bull pen at the rear of the courtroom.

Buddy Morgan and Li'l Arthur had been returned to the county jail after they had given their testimony before the court and jury, so

I was all alone in the bull pen when my friend, Jimmy Marshall, and Eve were led back to see me by the bailiff, who was in the same lodge with Jimmy.

I was pleased to have this opportunity to chat with both Jimmy and Eve. When the bailiff left us alone, I shook hands with Jimmy and kissed Eve through the bars. "It is sure great to have a buddy with some influence," I commented. "Most bailiffs won't let a prisoner have a visit like this unless there's a little monetary inducement."

Jimmy gave me a broad smile and winked knowingly. "In this particular situation, my lodge brother didn't get any inducement of that kind. He just did it as a favor."

"I wish you could have used your influence on old Judge Green. Because I don't care how fair and impartial he is reputed to be, the fact that he let that one joint confession go into evidence and not the other one I signed that Buddy made, which was totally inconsistent, deprives the jury of an opportunity to compare them and make up their own minds whether they were free and voluntarily made."

"Green probably believes that you're guilty as sin," Jimmy replied.

"Yeah. But the question of guilt or innocence was not at issue concerning the voluntariness of the confessions. The sole issue was whether they were made on my own volition, and whether they were true," I insisted.

"I see what you mean, cous, but lots of times, these judges don't follow the law when they think you're guilty, know what I mean?"

"Yeah. I know. It happens all the time—judges suddenly becoming legislatures and making their own laws on the bench to fit each individual case."

"Exactly, Jimmy! They do it all the time in the criminal court. You'd be surprised to see the many errors in some convicts' cases, but since the judges know that these poor cons can't appeal on a writ or error, they don't give a fuck what errors they make."

"Don't worry, honey, you'll be acquitted," Eve said optimistically. She gave me that beautiful reassuring smile, and I hoped that she was right because I would like nothing better for a coming- home present than to satiate my libidinous yearning for her that had been held in involuntary abstention for almost five long years.

"I sure hope you're right, sweetheart," was all I cared to respond. I was hopeful but not so optimistic after being disappointed by Judge Green's ruling on the confessions, which in my judgment caused him too to lose his credibility as a fair and impartial judge.

Jimmy and I were like brothers. We had known one another since early boyhood. We wanted to be as close as kinsfolk and therefore represented ourselves as cousins to almost everyone we met. There was only a thirteen-day difference in our ages, with Jimmy being the older.

The difference in Jimmy and me was perhaps a matter of common sense. Jimmy knew how to stay out of trouble with the law, and I didn't. He always seemed to have had a job as far back as I could remember—even as a youngster, he worked in a grocery store delivering grocery bags and helping to keep the shelves stocked. Today, he was in the insurance business working as a claims adjuster, and to illustrate his common sense approach to business, he had recently decided to enter the bail bond business.

I picked this opportunity to chide Jimmy good-naturedly. "So you're going to start making money on other people's misery by becoming a bondsman, eh, Jimmy?"

"Why not. It's suckers with money, not poor asses like you, Buddy, and Li'l Arthur who can make me rich. Everyone is making money on crime but the criminals. As fast as they get it, the lawyers, bondsmen, and courts take it away from them," he said with a note of seriousness.

"Why you old son of a gun, it's just like you to think about being a bondsman after I get in all this trouble. Where were you when I needed a bondsman?"

"I'm not a bondsman yet. I've told you before that I am only thinking about becoming a bondsman."

"Knowing you, cous, it won't be long before you become one now that you smell a buck in it for Jimmy."

"Don't forget the kids, cous. They have to be fed. It used to be when I fed myself, I fed my whole family, but things are different now. There's four other mouths besides mine."

"I agree wholeheartedly, Jimmy, that there is no bigger sucker in this world than a small-time hood carrying no weight behind him. Racket brothers aren't very reliable when you get uptight," I remarked.

"That's because racket brothers are usually uptight too. Now the smart hoods will always associate with guys a level or two above them financially. A smart hood worth five grand will hang out with another hood worth ten grand or more, and when he himself gets ten grand, he'll hang out with guys worth twenty. You get the idea, Blacky? Then if the smart hood needs help, he's got somebody to turn to with some dough to help him out," Jimmy concluded as he lit a cigarette.

"I got to hand it to you, Jimmy, you're never short on common sense.

"Hell, cous, it don't take a genius to figure that out. If you beat this rap, maybe you'll smarten up to the facts of life and quit hanging out with those poor-ass bastards that keep their hands in your pockets."

"True. But now, it's time to talk to my heart and soul." Looking at Eve, I went on, "Honey, I don't know when I've ever seen you looking so good."

She smiled. "You're really looking good yourself, you know."

"Anything with a skirt on probably looks good to old hot nuts here," Jimmy jeered at Eve.

She pretended to be peeved at what he said. "Well, I'm not anything with a skirt on, I want you to know that, Jimmy." Turning to me, she flashed an alluring smile. "Tell Jimmy that I'm something rare and special that can't be copied, imitated, or replaced, honey."

"You said it beautifully!" I exclaimed. "I couldn't have put it into words any better. Because to me, you're not only special, precious, and desirable—you're irreplaceable in my love and affection."

"Listen to him shoot the bull! He's just practicing his line on you, Eve, for the other chicks he's going to meet when he gets out of here. You've got to be a dummy to believe him."

We both knew that one of Jimmy's main jesting grounds was wisecracking and teasing couples about the pitfalls of love and marriage. He had already been married three times, and he hadn't celebrated his thirty-first birthday. One of his favorite sayings was "Love is a misunderstanding between two damn fools."

"Want to bet me that Blacky won't be with anyone else but me when he comes home? How about it, Jimmy? I'll even lay you odds of two to one."

"Dollars or men?" he quipped, then added, "If it's men, you win."

"Damn you, Jimmy! Can't you ever be serious?" Eve responded with feigned displeasure. She gave him a playful smack on the cheek, saying, "That's for insulting me in front of Blacky." Then she laughed at him and turned her attention back to me.

Eve's throaty laughter was always appealing to hear in its unpretentious gaiety. I reached through the bars and pulled her close. "Let me hold you for a minute or two, sweetheart," I said, reaching through the bars to draw her close to me. Then we whiled away the time talking, joking, and making plans for my homecoming. It was a little more than an hour before the bailiff returned.

"What's up, lodge brother, we got a verdict this quick?" Jimmy inquired.

"No, no. Nothing like that. I'm going to take the jury down to dinner and then they'll return for further deliberation. The judge said that he'll let them stay out late this evening if they think that they can reach a verdict. That's why I'm taking them down a little early for dinner."

"I'm getting a little hungry too. How about Blacky?" Jimmy inquired.

"Guess I could use a corned beef sandwich on rye," I replied.

"How about you, Eve? Want to go down for a bite to eat?"

"If it's okay, Jimmy, I'd just as soon stay up here with my man."

"How about it, lodge brother? Is it okay?" Jimmy asked.

"Sure, it's okay. If she wants to stay, I'll let her. But I'll have to lock her up in there with him until we get back. That's his wife, isn't it?" the bailiff chuckled.

"Yeah, she's my wife," I said, getting the message.

"Okay, Mrs. Jennings, get in there with your husband," he told her as he opened the door to the bull pen.

I couldn't believe it as Eve hurried inside and stood next to me. This was as close as we had been together in five years. "Thanks, man. You're one swell dude."

"Don't make no big thing out of it, Jennings. This way, I'll know you'll both be here when we get back. Make yourselves comfortable. The judge has gone down to dinner, and there's no one else in the courtroom." He locked the door and prepared to leave.

"Bring me a corned beef on rye too, Jimmy," Eve asked. Then she added, "If you can't bring two beers, bring us a couple of Cokes, okay?"

"Okay" Jimmy replied, and then they were gone.

We heard the door leading into the courtroom close behind them, and we knew that we were alone. Seizing Eve in my arms, I pulled her as close to me as I could, and I found her lips moist and appealing. We clung together with lips pressed tightly for what seemed like an eternity. The sheer pleasure of her delightful proximity, as her warm and cuddly body nestled in my arms, sent a flash of feverish passion coursing through my body. I knew that Eve could feel the throbbing protrusion pressing against her genitalia. We parted our lips long enough to draw a quick breath before sealing them together again.

One of the most dehumanizing things about prison was that it deprived a man of physical contact with a woman. Hell! Men weren't really meant to be celibates, voluntary or otherwise. It was contrary to nature for a normal man to be without a woman. Sexual fantasies, wet dreams, masturbation, perversion, or other erotic aberrations could not substitute adequately for the real thing—a woman with that right degree of sex appeal fashioned to the special needs of an individual male. Such was the pleasure and delight I had always found in Eve. Because she blended well into my desire for feminine companionship, she was in fact my beau ideal of what it took to please and satisfy me—"a lady in the living room, a good cook in the kitchen, and a strumpet in the bedroom." I had read something like that somewhere and accepted it as a classic of what I desired in a woman, never dreaming that I would find these three glowing qualities compounded in this marvelous personification of loving femininity that I held ever so close at this very moment.

Gently drawing Eve into the privacy of the toilet area that was enclosed from view with steel paneling, I began to fondle her in a more intimate fashion, touching her erogenous areas with titillating results. She responded to my love play with complete mutuality as she rubbed her hands over my body with firm and stimulating caresses.

In a moment of seething desire, I ran my hands under her skirt and pulled feverishly at her undies. She grasped my wrists murmuring, "Darling, can't we wait until you come home tonight?"

"I want you now, Eve. Who really knows at this time what the verdict will be? It could be a hung jury and I'll have to go through the process of another trial. They could find me guilty."

"Please, don't say that, darling. God knows I hope they don't. It's almost unbearable to even think about after the past five lonely years we've been apart," she whispered uneasily.

As she spoke, she relaxed her grip on my wrists. My hands slid her undies loose from her curvaceous hips, and they fell into a little crumpled pile around her ankles. She resisted no longer as she freed herself from the entanglement. Leaning back against the wall, she let me make love to her and responded with all of the enthusiasm that she could muster. In a few minutes, it was over and I was temporarily gratified. But within ten minutes, we were back in the same loving position until we consummated our desire for each other a second time.

When Jimmy returned Eve, and I were seated on the long wooden bench in the bull pen chatting and looking the picture of innocence. Jimmy shoved our sandwiches, soft drinks, and the evening newspaper through the bars, saying, "You two aren't fooling me.

I know you two mousies stole a piece of cheese while the old cat was away."

"Jimmy, why don't you give me your nasty little mind so I can flush it down the john. It'll be at home in the sewer," Eve kidded with him.

"Boy this corned beef is delicious! You don't get stuff like this in the joint," I commented before taking another bite.

"Save the pickle, Blacky, for your bride-to-be. She may be craving pickles after that five-year load you probably exploded with," Jimmy quipped.

"Oh, how I despise this horrible man!" Eve cried. "He needs a fetter on his tongue."

"Come on, honey, ignore that jackass and enjoy your sandwich before it gets cold."

Eve removed her sandwich from the bag and began to munch on it, still rolling her large attractive eyes at Jimmy with mocked disapproval.

Not long after we finished our sandwiches, the bailiff came and let Eve out of the bull pen. The cleanup crew had arrived to sweep and mop the area. I asked the time. It was ten after six. When the cleanup crew and bailiff left, I was all alone. Picking up the evening newspaper I settled back and began to read.

It was almost eight o'clock when the bailiff came to the door of the bull pen and informed me, "Jennings, the jury's got a verdict. I sure hope it's a favorable one."

As he opened the door, I got up nervously. "I certainly would like to get out of here tonight. If I could step out on the street a freeman tonight, that would be the greatest gift I ever got in my life," I said, walking ahead of him into the courtroom.

The jurors were already in the jury box. I glanced quickly in their direction, trying to detect some sign of favorable emotion. But their expressions were somber—a bad sign, I thought.

My attorney was already seated at the defense table. On the other side of the table sat James McGovern and Robert McDonald, the two prosecutors. Only Jimmy and Eve were in the spectators' section of the courtroom. They had waited all this time for the verdict.

Jimmy lifted his hand with crossed fingers. I nodded in his direction before taking my seat and facing the judge bench.

Judge Green, in his dark judicial robe, looked very stern and serious. "Has the jury reached a verdict?" he asked in a matter-of-fact tone, knowing damn well that they had.

The foreman of the jury stood up with a sheet of paper in his hand. "Yes, Your Honor," he replied.

"Will the foreman of the jury give the verdict to the clerk please," the judge ordered.

The clerk reached out and took the sheet of paper from the foreman and the judge added, "Will the clerk please read the verdict."

The clerk read, "We the jury find the defendant, Talbert Jennings, guilty as charged in the indictment."

I let out a sigh of disappointment just as Eve cried out, "Oh no!"

My attorney asked the court to poll the jury, and the court permitted each juror to personally acknowledge his finding of guilty. Then Judge Green thanked and dismissed the jury.

Attorney Leighton stood up and moved the court to defer sentence until he could file a motion for a new trial and a motion in arrest of judgment. Judge Green allowed his oral motion and set a date for the hearing of the motions; then court was adjourned.

I was permitted to embrace Eve, who was still crying and very upset over the verdict.

Jimmy took her by the arm, saying, "Keep fighting, cous. You'll make it yet. We're with you all the way." Then he led Eve from the courtroom.

Shaking his head sympathetically, the bailiff motioned to me to follow the deputy sheriff, who returned me to the county jail.

*   *   *   *   *

Several days after my conviction, I was preparing to return to court for my hearing on the motions for new trial and in arrest of judgment that my attorney had prepared. Leighton planned to argue these motions before Judge Green today. My feeling, however, was that the motions would be denied and that I would be sentenced to servitude back in the Illinois State Penitentiary system. Consequently, I had handprinted my own motion and affidavit in forma pauperis praying that the trial court grant me a copy of the trial proceedings without cost so that I could prepare a bill of exceptions and file an appeal for writ of error in the Illinois Supreme Court for a full review of my case. I knew though that this motion and affidavit would be denied. But it was necessary that I preserve this basic constitutional question in the record to show that I had made a timely and proper request for the records and transcript, which when denied to me would present a federal question of denial of equal protection of the laws that governed appeals in the State of Illinois for defendants who have funds available to them to file appeals and purchase their transcripts.

I had also caused many other prisoners in the county jail to file similar motions and affidavits to preserve the question for review in their cases. And now the time had come for me to personally take the initiative in my own case to set the stage for the most crucial and revolutionary drama in criminal appellate procedure that was ever played in the halls of justice in the sovereign State of Illinois. My battle cry was taken from a concept of law I had read, which held that "the state is sovereign. It neither needs nor can it accept any undue advantage over one of its citizens."

It was now up to me somehow to force the Illinois judiciary system to uphold that doctrine or concept of not taking unfair advantage of its convicted citizens, or any other prisoner, even if it meant carrying the fight all the way to the highest court in the nation.

At the hearing on the motions filed in my behalf by Attorney Leighton, Judge Green, following legal arguments, denied the motions and ordered me to approach the bench for sentencing.

"Before passing sentence on you, Mr. Jennings, have you anything further to say before the court?" I stood before the bar thinking of something to say. Realizing that I had covered myself sufficiently with all proper motions, I decided that contesting anything further would be anticlimatic as well as futile. I shrugged and said, "No, Your Honor, with the exception that I wish to thank the court in advance if the court will take into consideration the time I have already served in prison on this offense."

Judge Green smiled faintly before speaking, "Mr. Jennings, this court does not wish to make fish of fowl or fowl of fish. The court therefore has already decided to take into consideration the time you have already served in prison on the original ten- to twenty-five-year sentence." He paused thoughtfully to study some legal document before him. Looking up and straight at me with a blank expression, he went on, "It is the court's duty to sentence you to not less than three years or more than fifteen years in the Illinois State Penitentiary."

I nodded my head more in an acknowledgment than in gratitude. My attorney patted me on the shoulder a couple of times, saying, "I am sorry that things did not turn out better for you. At least under the terms of the new sentence, you'll be eligible for parole in about twenty-one months if that is any consolation to you. So now, let me wish you good luck and success with any appeals you take. The motion you filed for the transcript was a good move." He nodded knowingly as we shook hands.

"Thank you sincerely for all you have done, sir, in conducting a very good defense. You really fought hard for me, and I want you to know that I appreciate it."

Leighton simply acknowledged my gratitude with a little nod. Then I was led away to the county jail to await my return to prison. There was no inward cursing or rancor following the denouement of this trial. I would not waste my energy on such nonsense. I had a legal battle on my hands; and I needed all of my constructive wit and energy to buoy my intensive determination to give the State of Illinois holy hell in this upcoming legal battle for free transcripts to indigent defendants.

Now that I had lost my second quest for freedom, whether I won my freedom had become secondary to the crusade I now wanted to wage against the denial of the transcripts with which indigent prisoners needed to appeal their cases. I felt that if we could win this battle, the State of Illinois's judicial system for appellate review for indigents would be greatly improved. It would, in my opinion, compel trial judges to follow the law more closely in making their rulings in cases involving indigent defendants, not only on constitutional questions but all procedural questions as well. Because the indigent defendants could appeal all the manifest errors in their cases directly to the Illinois appellate courts or to the Illinois Supreme Court.

My time for return to the penitentiary on my new sentence came shortly after my last visit with Eve in the county jail. Her disappointment was still evident as tears still dampened her large brown eyes whenever she came to see me. We were now separated in a visiting booth with thick steel plate and glass windows. This was one of the booths used by prisoners visiting with their attorneys. I always paid the guard on duty a few dollars for the privilege of using the booth rather than stand at the regular visiting window shouting over the voices of several other prisoners having visits at the same time. The lawyers' booth was quiet, and there were seats to sit on. There was also an intercom system to facilitate intelligible conversation. But there was no way to make physical contact with a visitor.

I told Eve again that I was grateful for the intimate visit that we had enjoyed in the bull pen on the evening that I was convicted, and that the memory of that loving occasion would be a lasting one.

"I'll love you always, darling," Eve said in parting, as she touched her fingers to her lips and then to the glass that separated us.

"I love you too, sweetheart," I told her as I returned the symbolical kissing gesture. Then she was gone.

Chapter 12

GETTING READJUSTED TO PRISON LIFE was not too difficult.

I had been away from Stateville for several months during my retrial. Upon my return on March 20, 1953, my status took on that of a new prisoner. I was held for several days in the diagnostic depot at Joliet and given a new number (33507) before being shipped back to Stateville.

Once again I was placed in B-House and assigned to the coal detail until there was an opening for me in the prison barbershop. My popularity had not suffered with the inmates during my absence. If anything, I was more popular. It was as though the inmates were waiting to pounce on me no sooner than I arrived back in their midst. Because almost immediately came several requests for my free legal services—although the requests were always prefaced with a desire to remunerate me in some manner.

I had to postpone assisting anyone until I took on the task of challenging the legality of my own three- to fifteen-year sentence recently imposed upon me by Judge Green. So the first thing I did was prepare a petition under the Illinois Postconviction Hearing Act, setting forth the alleged denial of a free transcript of my trial proceedings as a violation of the due process of law and the equal protection of the law clauses in the state and federal constitutions. For added measure, I again challenged the legality of the coerced confession issue. It would now be necessary for Judge Green to once again pass on these federal questions before I could start my appeals rolling back to the Illinois Supreme Court and to the United States Supreme Court if necessary.

I put aside my own personal legal problems long enough to help one inmate who came to me terribly distressed because his wife was getting a divorce and she wanted to keep custody of their two children. The inmate did not want to contest the divorce. He did, however, want to contest his wife keeping custody of their two children. His reasons being that he knew that his wife was living in a house of ill repute with another man of unsavory character who was involved with prostitution.

The inmate had no money to hire an outside attorney to represent him or his interest in the divorce proceedings, and he prevailed upon me to do anything possible to stop his wife from having custody of the children. He was willing to settle for either his mother having custody of the children or that they be placed in a foster home. I immediately prepared a countersuit contesting custody of the children. The inmate filed the complaint, and it was heard by the court with him present at the hearing whereby he was able to have several witnesses subpoenaed to testify concerning his wife's involvement in prostitution. The court ruled favorably for the inmate and ordered that the children be placed in the custody of the inmate's mother as their legal guardian.

Within one month of each other, two of my jailhouse clients that were given hearings under the postconviction act were released by the courts. When the word spread around on the prison grapevine that I had prepared these liberated prisoners' petitions, I was hailed as a legal genius by many of the prisoners. This made me laugh because I knew that I was far from being a genius of anything. My success in preparing the petitions for these prisoners as well as for all of the inmates I helped was based on some solid legal knowledge, true enough, but the court-appointed attorneys that represented the prisoners in court deserved a large part of the credit for the successful outcome of these inmates' cases. I got them to court; the court-appointed attorneys got them new trials or got them out of jail. Because now that the courts had to hear many of these kinds of cases filed under the postconviction act, it gave the inmates, with court-appointed attorneys, a wonderful opportunity to sustain their claims of constitutional violations at their hearings. And although back in the prison, the other inmates overshadowed these attorneys' good works by constantly focusing the spotlight of credit on me, I still never failed to praise the attorneys to the prisoners who were successful in representing their clients in postconviction proceedings.

My name and reputation as a legal-eagle was ringing loud and clear around the state prisons. And soon, this adverse publicity began to have an undesirable effect on my security. The prison guards were shaking down my cell with unusual frequency in an endeavor to catch me red-handed doing legal work for some other inmate. I had become a marked man. And even though nothing was found in my cell to link me with helping other inmates with their cases after these shakedowns, I still felt the pressure of being constantly watched.

I always used a stratagem to foil detection whenever I was working on another inmate's case. And I am proud of the fact that I outwitted the warden's guards with this simple trick to prevent the screws from discovering another inmate's legal papers in my cell. My stratagem was to type my name on the lead sheet of the inmate's petition and records. I also never referred to the inmate by his name in the body of the petition. I always used such references as the "petitioner" or the "defendant" when referring to him. After I had completed the inmate's petition I would destroy the lead sheet with my name on it; then I would type the name of the inmate on the petition whom I was preparing it for. His name would also be typed in all other appropriate places before I sent the material back to him.

The officials were not fools even though I had fooled them by my ruse; they still knew that somehow, I was involved in the preparation of other inmates' cases even though they were unable to catch me at it red-handed whereby I would be subjected to disciplinary action.

One day, the prison disciplinarian, Captain Acord, sent for me. I entered his office and greeted him courteously. "Hi, Cap'n."

"Jennings," he began very seriously, "I'll get right to the point. I sent for you because I want to give you some good advice. So far, you have a good record, and I would like to see you keep it that way. You'll be going before the parole board one day in the not-too=distant future, and I would hate to see you lose some or all of your merit time." I listened without interruption as he continued, "There is a rumor going around that you are practicing law—that is, preparing petitions for other inmates. And that, of course, if true, is in violation of institutional regulations. You know that, don't you, Jennings?" Here, he paused, apparently waiting for me to say something. I simply nodded affirmatively and remained silent.

Captain Acord was prison wise with many years of penal experience behind him. He had a reputation for being fair-minded, but he was also a stickler for enforcing Warden Regan's rules. His nice old grandfatherly appearance could throw one off guard if he didn't know the captain's prison background. Because Captain Acord could be a tough old man if he had to lean on you heavily to make known a point crystal clear as to where he stood in dealing with a recalcitrant prisoner.

I therefore was not going to insult the intelligence of this prison-wise old "brass hack" by denying the rumor outright, nor was I going to admit to a violation of the rules either. I planned to "play him off the wall"—that is I would supply him with food for thought to establish a basis for the rumor without any direct admission of wrong doing on my part.

Captain Acord gave me a steady glance before asking, "Do you care to give any explanation for how this rumor got started, Jennings?"

I smiled pleasantly, shrugged my shoulders, and replied, "Not really, Cap'n—unless the little success I've had with my own case has branded me as a jailhouse lawyer. Some of the guys in here know that I won a substantial victory in the United States Supreme Court and also in the Illinois Supreme Court in getting the postconviction hearing law straightened out so that the inmates will stand a better chance to obtain hearings in the trial courts. And some of the guys exchange legal ideas with me at the courtyard sessions. Then too it is necessary that I work closely with my rap partners because our cases dovetail." I paused briefly to rally my thoughts more effectively. "Oh yeah, Cap'n, I'd like to point out that my cell has been searched several times lately and nothing was ever found to link me with working on another inmate's case, so I really can't say how this rumor got started, unless . . ."

"Unless what?" the captain cut in quickly.

"Unless it's because of some legal assistance I gave some of the guys in the county jail when I went back for my new trial."

"So then you helped other prisoners in the county jail," he said, showing interest in my admission.

"Oh yes, sir, Cap'n. There's no rule that I know of at the county jail that prohibits one inmate from helping another inmate with legal problems."

Captain Acord rubbed his chin thoughtfully, obviously not completely satisfied with my story. Finally, he said, "Okay, Jennings. But you do realize that we have a rule against that sort of thing here?"

"Yes, sir, I do!" I said with emphasis.

"Then for your sake, don't get caught violating that rule here, is that clear?"

"Yes, sir, crystal!"

"Now remember, Jennings, you have been warned. If you are ever caught helping another inmate, it will go hard with you."

I nodded my head acquiescently.

"That's all then. You may go."

"Thank you, Cap'n," I said. Then I turned and walked out of his office.

The officer on duty in the disciplinary building gave me the customary frisk before handing me back my pass to return to work. On the way back to the barbershop, I mulled worriedly over the warning that I had just received. I knew that from now on, I would be watched extra carefully by the screws, and I had to be on the constant lookout for a "bust."

One evening several days later when we were locked in our cell for the night and I was seated in front of the desk typing a petition for another inmate, a lieutenant and two guards suddenly appeared in front of our cell. The door was quickly unlocked, and my cell mates and I were asked to step outside on the gallery where we were searched. The lieutenant and one of the guards then proceeded to make a thorough search of the cell. This was very unusual to shake down a cell after inmates were locked up for the night—unless, of course, they had a tip from a stoolie.

The lieutenant was paying particular attention to legal papers that he found in the cell. And I kept my hopes up that my stratagem would foil any discovery that the petition and court records on my desk were not my own. As usual, my name was on the lead sheet, and the ruse worked again. I smiled complacently when we were told to reenter the cell—a signal that everything was all right.

"Just routine," the lieutenant remarked upon leaving. But I knew damn well that it wasn't routine. They were out to nail me. I made up my mind then and there to cool it until the heat died down. I would finish my work on the present case and not take on any more cases for a spell.

I decided instead of working on cases that I would do a little undercover work agitating against racial discrimination in the institution denying Negroes clerical and other jobs. Since the prison administration wanted to badger and plague me, I'd pay them back in turn. The time was ripe for such agitation because a Negro named Joseph Bibb had been appointed director of public safety for the State of Illinois when a new administration took over the governorship. The director of public safety was in charge of all state penal institutions and law enforcement agencies of the state, and in that capacity, he was Warden Regan's boss. I wondered how Regan felt having a black man for a boss.

I drafted a letter explaining to Mr. Bibb that the prison policy assigning Negroes to certain menial jobs was unfair and there should be equal opportunity practiced in the prison. Bibb was a Chicago attorney, and some of his old clients were currently serving time in Stateville. Some of them authorized me to use their names in a discreet manner in the event Bibb wanted verification and corroboration of the charges I was making against the administration.

When my letter to Bibb was finished, I got it smuggled out of the prison concealed in a bunch of legal documents that an inmate was taking back to court with him for a postconviction hearing. The censor department never read every document going out but only made a cursory examination of lengthy transcripts and documents, so the chances of the letter to Bibb being discovered was very minimal.

All went well, and the inmate turned the letter over to his attorney, who in turn mailed it to Mr. Bibb. Within two weeks, we noticed a sudden change in prison policy. A Negro clerk was assigned to an office in the administration building along with a Negro nurse who was assigned to the prison hospital. Gradually, more Negroes were given assignments previously reserved for white inmates. Suddenly too, a black guard showed up on the prison staff working inside the walls of the prison. We called him the token black hat, knowing that more would be added to the staff now that Bibb was aware of what had been going on.

A new inmate, named Louis Lomax, was assigned to the school. He taught special classes of typing and English grammar. Sometimes in prison, you can meet some very outstanding prisoners—men who are well-educated, of good character, and but for some unfortunate twist of fate should never have been imprisoned in the first place. One such person was Louis Lomax.

Lou, as we called him, was a hell of a nice guy; and I was proud to see a black of his intellect and caliber given the first Negro assignment as a teacher because I knew after talking with him that he was exceptionally qualified—*overqualified* would be a better description.

Lou had discovered that I was a highly touted prison lawyer, and he sought me out for a discussion concerning his case. This was quite easily accomplished since we both celled in G-House and shared the same recreation yard.

In talking with Lou, I learned that this rather short brown-skinned man was about the same age as I. He had a friendly personality and a fine sense of humor even when engaging in serious conversation. His wit was delightful indeed! He also had a brilliant probing mind that was keenly analytical as well as full of practical ideas and solutions to mundane problems in both national and worldly affairs. He could discourse on so many subjects with great wit and humor that it was always a pleasure to join in conversation with him.

Lou was born in Valdosta, Georgia. He graduated from high school there and enrolled at Paine College in Augusta, Georgia, where he was editor of the college newspaper; and he worked as a professional writer after graduating from college. He also did graduate work at American University and joined the faculty of Georgia State College in Savannah, Georgia, where he served as assistant professor of philosophy.

During our conversations, I discovered that Louis Lomax got one of the rawest deals from one of the worst judges in the Cook County Criminal Court. He had the misfortune to be tried and convicted by old Judge William "Railroad" Lindsay, an elderly man who wore a hearing aid and was reputed to have turned it off whenever testimony or a lawyer's argument bored him.

Judge Lindsay had a reputation as a stiff-sentencing judge. He even had a sign in his courtroom that read, "The man with the gun must go." And any poor defendant tried in his courtroom for burglary or armed robbery was sure to get a long sentence.

In spite of all the publicity Judge Lindsay got for being a stern judge, we prisoners noticed that most of his stiff sentences were meted out to poor prisoners with public defenders or court-appointed attorneys. Many of the prisoners with their own lawyers who had money were being acquitted, given probation, or handed down light sentences. If a defendant had money, Judge Lindsay seemed to be the most lenient judge on the bench. The word was therefore out that Judge Lindsay used his stiff sentencing of the poor defendants to cover up for his leniency toward the affluent defendants.

Louis Lomax happened to be down on his luck financially with the added misfortune of having been assigned Judge Lindsay as his trial judge. Being something of a "square" when it came to criminal know-how in demanding a change of venue from hostile judges with "hanging judge" reputations, Lou was a "sitting duck" when he stood trial before old Judge "Railroad" Lindsay.

The charge against Lou was larceny. The facts of the case showed that Lou had a purchase agreement with a car dealer to buy a used car; he made an earnest money down payment to the dealer who reneged on certain parts of the agreement. As a result, Lou kept the car without paying the dealer all the money until the dealer kept all his end of the agreement as guaranteed prior to the sale.

The car dealer, in a complaint, alleged that Lou had gained possession of the car by trickery. Lou was arrested and later indicted by the grand jury, tried, and convicted by Judge Lindsay and given an indeterminant sentence in the state penitentiary.

Were he actually guilty of the charge, his reputable background and lack of a prior criminal record should have made him instantly eligible for probation at the very least. Because the charge was a relatively temperate first offense and the car was returned to the dealer.

Having talked with Lou about his case, I couldn't discern anything in the nature of a substantial state or federal constitutional question that may have been in violation of his rights that occurred during his trial proceedings. There might possibly be procedural errors of a reversible nature in the trial transcript such as "his conviction was manifestly against the weight of the evidence" or that the judge erred in making certain rulings that may have prejudiced Lou's right to a fair and impartial trial. But to determine that would of course necessitate studying Lou's trial transcript—something he could not afford to purchase.

On the basis of what I had learned about Lou's case I decided to prepare a motion asking the trial court to supply the transcript without cost—knowing that Judge Lindsay would not allow the motion. Once the motion was dismissed, I could prepare a petition under the Illinois Postconviction Hearing Act and have Lou file it in the trial court. That way, we would preserve a substantial constitutional question in his case should the US Supreme Court eventually hold that the prisoners were entitled to free transcripts with which to file appeals on writ of error.

Lou and I became good friends. We discovered that we had a lot more in common than an interest in the legal outcome of our cases. We enjoyed discussing politics, civil rights for Negroes, literature, creative writing, and many other stimulating subjects.

At the time of our prison friendship, I recognized Lou's great talent as a writer. He helped me to renew my own interest in creative writing since I had cut down considerably on my legal activities of assisting other prisoners during the period that the officials had me under close surveillance.

I managed to write a mediocre novel and two plays as a pastime to substitute for the lull in my writ writing practice. My novel was fiction, and while Lou thought it a good first effort, he did not hold out much hope for its publication or success.

Lou wrote mostly political articles and social works dealing with civil rights for blacks. We exchanged our writings for constructive criticism and enjoyed a lot of fun and camaraderie in doing so. Lou was a tough critic. He would run through a gamut of things that I did wrong in my writing—from the subject matter being trite to excessive use of clichés, poor characterization and overly contrived situations and coincidences that had very little verisimilitude. Those were just a few defects in my lack of writing craftsmanship that Lou discovered. I took it all from him good-naturedly with a determination to improve my writing craft or technique. Because I trusted his judgment implicitly, knowing that he was being honest for no other reason than the desire to help me improve my writing. Consequently, he supplied me with many books on creative writing to study; and soon, my writing showed considerable improvement with his constant guidance and criticism.

It was a real pleasure to count Lou among my close friends in prison, as he was the rarest gem that I had ever encountered in prison. Lou typified courage in the face of adversity and the will to achieve greatness and success regardless of his misfortunate prison record. His optimism was eternal; that although we as blacks did not live in the best of all possible worlds, there was still much hope for change and justice if we as a race continued to strive and fight for our freedom and recognition as full-fledged citizens of America.

In his humorous witty manner, he had once said in effect, "I don't need to be rehabilitated, but I do need to be vindicated." Then he went on to say, "Notwithstanding this 'bum beef' that currently incarcerates me, I consider this to be an invaluable part of my education. For I have met some men in prison on the bottom rung of the ladder of character that I esteem far more than some men of whom I have met on the outside standing on the top rung."

His latter statement prompted me to recall the quotation that my foster mother often used: "There's so much good in the worst of us and so much bad in the best of us that it hardly behooves any of us to talk about the rest of us."

*　　*　　*　　*　　*

Judge Green issued a writ remanding me back to the Cook County Jail for further hearings on my postconviction petition that I had filed after my second conviction. I packed up my legal papers and a few law books, and on July 1, 1953, I was driven back to the county jail by one of the guard lieutenants. I was placed on tier D-3 this time. And it was good to get away from prison life for a spell. Even the countryside scenery during the short journey back to the county jail was refreshing. Judge Green had appointed the Cook County Public Defender to represent me at the hearing, and an assistant public defender, Mr. William Fitzpatrick, was assigned to my case. I found him to be a young, bright, alert, and sympathetic attorney when he visited me at the jail to discuss my postconviction hearing. And I could see from the beginning that we were going to get along very well together, as my attitude had changed considerably about the caliber of legal representation available in the office of the Cook County Public Defender now that it had a new head of that office who went on to become the most famous and proficient public defender to ever hold that position. His name is Gerald W. Getty.

Mr. Getty set high standards for administrating the Cook County Public Defender's Office and instilled a desire for excellence in his colleagues in representing indigent defendants. He himself, being an outstanding criminal lawyer, often participated as the defense counsel in many defendants' cases. His autobiography, *Public Defender*, should be required reading for all aspirants to positions of representing the indigents that come before the courts.

As usual, I met many inmates in the jail, some of whom were there for postconviction hearings and others with whom I had previously served time with in the penitentiary.

Jimmy Crenshaw was placed on tier D-3, and I was more than surprised when I found out that he was charged with armed robbery. I had served time with Crenshaw at Stateville, and we had worked in the prison barbershop together. He had a reputation as being a hell of a good pickpocket. Old Fingers McBride considered Jimmy Crenshaw one of the best dips in the business, and he had nothing but compliments for Jimmy's skillful ability to lift a "hide" with all the finesse of a master.

I had never met Judson Griffin, Crenshaw's condefendant, who also arrived on our tier, and I wondered how this Mutt and Jeff team ever got hooked up together. What a contrast, I thought. Jimmy Crenshaw was about five feet four inches tall, nearing sixty, and old enough to be Griffin's grandfather.

Judson Griffin was a handsome light-browned-skinned young fellow in his mid-twenties who was of slender build and stood about six feet three inches tall.

Crenshaw explained that he was facing a "bum rap"—that he and his codefendants did not commit the armed robbery that they had been accused of. One often hears the term *bum rap* bandied about the prison by the inmates disclaiming knowledge of the crimes they had been convicted for—just as I was currently claiming, so the terms *bum rap* and *bum beef* were taken with a grain of salt by most prisoners.

In Crenshaw's case, however, I found it difficult to believe that he had committed an armed robbery. He had been arrested many times but never for robbery, armed or otherwise. He was known to be a professional pickpocket, and usually, pickpockets and con men did not vary from their illicit professions. In fact, it was considered downright degrading to engage in what they termed "rough hustling" (muggings, stickups, and burglaries) to make a living. Therefore I was quite inclined to sympathize with Jimmy Crenshaw as being perhaps the victim of a mistaken identity or a trumped-up charge when I learned more about the facts of his case.

One thing I did know about Crenshaw was that he had a penchant for using narcotics, and I wondered, could his narcotic habit have driven him to such desperation as to make him rob someone at gun point? In any event both Crenshaw and Griffin were indigent men upon their arrival at the county jail. I loaned each of them a few dollars and suggested that they try their luck in the poker game, something that I rarely played anymore. Judson Griffin proved the better poker player of the two and paid me back the loan for both of them before the day was over.

I remained in the county jail several months awaiting my post-conviction hearing so that I could be near my counsel while the case was pending. There were delays because Judge Green became ill. His illness only afforded me more time to prepare my case and kept me away from the more austere confinement in Stateville.

Because of my prominence now as a legal troublemaker, I was accorded the red-carpet treatment by Judge Green—probably because the court and prosecution wanted to try and make doubly certain that I wouldn't find anything else to complain about after they were done with me this time. Old Judge Green insisted that I be treated fairly. He used the term *treated fairly* so much that it almost seemed as though he was being subservient, cynical or both. In any event, I didn't give a shit one way or another so long as the judge kept everything within the bounds of what was meet and just.

I didn't want to appear cocky. Although I knew that I could handle myself pretty damn well in this goddamned legal arena of bullshit and subterfuge that often turned out to be a display of chicanery and mock justice anyway. But still, I maintained a polite and modest attitude in the presence of the court and prosecution, while at the same time I kept a suspicious eye ready to zoom in on any funny business on the part of either the court or the state's attorney.

I had already been screwed around by the criminal court and the prosecution, and I had seen so much other screwing around in other prisoners' cases until at this point, I was suspicious of almost everybody affiliated with the criminal justice system in Illinois. No matter how popular I was with the prisoners, I was smart enough to realize that for the same reasons I was popular with them, I was equally unpopular with the opposition; and the gut feeling that the opposition was going to end up trying to screw me around again never left the pit of my craw.

One thing I could detect was that these officers of the court were not taking me lightly after the way we outslicked them in getting the United States Supreme Court to rule in the prisoners favor on postconviction hearings. Not only had we succeeded in getting their attention with that recent decision, but now, I had their reluctant respect also. If they were going to screw me this time, they would have to do it with grease—the same way I screwed them in winning my case in the United States Supreme Court. I wouldn't subject myself to anything less because I had girded myself for a fight to the finish.

A man couldn't be too careful in a courthouse where some judges and prosecutors played funny games like knowingly using perjured testimony of police officers to obtain convictions and then label it a "mistake" when pressure is brought to bear upon them to uphold truth and justice. I will never forget that incident, and the Illinois judicial system shouldn't forget it either because that is what made a jailhouse lawyer out of me. Were it not for that single incident in my trial, I probably would have settled down to serve my time without so much as making a ripple of protest over my conviction. But because of that one grossly unfair incident, I was inspired to raise a tidal wave of protest! And I had vowed to continue to erupt like a raging volcano, with all the indignation I could muster, to combat these purveyors of lies and false justice masquerading behind a facade of judicial respectability.

After extensive hearings, Judge Green finally denied my petition. And before returning to Stateville, I gave serious and sympathetic thought to Jimmy Crenshaw's case. It appeared that the little dark-skinned man, already in his late fifties, was facing the serious possibility of spending the better part, if not the rest, of his life in prison if found guilty on the armed robbery charge. And there was a possibility that he was innocent.

Certainly, from what I knew about Crenshaw and learned from his present case, the evidence concerning his identification as one of the participants in the robbery was not conclusive. The original offense report contained a notation that "there was no description as to one of the three robbers (Crenshaw)." This report was made shortly after the commission of the crime and before the arrest of the three suspects, Judson Griffin, James Crenshaw, and Richard Riles. Riles was on another tier in the county jail. Moreover, the arresting officer made a supplementation on the offense report four months after the robbery by adding that "such robber appeared to be about fifty years old." This to me demonstrated subterfuge on the part of the arresting officer to cloak the fact that a proper and prompt identification could not be made of the third bandit, who was purported to be Crenshaw. The arresting officer questioned the victims shortly after the robbery took place and took down their descriptions given of the bandits, and he clearly wrote on his report descriptions for bandits one and two, but he noted in the report, "No description," for the third bandit who was subsequently identified as Crenshaw. This taken with how Crenshaw was later identified by the victims who could not, right after the robbery, give the police a description of him indicated to me the old police trick of instigating the victim to make a positive identification of a suspect that the police assures the victim is the culprit beyond any doubt, and that without the positive identification, they cannot prosecute and win a conviction. This in such cases was as commonplace police procedure as wearing a badge.

Crenshaw told me that after his arrest, he was not picked out of a regular "police show-up" (a group of persons for the purpose of testing ability of witnesses to identify suspect as the guilty person). Instead, the arresting officer actually convinced the witnesses to make a positive identification inasmuch as they had already made positive identifications of Griffin and Riles.

The Chicago Police Department has always been notorious for its political appointments to the department of incompetent and mediocre personnel. The scandals for taking bribes, shakedowns, and engaging in unlawful activities and practices runs rampant throughout the department's history even to this very day. And it is often not just a single officer going bad, but a whole group of officers acting in concert to besmirch the department's image as a creditable police force. No amount of adverse publicity has reformed or effectuated a cleanup for any length of time in the notorious Chicago Police Department. The stigma seems to carry over from one administration to the next without abatement or a solution to the problem. And the ignominy of the Chicago Police Department has followed the notoriety and shame of its gangster-town reputation around the world—a condition that could only exist through the means of bribes, graft, and political bossism.

There was only one thing that I could do for Jimmy Crenshaw and his codefendants at this time. That was to prepare for them the same type of motion and affidavit in forma pauperis for the court records and transcript of the trial proceedings filed in my own case in the event that they were convicted.

I was shipped back to Stateville on March 23, 1954. Once again in prison, I decided next to redress my grievance against Detective Edward Piotter, Lt. Fremont Nester, James Brown, and John Phillips, the two prosecutors at my first trial, for violating my civil rights in the use of a coerced confession, illegally seized evidence, and the knowing presentation of perjured testimony to obtain my conviction.

The fact that in granting me the new trial, Judge Ashcraft had tried to cover-up the knowing use of perjured testimony by calling it a "mistake" made on Piotter's part had galled me beyond my power to forgive or forget. Because it struck me as being the evil root of a judicial system that condoned two standards of justice—one for the accused and one for the police or public officials. In short, what was perjury if committed by an accused was a "mistake" if committed by a public official while prosecuting the accused. I thought that as long as this type of justice prevailed, the police and prosecuting attorney would have no fear of violating an accused person's rights knowing that they could do so with impunity.

Far too often I had heard men in prison cry out against just such double standards of justice, and because it rankled their minds perpetually, some prisoners carried their bitterness against the police and other public officials back into the streets with them when they were released from prison. Having experienced an unjust judicial system, the ex-convicts invariably took their resentment out on society and became more desperate than ever to avoid facing a judicial system and law enforcement agencies that were patently unfair.

The word *cop-hater* was not coined because merely enforcing the law did not endear officers to the offenders. No. By and large, the term *cop-hater* was coined because of the unfair and oftentimes brutal treatment that offenders or suspects received at the hands of the police, who usually got away with flagrantly violating the rights of the accused or suspects.

Countless times I have heard inmates plan a life of crime following their release from prison simply because they had no hope of being given an even break in a society that was too indifferent to the poor quality of justice administered by its courts. No adequate means for assisting an ex-convict in so-called rehabilitating himself was another sore spot with men being released from prison who could not find work or who faced a situation that precluded them from being hired because of their past criminal records. These were the men who used the expression all too frequently in prisons "When I get out, I'm going to hold court in the street before I let 'em send me back here." It is simple to understand or define the phrase "hold court in the street" if you understand the words "kill or be killed."

Did not my friend LeRoy Lindsey hold court in the street like so many other ex-convicts have done when he helped to kill a policeman? Won't there continue to be court sessions held in the streets so long as our society lets law enforcement officials and the judges—that have offended and made a mockery countless times of the word *justice* through judicial negligence, prejudice. and corruption—continue to practice chicanery in courtrooms to infringe upon the rights of defendants?

Fortunately, I had learned to channel my bitterness against the law enforcement and judicial system through constructive means. Now that I had enjoyed some good results in fighting fire with fire—or more appropriately in my case, fighting law with law—I deemed it apropos to sue the police and prosecutors under the Federal Civil Rights Act to vent my profound contempt and bitterness with the pen rather than the sword toward these public officials whom I regarded as no less criminal than myself or the other prisoners who shared my walled environment.

I filed my complaint for punitive and compensatory damages in the United States District Court for the Northern District of Illinois. The suit alleged the commission of four acts depriving me of my constitutional rights while state officials were acting under color of state law. The acts specifically set forth in the complaint were (1) unlawful search and seizure of my property (the diamond ring used as evidence in the trial against me), (2) the use of a coerced confession to obtain my conviction, and (3) the knowing presentation of perjured testimony to obtain my conviction.

No counsel was appointed to assist me in this civil action, and it was necessary to handle this, novel to me, litigation all by myself. This of course called for a lot of additional study and preparation. Still, I felt equal to the task of venturing into what was a new branch of civil law practice for me. But before long, my complaint was on file in the federal district court.

This new legal thrust only tended to prove to me once again how the law works like a well-oiled machine when it comes to protecting the rights of law enforcement officials and the judiciary officials, while at the same time the law works like an old run-down rusty piece of machinery when it comes to protecting the rights of the poor, the weak and the oppressed. Because the law took special precautions to guard itself with immunity for judges and prosecutors while acting in their official capacities. This later made me realize all the more why some judges and prosecutors did not give a damn about the rights of an accused since they could violate those rights with apparent immunity—and impunity—to criminal or civil actions being brought against them. Such immunity tends to instill in some judges and prosecutors the attitude that so long as they act in their official capacities, they may not be right, but they are never wrong.

All judges and prosecuting officials feel comfortable with the aegis of judicial immunity that shields judicial acts of impropriety from prosecution or tort actions. And state and federal legislatures are not going to tamper with this immunity conferred on the judiciary for fear that legislative immunity conferred on legislatures might also be called into question. So where does all of this leave the little man who is damaged by misuse of judicial authority? Why, up that old proverbial creek without a paddle, of course! What else?

No matter what good reason there is for granting immunity to judicial officials, there can never be a good reason to excuse members of the judiciary of their willful acts of misconduct while acting in their judicial capacities. But the most galling experience for the victim is in determining when a judicial official's act is willful when it tends to violate a defendant's rights, because other judicial officials will be called upon to make a ruling on these kinds of questions, and they will usually lean over backward, like circus acrobats, to absolve one of their brethren of any willful wrongdoing while acting in his judicial capacity. And state's attorneys, when acting in their official capacities, are accorded the same protection of immunity as the judges.

We now see that the judiciary has injected itself with sufficient legal "inteferon" to fight off all efforts to penetrate its immune system no matter how badly a member of the judiciary infects others with the plague of misconduct and totally bad decisions of a willful nature. This might lead many to think, Do we really live in a country where there actually exist "justice for all?" Or are those just banal words of hypocrisy in our so-called Democracy to further mislead the thinking of the masses?

When the federal district court dismissed my complaint in 1954, for what it held was "failure to state a cause of action," I took an appeal to the United States Court of Appeals for the Seventh Circuit which is located in Chicago. Both parties were allowed to file briefs and written arguments. But no oral arguments were allowed when I had demanded my right to be present to argue my case. Although it appeared that the court of appeals was going to permit ex parte oral arguments by opposing counsel until I demanded a right to be present and argue my case too. Rather than let that happen, the court cancelled oral arguments altogether.

I had always been under the rather misguided impression that the federal courts could be depended upon to uphold the very essence of justice in the cases that came before its judges. But experience was soon to change that erroneous concept. While the federal courts did dispense a much better overall brand of justice than the state courts in most cases—due perhaps to better supervision and watchfulness of the United States Supreme Court—some federal judges, however, left much to be desired in their rulings where Illinois prisoners' rights were concerned. Then too it must be remembered that most of the federal judges have sat at one time or another on state court benches, and it's hard to break old habits. I don't specifically base this claim on the rulings made by the lower federal court on my civil suit in the instant case, although the judge had been a judge of the state court in Cook County Illinois before ascending to the federal bench. I do, however, as will be later demonstrated, base my conclusions on the manner in which the federal district judge and the judges on the federal court of appeals in Chicago handled my petition for writ of habeas corpus. In that particular case, I got the United States Supreme Court to overrule both courts' decisions that did not vaguely follow the applicable law and opinions available to them that had been passed upon by the high tribunal.

To me, the decisions of the two lower federal courts represented an inexcusable lack of deference to the US Supreme Court in the per curiam opinion in United States ex rel. *Jennings v. Ragen*. Evidently, feeling the same way I did, the high tribunal smeared egg all over the faces of the judges of the lower federal courts that sat in judgment on my habeas corpus petition and appeal. This was by far one of my greatest legal thrills, because the US Supreme Court appointed no lawyer to assist me and held no further oral arguments on additional briefs. The high court simply accepted my petition for writ of certiorari as being correct in every respect as to what the law should be in my case, and in upholding my position, the high tribunal wasted no words in telling the courts below that they were wrong in their judgment and rulings.

I respect the federal courts like all citizens ought to do. But a court is only as good as the judges that sit in those chambers of justice. We all know that man is a fallible creature; and we can forgive him for his inadvertent errors. After all, we as forgivers are fallible too. But in some cases, we find deliberate errors, omissions, remissiveness, and malfeasance on the parts of judicial officials that cannot be simply written off as an inadvertent "mistake."

Our judges are vested with awesome and stupendous powers! They are often held in almost godly fear and esteem by some people. I for one used to feel that way about some members of the judiciary.

Even during my present incarceration, I had come to look upon some jurist as idols. But today, I respect but do not revere these officials any longer. Because I have come to realize that all jurists are susceptible to all of the human frailties that abound within all of us lesser promoted mortals.

Perhaps one iconoclastic incident more than any other caused me to reject any notions of idolatry for certain members of the judiciary, living or dead. And it is not the criminality of this one judge in high office that turned me against all judges or jurists. For I am not against all of them. I, in fact, am of the opinion that the great majority of judges are, indeed, honorable men and women endeavoring to administer justice to the best of their abilities with fairness to all litigants and those accused of crimes. It is, however, that this one judge of the US Court of Appeals for the Seventh Circuit made me realize just how judges are. His name was Otto Kerner. He was governor of the State of Illinois before becoming a judge on the US Court of Appeals.

Judge Kerner signed a certificate when he was governor that restored my rights to citizenship after my release from prison in 1961. He later was appointed to the federal bench and sat in the same court where his father had sat as an esteemed jurist. And it was while Judge Otto Kerner was a member of the US Court of Appeals that he was indicted for criminal acts committed while he was the governor of Illinois. He was later tried and convicted and ignominiously sent off to prison where he emerged a broken, disgraced, and terminally ill person. He died soon after his liberation in 1976 while still on parole.

The US Court of Appeals for the Seventh Circuit, in handing down its opinion in the civil action brought by me titled *Jennings v. Nester. et al.* held in part,

> State's attorneys, when acting in their official capacities are protected by same immunity in civil cases which is accorded judges, and prisoner could not maintain damages action against state's attorneys under civil rights acts.

Civil rights acts create cause of action for conspiracy to deny equal protection, but do not create cause of action for conspiracy to deny due process of law, and there must be actual denial of due process before cause of action arises.

Where complaint, in action under civil rights acts charged police officers with unlawful search of plaintiff's person, seizure of certain articles of personal property, introduction into evidence of unlawfully seized property, and deliberate use of perjured testimony in trial, but there was nothing therein to indicate that every citizen was not potentially subject to same treatment, denial of equal protection of laws was insufficiently alleged. Civil rights acts were enacted to protect the civil rights of individuals and were not enacted to discipline local law enforcement officers for acts which are later corrected, and fact that new trial "is ordered under Illinois Post-Conviction Hearing Act, or a similar procedure in another state, does not give cause of action under civil rights acts where error is corrected at subsequent trial.

In determining whether a plaintiff's constitutional rights have been deprived so as to give him cause of action under civil rights acts, court must look to everything which has transpired; and where plaintiff had been convicted after second trial in which he had been accorded due process of law, and it did not appear that he had suffered any additional imprisonment due to first trial, plaintiff had no cause of action under civil rights acts against police officers for alleged abuse of his constitutional right to due process in first trial.

After reading all the opinion handed down by the US Court of Appeals and looking back over all the events that had transpired since my arrest and two convictions, I could not help but to recall a quotation from Shakespeare's play *Measure for Measure*:

> Man, proud man,
> Dressed in a little brief authority,
> Plays such fantastic tricks before high heaven As
> makes the angels weep.

My appeal to the United States Supreme Court was denied, and that abruptly brought an end to my suit for damages. I had tried and failed. But there was a steady stream of other legal activity to keep me busy—so busy in fact that the days and nights literally sped by with lightning speed. This was the way to do time and not suffer mentally. There was no substitute for staying busy so much with other people's troubles that you hardly have time to worry about your own troubles.

I had prepared appeals for my rap partners, Buddy Morgan and Li'l Arthur, because Judge Ashcraft had denied their petitions filed under the Illinois Postconviction Hearing Act. Li'l Arthur had already appeared before the Illinois parole board after serving the minimum of his five- to fifteen-year sentence less time off for good behavior. The board had given him a continuance, and he stood a good chance of being paroled the next time he appeared before the board. Should this happen, it would obviate the necessity of filing any more appeals on his behalf.

* * * * *

While enjoying a yard stroll on a lovely late spring afternoon chatting at random on various subjects, as we were wont to do, Lou got on the topic of education not being fully taken advantage of by the prisoners, since the prison administration offered a well-rounded source of academic studies and courses.

"You know, Counselor," which was his usual way of addressing me, "I can't imagine any man in here expecting to be released with serious intentions of earning an honest livelihood, not taking advantage of all this time and opportunity for self-betterment. And it is a shameful loss, indeed, that so many of the inmates in here fail to avail themselves of the richness of this repository for learning and vocational training. The hostile inmates can say all the bad things they want to about the warden and his staff and the harsh disciplinary practices that are enforced here, but the one thing that stands out conspicuously in Warden Ragen's favor is that he has made a sincere endeavor to provide his wards with every available opportunity to add richness into their lives by sharing in the learning process offered in this prison."

"Yeah. Guess you can give Ragen an E for excellence in educational facilities," I remarked agreeably.

"Which brings to mind, Counselor, your own particular situation."

I could tell by the tone of his voice that I was in for some type of professorial deprecation. "Yeah, come on with it, Lou."

"Well, Counselor, take you for instance—and I took the liberty of looking up your educational background in the school files—you have an exceptionally high IQ of one hundred and forty-nine, that's very superior intelligence. Yet you have never finished high school. Perhaps at this very moment, your self-educational process qualifies you somewhere in the upper college range of knowledge. Still, you don't have anything to show for it on paper."

"That may well be true. But what the hell do I need a high school or college sheepskin for? What can I do with it when you consider my fouled-up background?"

"Damn it!" Lou cursed before going on indignantly. "If I didn't know better I'd have to classify you with some of these other ignoramuses around here for making a remark like that. Why! you can do a great deal with a college degree when applying for employment on the outside."

"I can't be a lawyer even if I graduated from law school and passed the bar exam. I'd never get by the Committee on Character and Fitness that passes on new applicants before they are admitted to practice law by—guess who? Ha! Ha! The Illinois Supreme Court," I concluded with a laugh before Lou could answer.

"But there are a whole lot more positions that you could qualify for," Lou insisted. "And if you have the educational credentials, you would be surprised how that would facilitate your chances for success."

"Maybe," I muttered thoughtfully and somewhat dubiously.

"No maybe about it, Counselor. Now here is what I want you to do. Drop a request to the education director requesting an interview to sign up for the next general educational development test at the high school level. Perhaps you are aware of this method of obtaining an equivalent certificate of a high school diploma. These tests are sponsored by an official agency of the Veterans' Testing Service of the American Council on Education. Your other alternative would be to attend the prison high school classes full time. But I don't recommend that in your particular situation since you are doubtlessly qualified to pass the GED test."

"Is the test difficult?" I inquired with interest.

Lou grinned. "Counselor, do you realize that you are a phenomenal person?"

"You really think so? That's a compliment coming from a person like you, Lou."

"I certainly do. With your brains, it will be like eating pie a la mode passing the GED test. I'll give you some books to bone up on, and I'll tutor you as much as I can to prep you for the test."

"What about the certificate? Will it show that I got it in prison?"

"No, no, Counselor. There will be no stigma of prison attached to it. It will be issued by the American Council on Education."

"Good! I'll go for it."

Lou slapped me on the back. "That's great! And after you pass the high school level test and get your GED certificate, I want you to seriously think about signing up for the two-year college course. Man, we'll make something out of you yet," Lou concluded with a show of great satisfaction over his latest educational convert.

Lou was like a missionary—always seeking to spread the gospel about education. He particularly aimed his message at the black inmates and Hispanics who needed education the most. But his easy-going, friendly manner had enabled him to reach many poorly educated white inmates. This caused the prison officials to appreciate and recognize Louis Lomax as an excellent educator and an asset to the faculty. Now the door was open for other black teachers and instructors.

Lou said that, "the white man labors under such a superiority complex where blacks are concerned that he has to be educated into the reality of his own prejudicial stupidity and inferiority in believing that any one race of people is any more inherently superior to another race of people. Because we are all creatures of culture. Adopt an Australian Aborigine baby, place him in Buckingham Palace to be educated and raised as a prince, and that baby will grow up to be exactly that in every cultural aspect."

I agreed with Lou, because humans are not born to speak any particular language or learn any particular culture. We are only born as races to look like we look. From that point of origin on, throughout our cultural development, we act like we are taught to act. Man is a unique species unlike any other lower animal forms that are made up of many species. And mankind, being of the single human species, can interbreed with any fertile human being on earth no matter of what culture, whether it be the highest or the lowest.

Lou went on to say that "the best way to defeat the white man's so-called superiority complex is by a consistent black show of excellence on all fields of endeavor, and not just sports. True, blacks have excelled in most of the sporting events with shocking reality and consistency. But it remains for blacks to also use the educational arena to further explode the white man's mythical notion of blacks being intellectually inferior."

Before Lou was done making his point, he pointed to me as an example of how whites place no color line on knowledge when it can help them. For it was a reality that I was in no short supply of whites seeking my assistance and advice.

With Lou's help, I went on to pass the GED test with the ease he said that I would. My percentile rank in the scoring on all subjects greatly exceeded the standard score of a larger percent of the 35,432 public high school seniors that were used as a sample to establish norms for the test. And it gave me great pride to receive my certificate of which I owed a great deal of thanks to my friend Louis Lomax. Because without his advice and urging me on, I probably would never have taken the test.

Lou had a lot of racial pride. He naturally despised racial bigotry of any kind perpetrated against any race. He practically predicted the racial strife, unrest, and the freedom movement of the 1960s. I read several articles that he authored in his cell that dealt with these racial problems, their consequences, and solutions. I was amazed at this young black man's intellect and can remember almost verbatim him saying in effect that "America is built on a solid foundation of democracy. There can be no question about that. But the unfortunate thing is that the structure that was built on the foundation turned out to be a 'hypocrisy' because the white people that built it 'did not follow the blueprint after the foundation was laid.'"

Lou loved books almost as much as life itself. In fact, he loved books so much that he almost treated them as something human. While leafing through the pages of a book in his classroom, I accidentally caused a tiny tear on one of the pages.

A look of acute pain came over Lou's face. He immediately leaped to his feet, sought and seized a strip of transparent cellulose tape, and proceeded to apply the tape to the tear on the page with all the tender and loving care of a doting parent placing a Band-Aid on the injured flesh of a child.

When I mentioned his extraordinary reverence for books, Lou assured me that a book to him was not just an ordinary thing, that books were alive; and like humans, some books were dull and had little personality while others were stimulating, charming, and full of character and personality. "Some books die in their infancy," he told me. "Even as some babies die, and still other books are long-lived, depending upon their heredity passed on to them by their progenitors and the good fortune of fate in protecting them from destructive accidents."

*   *   *   *   *

A few months passed and Jimmy Crenshaw and his co-defendants, Judson Griffin and Richard Riles, were found guilty on the armed robbery charge. Crenshaw, because of his rather lengthy past criminal record as a pickpocket, was sentenced to serve from ten to twenty-five years in the state penitentiary. Griffin and Riles had sentences imposed upon them of five to ten years respectively. All three defendants were later shipped to Stateville to serve out their sentences.

I was working in the prison barbershop when they arrived, and since Giles expressed a desire not to become a part of a postconviction proceedings, thinking it might hurt his chances for parole, I immediately prepared a petition for Crenshaw and Griffin, which they filed with the clerk of the Cook County Criminal Court. The main question raised was denial of a free transcript with which to file an appeal.

The trial court wasted no time in dismissing Crenshaw and Griffin's petition, and I wasted no time in appealing the dismissal order to the Illinois Supreme Court.

With my case already on file in the Illinois Supreme Court, and now Crenshaw's and Griffin's case also on file, it should not be too long I thought before the court would make a ruling—little knowing at that time that my case would be pigeonholed in the Illinois Supreme Court for almost two years without a ruling being made. This indicated to me conclusively that the Illinois High Court recognized the seriousness of the issue raised on denial of free transcripts to indigent defendants. The court evidently realized too that since I had already won one substantial ruling from the United States Supreme Court, that any appeal I filed for a writ of certiorari would be given careful scrutiny by the nation's highest tribunal.

There was no way that I could compel the Illinois Supreme Court to rule on my appeal, although I did file legal papers with the clerk of the Illinois Supreme Court, protesting the long delay in having my case heard on appeal, but this action on my part was to no avail. This left me more upset and chagrined that the court would not rule so that I could pursue the matter to the United States Supreme Court. I knew I had the judges sitting on Illinois Supreme

Tribunal worried. But I did not have any confidence whatsoever of that court ruling in my favor.

The Illinois Supreme Court, probably thinking that perhaps an obscure case like Crenshaw's and Griffin's might not attract any attention in the United States Supreme Court, dismissed the petition and the Illinois Supreme Court affirmed, solely on the ground that the petition raised no substantial state or federal constitutional question for review.

This was the break I had been waiting for. I didn't care whose case I used to test the constitutionality of denying transcripts to indigent defendants so long as the issue properly reached the United States Supreme Court. With my own case still being pigeonholed in the Illinois Supreme Court, I promptly prepared a petition for writ of certiorari for Crenshaw and Griffin, and the making of legal history seriously got underway.

Feeling somewhat complacent now that I had succeeded in getting the issue properly raised before the United States Supreme Court, I crossed my fingers and turned my attention to other legal matters while awaiting the high court's decision.

Chapter 13

THE UNITED STATES SUPREME COURT granted the petition for writ of certiorari that I prepared for Crenshaw and Griffin. And the prison began to hum with the hope and excitement of winning free trial transcripts. A favorable ruling could certainly revolutionize appellate review for indigents in the State of Illinois as well as in other state jurisdictions that did not provide free transcripts to paupers.

Twice now, I had succeeded in winning reviews before the highest court in the land. Few practicing attorneys had ever achieved this distinction. The months and years ahead were to place almost unbearable pressures and demands on my time and intellect. I became so absorbed in my legal work that I put aside enrolling in the college course—something I have regretted to this day. But my first love was law, and there was something fascinating about its challenge. The thrill of winning was hot in my blood; the opportunity to match wits with highly trained attorneys made the whole thing seem like a game of chess or war. And it was fun! Because I wasn't beating run-of-the-mill attorneys. I was beating the very best appellate lawyers that worked in the office of the attorney general of Illinois and the office of the state's attorney of Cook County, since these were the attorneys who opposed my petitions for writs of certiorari and petitions for postconviction reviews.

Following the appointment of highly competent counsel in the person of Mr. Charles A. Horsky by the US Supreme Court to represent Crenshaw and Griffin on further briefs and oral argument, the case was set in full motion for the historical ruling that was to follow. Mr. Horsky was a member of the same prestigious law firm as Dean Atcheson, former United States Secretary of State in President

Truman's Administration; and to Mr. Horsky's undying credit, he prepared one of the most thorough and outstanding briefs that I have ever read in presenting the full scope of the constitutional issue of depriving the poor of appellate review who could not afford to purchase the transcripts of their trial proceedings. His legal research and outstanding presentation of the case spanned every state in the union with respect to appellate review available to paupers.

We only had a few months to wait before the good news struck like thunder and reverberated around the state prisons with echoes of hope ringing in the ears of indigent prisoners seeking to have their convictions given a full appellate review. The highest court in the nation had ruled in our favor with a wide-reaching decision, holding that "indigent defendants were entitled to a free transcript of their trial proceedings if they wished to seek appellate review." This was a crushing defeat to the Illinois judiciary's long-established unfair system of justice that was practiced, pervaded, and perpetuated by the judges and prosecutors in the State of Illinois.

I was extremely proud of the fact that I had, from the very beginning, concocted and orchestrated this legal coup that would equalize justice in state appellate procedure.

In handing down its opinion on April 23, 1956, in the case titled *Griffin v. Illinois*, the United States Supreme Court, speaking through Mr. Justice Black, said in part.

> Illinois law gives every person convicted in a criminal trial a right of review by writ of error; but a full direct appellate review can be had only by furnishing the appellate court with a bill of exceptions or report of the trial proceedings, certified by the trial judge, and it is sometimes impossible to prepare such documents without a stenographic transcript of the trial proceedings, which are furnished free only to indigent defendants sentenced to death. Convicted in an Illinois state court of armed robbery, petitioners moved in the trial court that a certified copy of

the entire record, including a stenographic transcript of the proceedings, be furnished to them without cost. They alleged that they were without funds to pay for such documents and that failure of the court to provide them would violate the Due Process and Equal Protection Clauses of the Fourteenth Amendment. Their motion was denied. They then filed a petition under the Illinois Post-Conviction Hearing Act, under which only questions arising under the State or Federal Constitution may be raised. They alleged that there were manifest non-constitutional errors "in the trial which entitled them to have their convictions set aside on appeal, that the only impediment to full appellate review was their lack of funds to buy a transcript, and that refusal to afford full appellate review solely because of their poverty was a denial of due process and equal protection. This petition was dismissed, and the Illinois Supreme Court affirmed, solely on the ground that the petition raised no substantial state or federal constitutional question. Held: Petitioners' constitutional rights were violated, the judgment of the Illinois Supreme Court is vacated, and the cause is remanded to that Court for further action affording petitioners adequate and effective appellate review.

The Illinois Supreme Court, in compliance with the mandate of the US Supreme Court, said in part in its opinion in the case titled *People v. Griffin* handed down on September 26, 1956:

So far as the present petitioners are concerned (Griffin and Crenshaw), disposition is not difficult. We were in error in holding that no constitutional question of substance was presented.

The judgment of this' court is therefore vacated and the cause is remanded to the Criminal Court of Cook County with directions to vacate its judgment in the postconviction proceeding. The constitutional objection, however, is one which does not affect the judgment of conviction, and that judgment need not be disturbed.

The trial court will enter an order directing the court reporter to transcribe his notes in full and to deliver a copy of the transcript to each of the petitioners without charge. Petitioners may then proceed in accordance with the rules of this court.

The impact of the decision of the Supreme Court of the United States is not, of course, confined to these petitioners. The net of that court's holding is that since Illinois provides a full review of all errors alleged to have occurred in the course of a criminal trial at the instance of a defendant who brings before the reviewing court a transcript of the proceedings at the trial, Illinois violates the equal protection clause of the fourteenth amendment (and perhaps the due-process clause as well) when it denies such a review to one who cannot afford to pay the court reporter for writing up the transcript. The scope of the decision is thus not limited to the case of the petitioners.

Following the aforementioned decisions of the US Supreme Court and the Illinois Supreme Court, the trial courts throughout Illinois were deluged with requests made by prisoners for copies of their trial transcripts without cost. I had already made my application to Judge Wendell E. Green, asking the court to enter an order that a transcript be allowed me posthaste without cost. And I could just picture the egg-smeared faces of all these judicial officials who were now eating crow after opposing and blocking my petitions in bringing about this great legal triumph. But I didn't give one tee-ny-weeny shit about their chagrin or how in the hell the ruling would affect the state treasury or another goddamned complaint that the officials might have. They had shoved this bullshit justice down my throat and the other prisoners' throats for years. And now this injustice had caught up with them, and they got their asses kicked good and proper by the highest court in the land, whereby they were compelled to mete out a little real justice for a change.

This was whoopee time! I was in a state of supreme euphoria! Cries from the inmate population rang out. "You really fucked 'em good this time, Counselor! Nice going, Mr. Precedent!"

"What this joint needs is a few more Blacky Jennings, and it won't be nobody left in this fuckin' dump."

On and on came an almost endless "blue" stream of congratulatory encomiums. Victory signs and fists balled up and shook high in the air in triumph were common sights when inmates passed me in line. And I would be a liar if I said that I didn't love every damn minute of it.

My name and legal work being associated with the *Jennings* and *Griffin* cases projected me into the legal limelight with such prominence that I became the knight in shining armor to these many happy prisoners whose constant adulation was beginning to cause me extreme embarrassment. Because I knew personally that I was not one iota as great as the prisoners made me out to be with their hyperbolical compliments and flattery. I was patted on the back frequently, my hand wrung constantly in congratulations, and I was pointed out to the "fish" (new prisoners) like a sideshow freak. The fish stared at me in awe, apparently just bursting with enthusiasm to tell me about the injustices in their cases first chance they got to corner me somewhere in the prison.

Everywhere I went in the prison, I was solicited and sought after for help or advice. Being a prison celebrity made demands on me that I could not hope to fulfill. But I ended up doing what most people do when they acquire a reputation for greatness, I tried to live up to my reputation by studying all the harder to merit my newly acquired fame, and I soon found out that to keep all this attention focused on me was a grave mistake.

On the recreation yard, I found myself giving lectures on law and teaching inmates how to prepare their own petitions. Prisoners recorded notes on pieces of paper. The screws kept a sharp eye on me at all times. Now and then a screw would ask a prisoner to see what he was writing—finding that it was not a kite, the guard would return the slip of paper to the prisoner and was therefore dubious as to what infraction of prison regulations he could make of it.

Before long Captain Bull Ryan, a tall, elderly official, with years of penal experience etched into his wrinkled and solemn features, accosted me on the yard. He advised me to cease those lectures that were drawing inmates into clusters around me. I made the mistake of quickly pointing out that nothing was being said about the yard evangelist who drew crowds of inmates around him. And I pointed off to a section of the yard where Brother Robinson, a self-acclaimed black inmate preacher, was preaching a fire-and-brimstone sermon at that very moment.

Old Bull Ryan didn't like my answer and started to walk me to the "hole" for insolence. The inmates around me began to grumble in a quiet and resentful manner. Mutterings of,

"It ain't fair."

"I thought Cap'n Ryan was fairer'n that."

"Shit! The counselor ain't did nothin' to get walked for."

Captain Ryan shouted, "All right, you inmates, break it up or I'll have you all marched over to isolation!"

The inmates slowly moped away, disgruntled.

Ryan and I were halfway to the isolation building when he stopped. "Jennings," he said, "you are letting these inmates use you." I turned around to face him in silence. He went on. "Maybe you like being a big shot around here. But you ought to start thinking about yourself. Sooner or later, we'll catch you red-handed breaking the rule to help one of these cons, and it could cost you dearly. You should be thinking about your chances for parole and get these fuckin' sycophants off your back. Don't let being Mr. Nice Guy blow your chances for parole. Because these cons don't really give a shit about you." I still remained silent. Ryan continued, "Come on. I'm giving you a break. Let's go to the cellhouse."

"Thanks, Cap'n," I muttered, and we walked to C-House in silence.

I knew there was no way I could stop being a vital force in the underground legal system no matter what the officials said or did. I knew that one of their favorite threats was to toss the parole board into a con's face when they wanted to kick him in line. And they could fuck you good with the board. Because Warden Ragen had the parole board by both ears just as he had the cons by both balls and the short hairs if they got their asses out of line. The more defiant a con got, the harder old Meatball squeezed his nuts, with deprivation of "good time" being one of the warden's harshest disciplinary measures. If a prisoner for instance had a sentence of five to ten years, with time off for good behavior, it used to be a prisoner would see the parole board in half the minimum of the sentence plus one year, three months, and fifteen days, that would mean that he would see the parole board in about 45 months on the five-year minimum of his sentence. If he had to serve the full ten years maximum, with time off for good behavior, he would only have to serve six years, three months, and fifteen days.

Elementary math should convince anyone that the bargain route through the front gate of the prison was the best buy. Yet many recalcitrant inmates did not buy that route and got socked with the maximum on their sentences when they were deprived of "statutory good time." I was a firm believer in the bargain route and tried to keep my cool and thereby my "good time" intact. To me, a low profile was the best way to conceal my resentment and frustration. Out of my mouth would always come politeness when a screw reprimanded me about something even if I thought that I did not deserve the reprimand. But silently, in the back of my mind, a steady stream of profanity would tell the screw where to go, how to get there, and what to kiss when he arrived.

I would, of course, always endeavor to be circumspect in breaking any prison regulation. Yet I had to take some chances because I was thrusted head-on into the limelight, like it or not, and there I intended to remain. I realized, contrary to what old Bull Ryan had said, the prisoners did give a shit about me. Fair exchange is no robbery. Every day, I witnessed prisoners willing to transport legal documents, steal prison goods, and go out of their way taking chances to do almost anything reasonable that I asked of them.

To punish me now for my legal activities would certainly brand me something of a martyr. Why, even one of the prison chaplains was soliciting my legal assistance on the QT to help some members of his prison parish. And he would return the favors by giving me all of the special letters I wanted to write to whomever I pleased.

I studied all the harder in my cell to keep abreast of the latest court decisions. Because I realized that soon, I would be delving into every phase and facet of procedural trial errors when those free transcripts started coming into the prison. I had gained the reputation of being one of the best, and to some, "the best" lawyer in the joint. Being a competitive person by nature, I would be damned before I would let my ego suffer any demotion in the limelight. My philosophy was to be sincere and sure of myself with the inmates seeking my help. There was no room for bullshit. They either had a case, or they didn't. When I told an inmate something about his case, I wanted to be precise, so I wouldn't later end up with egg on my face because I had given out the wrong advice. No nonsense. No bullshit. That was the only way to go; and I made this plain, simple, and clear to all my friends, assistants, and clients. One other thing I emphasized was "no fees." I really stressed "no fees" because hard as I might try to help some inmates, if the case did not turn out favorably, a hard loser might feel that he got bilked if he paid for my services. Besides, I always stressed the fact that although I believed that a case had merit did not necessarily mean that the appellate court or hearing judge would agree with my position or conclusion, because in most cases, they did not agree with me.

I had to squeeze the shit out of the state courts to get anything resembling a fair ruling on substantial constitutional errors, with the federal courts acting as a kind of watchdog over the state courts. But just going up on procedural errors was to prove difficult, indeed, to obtain reversals of convictions. The appellate courts and Illinois

Supreme Court could duck and dodge all they pleased because procedural errors were not reviewable by the federal courts in state court convictions.

It soon got to the point where the appellate courts and Illinois Supreme Court were calling almost everything "harmless error," and we started referring facetiously to those judicial bodies as the "Illinois Courts of Harmless Errors."

Transcripts were coming into the prison in such large numbers that it was impossible to peruse them all, or even a small portion of them. I had to arrange with other well-versed cell house lawyers to read some of these transcripts and refer any promising ones to me. I also revealed to them my secret of putting their names on the lead sheets while the transcripts were in their cells. This procedure worked out well; the screws were frustrated in their shakedown efforts to link a cell house lawyer with another inmate's case.

It took a lot of work to prepare an appeal to the Illinois Supreme Court. And I was happy when the courts started appointing counsel to file appeals in many of these cases. The results of our combined endeavors proved rewarding in winning a few new trials in which the defendants were later released when old witnesses could no longer be produced to testify against them. Some prisoners won outright acquittals while others, like myself, were convicted a second time and returned to prison with new sentences—usually shorter than their original sentences to compensate for time previously served for the same offense. But this too was in the discretion of the trial court judge, because if he wanted to, he could impose a more severe sentence.

Being involved in constant legal work caused time to literally fly by. I discovered that the most rewarding feeling in the world is to be able to help your fellow man. Whether it is caused by a subconscious feeling of superiority or self-aggrandizement, I cannot say for certain. God knows I tried to effectuate modesty. I extended credit liberally to all those involved in my cases who made substantial contributions. Even so, I could not hide from being the cynosure or idol of the prisoners who greatly appreciated what I had been instrumental in doing to improve justice for myself as well as them in the State of Illinois.

After all is said and done, I would still be a liar if I said that I didn't get some degree of selfish satisfaction in beating the state's best legal brains, causing them to eat crow and wipe egg from their faces, for this was the grandest thrill that I had ever gotten out of prison life—or out of life, period.

In a case decided by the United States Supreme Court titled *Johnson v. Avery*, Mr. Justice Byron White had the following to say in his dissenting opinion with regard to the jailhouse lawyer's power and influence over the inmates of a prison, "According to prison officials, whose expertise in such matters should be given some consideration, the jailhouse lawyer often succeeds in establishing his own power structure, quite apart from the formal system of warden, guard, and trusties, which the prison seeks to maintain. Those whom the jailhouse lawyer serves may come morally under his sway as the one hope of their release and repay him not only with obedience but with whatever minor gifts and other favors are available to them. Many assert that the aim of the/jailhouse lawyer is not the service of truth and justice but rather self-aggrandizement and power."

Mr. Justice White may be right in his logic. The jailhouse lawyer carries a lot of prestige among prisoners and can therefore wield a lot of power. But Mr. Justice White is wrong in his assumption if he subscribes to the statement that "the aim of the jailhouse lawyer is not the service of truth and justice but rather self-aggrandizement and power." Because I know that I am a true example to the contrary. I have, however, accepted favors from some prisoners, but the favors were not based upon any fee-like agreement or arrangement to perform any legal services. Some of the favors I received from prisoners came from men for whom I never did one piece of legal work. And never once did I voluntarily solicit or accept one gift from an inmate for any legal services that I ever rendered because I was very adamant in refusing gifts—for legal services. Gifts, however, were bestowed upon me, yes; but here, again, I had no way of stopping anonymous donations or returning gifts that were either mailed to me or placed in my cell with an anonymous note saying, "Thanks, Counselor" or "One of your grateful clients."

I, personally, was also an example of utilizing whatever intellect and legal talent I possessed to the service of truth and justice "rather than a conscious motivation of self-aggrandizement. The important cases that were initiated by me that won favorable consideration in the United States Supreme Court proves that I was instrumental in being the salient force that helped to restore a great measure of "truth and justice" to the Illinois judicial system. And the truth of the foregoing assertion can no better be attested to than by the opinions rendered in *Jennings v. Illinois* and *Griffin v. Illinois*, which emanated from the very court where Mr. Justice Byron White is a member. Because certainly, those two opinions were prompted by my personal pursuit of "truth and justice" with no thought whatsoever to anything else.

*　　*　　*　　*　　*

The letter hit me like a ton of scrap iron dumped squarely on my head. A sudden feeling of emptiness went straight to the pit of my gut. After waiting for almost seven years my Eve was finally calling it quits and getting married.

The news came as a shocking surprise, because she had visited with me only a few weeks ago, and everything seemed all right then. But as I read further into the letter, her explanation became quite simple. She was pregnant, and the baby's father wanted to marry her. She begged my forgiveness and asked for my understanding. She still claimed love for me but was at a loss to deal with her problem in any other way. She did not believe in abortions.

I laid the "Dear John" letter aside and contemplated my future without Eve. I didn't feel in a mood for conversation on the subject, so I did not reveal the contents of the letter to my cell mates. The hurt would pass. There was no enmity.

Eve had been a great lover, a wonderful source of comfort and companionship. I would truly miss her even though she suggested in her letter that maybe we could remain friends and continue to write to one another.

The picture was clear to me. If she was to find any kind of happiness in her marriage, it was best for me to get out of that picture completely. Therefore when I answered her letter, I told Eve that I was sorry to lose her and that I held no hard feelings in my heart whatsoever. I wished her happiness and thanked her for her past loyalty. Most of all, I assured Eve very frankly that I was understanding of the situation. I confessed that it was my own mistakes and undoing that had caused our separation and left her virtually imprisoned along with myself. She had suffered deprivation and frustration just as I had suffered, and were our situation just the opposite, I too could very well be in a similar situation of having to marry some woman who was pregnant by me. I closed the letter with, "In loving memories."

Several days later, I received another letter from Eve, thanking me for being so understanding and still expressing her love for me. She closed the letter with, "You will always be first in my heart."

That is a hell of a way to start off a marriage I thought, marrying one guy and loving another guy. But it happens all the time. This made me think about something I had read but could not remember from what sources: "Absence makes the heart grow fonder—or yonder." I don't know why that thought hit me at that particular time, but it was appropriate.

I didn't hear from Eve after that last letter, nor did I write to her anymore. Once in a while, my buddy, Jimmy Marshall, would run into Eve. Then he would include a little message about her in his letter. Sometimes she would call my foster mother just to inquire how I was getting along. The last word I received about Eve was that she had moved out of the state with her husband and their child.

*　　*　　*　　*　　*

Louis Lomax received a copy of his trial transcript, and I went over it very carefully; but I couldn't find anything to base an appeal upon. Of all the guys I would really have liked to help the most, there was really nothing I could do to help him.

Lou accepted the disappointing news philosophically, although just for the hell of it, I begged him to get a second opinion from one of the other top jailhouse lawyers that I recommended him to. But Lou wouldn't do it. He said that "I got all the faith in the world in you, Counselor. If you say nothing is there, I can live with that."

Fighting Lou's case would probably have proved useless anyway. Because by the time he filed an appeal and got his case heard, he would no doubt be out of prison on parole, and the whole damn case would be moot as far as getting his conviction overturned and going through the trouble of standing trial again with the risk of being convicted a second time. Vindication is always at best only a vague possibility. Parole, however, was an imminent futuristic reality for Lou in view of this being his first felony conviction because his prison record was exemplary.

Louis Lomax's first appearance before the Illinois parole board, several months later, did result in his freedom. Now and then I would receive a letter from him using an assumed name because parolees were not permitted to write to prison inmates who were not permitted to write to a parolee either. But we did not let that stand in the way of our friendship. More than once, I got special letters from the prison chaplain to answer Lou's letters. He was doing real well on the outside. He had moved to New York City, was writing professionally, and making a name for himself.

Li'l Arthur also received a parole on his five- to fifteen-year sentence when he appeared back before the parole board a second time. He opened a barbershop on Chicago's Westside and was managing to keep his nose clean if not his mouth from the word that got back to me from Jimmy Marshall.

My wife Juanita

My wife Juanita

Shopper

Talbert Jennings

Talbert Jennings with customer

Talbert Jennings

Shopper

Chapter 14

THE BEST WAY TO DO time is to break up the monotony of the daily regimentation as much as possible. In keeping with this philosophy, I transferred from the barbershop to the prison tailor shop. That move also caused me to transfer from C-House to D-House where the tailor shop crew was domiciled.

A job in the tailor shop paid a small wage, and the extra money would come in handy for purchasing legal materials.

And whenever the blood bank showed up at the prison, I sold a pint of blood for five bucks. Combining these sources of revenue with the few dollars I received from my friends and family, I was able to sustain my modest needs for commissary items and legal materials.

At Christmastime, I didn't know what to do with all the gifts I received from prisoners who sent me foodstuffs, tobacco, which I didn't need personally since I had stopped smoking; and other things such as toilet articles were bestowed upon me in larger quantities than needed. Because prison rules limited how many commissary items each prisoner could have in his possession at one time, I shared these gifts with my cell mates and other less fortunate inmates.

Some anonymous benefactor had been having a pint of ice cream and a pie delivered to my cell every Sunday evening for several months. I didn't know who in the hell was being so generous but guessed that it was from one of my satisfied clients who knew that I refused outright to accept any fees for my legal services.

Sending the goodies was one way of shoving a fee, so to speak, down my throat. Be that as it may, little things like extra foods, delicacies, and desserts meant a hell of a lot to a prisoner who didn't have too much else to look forward to in the way of pleasure. When

I transferred from C-House to D-House the, ice cream and pie followed me right to my new cell the first Sunday I was there.

This made me think about fat-ass Gooch over in B-House "shafting" the cons for goodies, and I deplored the thought of anyone comparing me with the Gooch. In law, if circumstantial evidence is what can be inferred as true from other events that logically coincide with some event, then the ice cream and pie might indicate that I was on "the take" also. And the following incident might also suggest that I was on "the make" if maliciously misinterpreted.

Doing favors in prison sometimes can put the good Samaritan in a bad light. Such is the case that happened to me when I stuck my nose in another inmate's business.

Slim Jones had a notorious reputation for going after the good-looking younger inmates. And he would use every trick in his perverted repertoire to seduce these naive newcomers. First, Slim would strike up the seemingly harmless friendship. Next would come assistance—especially if the younger inmate needed a few items from the commissary or felt the need of a strong protective security while being somewhat frightened in this tough new environment. Allying himself with Slim might seem a good thing to do to a scared "fish" who could see brute strength, toughness, and prison savvy in Slim Jones.

Once Slim gained the confidence of his unwitting quarry, he would urge the unsuspecting victim to put in a request for assignment to the tailor shop. With this accomplished, Slim would then bide his time until either an opening was available in his cell or the intended victim's cell. In either case, Slim would arrange to become a cell mate with the inmate he was baiting. When they were finally located in the same cell, wily Slim Jones would make friendly sexual advances to the new cell mate, which if not complied with in a reasonable period could turn Slim into a brutal monster in forcing himself on his victim.

Slim Jones was a tall hulk of a man standing almost six and one-half feet in stature. He weighed well over two hundred pounds. His solemn brown face with high cheekbones and droopy eyelids could make him look real ferocious when he got angry. The old-timers knew that Slim had forced himself on cell mates before with threats to kill them if they did not succumb to this sodomite's demand. And Slim swore too that if anyone ever stooled on him that he would kill them without mercy. Slim was known as the Asshole Bandit. But only inmates as tough or tougher than Slim ever dared to call him that to his face.

The young man he was after was about twenty-one years old. He had gotten into trouble at Pontiac, a prison for youthful offenders, and he was shipped to Stateville where he had been assigned to the coal detail before getting an assignment in the tailor shop. His name was Ricky, and he had talked to me a few time about his case when I worked in the barbershop.

My cell partner, Joe Wiggins, was an elderly inmate in his early sixties. And when we saw Slim move in with Ricky, we knew immediately that there was going to be trouble. It really wasn't any of our business, but we both hated to see a young man trying to keep his dignity and masculinity taken advantage of by a slob like Slim Jones. Had I an inkling beforehand that Slim was trying to get to the lad, I would have warned him to steer clear of the son of a bitch.

The next day in the tailor shop, I noticed that Ricky was very edgy, and I spoke to him. "Hi, Ricky. How's it going?"

He didn't flash his usual big smile, which made him such a charming individual. He mumbled almost incoherently when he returned my greeting. "Hi, Blacky."

"Something wrong?" I inquired solicitously.

"Naw—nothin's wrong. Why do ya ask that?"

"Oh, you just don't seem your usual smiling self this morning, that's all. But I'm glad everything is all right." I paused for a second. When he did not respond, I went on, "You and Slim get along all right?"

Ricky hesitated after first starting to say something.

He tucked in his lips and looked a little frightened. Then I asked myself, "What in the hell are you dipping into this about?" But I knew it was sympathy and nothing else that brought about my concern, other than perhaps I felt a strong aversion for guys like Slim Jones. What happened between two consenting cons was one thing, but a wolf artist like Slim was another thing that somehow rankled the unholy hell out of me.

"Look, Ricky, I know you got a problem with Slim. Wish I had known beforehand that he intended moving in on you. I could have warned you that he's bad medicine," I blurted out candidly.

Ricky. almost trembling with rage or fright, looked around to see if anyone was within hearing distance. "Blacky, I gotta get out of that cell today. I ain't no punk or fag, and I ain't no snitch. I swear I didn't know Slim was like that. He's crazy! Like I said, I ain't no snitch, but somehow, I gotta get out of there today. I don't know what to do. 'Cause if I leave, Slim's gonna get mad as hell! And if I stay, I'm gonna be in deep trouble. I—"

"Hold it, Ricky. Don't get yourself upset," I cut in. "Now listen to me. I think I know what you're up against. Just be cool, and I'll try to help you out of this mess."

"How? How ya gonna do that, Blacky?"

"Don't worry. I got connections. I think I can swing it. Now get back to your machine. I'll work something out at noon," I reassured him.

"Ya mean you can get me transferred somewhere today, don't ya, Blacky? 'Cause I gotta get outta there today. I don't want'a be a snitch, ya un'erstan', don't ya, Blacky? The motherfucker hit on me last night, and I ain't no punk," he concluded in a whisper.

"Okay. You've made your point. Now take it easy, Ricky. I told you I'd work out something. I got an opening in my cell. I'll try to get you in there today. But to do so means I'll have to use a gimmick. Don't worry though, I'm sure I can pull it off. I'll let you know for sure after lunch."

A look of profound gratitude spread over his smooth brown-skinned face. "Aw, thank ya, man. Ya don't know how much I 'preciate what ya tryin' ta do."

"Okay. Okay. Now get back to your machine," I told him.

At lunchtime, we went back to the cellhouse. I had a plan that I knew was feasible—it had been used successfully before. But not all cons knew about it or had the connections to pull it off. Most of the times the gimmick was used for hanky-panky reasons to get a temporary emergency cell transfer. But to pull it off a con had to have solid connections—something I had no problem with whatsoever.

Old Willy Niemoth was the cell house plumber. We were on very friendly terms because I had worked on his case. And only recently, Willy and I had been discussing filing a petition for executive clemency for him. When I stopped on the lower gallery to talk briefly with Willy, I told him to start a toilet leak in Ricky and Slim's cell just before we returned to the cell house after the yard recreation period. Willy knew the gimmick.

He would report that he was unable to fix the toilet because he needed a part that he couldn't get until the next day when the store house was open. The inmates in Ricky's cell would have to be given temporary quarters elsewhere until the toilet was fixed. Next Willy would get his friend the inmate cell house clerk to transfer Ricky into my cell. The clerk, with the knowledge of the cell house keeper, could make a temporary emergency transfer, but he could not make a permanent transfer. Only one of the lieutenants or a captain could order a permanent transfer.

Willy Niemoth was a little old gray-haired man with a good-natured mischievous grin on his wrinkled and ruddy countenance. He questioned my motive for getting Ricky in my cell until I explained to him what the situation was really about. His blue eyes lit up with mirth. "Hell, Blacky, for a minute there I thought you was snatching the fish out of the skillet into the fire," he chortled.

"Not me, you old rascal. I don't go that dirt-road route. You ought to know that, Willy," I said laughingly.

"Okay, I'll handle it for you, Blacky. But you know I don't give a shit what goes on in this goddamn joint when the lights go out," he chortled again before walking away.

Everything worked beautifully. Ricky was transferred into the cell with Wiggins and me. And I wasted no time in telling Ricky what our next move would be to get him permanent residence with us.

I typed a laconic note to the captain in charge of discipline and assignments requesting, as though I were Ricky, to be transferred permanently in the cell with Jennings and Wiggins. The reason given for the transfer stated that Jennings had agreed to tutor Ricky in study-ing for the GED test to acquire a high school diploma. I explained further that Ricky's other cell partners were not qualified to help him because they only had grade school educations, but that Jennings had already successfully passed his GED test.

The note having been couched in language as if Ricky had writ-ten it himself only required his signature under "Respectfully yours."

"Gee! Do ya think this will work, Blacky?" Ricky asked hopefully.

"Hell yes! It'll work beyond a doubt. One good thing about the warden, he's got these screws and brass hats so brainwashed about educating the cons and learning them trades that to deny you this privilege would be like going against Meatball's policy. You haven't got an ass-kissing, brownnose screw in the joint that will dare cross Ragen's policies. Besides, the Cap'n knows that Slim Jones is a big dumb asshole that couldn't teach you a goddamned thing construc-tive," I concluded.

"Amen!" Wiggins exclaimed. "Now, Ricky, you do what Blacky tells you, son, and don't ask no dumb questions. Just do as your ass is told—un'erstan'?"

"Sure. Sure, Wiggins, I gotcha," Ricky acknowledged politely.

"Trouble with most of you young devils is that you think you know it all, that's why you get yourselves in hot water 'round here. A heap sees but only a few knows." Wiggins unloaded with some of his provincial philosophy. "The only way a man can be a bigger fool is be a bigger man, and you is still a growin' boy." He added for good measure.

I looked up at Wiggins stretched out on the top bunk and cracked, "Now that the guru on Mount Bunk has parted with a cou-ple gems of his wisdom, will he please inform our young friend here of the cell rules."

"By the holy beard of a saint, I certainly will," Wiggins said with an important expression on his dark features. "Cleanliness is next to godliness," he said as though it were his own quotation. Then he went on to tell Ricky about the cleanup schedule for mopping the floor and cleaning the toilet every day. Each of us took turns each week doing these chores.

The plot I hatched went off without a hitch. The transfer came through the next day, and Ricky was given permanent asylum in our cell. But I had fortified myself to expect trouble from Slim Jones in the event that it did come. And I did not have long to wait either. Because Slim was pissed off to beat the band. He glared in our direction during the evening meal when we sat down in the dining room. He had demons flaring from his eyes as they peered out angrily from under their droopy lids.

The next day, Slim cornered me in the tailor shop, his hawk-ish-looking face was a ferocious mask of violent anger. "Just what in the fuck do you think you're pullin' off, nigger?" he blustered.

Since I had been expecting to be hassled by Slim, I had put some of my tougher friends on notice to back me. So in my most friendly manner, I said, "What's bugging you, Slim? Why are you coming down on me like this?"

"You know goddamn well why, motherfucker!"

I feigned surprise on purpose. "You mean this has got something to do with Ricky moving in with Wiggins and me permanently?"

"Yeah! That's exactly what I mean, you cock-blockin' bastard!

"Well, you see, Slim, Ricky just wanted me to help him with his case and his studies. He's trying to get a high school certificate. Besides, Ricky's all man, he hasn't got any sugar in his drawers."

"Don't give me that bullshit, man. You think I'm a goddamn fool!" He raved. "You just want him for yourself. I'm hep to you!"

I shrugged. "Look, Slim, I got to get to my machine. I don't want any trouble with you," I said, starting to walk away.

Slim shoved me hard against the wall. He was fighting mad! "Don't walk away from me when I'm talkin' to you, nigger. You might think your shit don't stink 'cause you're some kind of big shit around here. But I'll kick your motherfuckin' ass and chill your goddamned shit. Do you hear what I say, you yella motherfucker! I'll kick your yella ass 'til it's black as mine!"

"That makes five asses you gotta kick, Slim, if you don't unhand the counselor," Tree Top growled menacingly as he stood equally as tall as Slim with a much more imposing muscular build.

Slim Jones looked around to see Tree Top, Red Randolph, Pepper Bob, and Hank Jones all glaring at him pugnaciously. These were big men, two hundred pounders and upward. What's more, they had vicious reputations. Slim's attitude changed abruptly. "Now look, fellas, I ain't got no dispute with you guys."

"And you ain't got none with the Counselor either, is that clear, asshole bandit?" Tree Top growled, thrusting out his chin belligerently as he gripped a long pair of shears in his right hand.

"The Counselor's workin' on my case, mother-ass-fucker! And if you interrupt that, you interrupt my chance of gettin' out of here—and then I'm gonna interrupt your fuckin' breathin'," Pepper Bob spat at Slim.

"He ain't hardly lyin' either 'cause I'll help him take a piece out of your black ass before God can get the news if you fuck with Blacky," Red Randolph threatened him with a sneer.

"Goes for me too," Hank Jones snarled. Pushing himself up directly in front of Slim Jones, he added, "Nigger, you ought to know better than to fuck with the counselor! Has you lost yo' mind, fool?"

Slim had an unmistakable apprehensive expression on his face. He seemed relieved when one of the screws sensed a row and walked over, saying, "Break it up, men, and get back to your assignments or I'll call a white cap in here."

Everyone knew that a white cap meant a lieutenant of the guards, so my allies gave Slim a parting look of menacing stares before walking away. The guard followed them a short distance to see that they returned to their job assignments, and Slim Jones gave me an evil look. "I ain't forgettin' this, Blacky," he growled.

"You better forget it if you want to stay healthy. Like Hank just said, 'Nigger, you ought to know better than to fuck with the Counselor!'" I rejoined nonchalantly. Then I swaggered off and resumed sewing pockets on trousers. Slim Jones had been scared off but good! He was nearing the end of his sentence, and I was sure that he didn't want to chance any serious trouble with me or my allies. The coward son of a bitch didn't have a chance, and he knew it. We didn't have any more trouble out of him after that.

Later. Slim Jones was released from Stateville after completing his sentence. He committed a murder during a holdup not long after he was out. He was apprehended and convicted. His sentence was death by electrocution. But he cheated the chair.

The big bully hanged himself while awaiting execution in the Cook County Jail.

*　　*　　*　　*　　*

We called him "the Muslim." He was a young radical bent on serving the Black Muslim religion with total devotion to such men as Elijah Muhammed and Malcolm X, the two most revered leaders and ministers in the faith.

The spread of the Black Muslim religion was especially intense during the fifties, and its appeal to many blacks by condemning the white man for practically all of the ills in the world that caused the black race to suffer became a rallying force to those blacks who had shown a distrust and disenchantment with the conventional religious tenets propagated by the Christian ministry.

Naturally, Warden Ragen wanted to keep this type of religion out of the prisons that he administrated. Since the Black Muslim faith taught "hatred for the white man's ways"—not his race per se—many white people misinterpreted the true crusade of this fast-growing religion. Such terms as "blue-eyed devils" antagonized white people completely against the Black Muslims.

There were at the time only a handful of inmates in Stateville that professed a belief in the Black Muslim faith. Most of these inmates wanted to embrace the faith although they had never been members on the outside. Because they sensed the power, pride, and potential of this group that often referred to itself as a "nation" seeking change in the white man's world. To seek change in a social revolt or violent rebellion appealed to black prisoners—especially to those who wanted dearly to focus attention and pride on their desperate plight to be recognized as men and equals to the white power structured.

The Muslim was a tall, muscular brown-skinned man in his midtwenties. He was serving a life sentence for murder. Because of

250

his radical disposition, rebellious nature, and outspoken criticism of the prison administration denying him access to a Black Muslim minister, he was always in hot water with the officials. He had spent considerable time in the hole and isolation as well as working on the coal detail. Hard work, rigorous exercises, weightlifting, jogging, and shadowboxing had developed his body into fine physique with great power and agility that would be the envy of many professional athletes. He trained as though he had a purpose for preparing himself for some eventuality. He was aggressive and hard as a rock in body and spirit. It was only a matter of time before this resentful time bomb would explode.

I have seen many inmates, black and white, blow their tops and physically attack other inmates and the officials—sometimes inflicting, if not fatal, substantial physical damage to their victims. But I have never witnessed an attack as vicious and swift as the one the Muslim administered to two lieutenants who were attempting to march him to the disciplinary building for some infraction of the rules.

One of the lieutenants was called Big Mac by the inmates because of his huge and compact build that made him look like a professional wrestler. He used to be a screw in the barbershop when I first arrived at Stateville in 1949. And he was considered a nice guy by the inmates. Funny though how authority can change some screws. Big Mac got promoted to sergeant and later to lieutenant. With each promotion, it seemed that he would get tougher on the cons, as though his toughness and nitpicking about prison regulations would propel him into a captaincy role. Whatever his ambitions were, he was climbing the ladder of success at the expense of other people's misery, and this had earned him the enmity of the inmate body and the displeasure of some of his fellow officers whom he also supervised.

On this day, the other lieutenant, a nice-looking congenial young man, was accompanying Big Mac in walking the Muslim to the "hole" for some alleged serious infraction of the rules. The younger lieutenant, like Big Mac, had started off his career as a likeable screw. He worked as a cell house officer and was promoted to cell house sergeant. Later he made lieutenant. The difference between Big Mac and him was that he remained congenial and maintained his rapport and popularity with the inmates.

I don't know what exactly precipitated the attack that the Muslim made on these two officials. Because I only witnessed the assault from a good distance away. It was, however, later rumored that Big Mac made a racial slur to the Muslim during the walk to the "hole." In any event, the Muslim's attack was lightning-swift and brutally vicious! With one mighty punch, he broke Big Mac's jaw and rendered him unconscious. As he started to kick the unconscious form of the fallen hulk of humanity, the younger lieutenant tried to come to Big Mac's rescue, and he himself was quickly battered into a bloody pulp before other screws arrived to subdue the Muslim, who even then fought off his attackers with a fury and force that was daring and devastating as screws hit the ground and floundered around like a flock of scared chickens being attacked by a lone wolverine.

Needless to say, when the melee finally ended by the guards, overwhelming the Muslim by sheer numbers, he was taken to the disciplinary building and worked over good by his captors before being thrown into an isolation cell where he was kept locked up for years. But there was something about the Muslim's singular courage and rebellious nature that made him an instant hero to the inmates. Perhaps it was because he had sealed Big Mac's mouth for a spell, because his jaw had to be wired together for several weeks while it healed.

Not long after the Muslim attacked the two lieutenants, another black inmate erupted with violence in B-House, knocking out several teeth in a screw's mouth and belaboring another screw until his further agony was mercifully spared by unconsciousness. This attack was also rumored to have occurred over a racial slur.

Perhaps some screws hearing blacks calling one another niggers all day long in a meaningless fashion thought that they could do so too, without risking the ire of a Negro inmate. Most blacks of course ignored the slur with resentment while others known as blow tops would explode into anger and action immediately if a white man called them a *nigger*. After the two recent attacks made on the white screws, the word *nigger* seemed to suddenly disappear from the screws' vocabularies.

In prison one event can trigger another similar event—especially when an inmate has a psychopathic personality. For such an inmate is apt to react to a situation in much the same manner as some other inmate acted, deeming that to be the proper way to handle the situation; and the screws were getting leery of these sudden vicious attacks that they were prone to blame unjustly on the Black Muslim menace that seemed to be cropping up all over the prison. Persecutions and reprisals against the few self-acclaimed Black Muslim inmates were carried out by the officials. Some were placed in isolation and word got back to the other inmates that physical brutality was being administered to the inmates who either attacked the screws or threatened them. Because of the growing militancy among a large number of black inmates, who were not associated with the Muslim faith, the screws, nevertheless, blamed this sudden insurgency on the Muslims in the prison.

Now it was all right for the screws to use whatever reasonable force was necessary to subdue an inmate making a physical attack upon an officer or inmate. But once the offending inmate was subdued, no further physical force should be a part of the inmate's punishment. To do so would be in violation of the prisoner's civil rights.

Certain powerful factions among the inmates prevailed upon me to write a petition for one of the Muslims in isolation, charging the prison officials with denying him freedom of religion and subjecting him to cruel and unusual punishment in contravention of the due process and equal protection clauses of the United States Constitution. I prepared such a petition, and the inmate contacts got it into the Muslim's hands inside the isolation building whereby he was able to have it notarized and mailed by the prison officials to the court, because the officials did not dare refuse to mail an inmate's petition for fear of a contempt citation as a result of Judge Barnes's standing ruling that the prisoners were not to be badgered or denied free access to the courts.

Before long, there was a relaxation of the prison policy against inmates professing an affiliation with the Black Muslim religion.

Some inmates in isolation were released back into the regular prison population. The persecution abated, and the climate changed from one of sheer hostility to one of quiet toleration. And soon afterward, a provision had been made whereby the Black Muslims were permitted ministerial visits. Concessions were accorded the Muslims in their worship without judicial intervention, and our mission had been accomplished.

Physical brutality, which Warden Ragen naturally always denied, ceased being practiced in the isolation building. Judge Barnes had long ago put Ragen on notice that mistreatment of inmates in the "hole" or isolation could lead to the warden's undoing. Because the federal court would be alert to putting a stop to any such mistreatment. Judge Barnes had previously threatened to jail Warden Ragen for contempt because he was reluctant to follow the judge's orders. And it was a fact that the inmates in the Joliet-Stateville penitentiaries could thank Judge Barnes for receiving one meal a day while in the "hole." Because prisoners had been getting only three slices of bread a day and a meal every seventh day. Ragen knew that Judge Barnes was not to be provoked when he spoke about the rights of prisoners.

Perhaps again I was given more credit than I deserved for what legal contribution I had made in helping to initiate actions against the prison officials to bring about fairer consideration for the rights of the prisoners. But I had no control over how the word spread or the stories were embellished during transmission over the prison grapevine. One thing I realized more and more that I did not like was that many of these stories were reaching the hostile ears of the prison officials.

Roger Touhy pulled me aside one day when I came into the cell house. He told me that he had it on good authority that the prison officials were out to "bust" me out of business for good, that I should be on the lookout for it happening any day. Touhy warned me that there was talk of comparing the keys on my typewriter with the type on other prisoners' petitions to obtain proof positive that I had been doing work for them.

Roger Touhy, the notorious Prohibition beer runner, who, with a mob of convicts, escaped over the wall from Stateville in 1942, was perhaps the most maligned racketeer ever to be sent to prison and written about in the press. That he was framed for the kidnapping of John "Jake the Barber" Factor was fully brought out in Judge John Barnes's memorandum opinion handed down after an extensive habeas corpus hearing in the United States District Court for the Northern District of Illinois.

In rendering his opinion on August 9, 1954 in this saga of underworld intrigue, officially induced calumny, political corruption, and state court indifference to aid and abet in keeping an innocent man imprisoned for almost a quarter of a century, Judge Barnes wrote,

> THE COURT is of the opinion and finds and holds that the writ issued out of the Criminal Court of Cook County Illinois, where under Relator Roger Touhy is held for the period of ninety-nine years for the crime of kidnapping for ransom is void because issued on a judgment of that court which is void because the proceedings in that court antecedent to said judgment and said judgment were violative of the Due Process of Law Clause of the Fourteenth Amendment of the Constitution of the United States in that said judgment was procured by means of the use of testimony known by the prosecuting officers to be perjured and because the Relator was deprived in a capital case of the effective assistance of counsel devoted exclusively to protection of Relator's interests and compelled against his will and over his protests to accept the services of counsel who was compelled to serve adverse interests.

Following Touhy's release by Judge Barnes, the state officials broke their asses figuring out another way to get the poor guy reincarcerated, knowing now that Touhy had spent all that time in prison illegally. The state's attitude of "show him no mercy" led the Illinois attorney general to get the United States Court of Appeals to reverse Judge Barnes's ruling that the 199-year sentence given Touhy for aiding and abetting in the escape from Stateville was unconstitutional.

The US Court of Appeals neither held that Judge Barnes was wrong in declaring Touhy innocently imprisoned in violation of his constitutional rights nor that the 199-year sentence was not also unconstitutional as found to be by Judge Barnes; the court of appeals merely held that Touhy had not exhausted all of his state rights in having the Illinois courts review the constitutionality of the 199-year sentence imposed for aiding and abetting in the escape. This ruling placed Touhy back on the old merry-go-round situation. It could take years for him to get this phase of his case litigated in the state courts before returning to the federal court if the state did not find in his favor.

One can well imagine the torment and agony Touhy must have felt when he was returned to prison after such a short taste of freedom—only hours to be exact, or a little less than two days.

Roger Touhy was a rather smallish, aging little Irishman with sad brooding eyes—eyes saddened by the nightmare of suffering long years of imprisonment for a crime he never committed. Calling his case a travesty of justice would be putting it mildly. For it was a monstrous conspiracy engaged in by underworld mob characters, the police, the state's attorney, and a callous disregard for justice shown by some judges sitting in the lower and higher courts of the State of Illinois.

Touhy had the fighting courage of his ancestry ingrained deeply in his heart. He was what we called, in the parlance of a convict, a stand-up guy—meaning his word was his life-long bond, and he didn't back down come fire, wind, or high water when he had to fight for what he believed in. The little Irishman was a giant in courage as anyone would know who has known him personally, as I have, or who has read his book *The Stolen Years*, and the reams of newsprint written about him over the many years that have passed since he was originally imprisoned in 1934. Hollywood also made a movie based on Touhy's life in prison and his escape from Stateville.

Roger Touhy naturally formed a great distrust for law enforcement, judicial and prison authorities. There were very few in those capacities in Illinois that he had a good word for. Most of all, he disdained stool pigeons inside or outside of prison. And he hated injustices of any kind. The thought of framing a person literally consumed him with rage and indignation. Even though he had operated outside of the law by making and selling bootleg liquor, there was no evidence that Touhy had engaged in murders or crimes like the other mob leaders, Al Capone, Bugs Moran, and others of that ilk.

Without attempting to make Touhy resemble anything like a saint, it could be said about him, however, that certain reliable evidence showed that he was a devoted family man, a fair business man and a person with no past criminal record when he was framed for kidnapping Jake "the Barber" Factor, who was known to be a notorious swindler on an international scale. Touhy was tough and willing to stand up for his rights in resisting a mob takeover of his beer business, even if it should lead to violence in protecting his interests, but he was satisfied not to infringe upon anyone else's interests or territory in the bootleg business. And for the most part, he had no difficulties until the Al Capone mob tried to muscle in on his business. When he resisted, they framed him with the help of a swindler, crooked cops, and corrupt politicians.

I was fortunate and glad, indeed, to number Roger Touhy among my friends in the institution. Because of his esteemed stature as Stateville's most famous prisoner, who had taken the number one status and limelight from Nathan Leopold, the inmates and guards alike looked upon Touhy in awe. He, by far, in a quite a way, had perhaps the best tap of the prison grapevine that any prisoner ever enjoyed. For he got unbelievable information from both the inmates and guards. Perhaps because it swells some people's ego to be associated with celebrities, which was a prime reason for Touhy's source of information. In any event, when he told me about the keys on my typewriter being subject to an investigation to connect me with working on other inmates' cases, I gave him my immediate and closest attention.

Touhy was assigned to light work in the cell house—mostly doing nothing but playing cards or walking around, chatting with the other inmates assigned to servicing and cleaning the cell house. "Take heed, Counselor, I just got the info from the mouth of a guard who I can rely on," he told me as we stood off to ourselves by the office where he had called me aside when I came in from work during the lunch hour. As he went on to warn me of the pending danger that he was just privy to, I was all ears. "This guard that gave me the info hates this damn administration almost as much as I do, and he feels the cons should have the right to help each other with legal work since he sincerely believes that I was framed. Every now and then, you run into a 'Good Joe' in this dump. He only told me this because he probably figured I'd pass the word on to you," Touhy finished.

"I can't tell you how much I appreciate this information, Rog," I responded gratefully.

Touhy rubbed his chin with his thumb and forefinger in thoughtful silence for a moment, then he asked, "Do you know the Mex who is the instructor in the typewriter repair shop in the vocational school?"

"You mean Joe? Sure, I know him well. He used to be one of my barber customers."

"Then see if he can change the keys on your typewriter. Tell you what, Counselor, I'll get one of the runners to sound Joe out on changing the keys this afternoon. You get your typewriter down here in the morning and leave it in the office with a request to have it repaired. I'll take care of the rest"

"Thanks again, Rog. I'm sure Joe can handle it."

When I returned to the cell house after work the next day, Touhy nodded me over and told me everything had been taken care of and that I'd have the typewriter back in a few days with a new set of keys.

I will never know for certain whether the officials ever tested the keys against the type on another inmate's petition when I got my typewriter back with the new keys because an official could have easily gotten a sample from the typewriter when I was out of my cell.

It didn't matter though because I was now satisfied that the new keys could not be linked with any work I had done for other inmates, and I felt comfortable knowing that I had Touhy as a friend.

For precautionary reasons, I had to change my writ writing procedure somewhat in preparing petitions for other inmates. Once I prepared a petition on plain white paper, the inmate had to have it retyped on pink paper to comply with the prison rule before it could be sent out to the court. This, of course, prevented the officials in the front office from ever seeing the copy I had prepared. And once again, with the aid of a trusted ally, I had succeeded in outwitting the prison officials.

Chapter 15

IT HAS NEVER MADE SENSE to me, even before I started studying law, why a person accused of a felony that he claims he did not commit would put his fate in the hands of one man—the trial judge. A bench trial—a trial before a single judge or a panel of judges, usually three, who control the destiny of a defendant in considering the facts and the law of his case—certainly, in my opinion, gives the best odds to the prosecution that the defendant in most cases will be convicted. This of course does not always happen, so for the sake of argument, let's just say that it happens about 80 percent of the time.

The prosecutors will no doubt counter my argument with their own argument that convictions result more often because the defendants in most cases are in fact guilty of the crimes that they have been charged are indicted with having committed. Nevertheless, on the other hand, let us say for the sake of argument that only 50 percent of the jury trials result in convictions. The prosecutors will now probably argue, as I have heard them assert, that "jurors are swayed by sentimentality, ignorance of the facts of the case and being overly impressed with the phrase 'beyond a reasonable doubt' that most jurors find it difficult to reconcile what degree of doubt is beyond a reasonable doubt."

True, cases presented based on mostly circumstantial evidence—especially difficult to corroborate evidence—are extremely difficult for the prosecution to establish before jurors the legal requirement of convicting a defendant on evidence which they deem is beyond a reasonable doubt conclusive enough upon which to sustain their verdict of guilty. And if the state's case is weak, a good attorney—and even a mediocre attorney—can have a field day with the reasonable-doubt concept inherent in all criminal prosecutions that are contested. The foregoing percentages I have quoted are my own and can vary greatly in different jurisdictions, but they will remain constant in all state jurisdictions in that more defendants are convicted in bench trials than are convicted in jury trials. Federal courts usually achieve higher percentages of convictions in both bench and jury trials—simply because the feds try to make it a practice of only going to trial when they have a good case; this helps to make the federal system of justice of a higher quality than the justice practiced by the states that attempt to try almost any case in which an indictment is returned no matter how weak the evidence may be. I don't think that this can be fairly disputed by anyone.

At a jury trial, the defendant has twelve people to judge the facts in finding him innocent or guilty. And more than that, the defendant has the thirteenth person—the trial judger who can actually overrule the jury's verdict if they find the defendant guilty and the court believes that justice has not been done to the defendant. But the trial judge cannot overrule the jury's verdict if they find the defendant not guilty. In the face of all these odds in the defendant's favor—including that the defendant only requires one juror's confidence to preclude his conviction—why in the name of heaven or hell would any defendant let some lawyer talk him into taking a "bench trial" if the defendant wishes to assert his innocence? For the life of me, I cannot truthfully understand why—unless the lawyer has got a "fix" going for his client.

From my personal experience of having seen the most rank and unfair justice meted out by many judges sitting in sole judgment on some poor defendants, it is amazing why so many so-called innocent defendants accept that means of being tried—unless, as lawyers will often express to their clients, the intimidating prospect that should they take a jury trial and be found guilty, the state will ask for a stiffer penalty, and the trial court will usually impose a harsher sentence in the jury cases.

A jury trial of course takes longer because it is always more involved than a bench trial. But it is my personal belief that a defendant places himself in more jeopardy facing a single judge who might be biased than by facing twelve jurors who are not all likely to be biased. The judges, no matter how fair they might want to appear, belong to the same courtroom atmosphere as the prosecuting attorney who is sometimes assigned to try cases before one judge whom the defendant's counsel may or may not have ever tried a single case before that same judge. You may be certain, however, that, in any event, the defendant's counsel has not tried near as many cases before the same judge as has the prosecuting attorney if he has been prosecuting cases for any length of time.

Who then is in the best position to know the thinking, whims, or idiosyncrasies of the judge's courtroom behavior? The prosecutor, of course! But put twelve men and women, tried and true, in the jury box and the opposing lawyers are on an equal footing. Neither lawyer is personally acquainted with any of the jurors; otherwise those jurors would not be hearing the case—a peremptory challenge or the judge would have removed all jurors from the jury that admitted knowing personally either of the lawyers involved in the case.

Many times, prisoners in the county jail have asked me this question: "What kind of trial do you think I should take, Counselor?"

I always tell them without hesitation and without reservation: "If you claim you're innocent and you feel there is not sufficient evidence to prove you guilty beyond a reasonable doubt—for God's sake not mine, take a jury trial! And don't let anybody talk you out of it!"

Then too I would go on to explain what the risks were in getting a stiffer sentence but also what the odds were in winning an acquittal or a hung jury, whereby the prosecution would have to lower the terms considerably if there was to be any plea bargaining later on. It is a gamble either way which-ever trial a defendant takes. But since the best gamblers like the best odds in their favor, I recommend the jury trial every time. And most lawyers, if truthful, will have to agree with me that a defendant in most criminal cases stands a better chance of winning an acquittal before a jury than before a judge.

The trouble is that a lot of lawyers do not like to be tied up with one case for a long period—especially when he is representing an indigent defendant or a defendant of modest means. And it is difficult to condemn a lawyer for this because he does have to make a living out of his practice.

In my own particular case, each of the two trials was held before a jury, and each trial took three to four days to complete. These were relatively short jury trials. Had I taken a bench trial, my trial would have been completed in one full day, certainly in less than two complete days.

One method of demonstrating my point that most lawyers are in favor of jury trials rather than bench trials is vividly apparent when there is a tort action for monetary damages where trial lawyers really get down to the nitty-gritty—or to borrow a coined expression, "the needy-greedy." In these actions, the lawyers for the plaintiffs almost consistently elect to have their cases tried by a jury in a much greater proportion than by a judge. The lawyers don't give a damn how long the trial lasts, so long as the pot of gold looks good at the end of the rainbow. But let some of those same lawyers get a client with short funds in a criminal trial and the jury trial suddenly becomes taboo.

While in the county jail, other jailhouse lawyers and myself urged so many inmates to take jury trials that the public defender's office drew flak from the judges of the criminal court when their dockets were getting jammed; they thought that the PDs were at fault for this sudden large request for jury trials.

When it was discovered that we were responsible for urging the prisoners to take jury trials, we were called all kinds of agitating bastards by private lawyers, guys in the state's attorney's office and the judges too. But we didn't give one teeny-weeny shit about what they called us. Because we knew that these fuckers weren't acting in the best interest of the defendants if they complained. All the prosecutors wanted was to get some poor bastard over a barrel so that he could jam it in to the whiskers, and a lot of the defense attorneys were so busy brownnosing the judges that they were not about to offend His Honor by really making a lot of demands on the court's time.

It takes one hell of a lawyer, I'll tell you, to stand before the bar and belabor the shit out of a judge to uphold all of his client's rights—even if sitting there listening to defense counsel's lengthy arguments and presentation of the case irritates the shit out of the judge's piles.

This same type of good defense attorney has to be oblivious to antagonizing the judge or wondering whether the judge will penalize him with disfavor at that trial or at another trial.

The good lawyer—and I have known many—will stand up there and not kiss ass or condescend beyond common courtroom decorum. Because he is sworn to defend his client with all the fervor, diligence, energy, and competency that his intellect and body can muster.

In the end, the judge and prosecutor may not like the defense attorney for his stand, but they will damn well respect him for it if they are firm believers in the judicial code governing the lawyer-client relationship. Because as lawyers themselves, the judge and prosecutor would like to think of themselves possessed of those outstanding qualities of upholding the truest traditions of the legal profession in the defense of a client without fear of reprisals from the bench.

I raised the question of jury trial versus bench trial because one of my clients won a new trial under the Illinois Postconviction Hearing Act; and he, after seeking and being given my advice to take a jury trial in place of a bench trial, let his court-appointed lawyer talk him out of the jury trial in favor of a bench trial. He was convicted and returned to the penitentiary with as much time as he had left behind when he got the new trial.

Now this reconvicted clown comes back in my face, pleading with me to help him again. I just shook my head in disgust and walked away.

The other question that is most frequently asked of me is "Which lawyer is the best suited to try my case, the public defender or a court-appointed attorney in private practice?" This used to be a difficult question for me, and during my earlier days in the jailhouse practice of law, I usually leaned toward the lawyer in private practice. Because at one time, the public defender's office, perhaps unfairly so, was downgraded by so many defendants for placing too much emphasis on plea bargaining, bench trials, and also because the relationship between the public defender's office and the state's attorney's office was too chummy. In other words, too damn much "politicking" was going on in the criminal court building, often at the expense of the indigent defendant.

The "politicking" that went on between private lawyers, the state's attorney's office, and the judges was a horse of a different color. This "politicking" was at the expense of society. Because when the "fix" was in the guilty went free automatically or got taps on the wrists from the judges. "Fix" was not based on rumor. "Fix" was a reality. It existed. It was there. All it took was the right lawyer and the right amount of money.

Many miscreants with money have told me how easy it was to get a "fix" especially in those cases that did not create a lot of publicity; and they have pointed out to me cases in which obviously guilty parties were freed. The "fix" did not always depend on a bribe being given. The word of certain politicians was good enough to get a guilty defendant off scot-free or with a light sentence. And all the "fix" cases were accomplished at bench trials.

It was a known fact in the underworld and around the criminal court building who the lawyers were that could "put in the fix." There were two lawyers in Chicago that had such notorious reputations as being "fixers" that I watched their cases closely. They handled a lot of underworld characters' cases that were in organized crime, as well as those of other ordinary well-heeled lawbreakers; and sure enough, most of their cases ended up with either acquittals, or very light sentences after convictions at bench trials.

Chicago and its seat, Cook County, have both long been known for graft and corruption. It has been prevalent for so long that it has almost grown to be accepted by the populace like the chilled wind that blows off Lake Michigan's shores during the winter months. Political debts have to be settled in many ways, by influence peddling, money, political favors, and a license to break the law given to many crooks and racketeers to assure an ample supply of money coming into the political war chest of the party in power. This was the way of life under political-bossism rule in city and county government when I resided in Chicago and Cook County. And if I can believe what I read in the newspapers and what is written by ace reporters like Mike Royko of the *Chicago Tribune*, then even today. the corrupt city and county climate has not changed to any great degree for the better of what it was when I lived there.

Having watched cases over a period of years in which the public defender's office represented clients, I came to trust and respect many of the brilliant young lawyers or PD's that I came in contact with or gained knowledge of their courtroom exploits in representing their indigent clients. Most of them were dedicated to seeing that justice was done their clients, and with the trial courts now wide open to postconviction hearings and the state supreme court open to direct appeals by indigent defendants, this new legal weaponry gave the public defender's office some extra weapons to fight with—and they used these weapons with great skill in fully protecting the rights of their clients.

Consequently, my opinion about the public defender's office changed perceptibly. Because like the prosecutor, the PD was frequently present in the courtroom of the same judge; therefore he too could gain an intimate insight and knowledge of the judge's thinking, whims, and idiosyncrasies. And once a PD was assigned to a defendant's case, he was not under the pressure to meet other court schedules for other appearances as most lawyers in private practice are prone to suffer. The PD could concentrate on the one case from start to finish without interruption once the case was being tried. And other cases on his schedule could either be postponed or assigned to another PD. Moreover, the PD dealt strictly with criminal law, and he usually became an expert at his specialty.

My confidence in the PD's office, having been completely satisfied by the good work and dedication I observed, caused me to think of the PD as a definite asset and not the liability that previous persuasion had caused me to believe. Now when asked the question, which lawyer was the best suited to try an indigent's case or to represent him at a postconviction hearing or on an appeal, I unhesitatingly recommended the PD. To prove and illustrate my own confidence in the PD's office, I elected to have the PD represent me on my appeal to the Illinois Supreme Court.

*　*　*　*　*

Sometimes I would get so involved in some prisoner's case that I couldn't sleep well at night. Poor old Joe LaBostrie's was one of those cases. Here was an old man over seventy who had been given fifty years to life for selling narcotics. The judge may as well have had Joe executed on the spot. At his age, it was a death sentence.

Old Joe was drawing his Social Security, and he begged me to let him send out some money to his daughter so that she could send it to me to help him win his freedom. He had a hang-up about dying in prison. I, of course, told him to keep his money; I'd help him anyway.

I agonized over old Joe LaBostrie's case. I just had to help him, in every possible way with postconviction petitions and appeals; but always. I refused his generous offers of reimbursing me for my services. And as the months changed over into years, Joe's emaciated body became weaker. Hope was fading in his hollow sunken eyes, and his snow-white hair contrasted eerily with his crinkled black face, toothless mouth and cadaverous jaws. Pity struck a responsive chord in my heart when the Illinois Supreme Court upheld his conviction in *People v. LaBostrie*, and I saw him a few days later standing on the yard tired and forlorn.

Joe greeted me in a lackadaisical manner. "Hiya, Counselor. I got the copy of the court's opinion in my case if you want me to slip it ta ya."

I looked around cautiously before telling him to let me have the opinion. He slid his gnarled, old, arthritic hand inside his jacket and carefully pulled out the court's opinion. I took it from him hastily and slid it inside my shirt.

"Joe, I'll go over this and let you know if it's worth the effort to appeal the Illinois Supreme Court's decision to the US Supreme Court," I said. But I knew that it was useless to appeal the case because at that time, the US Supreme Court had not ruled specifically that the "exclusionary rule" of using illegally obtained evidence in violation of the Fourth Amendment to the United States Constitution was enforceable against the states per se. Although that court had ruled evidence obtained by illegal search and seizure could not be admitted in federal prosecutions. Still. I could not bring it upon myself to destroy what last vestige of hope remained in Joe's sunken old chest.

Then too I felt that one day, the US Supreme Court would make the "exclusionary rule" binding on the states, so I would go ahead and prepare a petition for writ of certiorari for Joe, and I told him so.

The old man placed one shaky hand on my shoulder. "Thank ya, son. Do what ya can for me. Ya know I 'preciate all y'all done. Ever'body has been so good 'bout tryin' to help old Joe. But I don't know what I'd do without ya, Counselor. And I 'preciate all y'all done, done," he concluded in a tired voice.

I tried to smile reassuringly. "Look, Joe, take it from me, this is by no means the end of the line. I'm going to prepare you the best petition for executive clemency that I ever wrote. You can depend on that. We'll file it with the Illinois Board of Pardons and Parole and see if they won't recommend to the governor a commutation of sentence. Hell, Joe, you're getting on up in years, they ought to give you a break. I'll tell them about your poor health too. We'll put in the petition about the heart condition, the diabetes, and the high blood pressure that you suffer from. I'll really make a good plea. If we can get them to mercifully cut some of that time off the fifty-year minimum of your sentence, maybe we can get you out on parole. How does that sound?" I concluded encouragingly.

"Mighty fine, Counselor! Mighty fine!" he responded with a faint smile of hope.

I watched old man Joe LaBostrie as he slowly walked away.

I knew that time was an exigent factor, so I went right to work in raising the question of illegal search and seizure, which was an issue in Joe's case, when I prepared his petition for writ of certiorari. No sooner had that been done than I prepared for him a petition for executive clemency and recommended to him a very trustworthy attorney that he could retain to go down to Springfield and argue his petition when it came up for hearing.

Not many weeks after old Joe was turned down for executive clemency he was taken to the prison hospital where he died a broken-in-mind-and-spirit old man. And when a couple Sundays passed by after his death without the ice cream and pie being dropped off at my cell, I knew then who had been my anonymous benefactor for the past few years.

Chapter 16

MY APPEAL FROM JUDGE GREEN'S court, both the second trial and the postconviction hearing, were heard and ruled on by the Illinois Supreme Court on September 19, 1957. The state supreme court affirmed my conviction and thereby upheld the legality of the confession being introduced into evidence against me at the second trial.

My appeal was represented by the Cook County Public Defender's Office, and Mr. John M. Branion, one of the best public defenders that ever lived, was assigned to my case. Mr. Branion devoted thirty-five years of his legal career to defending indigent defendants.

With him on the appeal was Mr. William F. Fitzpatrick, the exceptionally brilliant young lawyer that represented me before Judge Wendell E. Green at my postconviction hearing. Mr. Fitzpatrick was later in his career to become an associate judge in Cook County.

The Cook County Public Defender's Office was headed by Gerald W. Getty, perhaps along with Mr. Branion, could be called examples of what public defenders should be and do in defense of their poor clientele. Mr. Getty's book titled *Public Defender* clearly outlines these obligations based on his and Mr. Branion's long experience's in representing the indigent underdogs that looked to them for legal assistance. And I will be forever grateful for the interest that all of these attorneys showed in my cases.

In affirming my conviction, the Illinois Supreme Court held in part that

> [d]efendant (Jennings) directs attention
> to differences in Morgan's confession which he

signed in the morning of June 6 (1948) and the joint confession which he signed in the evening of the same day. The first states that defendant actually committed the robbery, brandishing a gun at Barr; the second states that Morgan announced the 'stick-up' and was the bandit who actually perpetrated the robbery. The discrepancies noted are immaterial in character and do not afford a basis for reversal.

I was very much dissatisfied with the "brush-off" type of decision that the supreme court gave this important assignment of error. Because the fact that I signed a so-called confession that was now admittedly untrue showed conclusively that I was not freely and voluntarily making a "clean breast of it," so to speak. The fact also that I was hid out in another jurisdiction's police station that had no charge against me whatsoever and shuttled back and forth to the Oak Park Police Station supposedly to keep me separated from Morgan, until I was compelled to make a joint confession with him, also indicated that I was under constant duress—especially when I had made the joint confession and was again returned to the secret custody of the River Forest Police Station. Why keep me separated from Morgan when according to the Oak Park police, Morgan and I were cooperating beautifully with them by truthfully and voluntarily making our confessions? Then too, didn't they have more than one cell in the Oak Park station?

All these acts and facts clearly suggested to me that the Illinois Supreme Court didn't give one teeny-weeny shit about my constitutional rights, that the court was probably pissed off because it was Talbert H. Jennings who got their unfair ruling in my postconviction case and the *Griffin* case on free transcripts overruled by the United States Supreme Court. This coming from the efforts of a lowly, untrained jailhouse lawyer probably presented a terrible insult to these learned, black-robed scholars of the law sitting at the highest level in the State of Illinois; and the judges evidently had not gotten over their pique or all the egg off their faces for their erroneous rulings in upholding the lower trial courts on the crucial issues raised in these cases. I therefore labeled the Illinois Supreme Court's ruling in my case a "reprisal decision."

For the Illinois Supreme Court to hold that signing an untrue confession, made by a codefendant in which I accepted blame that was not factual, "immaterial in character" with the joint confession I was later compelled to sign—and during the second trial this same confession was suppressed from the jury's factual consideration in comparing it with the so-called voluntary joint confession made by Morgan and I—this in itself was a flagrant disregard for truth and justice on the part of the Illinois Supreme Court. And this was the same unfair court that had pigeonholed and boycotted my postconviction appeal for almost two years, hoping the problem would somehow go away of allowing indigents free transcripts of their trials. But I pushed the *Griffin* case when they dismissed it because I was not about to let the problem go away. Had it not been Griffin, it would have been someone else's case. My determination was unalterable!

Now the august court of Illinois had spoken and my next move after filing for a rehearing and receiving a denial was to file a petition in the United States Supreme Court for writ of certiorari.

The United States Supreme Court denied my petition for writ of certiorari. But this did not mean that the high tribunal agreed with the Illinois Supreme Court's ruling. It only meant that four justices on the US Supreme Court did not agree that the court should review my case. It did not mean either that the US Supreme Court did not believe there was merit in my allegations. Because we will see later that when the case reached the federal district court and eventually ended back up before the US Supreme Court, that court, in remanding my case back to the federal district court, pointed out in its opinion that my allegations did in fact have merit if found to be true.

The following is the court's per curiam opinion handed down in my case United States Ex Rel. *Jennings v. Ragen*:

> The motion for leave to proceed in forma pauperis and the petition for writ of certiorari are granted. "Petitioner, confined under sentence

of an Illinois court following his conviction of armed robbery, sought a writ of habeas corpus from the Federal District Court. His petition contained allegations, primarily concerning the introduction into evidence at his trial of a confession coerced by physical mistreatment by police officers, which if true would entitle him to relief. Appended to the petition were various documents, including an opinion of the Supreme Court of Illinois affirming the denial to him of post-conviction remedies which he had sought in the trial court while his appeal from the conviction was pending. See People v. Jennings. 11 111. 2d. 610, N. E. 2d 612. In that opinion, the state court held that the evidence before it warranted the trial court's finding that petitioner's confession had been voluntary.

The State responded to petitioner's application and urged dismissal. The District Court, on a record limited to the aforementioned documents augmented by a 'report' prepared by an amicus curiae appointed by it, dismissed the application without a hearing. The Court of Appeals, in turn, denied petitioner's motion for a certificate of probable cause, 28 U. S. C. sec 2253, and dismissed his appeal.

It appears from the record before us that the District Court dismissed petitioners application without making any examination of the record of proceedings in the state courts, and instead simply relied on the facts and conclusions stated in the opinion of the Supreme Court of Illinois.

We think that the District Court erred in dismissing this petition without first satisfying itself, by an appropriate examination of the state court record that this was a proper case for the dismissal of petitioner's application without a hearing in accordance with the principles set forth in Brown v. Allen, U. S. 443, 463–465, 506. See also *Rogers v. Richmond*, 357 U. S. 220. It follows that the judgment of the Court of Appeals must he vacated and the case remanded to the District Court for further proceedings consistent with this opinion.

The foregoing opinion was handed down by the United States Supreme Court on January 12, 1959. This was my third victory before the highest court in the land—something almost beyond belief! Most of the best lawyers in this country will never in their lifetime get a single petition for writ of certiorari granted by the United States Supreme Court. Only a small percentage of the lawyers will get a single petition for writ of certiorari granted but will not win their cases; and only a very small percentage of the lawyers will get a single petition granted and win their cases. And for a single lawyer to get two petitions granted in his lifetime and win both of them is rare indeed! But to get three petitions for certiorari granted and win all three in a lifetime is so rare as to be almost unheard of. Yet I accomplished this legal feat of excellence by having all three of my petitions for writs of certiorari granted without having attended one formal law school class in my life, and the questions of constitutional law raised in all three of those petitions were upheld in our favor by the United States Supreme Court.

Needless to say, I had a right to be proud. For I had succeeded in getting the highest court in the country to overrule the criminal court of Cook County and the Illinois Supreme Court twice, both times creating lawmaking and far-reaching precedents. I had now succeeded all alone in getting eight of the United States Supreme Court justices to overrule in their per curium opinion the US District Court and the US Court of Appeals in Chicago, sending a message to those courts and all other federal courts that they cannot summarily dismiss state prisoners' petitions for writs of habeas corpus that presented substantial federal questions without making findings of fact and conclusions of law to support their decisions.

As one prominent lawyer in Chicago said, "The implications of the US Supreme Court's opinion is tantamount to saying to' the lower federal court judges, 'cant' you read plain English when we write opinions saying what the law is?"

Not a single lawyer in Illinois could match my record for successes in the highest court of this land; and to this day very few private lawyers, if any, in the whole country can match or surpass my record established in the United States Supreme Court of having three petitions for writs of certiorari "granted and upheld on review." It is therefore logical to assume that I must have been doing something right and that the courts that were overruled were evidently doing something wrong. In any event, truth and justice was ultimately established to be on the side of the prisoners—thanks to the United States Supreme Court.

*   *   *   *   *

Prisoners who had exhausted all their legal remedies in the courts without success were now turning to the Illinois Parole and Pardon Board in large numbers, seeking relief from long sentences. The object was to get a commutation of sentence whereby the prisoner would either immediately or in the near future become eligible for parole.

The pardon board had recommended to the governor of Illinois that he commute Roger Touhy's kidnap sentence from 99 years to 72 years, and his 199-year escape sentence to 3 years, making Touhy eligible for release on parole in 1959, after having spent 25 years in prison for a crime he did not commit. This in my opinion was the most shitty deal any man ever got in the history of the Illinois State judicial and penal systems, and I felt nothing but contempt for the state's judicial system as well as contempt for the state's administrative body for what I had seen of their indifference to truth in their mock justice system that was despicable and cruel. Touhy should have been freed outright in view of the incontrovertible evidence that was pro-

274

duced at his habeas corpus hearing before Judge Barnes. But the state officials were so damned cheap believing that Touchy might have to be reimbursed for all of the years he had spent in prison illegally that they seized upon the opportunity to release him on parole still under the stigma of having been convicted for the crime that never happened.

Notwithstanding my lack of confidence in these past-proven blameworthy institutions of the law, many other convicts deemed the time propitious for appealing to the Illinois Board of Pardons and Parole; and I, of course, was reluctantly pressed into action. Reluctant perhaps because I had already received a long continuance from the parole board on my three- to fifteen-year sentence. I would not be eligible to see the parole board again until the fall of 1961. To receive demerits now could be disastrous.

My rap partner, Buddy Morgan, had also received a long continuance from the parole board—probably because his prison conduct had not been good. Morgan loved to gamble, and he was caught with contraband several times. He also became moody and was easily provoked. This attitude cost him other demerits on his conduct record for insolence, fighting, and failure to adjust properly in conforming with the rules and regulations of the prison.

Morgan was bitter against the police, the courts, the parole board, the prison officials, and society as a whole. The prison experience was turning him into a man full of animosity, and he never talked about doing constructive things after his release from prison. His mind had reached that deadly impasse—to return to a life of crime and "hold court on the street" if that should become necessary. For Buddy Morgan had become far more dangerous to society now than when he was last on the street. It would be like rolling a barrel of TNT out of the prison gate with a short fuse when time came to release him, such as it was with so many other prisoners when they were released. Because the rate of recidivism at one time showed that for every one prisoner leaving prison rehabilitated at least two or more left prison and committed more crimes. But this was no true criterion either because no one knows for sure how many so-called rehabilitated prisoners turned out of prisons were actually breaking the law and simply not getting caught. This can be based on the logical fact that only a small percentage of malefactors are caught and punished in contrast to the large amount of crimes that are committed in America; whereby this calls to mind when I heard one wag sing this parody to our national anthem just before a sporting event:

> Oh, say does that star-spangled banner yet look
> O'er the land of the duped and the home of the
> crook?

The wag making a mockery of the national anthem probably did so with the knowledge that America is festered with crime and corruption in every walk of life from the lowest to the most lofty, and this is a country with a history of making heroes of crooks and suckers of their victims.

The prison officials and the psychiatric professionals evidently sensed a deep-rooted resentment in Morgan that was psychopathic. And he was transferred to Menard Penitentiary located in Southern Illinois near the Missouri borderline close to an institution called Chester that the state used for the criminally insane.

My prison record had been good—almost exemplary—when I appeared before the parole board. I therefore ascribed the long continuance that I received as a reprisal for my failure to show proper contrition in serving my time without making a nuisance of myself by stirring up all this legal controversy to the great embarrassment of the sovereign State of Illinois. And if in fact that were true, then the board should have paroled me the hell out of Stateville because sure as shit I was going to embarrass the state again, again and again, just as long as I could find something wrong to sock it to 'em about. And the funny thing about all of this was that I was getting one hell of a thrill out of making the officials eat crow as my own personal reprisal for keeping me in prison.

The Illinois Parole and Pardon Board had a chief clerk named Mr. Phillips who was a career employee. He had been around a long time and survived several gubernatorial administrations; and he was generally looked upon as the man who ran things in that office pretty much as he damned pleased with deference only to the chairman of the board.

Phillips was an ex-officio member of the board, in that he had been known to sit in on parole hearings if the board was short of manpower. And in his capacity as chief clerk, it devolved upon Phillips to answer most of the prisoners' correspondence. He was a hard man to bullshit, as well as being thought of as a hard man to get deserving sympathy from.

Some of the old-timers in the prison solemnly swear to the veracity of this anecdote:

A prisoner who received an exceptionally long continuance from the parole board took a course in Bible lessons and began to show a deep interest in religion. Several months after he had received his long continuance, he decided to petition the parole board for a rehearing with a view to being granted an immediate parole. In his letter, he outlined his penitence and described his sincere interest in religion. He even quoted from the Bible the eleventh chapter of St. Luke, verses 9 and 10, "And I say unto you ask and it shall be given you; seek, and ye shall find; knock, and it shall be opened unto you. For everyone that asketh receiveth; and he that seeketh findeth; and to him that knocketh it shall be opened." The prisoner closed his letter, "For the love of Christ."

Several days later, he got a laconic reply from Mr. Phillips. "Dear sir, in reply to your letter, please see St. Luke chapter 11 at verse 7." And Phillips closed his letter, "The Lord be with you."

The prisoner hastily fished a small New Testament out of his shirt pocket that he carried with him constantly. He opened it to the correct quotation that Phillip's had designated, and he read with great disappointment: "And he from within shall answer and say, Trouble me not; the door is now shut."

As one prisoner commented upon hearing the anecdote, "That man Phillips is as cold as my mother-in-law's love."

And I remarked, "If not that, he's certainly as cold as the iceberg that sunk the *Titanic*."

After a few unsuccessful attempts to get results from executive clemency petitions that I filed for other inmates, I finally hit pay dirt.

Willy Niemouth, the D-House plumber, got his life sentence commuted, and he became immediately eligible for parole. Old Willy had been a member of a gang of safe robbers. He and his confederates had burglarized a vault and stole over one hundred thousand dollars from safety deposit boxes, and Willy had been sentenced to life imprisonment as a habitual criminal after he was apprehended and tried. So it goes without saying that Willy was one happy old man when the gates of Stateville closed behind him as he egressed into the world of freedom.

My success with Willy's petition for executive clemency caused Peter Stevens, one of Roger Touchy's rap partners, to seek my services in preparing a petition for him. Stevens had an alias and was known to most of us as Gus Schafer, or just plain Gloomy Gus, because that sobriquet fitted him well since he seldom smiled. When he did smile it was a deadpanish sort of smirk. The smirk combined with his dry humor and quick wit made him a favorite with the prisoners. He was an easygoing, tall and rather slender, good-natured individual in spite of his gloomy appearance.

Gloomy Gus passed newspapers and magazines from cell to cell in the evening after the prisoners were locked up for the night. If a prisoner wanted to let another prisoner see his newspaper or magazine, he simply marked the number of the cell he wanted it to go to on the item and placed it in the door of his cell. Gus would come along, pick it up, and deliver the item.

Passing reading material between the cells was a privilege, and no contraband was permitted to be passed from cell to cell. This rule, however, did not stop Gus from taking chances for "all right guys," so it is fair to say that at times, contraband was passed between the prisoners by Gus.

Gus had received ninety-nine years for his alleged part in the Factor kidnapping hoax. Since he did not escape with Touhy, he had no other sentence.

Now that it had been established by Judge Barnes that the kidnapping was a hoax and publicity and public sentiment decried the frame-up that incarcerated Touhy, who was now free on parole, it was only fitting and proper that Gloomy Gus be given the same consideration. He probably could just as well have written his own petition for executive clemency and got favorable consideration. But as Gus said to me, "I want the Counselor's lucky touch on it, then I know it'll be proper."

Well, the Counselor prepared the petition, and out went Gloomy Gus Schafer on parole. He went to live with relatives in Oakland, California, and later moved to Berkley. He never failed to send me a Christmas card with a little note of gossip about himself. We kept up this mutual exchange of cards and notes for several years after Gloomy Gus's release and my eventual release from prison. Gus wrote to me once to tell me about his new bride. He was keeping his nose clean and doing all right.

One Christmas, I failed to hear from Gus, and I have not heard from him again. It is possible that he has gone to his great reward into the wild blue yonder where the good ex-cons gather. If such a place exists, I'll hope to see him again one day. And I can just visualize old Gloomy Gus soaring around the clouds with wings expanded, shouting, "Gee, Counselor, ain't it grand to be free like a bird!"

Poor Touhy, dogged most of his life by bad luck following his arrest and conviction for a crime he never committed, was murdered not too long after he was paroled. He was gunned down by assassins in gangland fashion in front of his sister's apartment building. His murderers were never apprehended and brought to justice. His was a senseless killing—probably done for revenge or out of fear that Touhy might take reprisals against some of the known people still living who had been instrumental in framing him. But knowing Touhy, I don't think he ever entertained the thought of seeking revenge once he was released from prison. After all, had Touhy wanted to seek revenge on anybody, he certainly could have done so after he escaped from Stateville in 1942.

With Gloomy Gus on my win list, it was just a matter of time before Basil "the Owl" Banghart would seek my services. He got his nickname the Owl because of his rather large slow-blinking eyes and his crimewise background. He was an old hand at breaking the law and escaping from his captors. His record for banditry stretched back a number of years, over a whole lot of territory and in quite a few jails and prisons, including a stay on "the Rock"—Alcatraz. Banghart also had a long record of escapes and attempt escapes. He broke out of the county jail at South Bend, Indiana, and he went AWOL over the walls from such maximum-security prisons as Atlanta, Menard, and Stateville. Crime and violence followed this man closer than his shirttail.

The Owl had received ninety-nine years for the Factor hoax, the same as Gus and Touhy. But his crime sheet was longer, and the escapes only darkened his "rap sheet" that much more with reasons to make his release from prison on parole questionable. Yet if Touhy had been framed on a "hoax"—a crime that never happened—then Banghard too was framed.

There wasn't too much I could say in the way of Banghart being rehabilitated, because to the parole and pardon board, buying that would be like buying the Brooklyn Bridge. I therefore launched into a theme of the injustice of his conviction for the crime that never happened. Apparently, I did a credible job because Banghart too got a commutation of sentence and a parole.

The Owl and I never exchanged cards or notes after his release from Stateville—although he later showed his appreciation with a money order I received through the mail from a lawyer; an enclosed note simply read, "The Owl said hello." I laughed because I always thought that owls said, "Hoo." At least that is what I would have told the officials had they ever questioned me about the note and money order.

When I was released from prison, I did have an occasion to visit Banghart and his wife. They were living on the Southside of Chicago, and he and his wife were custodians of a large apartment building. The Owl had fooled everyone; he had apparently retired from crime for good.

Willy Niemouth, Gloomy Gus, and The Owl were notorious inmates, and they only added luster to my success with executive clemency petitions, which caused many other inmates to seek my services in preparing petitions for them. But I had to decline many of these pleas for help because the workload was too onerous to bear. And I would tell the other inmates that there was nothing extra special in helping Gus and the Owl to win their freedom on parole since it was pretty much a foregone conclusion that if Touhy was framed for a crime that was never committed, then his codefendants, Gus and the Owl, deserved their release also. Even so, I was instrumental in helping several other prisoners to win commutations and paroles. Most of these other inmates had served long terms on their sentences, and they had good prison records that gave every indication of showing signs of making them good risks for release on parole.

There was one very worthy prisoner's case that I enjoyed greatly in helping him to win a commutation of sentence and a parole. His name was Marion Johnson, and I was so incensed with the foul injustice that he received at the hands of an old hanging judge named Dusher, who held court in Rockford, Illinois, that I was determined to do everything possible to help Johnson. When all efforts in the courts failed, I used executive clemency as a last resort to try and effectuate his freedom.

Marion Johnson was a quiet, well-mannered young man with no past criminal record. He had not been long out of the army when he returned home to Rockford and got into a fight at a party where he was attacked by an aggressor with a knife. Johnson shot and killed his attacker who had many rough and tough friends at the same party. They hid the knife and lied that Johnson had fired and killed their friend in cold blood, and they also threatened other people at the party not to reveal that their stories were not true. Old Judge Dusher sentenced Johnson to ninety-nine years for murder in a case at the very most was manslaughter and at the very least "self-defense." My involvement in Marion Jonnson's case became so devoted and dedicated that I kept working on it after my release from prison until I could personally go to Rockford and question some of the people who were at the party on that fatal day. I succeeded in finding two people to confirm Johnson's story that the man he killed did in fact have a knife on the night he was killed and that he had been the aggressor in the fight that took place. I returned to Chicago and turned over my information to a well-known criminal lawyer named Howard Savage, who journeyed to Springfield, the capital of Illinois, where he successfully argued the petition for executive clemency that

I had prepared for Johnson. The pardon board commuted his sentence, and he was released on parole shortly thereafter. Needless to say, the results in this case gave me a great sense of accomplishment and helped to renew my confidence that—in spite of all of the injustices that I witnessed in the State of Illinois—there was still hope that one day justice would prevail not just in isolated cases but in all cases that were clearly deserving of redress for justifiable causes of action.

*   *   *   *   *

Out of the several lawyers associated with me during my imprisonment, of whom I find no fault with any of them, if I had to pick a favorite lawyer, it would have to have been Attorney Sidney Z. Tepper. He practiced law out of the Chicago Loop in a law office with Attorneys Louis Kutner, Reginald Goodwin, and others. Kutner was well-known to the old-timers at Stateville for having helped to pioneer the rights of prisoners to petition the courts clear back in the early 1940s.

Tepper, besides being an honest and sincere person, was one of my greatest, fans in the legal profession; and he never seemed to get over the amazement of my accomplishments under the handicaps I was saddled with by being in prison. I explained that being in prison where I could concentrate on my legal work without the distractions of wine, women, and song together with my monastic existence was the perfect setting for serious study in dreaming up legal strategy to shake the very foundation of the Illinois judicial system.

I became associated with Attorney Tepper through one of my inmate clients who was fortunate in getting Tepper to represent him. And when Tepper reviewed the inmate's case and discovered that I had prepared it, he was so impressed that he made arrangements to visit me personally the next time he came to Stateville. He wanted to get more information on the inmate's case from me.

I thought that was very flattering. Following our visit Tepper and I developed a lasting friendship that continued after I was released from prison until his death. I was so impressed with Tepper's trustworthiness and sincerity that I recommended him with complete confidence to any prisoner who was able to retain an attorney to appear for him at a hearing before the clemency board or at a postconviction hearing. Because I knew that the prisoner's rights would be fully protected, he would only be charged a reasonable fee, and most of all, he would never be sold out. Some prisoners Tepper helped without charge, and the favors he did for me were many.

One evening while seated working at my desk, Wiggins was listening to his radio earphones. We were the only two in the cell because Ricky had recently been paroled and released from prison.

"Some nut has taken over the old Clark Street Federal Building, and he's holdin' the feds at bay," Wiggin's called to my attention.

Being preoccupied, I didn't show much interest. "Yeah, what's that all about?" I asked without getting up to put on my own earphones and listen to the news report.

"The commentator just said, 'The man fired some shots and is now barricaded in the men's toilet in the building."

"The federal court is in that building," I remarked. "I wonder is there any connection?"

"Could be. But whoever this guy is, he's got to be nuts to take on Uncle Sam," Wiggins commented.

"Maybe the guy is nuts. That's a hell of a thing—shooting up the federal building," I remarked before returning to my preoccupation before Wiggins interrupted me.

Later that night, I was listening to a newscast on my earphones when I was startled upon hearing the commentator announce that "the captured man who had barricaded himself in the men's toilet in the old Clark Street Federal Building has now been identified as James B. Jennings." The announcer went on to give James's home address and described the homemade pipe bombs, bulletproof vest, and other weapons that my younger brother had when he was captured.

"Holy shit!" I exclaimed. "This can't be real!"

It seems that James, to put it mildly, was a little upset over being fired from the post office job he held without being given a hearing or an opportunity to express his displeasure over his dismissal with some federal higher-ups. He therefore used violence to call attention to his problem. Fortunately. no one was injured or killed. Wiggins and I spent half the night discussing the event.

James had never gotten into trouble with the law in his life until he became antagonized by being fired from his job with the United States Post Office. He was a probationary employee who found it difficult to adjust to his supervisor.

James had appealed his dismissal to no avail because the Civil Service Commission's rules precluded that body from reviewing the dismissal of a probationary employee.

My brother was later given a psychiatric examination and committed to the state mental hospital at Elgin, Illinois, and he was thus spared a felony conviction and possible imprisonment for his act of terrorism.

James, a tall, thin person with benign features on his handsome face, looked anything but violent. But the old adage that "looks are deceiving" fitted my younger brother quite well. Because when something upset or disturbed him greatly, he brooded within like a volcano gathering strength just before an eruption. James would craftily devise a way to explode. He wouldn't just go off half-cocked. He was too original for that. He would carefully plan his detonation at the right time, the right place, and in what he deemed was the right way to gain a maximum amount of attention for his efforts— like the big news he had made with the reporters and television crews making him the cynosure of the day. He used to later point to that incident and said, "Talbert, I was a very important person when that happened. Everybody listened to me."

No one could deny that James did get everyone's attention. And whenever he spoke to me, I listened with both ears wide open! James had been a patient at the Elgin mental hospital for about two years. We exchanged correspondence all during that time. And when the doctors who treated James decided that he was ready to be trusted back into society, the government apparently thought otherwise.

James appealed to me to use all of my legal know-how to effectuate his release, or he was going AWOL right out of that hospital to demonstrate his further displeasure with the government. I therefore immediately turned the matter over to Tepper, who filed a habeas corpus petition and got James released from the hospital without further delay. And from then on, he was treated as an outpatient.

The electrical shock treatments that James had received in the hospital evidently affected his ability to function as a normal human being. He seemingly suffered from megalomania and became so obsessed with bringing peace to the world that he deluged the United Nations and Congress with letters and pamphlets suggesting how peace could be brought to the world, and he went so far as to write several songs in tribute to World Peace and the United Nations. This in itself, under normal conditions, would not be an indication of mental disturbance. In James's case though, it bordered on fanaticism; and when his letters did not receive favorable attention or consideration, James would become enraged. His subsequent letters would take on a threatening tone. As a result, when one of James letters reached the White House, the FBI and the Secret Service started keeping a close eye on my younger brother. James was delighted to know that he was that important to be "guarded" by the FBI and Secret Service.

Such hallucinations and obsessions with impracticable ambitions left James totally disabled to function in the normal work forces, and he subsisted off his Social Security disability benefits and infrequent odd jobs, painting and decorating on a self-employed basis. He never really resorted to actual violence again—even though on occasions, he threatened violence when he became greatly upset about something.

James simply went right on petitioning the United Nations and Congress—just as I went right on petitioning the courts. So my younger brother and I had much in common in that respect. We were trying to get the government to *listen*!

The will to fight injustice, real or imagined, lies dormant within all of us. It only takes a certain something to trigger our indignation and bring it to the fore. Whether we deal with the problem constructively or radically depends on each individual's concern and frustration. It is always easier to grab a weapon (symbol of violence) than a book (symbol of reasoning). James did it with a gun. I did it with law books. In either case, we both succeeded in getting the government to *listen*!

Chapter 17

SOME JUDGES AND PROSECUTORS REGARDED many defendants called before the bar of justice as just plain scum because they were the products of broken homes, uneducated, poor, and victims of the ghettos and slums. These court officials did not care or stop to think that the influential and affluent elements of society had actually created these conditions by their unwillingness to recognize and use their influence and affluence to try to change and rectify some of the inequities that existed between the haves and the have-nots. But the most pathetic thing about the concept of designating members of the lower-class "scum," when they appeared in courtrooms expecting justice, was all too often an innocent person, like virgin soil, would be washed down the river in this flood tide of indifference along with the so-called scum. Because the callous, unfair, and biased attitude of some police, judges, and prosecutors made the true dispensation of justice a farce, and sometimes because of these prejudicial attitudes they could not differentiate between the innocent and the guilty. As a consequence, innocent men and women were punished unjustly by being flushed into the stigmatic sewer of conviction and piped into the disposal plants of immurement for supposedly purification and reformation at places like the Joliet-Stateville penitentiaries.

While Roger Touhy and his codefendants were the most prominent prisoners that I served time with who were imprisoned unjustly, there were other innocent men that I was acquainted with that were equally victims of the state's cruel injustice by keeping these men imprisoned for many years for crimes they did not commit—even though the evidence was quite cogent in some of these cases in indicating that some prisoners, indeed, were innocent.

Were it not for Judge John P. Barnes compelling the State of Illinois to let these prisoners' cries of injustice be heard, these innocent men may have died in prison. And who really knows how many innocent men and women actually have died in prison because their cries of injustice were suppressed behind the sordid impassable walls of deprivation. But thank God today that all prisoners imprisoned in the penitentiaries have access to the courts and the tools to chronically protest their innocence.

One innocent prisoner that I was friendly with in Stateville was Earl Pugh. In fact, my acquaintance with Earl went back to 1939 when we were both inmates at Pontiac—an Illinois penal institution that housed mostly first-time felony offenders in their teens and twenties.

Earl was later transferred from Pontiac to Stateville. And I had no idea at the time that he was carrying such a tremendous burden—serving ninety-nine years for a murder that he did not commit, because I had never heard Earl mention his innocence until our paths crossed again in Stateville in 1949.

Earl Pugh was a nice-looking young man with a medium-brown complexion who had a pleasant personality. He was always interested in his music. He played guitar and sang well. Being always seemingly of a pleasant disposition. it must have been hell for him to conceal within himself the fact that he was spending the best years of his life in prison for a crime he did not commit.

To Earl, his case probably seemed hopeless since he was without funds or the necessary help to organize some kind of fight to prove his innocence. But once he reached Stateville and Judge Barnes's memorandum in the *Borgiorno* case, supra opened the way for prisoners to present their claims to the courts, Earl got his first encouraging opportunity to try to establish his innocence and thereby gain his freedom. But that was not to come soon because of the legal merry-go-round situation that existed in Illinois for many years as to which remedy was the appropriate one to raise questions of violations of a prisoner's constitutional rights to obtain his conviction.

As discussed earlier in this book, it was not until my case finally opened the way with a clear-cut procedure for an adequate postconviction proceedings that prisoners like Earl Pugh were given an opportunity to fully litigate their claims of wrongful imprisonment based on contravention of substantial constitutional rights that resulted in their convictions. And it was only then, in 1952, did Earl Pugh finally get his big chance.

The facts in Earl Pugh's case showed as shocking a disregard for his rights as one might find hard to believe in a civilized society—especially shocking because the police suppressed good evidence by credible eyewitnesses, which indicated that the guilty party could not have been Earl Pugh or his codefendant, Walter Fowler.

The facts developed at Pugh's postconviction hearing before Judge Daniel Covelli of the criminal court of Cook County revealed that Pugh had been arrested in September 1936 by the Chicago police. He was with another man named Walter Fowler, and both these black men were later accused of the murder of a white man named William Haag, who had apparently been stabbed to death while being the victim of a robbery.

Pugh and Fowler were locked in separate cells and held incommunicado. After that Pugh gave a nightmarish account of beatings, deprivation of food and water, threats to shoot him, and systematic torture that went on for six days. Reaching a breaking point when he was told that Fowler had signed a confession implicating him, Pugh also signed the confession. By this time, both men had endured a horrible ordeal at the hands of the barbarous Chicago police and were powerless to resist the dictates of their captors.

In January 1937, Pugh and Fowler were convicted solely on their confessions. The only witnesses to appear against them were the police and the deceased man's wife—neither of whom were present at the scene of the murder.

The court sentenced Pugh and Fowler to each serve a sentence of ninety-nine years in the Illinois State Penitentiary after they were found guilty by a jury. And it was not until seventeen years later that Earl Pugh was granted a new trial under the Illinois Postconviction Hearing Act.

The state refused to prosecute Pugh at a second trial, and he was set free. Fowler, his codefendant at the original trial, had died in prison in 1949 and was buried in the prison graveyard, or he too apparently would have been vindicated and freed from prison. Ironically, there is an inscription in the prison graveyard near Walter Fowler's final resting place. It read: "THEY PAID THEIR DEBT TO SOCIETY. MAY GOD REMIT THEIR DEBT TO HIM."

A fitting epitaph to those responsible for sending these innocent men to prison, after brutally coercing confessions from them and suppressing evidence in their favor, should read, "THEY STILL OWE THEIR DEBT TO SOCIETY. MAY GOD CONDEMN THEIR CRUEL SOULS TO HELL."

Fortunately for Earl Pugh, he had George N. Leighton to represent him at his postconviction hearing. This was the same attorney who represented me before Judge Wendell E. Green at my second trial.

Mr. Leighton produced evidence from the police file on the Pugh and Fowler case that the police had taken statements from two eyewitnesses to the crime. One of the witnesses, Henry Cooper, stated that he saw a man known to him pursuing a white man with a knife at the same time and on the same date and at the same place that the victim Haag was killed. This statement was made by Cooper on the same day that Pugh and Fowler were arrested.

A housewife, Mrs. Mildred Bradley, gave her statement on the day before Pugh and Fowler were arrested. She stated that she saw the same thing happen—a man known to her by name pursuing a bleeding white man with a knife. Both of these witnesses' statements named the man who had the knife and was chasing the wounded white man. The police, however, apparently never arrested the real culprit. They instead framed Pugh and Fowler as the perpetrators of the crime after inflicting callous brutality on these two men to coerce them into signing confessions.

On June 19, 1953, Judge Covelli granted Pugh a new trial based on his allegations of use of a coerced confession to obtain his conviction for a crime he did not commit. And he was freed from further prosecution and released on June 23, 1953, after spending seventeen years in prison.

Some people might think this case of Pugh and Fowler is an exaggeration and that the police, sworn to uphold law and order would not do such despicable" things as occurred in Pugh-Fowler case. They may believe what they will. But this is no isolated case. Here we have one man deprived of seventeen years of his prime life and another who suffered the ignominy of death in prison and burial in a prison graveyard—all suffered for a crime they did not commit.

The State of Illinois was so shamed by this grave injustice in the Pugh case that Attorney Leighton pursued the matter to that state legislature. The legislature approved a sum of $51,000 to be paid to Earl Pugh for the seventeen years of false imprisonment. This amounted to $3,000 for each year Pugh was incarcerated in a hellish nightmare of deprivation caused by the mental anguish of knowing that he was innocent.

I have seen Earl Pugh many times in the Cleveland area since my release from prison. We have visited one another at each other's homes. We have talked about the old days at Stateville, and we have compared the law today with the law of twenty-five and thirty years ago. While we both agree that many changes for the better have been put into force to protect prisoners' rights, some innocent men and women, however, still get caught in the web of overzealous police-work and malicious prosecution to end up being punished unjustly for something they did not do.

Since Earl Pugh and me both suffered brutality at the hands of the police and realize that even today, some police are not above using such illegal tactics, the courts ought not to ever let their guards down or close their eyes to the reality of man's inhumanity to man—even when he is a police officer sworn to protect those that he abused.

Roy E. Eaton is another old-timer who I was well acquainted with. We studied law together and shared in many yard-court sessions while serving time in Stateville. Our closeness can be seen in the same Federal Supplement that reported our civil rights cases in the same volume.

I sued the police and prosecutors in my case, and Eaton sued the warden, the head of the Illinois Department of Public Safety, and other state and federal officers for false arrest, kidnapping. and false imprisonment. The US District Court for the Northern District of Illinois and the US Court of Appeals for the Seventh Circuit said that Eaton did not state a claim upon which relief could be granted—just as they had held in my case, supra.

Roy Eaton, cagey little white man in his fifties was a feisty and scrappy fellow. He maintained his innocence and was in almost a constant feud with prison officials over his unlawful imprisonment and the means he employed to try and gain his freedom.

Neither Roy nor myself were getting very far with our latest petitions to gain our freedom, so we decided to employ a new approach to obtaining hearings in the federal court by endeavoring to sue the people responsible for our unlawful confinement in asking for compensatory and punitive damages. Hence, we ended up in the same law book without gaining the results that we had sought to achieve in those particular cases.

Roy Eaton, however, did finally receive a day in court under the Illinois Postconviction Hearing Act, and it was established that he had been deprived of his freedom for over fifteen years in violation of his state and federally protected constitutional rights. The evidence further showed that Eaton was innocent. He had been arrested and convicted for armed robbery in Rock Island, Illinois, in 1940. At all times, Eaton vigorously insisted that he was innocent. He constantly petitioned the state and federal courts for relief. He rode the Illinois legal merry-go-round until his head swirled with frustration and bitterness. But finally, justice under the Illinois Postconviction Hearing Act triumphed! Eaton was vindicated and finally liberated after fifteen years of cruel and undeserved punishment. Like Earl Pugh, he too received a monetary award approved by the Illinois Legislature because of false imprisonment.

Some readers may be familiar with the *Joe Majczek* ease. They may have seen the motion picture titled *Call Northside 777* starring Jimmy Stewart and Richard Conte. Some scenes of this movie were filmed on location at Stateville. The scenario of the *Majczek* case was based on a true life drama of an Illinois prisoner who served eleven years in prison for the murder of a Chicago policeman that he did not commit.

Majczek had been tried and convicted and sentenced to serve ninety-nine years in prison, and several years after that conviction, his mother, who had always believed in her son's innocence and never gave up hope of trying to gain his freedom, decided to place an ad in the old *Chicago Times* newspaper.

Mrs. Majczek worked as a charwoman and saved $5,000 from part of the little money she earned to help free her son. The ad placed in the *Chicago Times* newspaper offered a $5,000 reward to anyone who could come forward with information that might aid in freeing her son.

A reporter on the staff of the *Chicago Times* saw the ad and immediately interested himself in the case from a human-interest point of view. And it was through this reporter's long, tedious, and persistent investigation that he came up with sufficient evidence to establish Majczek's innocence.

Joe Majczek won a pardon and was freed from prison in 1945. A monetary award was approved by the Illinois Legislature for his false imprisonment. He had spent eleven years in prison for crime he did not commit; a codefendant Theodore Marchinkiewicz with Majczek was later pardoned. He had also been sentenced to serve ninety-nine years for the murder of the policeman.

There of course have been other cases of false imprisonment in the Illinois prisons, as well as in prisons all over these United States of America. The cases I have pointed out, however, are cases so clearly repugnant to the constitution and laws of Illinois and the federal constitution that no one can question their authenticity. The State of Illinois has commendably acknowledged the validity of the false imprisonment by awarding each misfortunate prisoner with a sum of money—money that will never fully repay these men for the anguish they suffered and the years they lost behind the cold concrete walls that shut them off from the free world for some of the best years of their lives. And in most of these cases, it was uncondonable police brutality, disregard for legal rights, and malicious prosecution that doomed these men to a living hell for crimes they did not commit.

I have pointed these cases out as support to the legal axiom that "there cannot be one set of rules for trying the innocent and another for trying the guilty." There can be only one set of rules to try a person under which a standard of justice to assure the fullest protection of an individual's rights must be vigorously upheld and adhered to.

My case differed from Pugh's with respect to the coerced confession issue in that Pugh was innocent and I was actually guilty. But that does not excuse the police brutality that I and my codefendant Buddy Morgan suffered at the hands of the Oak Park police because they had no right to use brutality to obtain an involuntary confession in either case. I could have been innocent as so many other men have been. The law is therefore clear that innocence or guilt has no bearing on the fact that a coerced confession is not admissible evidence. The test is "whether the confession was voluntarily made." But I did profess my innocence from start to finish with the exclusion of having been forced to admit guilt under the pressure of coercion and brutality, which I promptly retracted when I was safely out of harm's way.

Power is a heady thing indeed! And all too often, the police take the law into their own hands and try to be three things that they are not—judge, jury, and prosecutor. Sometimes they take on the role of executioner also.

It is not my purpose to condemn all law enforcement officers for what many do (and notice I did not say a few) in violating rights of suspects and accused. Many such police officers think that their badges give them a license to impinge upon the rights of others with impunity. These kinds of police officers are bullies with badges, billies, and bullets that are oftentimes guilty of misconduct in purported/enforcing the law; and their misdeeds breed animosity among the citizenry as well as among the people they send to prison. Consequently, law enforcement suffers a bad image and loss of respect everywhere.

Reissfelder won a new trial in June 1982 because of a deathbed statement in 1972 made by his codefendant, William Sullivan, who was dying from leukemia.

The most interesting and repugnant thing about this case is that five policemen, an FBI agent, and a probation officer all submitted statements that original investigators knew Reissfelder was not Sullivan's partner in the robbery.

We thus see that nothing has really changed in the many intervening years since Touhy, Pugh, Eaton, and Majczek were illegally imprisoned by conniving law enforcement officials. It seems to be a consistent fact that in all these types of false imprisonment cases the police either used brutality to obtain confessions, perjured themselves or suppressed vital evidence that they were aware of that could have spared the defendants an undeserved trip to prison.

We experienced lawbreakers and ex-lawbreakers know that the conditions for sending innocent people to prison were and still are prevalent within the ranks of law enforcement officials and indifferent court officials. This is something that has been going on for scores of years in America and is not peculiar to any geographical area. And although suspects and defendants can expect their rights to be protected better today than ever before—the sad fact still remains that innocent people are being convicted and sent to prisons for crimes they had no knowledge of. One only has to pick up the newspaper to read all too frequently about cases of false imprisonment.

＊In November of 1980 Floyd "Buzz" Fay was freed after spending two years in prison in the London Ohio Correctional Institute. Efforts by a public defender named Adrian Cimerman led to new information in the March 1978 robbery-murder of Fred Ery, owner of a Perrysburg, Ohio carry-out store, and a William Quinn, nineteen, of Perrysburg was charged with the crime that Fay had been falsely imprisoned for. Now authorities say that they are convinced of Fay's innocence. The trial judge said, "I'm just glad Ohio didn't have a death sentence then. If we would have had one, Buzz would be dead right now."

In October of 1982 Ohio, got another shock when it was discovered that William Bernard Jackson had served more than four years in prison for two rapes the state now concedes he did not commit. Another man named Edward Jackson was apprehended and charged in Columbus, Ohio with thirty-six counts of rape and forty-six counts of aggravated burglary including the two rapes that William Jackson was unjustly convicted for. William Jackson was the victim of mistaken identity because it is alleged that he resembled

Edward Jackson; others, however, say that the two men do not really bear a striking resemblance.

In November 1982 the newspapers are out with the story of Isidore Zimmerman who spent twenty-five years in prison and nine months on death row for a murder he did not commit. Zimmerman contends that a state prosecutor had tried him for a murder the prosecutor knew he didn't commit and suppressed evidence that proved him innocent. Zimmerman was convicted of killing a policeman on the Lower East Side of New York in 1937 when he was only nineteen years old. He was an hour away from dying in the electric chair when then Gov. Herbert Lehman commuted his sentence to life. For twenty-four years and eight months Zimmerman stayed in prison where he smuggled in law books that in those days were considered contraband for prisoners. He finally was able to prove his innocence.

In January 1983 the newspapers are back again with the story of an innocent man being imprisoned. He is Steve Titus who was convicted of rape and faced ten years and four months in prison. Titus was innocent although he almost went to prison for another man's crime. He was spared from prison by his own determination and a newspaper investigation of the charge against him. Titus was the victim of a mistaken identification, but he was also the victim of poor police work. Among the discrepancies gathered by Titus and the *Seattle Times* newspaper reporter, Paul Henderson, who won the Pulitzer Prize in 1982 for his efforts on Titus's behalf, were these facts: The rape victim and her friend changed their stories about the time the attack occurred. The changes worked against Titus's account of his whereabouts. In court, the victim changed her recollection of the attacker's license plate to fit that of Titus more closely, and an investigator wrote that the victim "pointed out the exact location where the suspect vehicle had parked" and there were "fresh tire tracks where the vehicle would have traveled."

But they did not match Titus* tires. Another new suspect was arrested who eventually admitted the rape that Titus had been accused of, and when the victim viewed the new suspect's picture, the seventeen-year-old who had implicated Titus looked at it, cried and said, "Oh my God, what have I done to Mr. Titus?"

Titus lost everything, his fiancée, his job; and his family lost their life savings of $9,000 to help him with his defense. The thing that hurt him the most though was that "No one ever apologized," he said. He filed a $20-million damage suit against the Port of Seattle, alleging that an investigator lied and persuaded witnesses to change their testimony.

Some people like to shrug their shoulders and say: "Sure there's a few cases where someone is falsely imprisoned, but most of "'em are guilty as sin." I often wonder how the people that make similar statements would feel if they found their asses in prison for a crime that they did not commit. Even one case of false imprisonment is too many! And God only really knows how many people are actually suffering false imprisonment; because if you listen to the prison populations in America, over half the inmates inside the walls claim to be innocent. We of course know that that is a greatly exaggerated figure. Yet who can say truthfully just how many really are innocent. Once a person arrives in prison the natural thought that enters most people's minds is that he belongs there. And one of the most difficult things in the world is for the innocent person to prove that he does not belong there.

These innocent people in prisons could be helped considerably if the law in the first place would take every precaution to see that all laws are enforced to assure defendants the fair and impartial trial that the law guarantees them. The legal maxim that says, "Better ten guilty go free than even one innocent be wrongly convicted" is a good one. It should be adhered to in considering a person's guilt or innocence beyond a reasonable doubt.

In a subsequent chapter in this book I will demonstrate conclusively how easy it is to build a false case against a defendant and start him on his way to prison. Only in this case it is not going to happen. Because given the right know-how and expert legal assistance, with a bit of luck, cases founded upon circumstantial and manufactured evidence can be exposed before a jury in open court for what they really are—frame-ups.

*   *   *   *   *

My own case, *Jennings v. Illinois*, supra, and other precedent setting cases like it that opened the gates of the prisons for others but did not open the gates for the person/s whose case set the precedent proved to hold true in the *Griffin* Case, supra. Because the Illinois Supreme Court, upon finally reviewing the trial court transcript on writ of error, held in a ten-page opinion handed down in January 1959 that there were no reversible errors in Judson Griffin and James Crenshaw's case. The court thereby affirmed the trial court's judgment of conviction.

The news came as a hard blow to James Crenshaw who was suffering from cancer. Not long afterwards he died in the prison hospital in Stateville. Judson Griffin and Richard Riles, the other two codefendants, were subsequently given paroles, and the case was closed as far as they were concerned. But the wonderful precedent that the *Griffin* case set will never die or be closed to indigent defendants who believe that they have been unfairly convicted and wish to appeal their cases directly to the higher appellate courts. And the *Jennings* and *Griffin* cases will always be remembered the most by the many prisoners the cases helped to win new trials that eventually led to their freedom.

A whole decade had gone by, and I was still in the midst of battle over my conviction. Much had been accomplished for others in winning their freedom, but not very much had been accomplished for me. The time had passed so swiftly that I found it difficult to believe that I had been incarcerated over ten long years. My mind was never idle during those years, and this made my ordeal a lot easier.

My foster mother, during one of our visits, had told me that God was using me "to help others and to combat the evil of the Illinois judicial system as a token of remission" for my own sins. And she went on to quote the Bible that "the truth shall make you free." She told me that "before there could be justice there first must be truth; that the truth was hid inside me concealed from everyone" but God and myself. I would therefore have to be truthful with myself in acknowledging my sins and pray to God for forgiveness, strength, and guidance. Then when my purpose in prison is finished according to His Plan, God would see to it that I was delivered from my imprisonment.

I pondered in essence what my foster mother had related to me; and I knew that this wonderful old lady, steeped in her unwavering faith in God and wise in the knowledge of the ways of mankind, was telling me what was wrong in my life; and that if I couldn't admit my faults and sins to others to at least admit them to myself before I could be free of the evil thoughts and things that had brought this imprisonment upon me.

There was much truth in what my mother had said. I had been so busy fighting the injustice of my conviction that I had lost sight of the guilt involved. "Two wrongs don't make a right." It was wrong for me to commit a crime, and it was equally wrong for the officials to convict me on a coerced confession and perjured testimony. Two wrongs. Yet the only right was in the truth. I was paying my debt by serving an exceptionally long sentence for a crime in which no violence was inflicted—not a single scratch did the victim suffer. And prisoners came and went who did far worst crimes and served far less time for their crimes. But the State of Illinois was paying its debt too, paying it in time, money, and embarrassment by keeping me in prison. The cost alone for transcripts for the poor would eventually run into millions of dollars combined with other court costs for post-conviction hearings and appeals. Yes, the state was being punished. "Fair exchange is no robbery," I thought. The State of Illinois and I are both guilty as hell! There, I have admitted it for both of us. My conscience is clear, and the whole experience has been a learning process from the very beginning. I'm a better man for the experience. I am wiser, stronger, and full of self-confidence. I have nothing to be ashamed of. I can hold my head high. My resentment had paid off in a constructive way. And I could leave it behind as a memento to the sovereign State of Illinois that if crime doesn't pay the criminal, then injustice doesn't pay the state either. I could therefore leave prison not as a loser but as a winner of the highest degree.

Attorney Sidney Tepper wrote me a letter advising me that *Ebony Magazine* was interested in doing a story about me. He and Attorney Reginald Goodwin had been in conference with the editors and Warden Ragen. Only my permission was required before a writer and photographer could come out to the prison to take pictures and interview me. The publicity could be a help I thought, and I gave my permission for the interview.

Several days later, I met Mr. Larone Bennett Jr., who wrote the story about me. And the story was published in the 1959 September issue of *Ebony*. It was a good article that brought me many kind and sympathetic letters from all over the country. One of the letters I received was from a lady I had met before my imprisonment. She recognized me in the article and wrote me a long letter full of praise and encouragement for the legal battles that I had waged and won. I couldn't reply to all of the letters I received as a result of the *Ebony* story, but I did manage to reply to some with the help of special letters issued to me by my friends, the Catholic priest and my own priest. I answered the letter that I received from a schoolteacher. Her name was Juanita and she lived in Cleveland, Ohio.

Juanita had a sister and other relatives living in Chicago that she visited on occasions, and she wrote in one of her letters that the next time she visited her sister in Chicago, she would like to also visit me in Stateville. I of course encouraged her to do so. In the meantime, I had Juanita added to my regular list of correspondents and visitors so that we could continue writing to one another on a regular friendship basis.

Following the *Ebony* story, Gladys Erickson, a reporter on the staff of the old *Chicago American*, did a feature article about me. She is also the author of Warden Ragen's biography titled *Warden Ragen of Joliet*. Some other newspapers also got in on the act and the outside world was beginning to learn about my legal exploits.

More letters of encouragement reached me; and for the first time that I had been in Stateville, Warden Ragen, who was no stranger to publicity himself, showed an interest in me. He laughed off the fact that I had emerged unscathed by prison discipline after doing all that legal work in his prison in violation of the rules. In front of the reporters, he let bygones be bygones in favor of sharing my publicity favorably by taking credit for the rehabilitation factor in my prison life, such as finishing high school, the barber trade, and the training I received in the prison tailor shop. He even whispered to me while the *Ebony* photographer was taking our picture together: "This might help you get a parole, Jennings. Play up your rehabilitation efforts. You don't have a bad prison discipline record. I'll put in a good word for you."

True, I did have a good prison record with only one major blemish that was caused by a fight I had with one of my cell mates who resented the noise I made typing all during the evening. He had a history of mental illness during his incarceration, and he was serving life as a habitual criminal. He was the type of prisoner that we inmates referred to as being a "touch hog," meaning he was apt to fly off the handle under the slightest provocation.

During the dispute over my typing so much, he suddenly made an attack upon me. I of course defended myself against his attack with all of the ferocity that I could muster, and my assailant ended up being treated in the prison hospital when I was finally able to subdue him with a well-placed stool on his semibalding cranium. I was immediately thrown into the hole by the officials where I spent several days before being given another assignment on the coal detail in B-House. A few months later, my punishment was lifted, and I was assigned as a clerk in the B of I (Bureau of Identification) where the records of all incoming and outgoing inmates were processed.

You had to hand it to him because Joe Ragen was his own best public relations man. For all of his pretentious modesty, he sure knew how to milk the press for publicity. At one time, he had the public believing that he even had Basil "the Owl" Banghart supposedly eating out of his hand when he returned to Stateville after serving his sentence in Alcatraz. Following his escape with Touchy and after his capture, the federal government had Banghart taken into custody on an old warrant to serve time that Banghart owed Uncle Sam. When he satisfied that debt, Banghart was returned to Stateville to resume his sentence for the alleged kidnapping conviction that he had been serving time for before his escape.

The Owl was prison wise and extremely deceptive. While Warden Ragen might have thought that he was using The Owl, The Owl was also using him to stay out in the prison population instead of being thrown into isolation. That way Banghart would be in a position to better take advantage of any opportunity for escape that might present itself in the future, so he continued to say nice things about the warden.

Roger Touhy, on the other hand, was one man that the famous Warden Ragen could never reach. He never lied about his dislike for the warden. Touhy was never two-faced with anyone. He was a man of strict principles and of good character no matter what anyone might say to the contrary. I never heard one single convict say anything bad about Roger Touhy; they all had nothing but praise for him.

Touhy was the victim of the corruptive system that prevailed during his time in the politically dominated judicial system and the controlling underworld influence with governmental law enforcement agencies in Cook County and Downstate Illinois. The truth finally made Touhy a free man. But what a price he paid before the truth set him free—only to be cut down by the bullets of assassins lurking in a basement across the street from where he resided with his sister.

Chapter 18

WINNING VICTORIES IN THE *JENNINGS* and *Griffin* cases that opened wide the doors of the state courts to indigent prisoners' appeals gave me immense satisfaction. But when the United States Supreme Court reversed the United States Court of Appeals of the Seventh Circuit and the United States District Court in Chicago, that was by far my greatest hour! My grandest triumph! It was the coup de theatre as the final curtain descended on the drama of my fight for justice for myself and the other prisoners. The US Supreme Court's decision left a cul-de-sac that closed off the lower federal courts escape from the responsibility to hear and decide a prisoner's federal questions of alleged infringements upon his constitutional rights.

One thing, however, that had always puzzled me throughout the state courts and the federal courts that I petitioned was how the judges of these courts failed to make the correct interpretations of the opinions of the United States Supreme Court in their applications to the questions of constitutional law that were raised in the petitions I prepared for myself and the other prisoners. For some of these judges seemingly left themselves open for surefire ridicule from the high tribunal. Certainly, I would not dare profess to being smarter than these highly educated and experienced practitioners of the law.

Still, these jurists failed to make the correct interpretations of the high tribunal's rulings. Could it then be that an inner prejudice or intolerance was created by these judges' impatience with the prisoners constantly filing petitions in their courts? Is this why the state and federal judges so often endeavored to summarily dismiss or deny the prisoners hearings on their allegations? Was I regarded by these judges as a nemesis to their willingness to bend the law unfairly in trying to stop the prisoners from exerting their inalienable rights to hearings in the state and federal courts on substantial constitutional questions?

Certainly, my own claims of constitutional violations were never frivolous. They were all well-founded claims. But if it were these lower court judges and state supreme court judges' intentions to stymie my efforts by their poorly founded rulings, then thank God the US Supreme Court, that guardian body of the law and constitution, was watching all of these judges' actions with apparent disapproval.

Every judge ought to be made to spend some live-in time in prison as an observer before taking on the responsibility of judging and jailing other citizens. Likewise, all lawyers, police officials, and prosecutors also ought to be made to spend some time in prison as observers before arresting, defending or prosecuting accused persons subject to confinement in the penitentiary. Because the knowledge that these officials would all gain from their prison experiences would make them far better qualified to take on their responsibilities of participating in criminal trials.

It did not surprise me when the judge of the federal district court grudgingly reviewed my case without calling me into court for a plenary hearing on the allegations raised in my habeas corpus petition after the US Supreme Court had reversed the lower court's decision and remanded the case for further proceedings consistent with their opinion because the judge in the lower court was too damned embarrassed to face me after having been overruled by my appeal which brought down a per curiam opinion by eight justices of the highest court in the land literally telling the judge that he had been unable to interpret their established decisions on the points of law raised under the circumstances, in my petition for writ of habeas corpus. Under the circumstances, what the high court's opinion amounted to was a slap in the face.

I was very happy with the high court's per curiam opinion because I had detected in the lower federal district court judge the same prejudice and reluctance that I had long ago detected in the state court judges to fairly hear and rule on my charges of constitutional violations. Then too these judges realized that it would not be long before my sentence would be complied with and that I would be released from prison and therefore be out of their hair for good. But I considered the trouble and embarrassment that I had caused them and the attorney general of Illinois a moral victory to say the least.

When I advised Attorney Tepper of the federal district court judge's denial of my latest petition for writ of habeas corpus, he wrote to me the following letter:

> Dear Talbert,
>
> I wish to advise you that the time, as you well know, is a little over a year off before you will be appearing before the Illinois Parole Board. Mr. Goodwin and myself plan to appear before the board on your behalf. We therefore believe that it would inure to your benefit to cease petitioning the courts for redress. And our reasons therefore are as follows:
>
> Your legal feats are damaging to yourself. A judge finds it difficult having his decisions overruled on appeals filed by learned practicing attorneys. But when, in their opinion, a defiant convict upstart like you gets high court judges in both the state and federal courts overruled, you are not apt to build up much goodwill with the judiciary of either jurisdiction. And if a judge was not fair with you in the first place, what makes you think that after the judge has been overruled, he will be fair with you the second time your case appears before him?
>
> In all candor, you should devote all of your efforts to seeking parole rather than trying to pursue further actions to gain your freedom through the courts. Because the best you can hope to win through the courts is no doubt another trial. Why risk that now with so much service on your current sentence? You have made your point and

legal history. It is now time to close the book on the legal aspects of your case.

I talk with lawyers every day, and often your name is the topic of discussions. Some of these lawyers are amazed that you have accomplished as much as you have under seemingly insurmountable odds.

We all agree that you have been a thorn in the sides of both the state and federal courts and that you have been highly instrumental in dealing very devastating defeats to the offices of the state's attorney of Cook County and the Illinois attorney general. It therefore would be foolish to keep irritating these two powerful offices when you are about to receive a hearing before the parole board.

Again, I urge you to put your best efforts into winning a parole. Mr. Goodwin and I will do all that we can to help you.

Sincerely,
Sidney Z. Tepper

I accepted Tepper's advice and retired from the legal scene so far as my own case was concerned. I also had to be very circumspect in handling any other prisoners' cases. Because I could not afford to be caught and punished this late in the game now that my parole hearing was coming up.

The time passed swiftly as always for me, and my date with the parole board was drawing very near now. The prospect of freedom was good. But there was also a legal matter to be resolved with the parole board concerning my sentence. Under the "good-time" regulations in effect when my crime was committed, it was regulated with the force of law by the Illinois Department of Public Safety that on a fifteen-year maximum sentence a prisoner was entitled to his complete discharge after serving one-half his sentence plus one year, three months, and fifteen days. I was therefore only required to serve eight years, nine months, and fifteen days to be eligible for my discharge from confinement.

Having been returned to prison to commence service on my new sentence of three to fifteen years on March 20, 1953, I had served about eight years and nine months, almost the maximum of my sentence under the terms of the good-time regulations in force when my crime was committed in 1948.

The state, however, had changed the old good-time regulations in the early 1950s after my crime had been committed. The new good-time regulations adopted were more drastic in lessening the amount of good-time a prisoner could earn off his sentence. And the Illinois Parole Board wanted to enforce the new good-time regulations in crediting time served on my sentence. This, however, was manifestly unfair and contrary to the ex post facto provision contained in Article 1, Section 9 at Paragraph 3 of the United States Constitution, which holds that "no bill of attainder or ex post facto law shall be passed."

I called this legal question to the attention of the parole board that was determined to deny me my release in accordance with the law in effect at the time the crime was committed for which I had been imprisoned.

I had also appealed to the court questioning the constitutionality of crediting my sentence against the provisions of the new good-time regulation contrary to the ex post facto provisions in both the state and federal constitutions. The appeal got stalled in the process of being heard, and I knew that time would defeat my purpose before the court would hear the matter. I was back between a rock and a hard place, or as the cons preferred to express the situation, the court was playing the old game of "hold 'em and fuck 'em."

Since the officials and the court did not want to resolve the issue fairly and promptly, I said to myself, "To hell with them!" I made up my mind to ignore all the rules and regulations contained in my parole agreement once I was out on the street. Because I was good and tired of the State of Illinois and its bullshit justice. I had been fighting the state since day one right up until my last days in prison. The state had kicked my ass good in thirteen years. But I had retaliated with a few well-directed kicks of my own straight into the unjust balls of the state's judicial system that had prevented the officials from screwing us prisoners around on a couple of crucial issues concerning our rights.

What the state officials had done to me would soon be forgotten. What I had done to the state would live forever on the pages of law books as a symbol of real justice for the poor, the weak, and the oppressed. With these sentiments aglow within me, I was ready to bid adieu to Stateville and step out into the free world.

*   *   *   *   *

On December 6, 1961, exactly thirteen years and six months from the date I was arrested on June 6, 1948, I walked out of prison on parole a freeman. New Year's Eve, I would be thirty-nine years old. Thirteen unlucky years? Maybe. But those thirteen and a half years had made a great impact on my life in changing it for the better, I think. Others close to me seemed to think so too.

Attorney Reginald Goodwin said in the *Ebony* article about me, "What a blessing that this man was taken off the streets. Sometimes, things happen in a strange way. Through his arrest and incarceration, a great talent has been discovered. If he had not gone through this, he never would have developed a personal interest in the law. Today, he would be an asset to any law office. He thinks legally. His clarity of thought comes from exposure to law courts. It is a pleasure to read his documents."

And Gladys Erickson said in her feature article about me that appeared in the *Chicago American* August 18,1959, "This was the beginning of a new era for Jennings although he was unaware of it. The rehabilitation process had begun."

Tepper said in the *Ebony* article, "His (Jennings) appeals are letter perfect. He makes citations and argues law, all as if it came from the mouth of a Harvard professor." He also said in the same article, "Jennings not only knows law, he has made law."

The *Chicago Defender*, on August 22, 1959, said in a news item, "The most spectacularly successful lawyer in Illinois, and perhaps in the United States today, is a thirty-six-year-old Chicagoan with no formal legal training . . . the man is identified as Talbert Jennings. Three times Jennings has gone to the US Supreme Court and established, as one noted lawyer said, 'the greatest revolutionary precedents in the annals of the state's criminal procedure . . .'"

With all of these encomiums still locked in my mind, I was somewhat reluctant to leave my legal career behind me when I left Stateville. Because it was disappointing to realize that I could not practice law anymore the way I had done in prison. And I had developed a deep love for the law coupled with a fervent desire to see it work in the letter and spirit of justice for all—the way it was meant to work in all of its virgin glory without being prostituted and manipulated by some pimps with law degrees.

Rehabilitation. The word had no meaning to me before I entered prison in 1949; but now, it did. I felt and acted like a new man, not so much that I was intimidated by the dear price I had paid by being locked up over thirteen years, but because I had changed myself. Those were not lost years. They were eventful years. I had something grand and good to show for those years. Indeed! The truth had set me free in many ways. Free from my selfishness, free from my inclination to be a malefactor upon my return to society, free from my own doubts and fears that I could accomplish something to be proud of. And most of all, free from the horrors of the past. Because this time when I emerged from prison, I had the prospect of a real future.

If members of the justice system and the parole board sought to punish me by keeping me in prison longer than necessary because of my stubborn adherence to exacting the very justice that the judiciary had sworn to abide by and uphold, then so be it! But in doing so, they only gave me the time I needed to help overhaul the system where it was lacking in justice in postconviction and appellate procedures. I wasn't doing anything useful with my life anyway until the injustice in the system gave me the courage and the incentive to try and change it. At least I had been the catalyst that had started some of the forces of law and justice working in favor of the prisoners.

Ordinarily I would have considered my legal work complete when I walked out of Stateville, but there was still the matter of a prisoner called Marion Johnson to be redressed. I had prepared his petition for executive clemency, but I wanted to go to Rockford, Illinois, where he had been convicted and do some investigative work on Marion's behalf to further substantiate his contention that the killing for which he had been imprisoned to serve ninety-nine years was an act of self-defense and not murder.

I had promised him that I would do this, and I had every intention of keeping my word. When I got out of prison, I kept my word. Marion Johnson got his ninety-nine-year sentence commuted by the governor, and he was released on parole not long after my release.

Father James Jones, who at one time had been the Episcopal chaplain at Stateville, had succeeded in opening a halfway house on the West Side of Chicago for ex-convicts who needed a place to stay until they found employment and could provide for themselves. And since it was a condition of the parole board that a prisoner had to have a job and sponsor before he could be released on parole, Father Jones agreed to accept me immediately to facilitate my release so that I would be home for Christmas. He therefore had Father Clark drive me to the halfway house after my release from prison on parole. Father Clark was the Episcopal chaplain assigned to Stateville at that time.

Before I left the prison, I made arrangements to give all my law books away to the inmates whom I thought could make best use of them. My typewriter and voluminous personal legal papers and correspondence were carefully packed, and I took them with me.

*   *   *   *   *

The halfway house was a large mansion with many bedrooms, a large kitchen, dining room, and recreation area in the basement. At the time I arrived, it housed about fifteen ex-prisoners who, like myself, had been released on parole to the facility that was provided by the Episcopal church and administrated by Father Jones. I was assigned to a room on the third floor and spent the day getting acquainted with some of the other inhabitants, although there were some men there that I had met in Stateville.

Later that afternoon. Father Jones arrived. and we had a long chat about my plans for the future. He reassured me in his pleasant manner that I could rely on him for any help he could provide to assist me in finding employment. I in turn assured him that I would do everything possible to find employment and that I already had a choice of two places to live—either at my foster mother's home or with my brother James until I was able to find a place of my own.

I realized that there were prisoners that needed shelter in the halfway house far worse than I, and that Father Jones had done me a special favor to effect my prompt release from prison when I was granted parole. Because my release could have been delayed for weeks pending my finding a job before I could be let out of prison.

I also spent much time contacting my friends and relatives by letters and telephone calls to convey to them the good news of my release. I, of course, wrote to Juanita who lived in Cleveland, Ohio. Because once we had started corresponding with one another and seeing one another on occasional visits, I had grown quite fond of her.

I talked with Li'l Arthur over the telephone the first day I got out of prison. He wanted to come right over to the halfway house to pick me up for a big celebration. His barbershop was located on the West Side not far from the halfway house. He told me that because of his criminal record his mother, acting as a cats-paw, owned a tavern called "the House of Sound," which was located down the street from his barbershop on California Avenue; but, in reality, Li'l Arthur was the real owner of the tavern. Li'l Arthur also told me that he had completed his three-year parole supervision and had received his discharge from parole; he was now clear of all restraints on his liberty. I agreed to meet with him the next day sometime during the early evening, and we could go out for a little celebration.

The next day. I visited with my family before going downtown that afternoon to check in at the parole office and meet my parole officer. After that, I found time for a short visit with Attorneys Sidney

Tepper and Reginald Goodwin. Because I wanted to thank them personally for all of the assistance that they had given me.

Li'l Arthur, looking well-groomed with a neatly trimmed moustache, picked me up as planned about eight o'clock in the evening. He was driving a new car and looked prosperous in his flashy clothes and sparkling jewelry. which caused me to comment facetiously, "You haven't knocked off any jewelry stores lately have you?"

He looked at the two diamond rings on his fingers and laughed. "Shit naw, man! You think I'm crazy? I got these gems on the legit. I got connections with the right people, and the price is always real nice. The West Side is where it's at."

To Li'l Arthur, getting something of the legit didn't necessarily mean that it wasn't stolen; it simply meant that he didn't steal it, he just bought it "hot." I told him so, and he laughed before conceding I was right. "You sure know me, don't ya, Blacky?"

"That I do, my man. And I could make you a twin too if I could rake up enough bullshit in a cow pasture." I let my remark sink in before asking, "Now what's the first stop?"

"I got a little somethin' planned for ya at the House of Sound tonight, and I'll show ya my barbershop tomorrow. I'm gonna be spinnin' records—"

"Spinning records?" I cut in. "What are you talking about?"

"Well, goddamnit. Let me finish," Li'l Arthur said testily. Then he explained, "I'm what they call a tavern disc jockey. I play records, requests, and things like that. It's cheap entertainment. We don't have live musicians to play music for the customers to dance by, so I play records."

"What about the jukebox business, isn't that still going on?

"Sure. We got a jukebox in the joint, but spinnin' records is special entertainment. People can hear their old-time favorites. I must have damn near a thousand records in my library."

"Now I get the picture," I said. "This wasn't going on when I was on the street before getting sent up."

"Yeah. It's sort of a growin' business spinnin' records. I work other taverns besides my own, and I got a couple of other guys who work for me spinnin' records. I book 'em out to other taverns."

"Boy, you're still the same old hustler," I commented.

"Anything to make a buck or two, I'm for it. But I'm not doin' nothin' rough. My hustlin' these days is strictly cool. Real cool! 'Cause I don't wanna take no fall. We do a little gamblin' in the back of the barbershop, and I let a few whores trick in a couple rooms over the shop—for a fee, of course," Li'l Arthur commented as he cruised his Imperial Chrysler down California Avenue.

"I'd heard about you from Jimmy Marshall and some of the new cons coming in the joint," I told him.

"Well, Blacky, ya know, I never was one for writin'. But I'm gonna take care of ya now that you're out here. But remember, you're out here on 'paper,' so ya gotta be cool."

"What do you mean be cool? Why, I'm violating my parole already associating with a crooked little swelled-head bastard like you," I told him.

"And before the night's, over you'll violate parole a hundred times," he laughed before adding, "The knack is in not gettin' caught. So whenever there's a situation that looks like the 'man' might get involved, hightail your yella ass away from wherever you're at. Don't get picked up by the police, know what I mean?"

"Yeah, I know," I nodded my head as I replied. And just then, Li'l Arthur pulled up to the curb and parked in front of the House of Sound. Large signs in the window announced that "Li'l Arthur—the King of Sound—is spinning records tonight."

"How ya like it, Blacky? Nothin' fancy, but we keep the place jammed with customers, and that's where it's at, huh, man?"

"Yeah. That's where it's at. And this ain't a bad little joint," I remarked.

"C'mon inside, Blacky. Everything's on the house. Ya name it. I'll claim it! This is your night to party. It's really great to have ya back in circulation."

"It's great to be back," I responded in a low voice as I looked around the place and was impressed with Li'l Arthur's business acumen.

The bar was half full with patrons, and several couples were seated at tables. Most of the customers were black, but a few were

Hispanic and Appalachian whites. A small stage was up near the front of the place with a table, record player, microphone, and record rack containing a variety of recordings. Sound amplifiers were all over the place.

We took a table near the front. And L'i'l Arthur said, "I'm gonna have some scotch. What's your pleasure, Blacky?"

"Guess I'll have CC and ginger."

"This your first drink since ya been out?"

"The first, and by no means the last."

"Guess ya ain't got no pussy yet either, huh, man?"

"Not yet." I grinned.

"Well, Blacky, I got news for ya. See that fine bitch over there by the bar," he said pointing to a tall, voluptuous brown-skinned young woman with a pretty face that was a bit overly made-up.

"Yeah. I see her."

"How ya like that? Nice, Huh?"

"She looks like a fine situation from where I'm sitting," I acknowledged.

"That's Maxine Hightower. If ya dig her, man, and want her to turn ya on tonight. ya can go ta one of the rooms over the barbershop. She won't miss a thing on your body you don't want her to miss," Li'l Arthur offered knowingly.

"I'll think about it."

"Think what, nigger! That's some of the best pussy in town. and you're gonna think about it sittin' there on your tender-dick ass fresh out of the penitentiary. You must be stir crazy! Now I'm lookin' out for ya, man. Whatever I tell this bitch to do, she'll do. Ya can make book on it. Now—"

"All right! All right! Don't be so pushy, little nigger. Let's just sit and rap a while. I'll warm up to the atmosphere as I go along, okay?"

He shook his head, apparently displeased that I didn't get suddenly excited over his proposal. "Okay, I guess. But you're a stupid son of a bitch sometimes." He reached in his coat pocket and pulled out his wallet. Slipping out two one-hundred-dollar bills. he shoved them across the table and let them rest in front of me. "Here's two

Cs. Take 'em for pocket change. But remember, you're not spendin' nothin' in here, un'erstan'?"

"Thanks," I said, stuffing the bills into my shirt pocket.

"Tomorrow, I'll get ya a couple suits and a topcoat. So give me your size."

"Forty-two long," I responded.

"Good. I'll have my salesman come over to the barbershop tomorrow with some forty-two longs. You be ready for me to pick ya up when I call ya. By the way, what's the number at that home for ex-cons?" He paused to write down the number when I gave it to him. Then he inquired, "What time ya gotta be back there tonight? Or can ya hang out all night?"

I sipped my drink before making up my mind. The Canadian Club whiskey and ginger ale was soothing to my taste buds and warmed my insides. I was beginning to feel good. "Think I'll hang out with you. But I'll have to call the halfway house and tell them I'm going to spend the night at my mother's."

"That's great!" Li'l Arthur exclaimed. We can make a night of it." He took a drink and set his glass back on the table. "How long ya think before ya can leave that home?"

"Soon as I get a job."

"I wish ya could work in my shop. But ya know, the parole authorities would never hold still for that."

"Nor for me sitting here drinking with you either."

"Look, Blacky, I know a guy on Seventy-fifth Street near South Park. He's got a barbershop. His name's Ed Floyd. Maybe I can get him to give ya a job, or at least front for ya. I'll call him tomorrow."

"Sure. Why not," I responded hopefully. "The quicker I get a job that my parole officer approves, the quicker I can leave the halfway house. I don't want to cause Father Jones any embarrassment since I'm not abiding by the parole regulations."

"Just leave it to me, Blacky. I'll find somebody to give ya a job that they'll approve. I'll go the limit for ya, ya know that. But I wouldn't do shit for Buddy Morgan. That nigger ain't got nothin' cornin' from me for tryin' to say I ratted."

"I know there's bad blood between you two—been that way since we all got 'popped.' But I'm lettin' bygones be bygones myself. Buddy is doing the max on his sentence because he kept fuckin' up in the joint. But he should be coming out next year if he doesn't blow any good time," I said before sipping my drink.

"He's still down south in Menard?" Li'l Arthur asked.

"Yeah, that's right—still in Menard."

Li'l Arthur looked at his watch. "Say, man, it's gettin' late. It's time for me to do my thing. I've gotta go ta work. Look, Blacky," he went on as he stood up, "order what ya want. We can send out and get ya some ribs, Chinese food, shrimp, chicken, or anything ya want. You name it, and I'll claim it. I'll have the food picked up and delivered right to our table. Now hold tight. I've got to get busy." He walked over to the lady called Maxine. She looked over in my direction with a smile as he talked to her. Then with glass in hand she came over to the table and sat down.

"Hi, Maxine. I'm Blacky."

"Yes, I know," she said. "And I see you already know my name."

"Li'l Arthur gave me your name. He thought we'd enjoy one another's company this evening," I remarked casually.

Maxine gave me a coquettish glance. "Just this evening? I was hoping that our acquaintance would last longer than that."

"Well, we'll see now, won't we?"

"Yes, we'll see," she replied, still giving me that flirtatious look that caused her attractively mascaraed eyes to flutter.

Li'l Arthur mounted the stage and announced his first record selection, which was one of my favorites. "Ladies and gentlemen, good evenin'. This is your disc jockey, Li'l Arthur, the King of Sound, up with it, down with it, and about to get started with it. Yes, indeed, folks, we got some jams to spin so let's begin with Count Basie's 'One o'clock Jump' for my old friend Blacky Jennings, who just got in from the Big Apple. There he is sittin' and jivin' with our very own Miss Fine Brown Frame, Maxine Hightower! C'mon, let's welcome Blacky Jennings!"

I was shocked to hear the patrons applaud me like I was some kind of celebrity. Then the music seemed to come from everywhere as Count Basie and his band started playing on the recording. The audience screamed and hollered with delight. Some got up to dance, and I too felt like joining them on the dance floor. I took Maxine by the arm and led her away from our table. A moment later, we were jitterbugging to the beat of the rhythm.

All of sudden, I was having a lot of fun. I felt carefree. My recent immurement seemed unreal at that moment. It was as though I had never been off the streets for all those years. The alcohol I had consumed had taken over my mind in helping to blot out temporarily the past for this joyous occasion. All I could think of now was how sexy Maxine looked when her dress swirled high above her knees, revealing shapely legs and thighs, as I spun her around and she twisted her curvaceous hips to the beat of the rhythm. I knew then beyond any doubt where and with whom I would be spending the rest of the night.

Chapter 19

ED FLOYD'S BARBERSHOP HAD ONE other full-time barber besides Ed. I was hired to work on Fridays and Saturdays, the busiest days in the week. The arrangement was temporary until I could find full-time work. My parole officer, however, was under the impression that the job was full-time. Nevertheless, it was sufficient to get me out of the halfway house, and I listed my mother's house as my home address although I had actually moved into an apartment on Drexel Boulevard with an old friend named Walter Brown. This arrangement allowed me more freedom of movement without permitting my family to observe directly my lifestyle in readjusting to a free society that included some of my associates that they would not approve of.

It was, however, through these old associates, like Li'l Arthur, that I acquired the most help in getting gifts of money, fine clothes, and free access to a six-room, well- appointed apartment until I was able to become completely self-supporting and independent.

My reputation as a successful jailhouse lawyer gave me much prestige when I ran into some of my old underworld acquaintances. They had read about me or heard stories about me from other released prisoners. I had no idea that my fame had spread so extensively beyond the pale of prison walls and jail cells. The stories in *Ebony* and the news media had done their share to project me into the local limelight among the Chicago underworld element—especially on the South Side.

Some of my old acquaintances that I had known on the streets before my recent incarceration, as well as men whom I had met in prison that were now free, offered me propositions to join with them in illegal activities, which I politely declined. Still, others gossiped about the activities of some associates, and it was through these conversations that I first heard the rumor that Li'l Arthur was involved with trafficking in narcotics.

When I asked Li'l Arthur about the rumor, he said, "It's a fuckin' lie, Blacky. The stuff is everywhere, but I'm not dealin' in it." He knew that I never wanted to get involved in the narcotics racket. I had always contended—and rightly so—that the racket was too easily infiltrated by informers, and the low-breaking point of the users afforded the police an excellent source of stool pigeons to aid them in the arrest of the pushers who, in exchange for leniency, revealed information in helping the police to arrest the big suppliers of drugs. It was a dirty business that never appealed to me even when I was actively involved in a life of crime.

Jimmy Marshall, my best friend, stopped by the barbershop for a haircut one Saturday evening. During our conversation, he informed me of a proposition that looked promising. "Blacky," he said, handing me a business card, "I want you to go see this lawyer. His name is Ron Friedman.[†] If you're interested in working for him in securing accident cases, he will put you to work. Ron is a close associate of mine and I told him that you could be trusted. I also told him all about your legal background, and he was greatly impressed. This could be a big opportunity for you."

"What it amounts to is ambulance chasing, right, Jimmy?" I asked as I clipped away at his hair.

"Yeah, I guess you could call it that. But I prefer the term *legal investigator* or *legal assistant*, because that in fact will be a large part of what you will be doing other than actually soliciting cases," Jimmy euphemized.

"Sounds interesting. Go on, Jimmy."

"Now if you're good at this business, you can make a real buck out of it. And if you make a deal with Ron, be sure to ask for a percentage deal with expenses. What I mean is ask for a percentage of what he recovers in fees from a client's case. Usually, he'll work on a

---

[†]   The actual name of the attorney is not used in this book in order to protect his privacy and his professional standing as practicing attorney

contingency fee basis, taking one-third of what is recovered from an accident claim. Sometimes, he works for 40 percent if the case goes to trial. You get the picture?"

"Yeah. I get the picture. Go ahead, Jimmy. I'm all ears."

"In the legal profession, this, of course, is considered to be unethical," Jimmy went on. "But many lawyers find it profitable, as well as expedient, to work with legal assistants. Why, a buddy of mine who died just a few months ago from a heart attack made out like a bandit working as a legal assistant to Ron. I know some of his old connections, nurses and other hospital personnel. Some of these people can give you daily reports on auto accident cases as well as other kinds of accidents, including the names, addresses, telephone numbers, and nearest kinsfolks of accident victims. As you probably know, Blacky, this is confidential information, so all you have to do is shell out a little dough to the advisers. You get the picture?"

"Sure, sure. You bet I get the picture. Go on, Jimmy."

"You probably know the rest. Contact the wife, husband, or other kin and get out to the hospital with them to talk them into retaining Ron Friedman. Or you contact the accident victim directly at home if he is released after emergency treatment."

"I'll need a car," I said, giving the matter serious thought.

"That can be arranged. And as soon as you start bringing in business, you can depend on Ron to give you a draw against the percentages that you'll be earning and building up, plus, he'll give you expense money."

"This has got to be the best deal I've heard since I've been out of stir."

"Ron's a good guy to be associated with. I'll call him Monday and make an appointment for you to go in and see him. What do you say?"

"Do it! Do it, Jimmy!"

"Good boy! You're as good as in. And don't you forget, Blacky, kick the word around among your crime pals that 'Downtown Jimmy' is the best bail bondsman around town. I'll give you a stack of my business cards to pass out. You scratch my back and I'll scratch yours."

"It's a deal!" I exclaimed, excited over the possibility of what we had just talked about.

Christmas was only a few days away, and Juanita was arriving from Cleveland, Ohio, on the New York Central that evening. I had to meet her at the Sixty-third Street Station, a stop the passenger train made just before its final stop at the LaSalle Street Station in Chicago's Loop. Jimmy, accommodating as usual, offered to drive me to the station to pick Juanita up. After finishing his haircut, I left the shop a little earlier than usual that day so that I would be on time when her train arrived.

*   *   *   *   *

My first Christmas at home was something I had looked forward to for many years. It was the first time that I had been together with the whole family since my release from prison, and the only one missing was my foster father who had died a few years earlier from a stroke.

We enjoyed Christmas dinner, opening gifts. and other Yuletide festivities at my mother's home, where Juanita was introduced for the first time to all the members of my family. Mom liked her very much and hinted that she would make me a good wife. My brothers and sisters could find no fault with her either, and I was pleased that everything was going well for me in the few weeks that I had been released.

My family thought that it was great that I was working for a lawyer as a legal assistant. They did not, however, fully comprehend what my real duties were, nor did I bother to describe my work to them—not because I was ashamed in any way of what I did, but because the term *ambulance chaser* had a misunderstood connotation and insinuation that someone was being victimized or that there was something dishonest involved in soliciting clients for lawyers when in truth, there was only a question of ethics involved. Because any accident case that I might solicit for Ron Friedman was handled in the very same ethical manner in which it would be handled if any other lawyer of good reputation was retained directly by the client to handle his case. And the only complaint against what I was doing was in the fact that the code of ethics of the legal profession precluded an attorney from soliciting business in the manner under which I was assisting Ron Friedman. The clients themselves were not taken advantage of or the insurance companies involved because the accident cases were all based upon legitimate accidents in which clear-cut liability was established and predicated upon some form of negligence.

Before leaving, Juanita and I said good-bye to all the family. But Mom followed us to the door with a sweet smile on her light-skinned face which was characterized by her benevolent disposition. She stood in the hallway for a last-minute bit of conversation. "Now, Talbert," she said, "you be careful and remember to take good care of Juanita. Because we all think that she is just a wonderful and adorable person. God is bestowing His blessings on you already in so many ways. You must remember to thank Him constantly."

"Sure, Mom. I do thank Him, and you too for being such a wonderful mother," I responded with a kiss on her cheek.

Juanita held on to my arm with a pleasant smile on her winsome face that was radiant with joy on the surface of her smooth medium-brown complexion. "It has been a beautiful Christmas! We all have so much to be thankful for, Mrs. James, now that Talbert is home. And I hope that the New Year will bring us all much joy and prosperity."

"Yes, I hope so too," Mom responded before asking, "Do you plan to spend New Year's with us, Juanita?"

"I really haven't decided. But I don't have to be back in Cleveland until after the New Year for the upcoming school term."

"Well, if you are still in town, I hope Talbert will bring you back by to see us."

"You can depend on it, Mom," I said, this time kissing her good-bye. Juanita also planted a kiss on her cheek as she said good-bye.

Outside at the curb, we got into a car that I had borrowed from my older brother. "Mom really likes you a lot, Juanita," I told her as I drove off in the direction of Juanita's sister's home.

"I like her very much too. But all of your family treated me extremely well. I'm very happy to have met them."

"Mom thinks that I ought to seriously start thinking of marriage and settling down to raise a family because I'm just about a year away from being forty."

"Your mother is right, you know," Juanita said in a serious tone of voice.

"You wouldn't by any chance have anybody in mind with whom I could spend a lifetime of marital bliss, would you, Juanita?" I asked facetiously, but I was really seriously feeling her out.

"There is no such thing, Talbert."

"What do you mean?"

"I mean no one in their right mind should expect a lifetime of marital bliss. Too many couples get off on the wrong foot thinking like that. Because life has its ups and downs and its highs and lows. The most anyone can hope for in a successful marriage is that no matter what adversities they face—and there will always be some—the couple will somehow find enough love strength and devotion to hold their marriage and family together, if they are so blessed to have children," she concluded solemnly.

"My, my! Aren't you the serious one," I exclaimed.

"Marriage is a very serious thing, Talbert."

"Is that why you have never tried it?"

"I suppose you could say that. But it's just that I never felt that I met the right person. There of course have been other men in my life. But even if I were right for them since I did not love any of them enough to accept a proposal, they were not right for me."

"Then love is all important in your concept of marriage?"

"Definitely! Without love, I don't believe that there can be a lasting and workable marriage."

I was thoughtful for a spell as I contemplated what Juanita had just said. All during the time I had known her and during our correspondence, she had only closed her letters "Sincerely," and I closed mine "Affectionately yours." There never was any serious references to love during our visits or in the letters we exchanged. We were certainly different in almost every respect. She was an introvert while on the other hand, I was an ambivert.

I searched my mind to come up with some ways in which we held things of life in common. When I was done making a comparison, I discovered that what we lacked in common far outweighed what we held in common. Yet I was extremely fond of Juanita—so much so that I often wondered if what I felt was really love. She was certainly different from any other girl I had ever known. She appeared to be neither prudish nor unsophisticated, although she did seem to position herself in that old-fashioned type of girl "that married dear old dad." And for the life of me, I couldn't tell whether this particular trait was sincere or pretentious. I ended up giving Juanita the benefit of the doubt when she turned down my offer to spend the night with me the same evening that she had arrived in the city.

Perhaps it was egotistical of me, but I labeled her old-fashioned when I couldn't coax her into spending the night in my bedroom. Still, I sort of clung to liking the idea of going with an old-fashioned girl for a change. Juanita definitely presented a challenge that made me feel a bit unsure of myself.

I finally opened up again. "You know, Juanita, I used to have a recurring dream that I was married, living in Ohio, and my wife and I had one son that resembled me very much, right down to the birthmark on the left side of my chest. I'm not making this up. I actually dreamed this several times. But not once did I actually see the woman I was married to."

"Did you have this dream before or after we started corresponding with one another?" she asked. You know, sometimes dreams can be meaningful. Sometimes, a dream can be the longing for the fulfillment of a subconscious desire."

"I see you're into Freud."

"Jung and Adler too," she laughed.

"Well, I'll be damned. Another point in common. I'm into all three too. The gap narrows," I muttered, more or less to myself.

"What?"

"Oh, nothing. I was just thinking out loud."

*   *   *   *   *

The very first personal injury case I managed to secure for Attorney Ron Friedman was through a contact I had made at the Cook County Hospital. Jimmy Marshall had set me up with the contact who worked in the emergency room, and subsequently, I was able to establish contacts at two other Chicago hospitals. These contacts also resulted in cases I was able to refer to Ron. All these cases involved automobile accidents. One of the best cases I got for Ron Friedman came about by happenstance. Li'l Arthur was driving me over to the House of Sound for a cocktail party when we came upon a nasty two-car collision that was blocking traffic. I got out and walked down to the scene of the accident to observe the situation.

Both cars were demolished beyond repair. One car was turned over on its side; the occupants, a man and what I learned later were his wife and their two children, were being removed from the car by police officers. The driver of the other vehicle was standing near his car in a dazed condition, holding a bloodstained scarf to his injured head.

It was a cold day, right after the New Year, and I rubbed my hands together as I watched the wife of the man taken out of the overturned car. She appeared to be unconscious as the police laid her on the pavement. The two children, a girl and a boy, were bleeding from facial cuts. The boy, about seven years old, could only stand on one foot as one of the police officers held on to him. The father covered his wife with his overcoat and stood shivering from the cold. Shortly thereafter, the police placed the children in a patrol car.

I accosted the father who appeared to be in his late twenties or early thirties. "Are you hurt very badly?" I asked him.

"I don't think so. But I wish an ambulance would hurry up and get here for my wife and children," he replied. He was shivering rather violently from the cold. I slipped off my coat and draped it around his shoulders.

"You ought not to do that," he protested. "You'll only get cold yourself."

"I don't mind. I can always get in a warm car. But I realize that you want to stay here close by the side of your wife."

"Yes, I do," he said, kneeling down beside her.

I heard a man a few steps from us telling some other people that the other car ran a stop sign and hit the car that the family was in. One of the police officers returned to examine the injured woman, and he assured her husband that they had called for a couple of ambulances.

I walked away to question the man that had apparently witnessed the accident. I jotted down his name, address, and telephone number before quietly going about asking other people in the crowd whether any of them had witnessed the accident.

Two more people, who corroborated the first witness, gave me their names and addresses.

Two ambulances arrived and started loading the injured into the vehicles just as Li'l Arthur walked up to me and said testily, "These goddamned cars got me blocked in. I wish the hell these cops would clear all this traffic out of here so I can get out of this jammed-up mess."

"Now take it easy, partner. This could be a big break for me. I'm going to try and land this case for Friedman," I told him as I stood shivering from the cold.

"Where in the hell is your coat?" Li'l Arthur wanted to know.

"I loaned it to the man driving the overturned car. He just got in the ambulance with his wife."

"Well, git your fuckin' coat from him before the goddamned ambulance leaves, fool!" Li'l Arthur urged before adding, "Ya good Samaritan niggers kill me meddlin' in white folks' business."

"This is anybody's business that wants to help. Like I said, this could be a good case for my business."

"If you don't die from pneumonia. Now git that coat that I bought ya from that honky and let's git outta here."

"No way! The coat will be an excuse to contact him later. Now let me find out what hospital they're taking these people to," I said before hurrying over to the ambulance driver to inquire of his destination.

When I returned to join Li'l Arthur, I told him, "St. Luke's, that's the hospital they're taking them to. Now let's get the hell out of here before I freeze my balls off."

"It would serve a dumb son of a bitch like ya right to freeze 'em off," Li'l Arthur said, showing a scowl-like grin on his irritated features.

The police were beginning to direct the traffic around the accident scene. In a few minutes, we were underway headed for the hospital. When we arrived there, we went straight to the emergency room. I was able to talk one of the attendants into letting me in to see the father of the children to recover my coat.

The father's name was Robert Allen. He was grateful that I had loaned him the coat. He complained of chest pains now and also a neck injury, but he was more concerned about his wife and children. They were being treated inside the operating room. I told him about the addresses and names of the witnesses that I had obtained at the scene of the accident, and I explained to him that they all said that he had the right of way when the other driver ran the stop sign and hit his car.

Mr. Allen seemed very pleased and surprised over my interest in wanting to be of help. I told him that I was a legal assistant who had just happened to stop at the scene of the accident. He gave me his address and telephone number when I asked him to let me keep in contact with him. I in turn wrote my name, address, and telephone number on the back of one of Ron Friedman's business cards and gave it to Mr. Allen, telling him that I was going back to the scene of the accident to try and get some photographs while searching for other evidence. I advised him at the same time not to discuss the case with anyone other than the police until I was done collecting evidence for him. I was very careful not to mention anything about Ron Friedman or representing him at this time. I wanted to convey the impression that whatever I was doing was being done for Mr. Allen personally without applying any pressure whatsoever to accept a lawyer that he had probably never heard of. My first thought was to get his confidence. Once that had been accomplished, the rest was easy.

Li'l Arthur and I left the hospital and drove to the House of Sound to get a camera. But when we got back to the accident scene, the cars had been tolled away. I cursed and made up my mind then that if I was to stay in this business, I would always keep a camera close at hand. Before leaving, I diagramed the accident scene as best I could remember it, including the intersections, the positions of the two cars involved, and the point of impact.

Later that same evening I checked with the hospital's emergency room and was advised that Mrs. Allen was hospitalized in critical condition with a brain concussion. The young lad was also hospitalized with a broken leg besides the lacerations and contusions he suffered in the accident. His five-year-old sister only suffered minor facial lacerations and contusions of her body. The father suffered two broken ribs and a neck sprain. His rib cage was taped and, he was placed in a neck brace before being released along with his daughter.

The next morning, I called Attorney Ron Friedman and filled him in on the accident case. He advised me to obtain copy of the accident report as soon as possible and to try to get Allen down to his office right away before he was approached by some other solicitor, or before he thought of contacting his own lawyer in the event he had one.

Being new in the business, I still had much to learn, and I relied heavily on Ron for advice during this training period. I therefore hurried over to the police station to get a copy of the accident report. The report revealed that the man who had hit the Allen car was cited for running the stop sign. It further disclosed that he was insured by a good insurance company. This was a clear-cut case of negligence.

Before leaving the police station, I called Mr. Allen and got him to agree to accompany me downtown to see Attorney Friedman. Hopping in my old struggle buggy, I headed for the Allen's apartment. I certainly intended to ask Ron for a draw against my commission once he signed Allen to an agreement to settle his claim, because the old car I was driving coughed, spat, and shook like a tubercular patient not long for this world. I had only paid seventy-five bucks for it.

Ron Friedman was a tall, thin man in his early forties. He explained to Mr. Allen how he could help him recover damages on a contingency fee contract—meaning that one-third of the settlement would go to the attorney and the rest to Allen and his family and that they would not have to pay the attorney anything if no settlement was reached. In the event the case went to trial, the attorney would keep 40 percent of what money was awarded. No matter what the outcome of the case, Mr. Allen would not have to pay any fees or expenses out of his own pocket.

With the slightest urging from me, Allen agreed to retain Friedman on a contingency fee basis. It all seemed too easy to even be called work. But I was later to learn that all cases were not that easy to land. Some cases took long hours of investigation to locate witnesses in order to take their signed statements so that we could establish justification for making a claim against someone who was responsible for causing a personal injury. But for the nonce I could bask in the financial prospect of having secured for Ron a case with unquestionable merit.

*   *   *   *   *

With Jimmy Marshall acting as my cosigner, I was able to trade in my old car and purchase a white 1960 Ford Thunderbird that was only two years old and in excellent condition. Ron Friedman had been generous in advancing me the down payment after receiving the Allen family's case. Now I couldn't wait to show off my car to Juanita, who had postponed returning to Cleveland when we decided to get married.

Ours was to be a secret marriage because I did not want to apply to the parole authorities for permission to marry for fear that permission would not be granted. The parole officials would no doubt reject the request on the grounds that I had not established sufficient security to be considering matrimony so soon after my release from prison. But Juanita and I had confessed our love for each other, and we were both determined to not let anything stand in our way. We therefore decided to have a quiet wedding ceremony in the city hall building and announce our marriage after her current teaching contract expired in Cleveland. By then, I would be off parole. She could then return to Chicago and apply for a teacher's position with the Chicago Board of Education.

It was one of those crispy-cold winter evenings when the sky was clear and the stars were bright and plentiful in the firmament. The beauty of it added romance to our drive as we cruised along the shoreway with the car radio, playing soft music. Lake Michigan was ice-covered and coated with a thin layer of newly fallen snow, and the moonlight glistened across, its wide expanse like the reflection from a million gems. It was indeed a beautiful night!

We had already applied for our marriage license. and our waiting period would be up tomorrow. We planned to say our vows the same day and spend our wedding night together in the Conrad Hilton Hotel. My bride-to-be was really old-fashioned. She was holding out until the very end. The thought of this made me smile when I associated it with the lines of some poetry I recalled:

> The lover's pleasure is like the hunter's,
> It's in the chase.
> And the brightest beauty loses half its merit,
> As the flower its perfume,
> If the willing hand can reach it too easily,
> Or touch it too soon.

The poet responsible for those lines escaped me, and I did not know whether the lines were exactly as I had once read them, but they were beautiful and meaningful as they flashed through my mind during our drive. Suddenly, the Conrad Hilton loomed on the distant skyline and caused me to comment, "There's our honeymoon manor over to the left, dear. That'll be home come tomorrow, and the time can't pass fast enough to suit me."

"Oh yes! I see it! There it is over there!" Juanita responded excitedly, pointing a gloved finger toward the large hotel.

"We can always move the date up if you have a mind to join me for some prenuptial bliss," I teased.

"Never mind, Talbert. I can wait if you can't. And you really don't have a choice," Juanita rejoined with that ever-present serious look on her face.

"Know why I'm going to marry you?"

"I hope because you love me."

"Not just that alone."

"Then what else?"

"Well, you're a schoolteacher, see, and school teachers make you do it over and over until you get it right, don't they?" I said, laughing at the old joke.

Juanita didn't laugh. She just sat there with that serious look on her face. "Come on! Don't you get it?" I asked.

"Get what?"

"The joke. Do it over and over until you get it right, that's the punch line."

"What does that mean?" she asked with a genuine puzzled expression on her face.

"Hell! Where is your sense of humor? You can't be that naive. I'm talking about making love to you in bed."

I couldn't help but notice the stern look of disapproval on her face as she responded, "You call that humor?"

"What do I have to do, tickle you under the arm to get a laugh?"

"You better not. Keep your hands on the wheel. This is no time to be tickling anyone."

"God! Are you always so serious?"

"No. You've seen me laugh lots of times."

"I won't argue the point further. Just get it altogether for tomorrow night because we'll be checking in that hotel if all goes well."

"What do you mean if all goes well?"

"I mean if we can get in and out of marriage court without delay. There may be other couples ahead of us, you know."

"This isn't exactly the marriage season, so it probably won't be too crowded," Juanita said thoughtfully.

"I don't know, honey. There may be a lot more couples like us that want to start the New Year off with wedding bells."

"We'll see," she said happily, and she surprised me by leaning a bit closer until her shoulder touched my arm.

I squeezed her hand reassuringly, feeling the engagement ring under her glove that I had recently given her. Too bad I couldn't tell Mom about our wedding plans. It would have made her very happy to know that we were getting married. But Mom would have to wait like everyone else until we were ready to make the announcement.

We stopped and enjoyed dinner with cocktails at a downtown restaurant before returning home. Tomorrow was going to be a busy, busy day, and one of the most important days in our lives.

Chapter 20

IN ALMOST A YEAR OF so-called "ambulance chasing," I had prospered rather well, and Attorney Ron Friedman had also increased his fortune by a good margin. He was delighted with the business I had brought into his office through my aggressive but diplomatic approach to acquiring clients.

Juanita and I had announced our marriage to all of our relatives and friends in June of 1962. I had been discharged from parole, and Governor Otto Kerner had issued a signed certificate restoring all my rights of citizenship. At last, I was a completely free man with no conditions or restraints on my liberty whatsoever.

During our secret marriage, I had commuted on weekends by driving the 365 miles from Chicago to Cleveland, Ohio, to spend a few days with Juanita. When school terminated for summer vacation, Juanita returned to Chicago to live with me and to apply for a teaching position with the Chicago Board of Education.

It was during Juanita's medical examination for the job with the Chicago Board of Education that it was discovered that she had a small breast tumor. She was advised to have an operation before she could be cleared medically for consideration as a teacher in the Chicago school system.

Juanita decided to return to Cleveland to be operated on by the brother of her personal physician, who was considered an outstanding surgeon in the kind of operation she needed. This of course postponed our plans to make our home in Chicago. It also meant that I would have to continue making weekend trips to Cleveland at least twice each month until we finally established a permanent home to settle down in.

Juanita had the operation performed. A small benign tumor was removed, and she recovered quickly from the operation. But she had to wait until the following year to reapply for a position with the Chicago Board of Education. In the meantime, a sudden turn of events caused me to make some fast changes in my livelihood and environment.

Certain enemies of Ron Friedman in the legal profession set out to cause his undoing by revealing the so-called unethical manner in which he used assistants like myself to acquire clients in personal injury cases. There was talk of an investigation that would include Ron and other lawyers suspected of using "ambulance chasers" to acquire business. Complaints had been made to a local bar association and the state's attorney.

Ron set out immediately to clean up his act, hoping that by doing so in time, it would not be too late to forestall any charges being brought against him as a result of his enemies making a malicious assault upon his integrity. And when my name became linked in the investigation, I was advised that an investigator from the state's attorney's office wanted to interview me. It was at this point that Ron and I agreed that it would be very prudent to part company. In fact, it would be even more prudent if I disappeared, got lost, and sort of vanished to Cleveland for a spell.

Ron gave me a bonus and promised to send me my percentage share in all the cases that I had worked on just as soon as the cases were settled. After that, there was nothing left to do but pack up and point the hood of my Thunderbird toward Cleveland. Before I left, however, I advised my family not to reveal my location to anyone who might show up to make inquiries about my whereabouts.

Juanita was more than pleased when I told her that I had decided to move to Cleveland permanently so that we could have more time to spend together. I gave her an inkling of my real motive for leaving Chicago, but at the same time, I assured her that it was important that we be together if our marriage was ever to be meaningful in the truest essence of matrimony.

Establishing myself in Cleveland did not take long. Juanita and I shared her small apartment on the East Side. She continued with her teaching position, and I found a clerical job with a fabricating company. My social life at first revolved around Juanita's friends in the Cleveland area, but I soon began to make friends of my own.

Leonard, our first and only child, was born on February 27, 1964. Shortly after his birth, Juanita's mother came to live with us to help take care of our son while we continued to work at our jobs.

It was now necessary to move into a larger apartment. Our combined incomes allowed us to lease a modern apartment in a quiet middle-class neighborhood. Several years later, we purchased an eight-room house in Shaker Heights, one of Cleveland's finest and most affluent suburbs that boasted the twelfth best high school in the nation. This was an ideal environment in which to raise a family, and we were happy and proud of the progress that we had made.

I never missed living in Chicago too much after the first few years I resided in Cleveland. What nostalgia I did feel was cured by occasional visits home to visit with my family and friends.

Ron Friedman survived as a lawyer, but he had to cease being associated with the so-called "ambulance-chasing" mode of soliciting personal injury cases. And I always found time to visit Ron whenever I was in Chicago. We would usually have lunch together. Sometimes, Jimmy Marshall would join us. I had always found Ron to be a fair, decent, and trustworthy human being. Not once did I ever notice any tendency on his part to bilk any of his clients or any of the many insurance companies that he had done business with. To the contrary, Ron had always been on the level with his clients and the insurance companies by his insistence in handling only valid accident cases that were easily recognizable by obvious negligence. His only shortcoming in his law practice, if it could be called a shortcoming, was his desire to go after business instead of letting business come to him.[‡]

The passing years had taken their toll on some of my old friends that passed into eternity. Attorney Sidney Tepper died in the line of

---

[‡] Today the United States Supreme Court is in favor of lawyers advertising for clients. Prior to The High Tribunal's ruling that it is all right for lawyers to advertise, lawyers were prohibited from advertising by the Code of Ethics of their profession.

duty when he suffered a fatal heart attack in a Chicago courtroom. His passing was sincerely mourned by me. I had the greatest affection/esteem for this kind and altruistic man.

My old friend Louis Lomax was killed in an automobile accident in Mexico, ending all too soon a successful writing career. I was very fortunate to have seen Lou a few years before his demise. He was on a lecture tour in 1963 that brought him to Cleveland. He spoke on "racial tension in America" at one of the Jewish temples in our area.

Lou's appearance drew a huge audience of which my wife and I had the pleasure of attending. After his lecture, Lou and I had a long chat about where our lives had led us following our release from Stateville, which Lou humorously referred to as our alma mater.

My younger brother James made a special trip to Shaker Heights from Chicago to personally decorate our home when we purchased it. He did a beautiful job in the month that he spent with us, and when we moved into our home, James was as proud of his work as we were. He returned to Chicago for several months before returning to Cleveland, where he moved into a small apartment and remained close to us until his death in 1972 from sclerotic coronary disease, probably brought on by James's chronic mental stress. We buried my brother in a suburban cemetery only a few miles from our home with the hope that James would find far more peace in eternity than he found during his mundane existence in a world that often left him troubled by the complexities of life.

The entire family had showed up for James's funeral. It had been like a family reunion. And I was especially gratified to be with my family since it was not often that I got an opportunity to see everyone as often as I would have liked to.

Most of all, I was glad that my mother was able to make the trip because it was not too long after that that she too was taken from us to find a resting place in the hands of God.

Jimmy Marshall and Li'l Arthur both showed up for James's funeral and used the occasion to stay over a few days for a friendly visit. They filled my head with stories about what was going on in Chicago concerning people that we knew on the seamy side of life.

One of the stories involved Buddy Morgan. He had continued to live a life devoted to crime following his release from prison until he was found shot to death in a New York motel. His murder was never solved.

I continued to make it a practice of avoiding trouble with the law in favor of a constructive lifestyle that would give me peace of mind and the least unhappiness. Many times, I met men in the Cleveland area with whom I had served time in prison. Most of these chance meetings were usually just friendly hellos with a little exchange of passing conversation. Others, however, were of a more sinister nature in which I was offered propositions to join in some illegal proposals. These kinds of meetings I did not enjoy. But before the meeting was over, I usually made myself quite explicit in not wanting to get involved in whatever unlawful propositions were called to my attention.

In 1977, I opened a paralegal business doing legal investigative work to supplement the income from my regular job. None of my activities in my capacity as a legal investigator involved ambulance chasing. I had acquired bona fide credentials by completing a course in legal investigation at an accredited educational school. After graduating and getting my diploma, I enrolled in evening classes at the Cuyahoga Community College to study real estate law, practice, and procedure. I took the real estate course because a friend of mine, who was a real estate broker, wanted me to become his office manager.

I had always been a congenial and gregarious person who was fond of a social life that included drinking alcoholic beverages at parties and bars. My drinking had always been of a social nature and had created no problems for me all during the many years that I used alcohol in moderation. But alcohol, being the insidious drug that it is, lies in wait for its unsuspecting victims to find a constant need for its dependency brought on by emotional problems, stress, or psychogenic complications; then alcohol takes over to rule the body, mind, and spirit.

The exact cause of my alcoholism I could never pinpoint. At first, I thought that perhaps it developed from overwork and my trying to do too many things at the same time. Because it seemed to me that the more work I did, the more alcohol I consumed. Still, I could not be absolutely certain that my alcoholic dependency developed from an overactive lifestyle. I could just as easily have become the victim of overuse: addiction brought on by social abuse of liquor. Be that as it may, I got hooked and hooked bad! It did not occur overnight either. The disease developed gradually—perhaps from a combination of mental, moral, and hereditary factors that seized upon the right moment with the right chemical (alcohol) to make me a dependent. And I should have become immediately aware that I had a drinking problem when there was a sudden change in my drinking habits, such as drinking in the morning to "get started to work," drinking during lunch for a "pickup," and excessive drinking during the evening hours, either at my favorite bars or with friends inside a residence. But I was probably too high most of the time to make a rational conception of just how serious alcohol was dominating my life.

Prior to the onset of the disease of alcohol abuse, I had only drunk moderately, mostly during evening hours after my work was finished. When I finally realized that I was hopelessly addicted to alcohol and I no longer had any control over my drinking, my life began to fall apart. I became miserable with periods of depression that caused me to question my own personal worth and ability to function as a normal human being.

Once I admitted to myself that I was an alcoholic, I finally accepted Juanita's advice and sought help for my problem. The treatment consisted of detoxification (withdrawal from alcohol), taking disulfiram, a drug called "antabuse" that if mixed with alcohol would make me extremely ill. Counseling and becoming a member of Alcoholics Anonymous also played a great part in my initial recovery.

I used the term *initial recovery* because I was later to learn through a relapse, when I returned to drinking more alcohol, that only total abstinence from alcohol could control or arrest my drinking problem. Because there was no way that the disease could be cured whereby I could return to even moderate drinking. Once I got started back on the bottle, my drinking habit had reached the point where "one drink was too little and a thousand drinks not enough."

My urge to take a drink would return occasionally, and in times of great stress or despondency, the urge to take a drink would be almost intolerable! At such times, the urge could be controlled if I immediately took an Antabuse pill and continued the prescription medication until my emotional affliction was stabilized, whereby I was able to cope with the problems that come with daily living without the use of alcohol.

During my periods of sobriety, I functioned normally in my domestic, social, and business conduct—being responsible, resourceful, and respectable. It was therefore clear to me that if I wanted to continue to lead a normal life, I would have to abandon the use of alcohol altogether—or suffer the tortures of the damned!

*   *   *   *   *

I have always been fascinated by astrology and occult subjects for as long as I can remember, and I have always kept an open mind on these so-called pseudosciences. Because I could neither find reason for total acceptance nor total rejection of the preternatural phenomena that I had become aware of in my lifetime.

It is recorded that astrology has been believed in by mankind for over five thousand years—or three thousand years before the origin of Christianity. What made astrology unique in much of mankind's beliefs was the fact that it could be traced to every continent in the world, and the additional fact that it correlated the birth and existence of mankind with the universe—meaning that mankind is not a worldly creature but an intrinsically universal being tied into the cosmos.

The grounds for truth in the astrological mystique concept of creative influence on one's being at birth did not seem as far-fetched to me as the concept of the virgin birth tenet. At least I could keep an open mind on astrology. Because my belief in God—as the unseen ruling force of the universe from which all living things emerged—had a tendency, in my opinion, to lend credence to the astrological belief that the major planets of the universe and the moon does indeed play a significant role in the influence of one's life.

It is an accepted truth that the moon has an effect upon the tides of our seas. There is also considerable evidence that the full moon influences behavioral patterns in some people's lives—and perhaps all people's lives on a higher observable degree or a lower degree that might be imperceptible to human observance or understanding at this time. An analogy may be found in epilepsy in which attacks range from "grand mal" to "petit mal," in which the sufferer may not even be aware of a seizure. Who then can truly say that the moon or planets do not have some influence upon our lives and behavior—and be absolutely right?

The way I look at the subject of astrology, there may be pros and cons as to whether or not it is a true science, but there is no conclusive evidence either way for me to predicate a firm and true belief whether astrology is real or unreal. Therefore what I cannot absolutely believe or disbelieve I always keep my mind open to further contemplation and evidence.

My first inkling to get into the astrology business came about one day when I was shopping for a birthday gift for a friend. I wanted to buy a gift with the friend's zodiac sign on the gift, such as a pendant or other piece of jewelry. Searching for such a gift took me into several stores. Most of the stores, however, only carried one or two items of zodiac gifts where I attempted to shop. The stores that carried jewelry items did not have in stock the item with the birth sign I was seeking, and I gave up trying to locate the kind of zodiac gift I wanted to purchase.

The experience of looking for the zodiac gift and not finding it gave me the idea that it might be a real shopper's service to open a specialty shop with numerous well-stocked zodiac gift items in combination with books on astrology and other occult subjects.

As time went on, the germ of the idea fertilized itself in my mind and soon grew into a reality when my wife and I decided to make the necessary investment from our savings to open such a shop in 1979. Consequently, Zodiac World Incorporated came into being with the hopes and expectations of growing from a small family retail business into a nationwide franchise with similar gift shops located in all of the major cities in America.

It was a big idea within the concept and feasibility of the American dream. Through hard work and determination, we succeeded in opening our first store in one of America's largest strip shopping centers. This was a modest beginning. But we were confident that we were on the right track to see our dream flourish and culminate into the greatness that we had anticipated.

By keeping a level head and low profile through the passing years, I had managed to enjoy almost two decades of uninterrupted freedom combined with some success in earning a good livelihood that included property and a few luxuries. Then suddenly! The threat of destroying that streak of good fortune came about with a catastrophe that brought a terrible nightmare into my life, leaving a new threat of imprisonment looming before me like a dark cloud portending my doom.

Part III

(Conclusion)
The Truth Shall Set You Free

Chapter 21

DROWNING MY TROUBLES IN ALCOHOL had always been an ephemeral escape at best. Because the same troubles that I went to bed with were always still there to stare me in the face and plague my mind when I awoke from my alcoholic stupor. Today was to be no different. I arose and sat on the side of the bed, rubbing my trembling hands over my face, and head in an endeavor to push the mental agony from my reeling brain. Like a projector, my brain had flashed much of my past into focus during my fitful slumber, as though it were meaningful for me to review my life in order to chart a course of action in coming to grips with the reality of the arson charges that had been brought against me.

It was barely light outside. A little preview of dawn slipped through the edges of the window shade. I glanced at the clock on the dresser. It was a few minutes after five. I raised the shade to let in more light and was greeted instantly with a clear summer sky. The chirping of birds in the big elm tree out front suggested a nice day in the making.

God! My hands were shaking as I wrung them together to still the awful tremors. I looked around the room anxiously until my eyes came to rest on the bottle of gin on the floor near the bedside. Eagerly, I seized it. In a moment, the neck of the bottle was tilted against my lips with both of my hands holding it in a steady grasp. I let the warm liquor trickle down my throat until I had to catch my breath. Pausing for a few minutes. I raised the bottle again and again until my hands and body felt the tingling calm that some drinkers like myself refer to as a "glow."

"Ah!" I sighed, thinking, "what makes you ill makes you also well."

It was now time to meet the challenges of the day. The thought of my indictment crossed my mind, and I cursed angrily. "I'll show those damned devils a thing or two about trying to bum rap me." But first, I had to talk to a lawyer. So I decided to go see Attorney Stanley Tolliver and tell him all about myself. I had an old copy of *Ebony* with my story in it. I could hardly believe that over twenty years had gone by since that story was written. My God! How time does fly! I'd show Tolliver the story about me. That should convince him at the very least that I'm not stupid.

Once Tolliver got to know all about me, he should be able to easily see that I wouldn't commit such a grossly stupid crime by burning my store with gasoline, an easily detectable flammable liquid, on a Sunday afternoon with hundreds of shoppers milling about in the shopping center. This just isn't done by naive businessmen, much less by an ex-criminal, well-schooled in the law, with a diploma in legal investigation. As any fool should know, I reasoned, arson for profit is usually done in the dark of the night when no one is around. And Tolliver would understand, once he had all of the facts, that I was indicted and being put on trial on trumped-up charges. We would fight this case and win it easily, I convinced myself before heading for the bathroom.

A half hour later, after a shave and shower, I was downstairs having strong black coffee in the kitchen. I perused the indictment once again. "Criminal tools—gasoline." I stared at those words in the indictment before cursing out loud. "Why, those damned devils are crazy as hell if they believe they can stick me with such bullshit!" Hell! I took on the State of Illinois and turned that state's legal system upside down. No bullshit state and suburban arson investigators were going to hang a bum beef on me, I reassured myself. I'll beat this phony rap and throw it back in their faces with egg.

At six thirty, I got up to fetch the morning newspaper lying at our front door. I turned on the television set in our living room, dialed the morning newscast, and settled back in a comfortable chair to read the paper and listen to the news simultaneously.

Juanita, dressed in a housecoat, came downstairs. and we greeted one another with good-mornings before she said, "I hope you had a good-night's rest so you can get your head together on what has to be done. To be absolutely frank, dear, I did not rest too well myself for thinking about this mess. It's embarrassing, and certainly, it's an ordeal that we shouldn't have to undergo."

"Well, thank goodness! There's nothing in the paper or on the news about my indictment. I sure don't want any publicity if I can avoid it. What's more, honey, don't tell any of our friends or relatives about it either," I cautioned her.

"But why, dear?" she asked with a look of puzzlement on her worried features. Before I could say anything, she went on, "Surely our people will be understanding about this matter."

"No! No!" I cried. "Do as I say. Don't mention it to anyone. It will only upset our relatives, and it is hard to tell who really are your friends these days. So why bring other people into it if we don't have to—at least until the trial comes up. Because I'd go nuts every time someone asked me in a solicitous tone, 'How is the case coming along, Bert?' I just can't take other people's constant concern over my problems. I'm not looking for sympathy. Besides, I bet half the people I know around here would believe I'm guilty. I say that on the premise that most people pretending to be friendly really want to think the worst of you in situations like this. You ought to have heard the kidding I took from some of the guys in Woody's bar."

"Well, what do you expect from such riffraff. You'd do well to stay away from those drunks and get back on the wagon right away. You're beginning to sound paranoid," Juanita responded with stern disapproval.

"I'll dry out. Just give me time, woman."

"At least we can tell Leonard about the indictment, can't we?

"Sure, sure," I said "I'll tell the kid. Let me handle it."

"All right, dear. Now, can I fix you any breakfast? How about eggs and sausage this morning?"

"No, thanks. I'll just have some dry cereal, a piece of toast, and more coffee. I'm going to take the day off and go see Tolliver."

"Yes. I think you should. Do you want me to go with you?"

"That won't be necessary. I just want to get his thoughts about the case before deciding whether he's right for handling my troubles."

"Oh, I see. Well, just relax with your paper while I fix breakfast. Everything is certain to be all right if you have to go to trial," Juanita said optimistically before cautioning me, "Now, Talbert, please don't go into Tolliver's office with liquor on your breath. Be serious."

"Hell, woman! I am serious! What do you keep bringing up liquor for anyway? I know how to act in situations like this," I blurted out in a peevish manner.

"It's just that this thing is too serious to be mixing with heavy drinking. I can smell alcohol on you this morning, and you shouldn't be drinking, and you know it!"

"Okay! Okay! Knock it off, will you! You're bugging the shit out of me!" I shouted.

Juanita grew sullen and walked into the kitchen. I knew she was right about drinking, but I got edgy just thinking or relinquishing my liquid crutch. Somehow, though, I knew that I would have to get back on the wagon—and soon! But I also knew that I could not quit drinking today. I'd be nervous as hell without a drink. In fact, I needed a little bracer that very moment. Getting up from my chair, I went to my room and finished the bottle of gin. Then I used a strong mouthwash and went back downstairs.

Juanita and Leonard were both on vacation from school for the summer. The boy was still asleep when I looked into his room. I had told him about my past criminal record when he was thirteen and old enough to understand because I did not want him to hear about my past from someone else. I therefore had personally prepared him with knowledge of the shady life I had once led. Now I would have to explain about the indictment to him. But he was a good kid and would be the first to stand up and defend me against such trumped-up charges. Because he knew I had always been on the level with him.

When my sixteen-year-old son, Leonard, came downstairs that morning looking for his breakfast, I put my newspaper aside and asked to speak with him for a few minutes. The lad sensed something serious in my attitude and turned his full attention upon me.

"Yeah. What's up, Dad!" he asked with a curious expression.

"Sit down, son," I said, pointing to the sofa in the living room. When he lowered his tall slender frame onto the cushion, I went on, "Your father's been indicted and must stand trial on charges that he burned our store in an attempt to defraud the insurance company," I explained matter-of-factly.

"What!" the boy exclaimed. Then he smiled with obvious disbelief. "Ah, c'mon, Dad, be serious. You're kiddin'."

"Not really, son. I'm very serious. Here's the indictment," I said, handing him the copy.

Leonard's handsome brown-skinned face was drawn into a sober mask of concentration as he read the indictment. When he was finished, he laid it on the cocktail table in front of the sofa, commenting, "This is really unbelievable! Dad, you never burned that place."

"I'm sure I didn't. But I've got a fight on my hands to convince a jury that I didn't do it. I'm going to see Mr. Stanley Tolliver today. He's a good criminal lawyer, and we'll get to the bottom of this mess. But I just wanted you to know what's happening, son. And I'd also appreciate it if you wouldn't discuss this with your friends or other members of the family at this time. There's no need to upset anyone else. This is my personal problem."

"Sure, Dad, whatever you say. You know Mom and I will stand by you all the way. We know you're innocent."

"Thanks, son. It'll come out all right in the end. I—"

Leonard cut in. "I always figured there was somethin' funny goin' on when those fire investigators switched the fire from the empty store to our store as the place where the fire was supposed to have originated. Yeah. There's somethin' awful fishy about this indictment, Dad. Those firemen are out to get you 'cause you're black. They're all prejudiced in Maple Heights. Everybody knows that around here. I told you about the run-in I had with those guys when I tried to protect the property in the store window, so I know those fireman aren't right."

"Perhaps that's true," I responded thoughtfully. "Because I'm sure the fire investigators and the insurance adjuster aren't bothered too much about trying to get at the truth as they are about trying to get after me. They were looking for a scapegoat all the time, and now, as it turned out, I am the scapegoat. But they have underestimated me if they think I'm going to be a sitting duck."

"You ought to sue those jokers, Dad, for false accusations," Leonard said, rising from the sofa with a look of disgust.

I smiled at him reassuringly. "First things first, my son. And the first thing right now is to win an acquittal on these phony charges before bringing any charges of my own. Now you run along and have your breakfast."

When Leonard went into the kitchen, I remained thoughtful for several minutes. I had never told any of the friends I had made in the Cleveland area about my past. And the few people who did know about it were ex-cons I had served time with that I would chance to meet from time to time. But those guys were discreet. They were also as anxious to conceal their own criminal records as much as I wanted to conceal mine.

I had been cool and stayed out of trouble. Not once in the eighteen years since I resided in and around Cleveland was I ever arrested for anything. The cops didn't have a damn thing on me downtown at the detective bureau. I was clean. Soon, however, I would be dirty again once my FBI file came back from Washington. Because after I was arraigned, I would be taken into custody, then mugged and printed before I could make bond. Chances were good though that the arson investigators or the insurance company's lawyer had already found out about my criminal record if they checked me out through the Chicago Police Department or the FBI. Be that as it may, if the shit hadn't already hit the fan, it wouldn't be long until it did, and I would be splattered all to hell before they were done with me.

*   *   *   *   *

Stanley Tolliver was a tall brown-skinned man with long sideburns that tapered into a thick moustache. He was in his midfifties and had rather large dark-brown eyes that stared at me candidly as he listened quietly while I went over my past history and the facts surrounding my arson case. Occasionally, Tolliver would ask a question. But mostly, he just leaned back and listened without interruption.

The *Ebony* containing my story was on his desk. Now and then, Tolliver would glance at the magazine and then at me as though he were trying to fathom how the man in the magazine story could be the same man across the desk from him pouring out his agony, indignation, and innocence in such a plaintive manner. Maybe I wasn't coming across very well. Most criminal lawyers on first meetings have a tendency to believe that their clients are guilty, and I wondered what Tolliver was really thinking when the brow beneath his receding hairline would furrow between his eyes as he sat there with an intense probing look on his countenance.

I had been drinking rather heavily and was feeling somewhat depressed and sorry for myself instead of sounding confident and aggressive, the way I usually do when I get indignant over something. I also wondered whether Tolliver could detect that I had been drinking as his chilly gaze never left my face. I decided then to tell him about my alcohol problem and about how I fell off the wagon the day of the fire.

Having heard me out, Tolliver thanked me for being candid with him about my past and the facts of the case. He then acknowledged that he would accept the case. We agreed on a retainer fee, and he advised me how the legal procedures would be handled. There would be a pretrial hearing where the prosecution and the defense would produce what evidence each intended to use at the trial. He also told me about the prospect of plea bargaining at pretrial hearings, even though he felt that I would hold true to my course in demanding a jury trial. I assured him that I had not thought whatsoever of doing anything else but that.

When Tolliver was done advising me, he seemed neither impressed nor unimpressed with me or my legal background. He had been very matter-of-fact in his approach to the case, and I still did not know what his thoughts were as to my guilt or innocence on the basis of what I had told him.

Before leaving his office Tolliver and I chitchatted about things other than law for a few minutes. Suddenly, he became very warm and friendly. I noticed several trophies for marathon running on shelves in his comfortably appointed office. It was then that he expressed his fondness for jogging daily and competing in marathon races even at his present age.

Tolliver was also very prominent in civic and community affairs, and I felt satisfied when I left his office that he would be more than capable of defending me against the charges in my indictment.

A few weeks later, I appeared in court and entered a plea of not guilty at my arraignment. Bail was set at $5,000. Judge Lloyd O. Brown was assigned as my trial judge. This I considered to be a break because he was a distinguished black jurist who had sat on the Ohio Supreme Court at one time, and he had a reputation among his colleagues as being a legal scholar. Lawyers also held him in high esteem for his brilliance as well as his fairness in presiding over judicial proceedings. Since all I could ask or hope for was a fair trial, it was comforting to know that I had been assigned a trial judge capable of giving me just that.

Following the arraignment proceedings, I was held in temporary custody in the receiving room at the Cuyahoga County Jail, which was also located in the Justice Center. I remained there for well over one hour before Tolliver was able to arrange to have me released on a $500 bond. That was the first time I had been in jail in one hell of a long time. Even though it was for only a short period, I still dreaded the thought of being locked up again even for a minute, much less an hour or two.

"Holy shit!" I thought. "Man, you got to get on the stick and beat this bum beef with your feet on the street, because experience has taught you, guilty or innocent, once you're in, it's tough as hell to get out!" I told myself.

Tolliver had won hundreds of cases in his long legal career. But one case he won probably pleased him more than any of the others, simply because he rescued an innocent man from the penitentiary who, like other innocent men pointed out in the foregoing chapters of this book, had spent part of his life in prison for something he did not do.[§]

*   *   *   *   *

With determination and help from my doctor, I was able to withdraw from the use of alcohol and get back into the AA program. Soon, my mind was restored to complete sobriety, and I was able to devote full concentration to making preparations for my upcoming trial.

I spent a lot of time in the main public library downtown researching and studying arson and arson investigation. Fortunately, Cleveland has one of the nation's best library systems, and I was able to find a wealth of information on the subject I was interested in. I took home for perusal such outstanding volumes as *Physical and Technical Aspect of Fire and Arson* by John R. Carroll, *Fire Investigation* by P. L. Kirk, and *Principles of Fire Protection* by Percy Bugbee. Those three books told me just about all I wanted to know about fires and arson investigation.

Prior to the fire that destroyed my store, I knew hardly anything at all about arson investigation. But when I was done reading

---

[§]   Dale A. Sutton, a twenty-six-year-old black man, was convicted by jury in the United States District Court in Cleveland for the alleged holdup of a United States postal station. The US postal inspectors enlisted the help of a dog trainer whose German shepherd was given a scent from Sutton's bedsheet and the dog, having been used in other federal criminal investigations around the country, placed Sutton at the scene of the crime. And the jurors chose not to believe Sutton's relatives and friends, who placed him many miles away in another county at the time of robbery, but instead elected to believe the dog. Whereby Sutton was convicted and sentenced to serve twenty-five years in the federal penitentiary. Tolliver produced evidence that another man had committed the crime for which Sutton was imprisoned, and Sutton was freed when the authorities obtained a confession from the man who had actually committed the robbery. On March 15, 1983, Sutton walked out of the federal prison in Terre Haute, Indiana, and Tolliver had this to say: "As a practicing lawyer for thirty years, I have never been one to try to defend this legal system. If you've got money, you get justice. If you don't have money, you get justice. If you don't have money, you don't get justice. Sutton's family is very poor."

at the library and at home, while at the same time making copious notes from the material, I knew all the basics for a thorough arson investigation as well as the natural causes of fires that involved faulty electrical systems, carelessness, and other accidental reasons. This information greatly aided me in making determinations of what the arson investigators in my own case may have overlooked or failed to do in making their own investigation when all the facts of their investigation were divulged.

My own training as a legal investigator helped me enormously in understanding what a full and fair investigation entails. If Joe Scharfenburg and Pete Petronis, the two arson investigators, deemed this an open-and-shut case and this defendant an ordinary person, they were in for one hell of a surprise! Because I came across numerous deficiencies in their investigation through both their inadvertent and willful neglect while trying to build a case against me.

I had done my homework well. Now I was ready to pit my legal skills and newly acquired arson knowledge against the case that had, in my opinion, been mostly constructed on manufactured evidence, which was cleverly presented as circumstantial evidence to obtain my indictment and hopefully my subsequent conviction. For I knew beyond all doubt that there was no flammable gasoline in my shop on the day the fire occurred.

Attorney Tolliver, in pretrial conferences with the prosecution, was able to obtain copies of documents to be used as evidence against me. One such piece of evidence was the "Arson Laboratory Report" that the deputy state fire marshal obtained. The report consisted of the findings made from samples of evidence taken from our store, Zodiac World, by Investigator Petronis for identification of accelerant, explosive, fuse, and electrical examination. These items taken from our shop exactly as they appeared in the report consisted of the following:

1. Gal. Can with fire debris from rear reading room baseboard.
2. Gal. can with carpet debris from reading room and hallway.

3. Qt. can with fire debris from hallway area.
4. Plastic bag with baseplug from reading room.
5. Plastic bag with 3 battery pack.

Findings:

Gas chromatographic analysis of extract samples revealed

a) Exhibit #1 to contain a hydrocarbon identified as deteriorated gasoline.
b) Exhibit #2 to contain a hydrocarbon identified as a mixture of gasoline and multi-component hydrocarbon which does not match current laboratory standards.
c) Exhibit #3 to contain a multi-component substance which could not be further identified.

Examination of Exhibit revealed an open circuit through the 6 inches or so of attached wiring. This outlet and its wire did not overheat electrically, and the damage to the front of the duplex outlet is a result of the fire.

Examination of Exhibit #5 revealed what appears to be three size 'D' batteries held together by molten plastic. This could be part of a 'device,' but it is more likely to have been a power pack for something requiring considerable power such as a toy, tape recorder, electronic flash unit, etc.

Here, again, I knew positively that there was no flammable gasoline present in the rear reading room at the baseboard or on the carpet in the reading room or so-called hallway where the investigators had established the "point of origin" of the fire. I knew this beyond all doubt. This report therefore only reinforced my belief that these investigators had deliberately manufactured evidence to create the "point of origin" of the fire near or almost in the same spot where I had told them that I first observed flames on the floor and wall.

Since I had admitted that I was the only one in the store on the day of the fire, Scharfenberg and Petronis were trying to lock me in the corner, so to speak, where I admitted being when I observed the first signs of fire in the shop. Next, they wanted to establish this area as the "point of origin" and then show evidence of a flammable liquid (gasoline) having been poured in the area. The picture of what they were trying to do was all too clear to me.

The noose was tightening fast to snare me in a trap contrived of manufactured evidence. It would be near impossible to convince anyone other than my wife and son that these two so-called highly respected arson investigators were literally framing me to make a case of arson. Perhaps they sincerely believed that I was guilty and wanted to make certain that they had sufficient evidence to prove their case, so they apparently started manufacturing some evidence. A finding of gasoline at the spot where I admitted seeing fire would be the clincher, they evidently thought. But if I didn't put gasoline there, who did? Or, in fact, was there ever any gasoline in that area of the store? No. I knew that there was no gasoline in that area or anywhere else in the shop on the day of the fire. This therefore had to be a frame-up.

Tolliver had an extremely worried look on his face when he told me in the corridor of the Justice Center, "Mr. Jennings, the prosecution feels that they have a very strong case of arson against you. I have examined much of the state's evidence, and I have shared it with you. Now I must share my thoughts with you regarding that evidence in telling you that we are going to be up against a very tough case."

"I appreciate your frankness and concern, Mr. Tolliver." I replied. "I do not expect this to be an easy fight. But I do believe that we can overcome their evidence and so-called motive that I was in financial trouble when the fire occurred. I believe that we can present sufficient evidence to overcome all of their charges."

"Well, I should truly hope so," Tolliver responded with an ambiguous look on his face that was unmistakable.

"In any event, sir, I want to point out now, and point out very clearly, that I intend to fight this case all the way. I am innocent—no matter what the state's superficial evidence looks like at this time. And I would never, not for one moment, bargain with the state over my liberty in this matter—under no circumstances will I do that! No! Never!" I exclaimed with firm resolution.

Tolliver raised his brow in a thoughtful manner before he replied, "Just as you say, Mr. Jennings. I'll do my very best when we go to trial, you can bank on that."

"Thank you, sir. I'm sure I can. Your best is all I could hope for," I quickly responded before he excused himself to take care of other legal business on his schedule.

I stood in the corridor for a few moments after Tolliver had left. Once again, I wondered what he really thought about my claim of innocence. I could tell from his expression that the arson laboratory report had diminished much of the previous confidence that he had shown. This was understandable, because when I originally talked to Tolliver, I had no knowledge of the arson report or where if any place the investigators would try to say gasoline was used to start and fuel the fire.

Certainly, if I assumed that the investigators detected obsolete gasoline on the carpet that may have leaked from my son's moped, then the gasoline would have been inert and incapable of starting a fire, or even fueling a fire for that matter. Because the moped had not been in the store for several days. Only fresh gasoline could start and fuel a fire to create the "point of origin" that the investigators were trying to establish. And once again, I knew positively that there was no fresh gasoline in our shop on the day of the fire.

Scharfenberg and Petronis were gambling on their word and esteemed credentials as fire investigators over my word as a businessman, having so-called financial difficulties and a questionable reputation, who they could place at the exact spot where the fire is supposed to have been started by use of a flammable liquid. It was not difficult to see that this was a damning situation.

But as said before, "I had done my homework well," and I was ready for almost any eventuality. Tolliver, on the other hand, would have to rely on my newly enlarged knowledge about arson investigation in conjunction with the facts of the case known to me personally as much as I would have to rely on his many years of trial experience in defending criminal cases. I was concerned, yes. But I was not intimidated by the state's case or deeply worried over the "arson laboratory report." For I firmly believed that it could be overcome by factual evidence for the defense presented at the right time and in the right manner.

Chapter 22

OHIO LAW PROVIDES THAT "A person against whom a charge of felony is pending ***shall be brought to trial within two hundred seventy days after arrest."

If the defendant does not cause any delay on his part in being brought to trial within the statutory provisions for a speedy trial, it is incumbent upon the trial court to dismiss the charges against the defendant.

In my own particular case, I caused no delays in being brought to trial within the 290-day period, so when the date to be tried ran right down to the wire, Judge Brown summoned my attorney and me into court on April 2, 1981, and the judge announced that I would have to be tried on that date unless I signed a waiver of my constitutional and statutory right to a speedy trial. I of course refused to do so even though Tolliver complained that he was not prepared to try the case on that date. Tolliver advised me that if I signed the waiver, the judge would set a date for trial in the near future. But I remained adamant in my refusal to waive my right to a speedy trial, and I demanded that I either be tried immediately or that the charges against me be dismissed.

I had waited long enough for trial and was well aware that if I signed the waiver, I would be placing myself at the mercy of the prosecution to try me whenever they damned well pleased should Judge Brown become ill, expire, or leave office before being able to try my case. No, I could not chance any of those things happening. It was now or never.

Going to trial unexpectedly was something of an imposition on my attorney. Because Tolliver had other obligations on his trial calendar that would have to be cancelled. He nevertheless had no alternative but to try the case on the date we were in court since I had demanded trial. Judge Brown therefore ordered a panel of prospective jurors be brought into the courtroom for examination.

The trial got underway after the selection of a jury. Although I did not know at that time that two of my most crucial witnesses would not be available to testify in my behalf at the trial. This was later to prove a great handicap to my defense.

Following the opening statements to the jury by counsel, the assistant county prosecutor, Mr. Edward J. Sullivan, and my attorney, Mr. Stanley Tolliver, girded themselves for the legal battle ahead of them.

The state put their first witness on the stand. He was the police officer that arrived on the scene shortly after the fire had started. The officer testified that he responded to a holdup alarm—not a fire alarm—when he arrived at the scene of the fire. It was theorized by fire officials that the fire had burned through the burglar and holdup alarm wires in our store to trigger the alarm system.

The officer also testified that he went straight to Zodiac World and observed smoke in the store, and he did not observe any smoke coming out of the empty store. The stage was therefore being set very early in the trial proceedings to discredit my statement that the first signs of smoke and fire emanated from the empty store next door.

As the trial progressed, other witnesses for the state, firemen and the arson investigators, all testified that there was no evidence that the first signs of fire came from the empty store.

The captain in charge of the first fire truck to arrive on the scene testified that his fire truck arrived within two or three minutes after receiving the alarm, because the fire station was located only a short distance from the shopping center. He further testified that the fire had a good start when he and his men arrived. He stated that the fire had probably been "cooking" in the rear of Zodiac World for about an hour before the alarm was received. This of course was more of a hyperbole than an attempt at perjury. The captain's statement, nevertheless, indicated to me the zeal and dedication that was obviously being employed to try to mislead the jury of the true facts in the case. The captain also gave misleading testimony that he and his men started using water to fight the fire almost immediately after they arrived on the scene.

The pattern of misleading, false and exaggerated testimony continued as I sat and listened with disgust while these state witnesses seemingly wove an arachnoid net of circumstantial evidence around me to indicate that I was the arson culprit responsible for this conflagration that caused an estimated $750,000 in damages to the three stores that were completely destroyed.

Pete Petronis, the deputy fire marshal, endeavored to convince the jury by reciting his long-experienced background as a fireman, an ex-captain commanding a fire station in Cleveland, and his wealth of experience gained as an arson investigator with the state of Ohio as being prime factors that his word and investigative skills were infallible. His testimony was therefore extremely important to the state's case; and the state, through direct examination by the prosecuting attorney, Mr. Sullivan, elicited the following damaging testimony from Petronis:

That the burn pattern in Zodiac World indicated that the fire definitely started in our store and spread to the two stores next door on either side of it.

That the fire was started by gasoline (as indicated in the arson laboratory report).

That the gasoline was poured on the floor a few feet on either side of the rear doorway leading from the front of the store to the rear of the store.

That this was described as a "trailer" of the flammable liquid at the point of origin of the fire.

That I was the only one present in the store on the day of the fire by my own admission—and therefore I was the only one who could have set the blaze.

Admittedly, Petronis sounded very scientific and professional in giving his testimony—the result no doubt of testifying at numerous trials on the causes of fires and arson. Yet there were glaring flaws in his testimony and investigative technique as to the thoroughness of his investigation, which now was apparent to me from my newly acquired knowledge of arson investigation.

All during Petronis's testimony, I had been making notes of the defects in his statements. I now turned my notes over to Tolliver before he commenced his cross-examination of the witness.

Tolliver studied the notes very carefully before he stood up to start his cross-examination. Occasionally, he would return to the defense table and glance at the notes before continuing on with his relentless cross-examination. It was easy to see that Tolliver was an old pro when he went into action digging for flaws and skillfully leading the witness into a false sense of security by cleverly injecting humor into some of his questions in a carefree manner that was almost disarming.

MR. TOLLIVER. Now, Mr. Petronis, when you found out that Mr. Jennings' son owned a "mophead"—

The whole courtroom exploded with laughter.

THE COURT. That's "moped," not "mophead," Mr. Tolliver.

MR. TOLLIVER. Ah yes, Your Honor, "mopehead."

THE COURT. No, no. It's "moped."

MR. TOLLIVER. Yes, "moped." Thank you, Your Honor.

MR. TOLLIVER. Well, Mr. Petronis, when you found out about the "mopehead" did you ask to examine it to see whether it had a leak in the fuel tank or motor?

MR. PETRONIS. No, sir.

THE COURT: Again, I must remind you, Mr. Tolliver, it's a "moped," not a "mopehead.

By now, the courtroom was in stitches as Tolliver feigned puzzlement. When the laughter subsided, he went on to bring out the following things in his cross-examination of Petronis:

Petronis conceded that although he had knowledge that a gasoline forklift truck was parked in the empty store next door to Zodiac World, he did not take any samples of fire debris from the store for submission to the arson laboratory to determine whether hydrocarbons (compounds found in gasoline, oil, paint, and like materials) were present.

Petronis further admitted that although he was aware that I had told him of sparking in the electrical panel box when I turned my outside sign on, he, nevertheless, did not submit the panel box to the arson laboratory for examination by an electrical expert—although he did submit one electrical outlet to the laboratory taken from where I had told him that I was using it to power my calculator when it ceased working.

Since my research of the causes of fires had taught me that electrical fires ranked first among fires in hospitals, bowling alleys, motion picture theaters, motels, schools, shopping centers, and supermarkets, Tolliver evidently took heed from my notes, because he pressed hard to bring out the fact that Petronis only paid cursory attention to the electrical problems I had had with my sign—especially since the sign, not quite a year old, had blown two ballasts. Tolliver wanted to know if he was such a competent, qualified, and thorough arson investigator, how did he happen to overlook so important a thing as the sign panel box that sparked when he submitted his other evidence to the arson laboratory?

Petronis was caught off guard. He never gave a satisfactory reply to the question about submitting the sign panel box to the laboratory. When he left the witness stand, he did not appear half as confident as he had demonstrated under direct examination by Mr. Sullivan.

Scharfenberg had been permitted to remain in the courtroom to assist the prosecuting attorney with whom he sat at a table across from the defense table where Tolliver and I sat. All other witnesses had to remain outside the hearing of the witnesses testifying in the courtroom until they gave their testimony. Scharfenberg, however, had reaped the benefit of hearing Petonis's testimony and could anticipate therefrom what to expect by way of cross-examination.

When Scharfenberg took the witness stand to give his rather long testimony that included the showing of over one hundred slide photographs of the fire scene that he had taken, he too appeared confident as he gave his testimony under direct-examination.

Much of Scharfenberg's testimony corroborated Petronis's testimony. He testified, however, that he did make a routine examination of the empty store with a "sniffer," the nickname of a gas detector device used to detect hydrocarbon. Scharfenberg nevertheless failed to detect any hydrocarbon present in the empty store—even though the hydraulic hoses on the forklift truck had burned and spilled oil onto the floor, Scharfenberg endeavored to use his numerous photographs taken at the scene of the fire to establish that the hottest part of the fire centered in Zodiac World, even though from the angles, some of the photographs were taken it was extremely difficult to determine, if not outright impossible, exactly from which store the most flames and smoke were coming through the roof. This was because the three stores involved in the fire all shared a common roof. Scharfenberg, nevertheless, would point to smoke and flame and repeatedly refer to Zodiac World with monotonous regularity in his calm presentation of the evidentiary slides. But I could easily sense that inner cunningness underneath the mask of calm persuasiveness that endured all during his direct testimony when he pointed out the discrepancies he found in my statements about the purchase of the jar of instant coffee on the day of the fire.

Scharfenberg testified that although I had mentioned buying coffee at the K-Mart store, he had examined all the cash register tapes during the time I claimed to have purchased the coffee, and there was no record on the tapes to verify the sale that the tape receipts were recorded by a computer register that showed the date and time of purchase as well as recording the code numbers of items sold.

Scharfenberg also testified about the contradictions in my statements that I made when I stated that I had purchased the coffee at the Fazio's supermarket, which had been closed on the Sunday the fire occurred.

Scharfenberg gave the false impression in his testimony that I was accorded every courtesy in having access to my store after the fire was extinguished. He insisted that their investigation of the fire was completely thorough and fair. And he too testified that it was the result of a holdup alarm that drew the response from the police and fire departments. He went so far as to assert that I did not have a working fire alarm system in my store at the time of the fire.

Attorney Tolliver, standing tall and erect, wasted no time in bringing out the fact from Scharfenberg that he had mentioned that the officer who first arrived on the fire scene would be appearing in court—even before Scharfenberg had actually begun his physical investigation of the stores involved in the fire.

Scharfenberg's calm demeanor was slightly ruffled as he sought to justify his obviously prejudicial remark about "court" by falsely testifying that prior to the taking of the tape-recorded statement I had asked him outside in the parking lot that "if the fire was found to be deliberately set by someone, would the guilty party be prosecuted?"

I of course never made such a remark to Scharfenberg, and by him testifying to this outright lie made me completely convinced that I was being deliberately framed. It was therefore very clear to me now that they would go to any length to try to obtain my conviction. I noticed, too, that Judge Brown—who had been reclining in his chair at ease behind the bench, patiently digesting the evidence—suddenly drew himself forward with a profound thoughtful expression on his dark-brown countenance. The jury also appeared to be deeply interested as Tolliver brought out the fact that Scharfenberg was thinking arson and court before he had actually made a physical investigation of the fire scene.

Tolliver went on to further bring out during his cross-examination of Scharfenberg that although he spent a lot of time investigating the purchase of the coffee, he did not show any interest in investigating my son's moped that I had called to their attention in the deposition I made to the Nationwide Insurance Company's attorney, Mr. Harold Reader.

I had told Mr. Reader that the moped had been in the shop several days before the fire and that the moped leaked small quantities of gasoline on the carpet. This of course could have explained any traces of gasoline that was found on the samples of carpeting submitted to the arson laboratory. Scharfenberg did not therefore want to involve himself in anything that might shed light on my innocence.

When the manager of the K-Mart store was called to give his testimony corroborating that the cash register tapes did not show the purchase of the coffee during the time I claimed I had bought it, Tolliver, on cross-examination, very cleverly elicited from the manager that it was customary that there were shortages and overages when the registers were checked at the end of the day, and that there were more often overages than shortages in the registers.

Tolliver, obviously recalling that I stated in the deposition made in Attorney Reader's office that I "picked up the coffee and walked through the cashier," after plucking down the exact amount of money to pay for the purchase, I therefore never got a receipt as I hurried out of the store so that I could open Zodiac World on time. The statement in the deposition was made long before my indictment. But the investigators were using anything and everything against me that might prove a contradiction or false statement no matter how immaterial or undeliberate. At the same time the investigators sought to suppress or ignore anything of substance that might be in my favor, such as investigating the leaking moped.

Common sense should have told Scharfenberg and Petronis that I had nothing to gain by saying I purchased the coffee and was thereby away from Zodiac World for a short period. I could not use my brief absence from the store as an alibi because I had locked the store before I left and had already admitted that no one was in the store or had access to the store other than myself from the time I opened the store until the time I discovered it on fire.

It was obvious now that in my eagerness to be as truthful as possible with the investigators, I had opened avenues that, by unforeseen circumstances, could be exploited as either lies or deliberate contradictions. But in this particular instance, the redeeming factor fortunately turned up in my favor when I stated that "I walked through the cashier" when I purchased the coffee.

Under such circumstances, it could be reasoned that the sale was not recorded properly. The manager of K-Mart acknowledged that it was not unusual for a customer to make a purchase in that manner, although it was not a policy of the store to encourage such transactions.

Mr. Sullivan was highly regarded as one of the most resourceful prosecutors on the staff of the county prosecutor's office, and Sullivan evidently meant to keep from the reach of the defense attorney any witnesses that might prove damaging to the state's case under cross-examination. He therefore did not call as a witness for the state the Maple Heights fire chief. The chief had been quoted in the press as saying, "It was first thought that the fire started in the empty store." Nor did Sullivan call the president of the shopping center to the witness stand who had negotiated the lease with me for the store that was to become Zodiac World. Instead he called the manager of the shopping center to give testimony concerning my arrearage in rental payments. The purpose was to indicate to the jury that I was in financial trouble and operating my business at a loss. The manager, however, did not have a true grasp of the facts concerning my lease or the arrangements I had made with the president of the shopping center.

It developed at the trial that it was the brother of the shopping center manager who held the contract to remodel the empty store, and the brother testified that he was present in the empty store on the day of the fire, a couple hours before the fire was discovered. At the time he was present inspecting the empty store, he testified that he found nothing amiss. He did, however, admit to garaging the gasoline forklift truck in the empty store, although he denied that any gasoline was kept in the store to fuel the forklift truck which was loaned to him by the shopping center management.

Tolliver, on cross-examination, tried to leave the impression that if the fire had in fact started in the empty store there may have been a cover-up attempt to escape liability by the Southgate Management Company and the brother of the manager of the shopping center whose company was doing the remodeling work.

Tolliver, known to be a vigorous civil rights proponent, really wanted to bring out the fact that as a black businessman, I was never actually welcomed at Southgate. There were four black jurors on the jury, and this would obviously provoke them to profound contemplation and probably stir the consciences of the white jurors as well that maybe there was some hanky-panky going on to oust the nigger. But by not calling the president of the Southgate Management to testify, the prosecution had cleverly precluded that possibility.

We thought of calling the president of the shopping center, but Tolliver, on second thought, very wisely decided against it, no doubt basing his decision—which I certainly agreed with—on the legal truism that "an attorney should never ask a question of a hostile witness called for the defense unless he knows what the answer will be."

The insurance adjuster for the Nationwide Insurance Company, Mr. James Morman, was called as another state witness to establish that I held an insurance policy with Nationwide and was attempting to recover my fire loss based on that policy.

It had been obvious to me from the beginning when I first met Mr. Morman, a few days after the fire, that he was partial to Petronis and Scharfenberg's investigation. Because if the investigation could produce sufficient evidence to charge me with arson, Nationwide would not be obligated to pay my claim for the fire loss.

It therefore came as no surprise to me at the trial when Norman testified against me. He particularly testified that I asked him whether or not I had "business interruption insurance." The implication was meant to establish that I burned the store down thinking that I had business interruption insurance as well as insurance on the contents of the store. To the contrary, this should have indicated to any fair-minded person how uninformed I was about business insurance. Because no sensible arsonist would burn his property for insurance unless he actually was aware that he had ample insurance in force when he committed the act. But this was the type of low-mentality person that the arson investigators, the insurance company's attorney, and their adjuster apparently underestimated me as being; and if they sincerely believed that I was actually a person of such stultified intelligence, they surely found themselves the victims of their own surprise before the case was closed.

I had only become aware of the question of business interruption insurance after the fire when I was asked by Bill White whether it was included in my insurance policy. Since I had turned all of my insurance papers over to the Alex Sill Company to adjust my claim, I did not know for a fact whether the policy included business interruption insurance. I therefore had asked Morman whether he knew if I had it simply because he was a representative of Nationwide. As it turned out, I didn't have business interruption insurance; and the prosecution, through Morman's testimony, tried to make it appear that I actually thought that I had it before burning the store.

When the prosecution rested its side of the case, even though the burden of proof was on the state to prove me guilty beyond a reasonable doubt, I realized that I was still saddled with a tremendous burden to offer sufficient proof to refute and contradict the evidence presented by the prosecution. Because the manufactured, circumstantial, and false evidence presented against me could be devastating if not convincingly met with a preponderance of evidence to substantiate my innocence.

Judge Lloyd Brown had very fairly and commendably ruled before the start of the trial that the state could not use my past criminal record against me during the trial proceedings before the jury; because my prior conviction was too old. The crime for which I had been convicted occurred over thirty years prior to my trial in the instant case. I had fully paid my debt for the old offense and had not been convicted or accused of a crime since my release from prison until accused of the current offense.

To raise my past record at the trial would have been purely prejudicial and would not have served to provide any proof of my guilt whatsoever. And the only way that the state could bring my past criminal record up at the instant trial would be to question my character if we called any character witnesses. Needless to say, we had no such plans. And not being able to bring up my past record during the trial was evidently a great disappointment to Petronis and Scharfenberg.

In lieu of trying to present me as a person of exemplary character, our strategy was to truthfully level with the jury right from the start and relate to them my alcoholism, which I had always tried to conceal because I deemed it a character weakness.

In this instance, however, we deemed it advantageous to use my alcoholism as a part of my defense to show that because of it, I was vulnerable to forgetfulness and periods of disorientation in times of stress. This could well explain the self-contradiction concerning where I purchased the coffee on the day of the fire.

To the great surprise of the prosecution, we called to the witness stand the bartender of the Touch a Glass Lounge, a bar in the Southgate Shopping Center located a short distance from Zodiac

World. The bartender, a friendly and easygoing young man, testified that on the afternoon of the fire, I came into the bar and ordered a drink. He had never seen me in the bar before but remembered me because I mentioned that I was the owner of Zodiac World, which was one of the stores on fire at the time. The bartender went on to further testify that I appeared upset and that I drank more than one drink while in the bar, but he could not recall exactly how many drinks I had.

The testimony of the bartender was not sufficient to prove that I was a full-fledged alcoholic. And unfortunately, my personal physician was out of the state involved in medical refresher studies. Without the testimony of the physician, Judge Brown would not allow the certified medical records of the physician's diagnosis and treatment to be admitted into evidence. This was my first bad break. The second and most crucial bad break came when my accountant, who had promised to be in court to testify, did not show up to do so. I had made the mistake of trusting him and, therefore, did not have a subpoena served on him to appear in court. The accountant consequently elected to go on a business trip with the assumption that he would be back in time to testify at my trial, but he did not arrive back in time.

Tolliver and I had placed a great deal of confidence in the accountant's ability to demonstrate to the jury that my net worth exceeded the $20,000 insurance that I carried on the contents of the store. Now, without his testimony on record, our defense had been seriously deprived of a vital piece of evidence.

Delores O'Bryant made an excellent witness in testifying that she and I had a verbal agreement to sell her the store as a franchise, and that we had just about worked out final negotiations for the sale when the fire destroyed the store. Here, again, we needed the accountant to corroborate Delores's testimony, because he had been retained to make a final accounting of the assets and liabilities of the business in preparation for the transfer of the business to Delores O'Bryant.

Dick Howell, the optician, appeared and testified that Delores and I endeavored to lease a store from him shortly after the fire to continue doing business as Zodiac World. This part of our defense was to show that I had no plans to discontinue the business after the fire.

Leonard and my wife's testimony established that our son's moped leaked small amounts of gasoline and that Leonard had parked the moped in the rear of the store until I discovered it being parked there and ordered him to park it outside.

I testified to the pertinent facts concerning the fire as previously written about in this book, and Mr. Sullivan, the prosecutor, put me under relentless cross-examination but was never able to knock any material holes in my testimony.

We called as a defense witness the manager of ADT, who was in charge of supervising the monitoring of the fire and theft alarms in our store. Contrary to what Scharfenberg and the police officer had testified to concerning the alarm system in Zodiac World, the manager of ADT testified that I did indeed have a working thermo-heat fire detector alarm system in the store on the day of the fire, and he further testified that he personally received the fire alarm on the day of the fire and relayed it to the Maple Heights Police and fire authorities. He concluded testifying that he did not receive a burglary or holdup alarm over the alarm systems in Zodiac World. This of course contradicted what the police and fire investigators had previously testified to.

The manager of the Buddy Simon Sign Company testified that I did have electrical problems with the outdoor sign, that the sign had to be repaired because one of the ballasts burned out. He also testified that an examination of the sign after the fire also showed that another ballast had burned out. He acknowledged that I had complained of sparking in the panel box that housed the switch for the sign and that it was possible that a short circuit in the box could have been responsible for blowing out the ballasts but that he could not say truthfully that that was the reason that the ballasts in the comparatively new sign did burn out. His testimony was helpful if not conclusive in establishing a short circuit in the switch.

Tolliver made a brilliant closing argument in my defense to the jury. But when the jury went out to deliberate, he expressed his dismay that my physician and accountant had not been present to testify.

Perhaps it was his trial instinct, drawn from many courtroom battles in criminal cases, that gave him a qualmish feeling about winning an acquittal in my case. He seemed hopeful but not too optimistic that we would win the case. Because he said, "Whatever happens, I believe we have someone friendly to our persuasion on that jury."

I tried to appear optimistic and almost confident that the state had failed to prove me guilty beyond a reasonable doubt. But I too would have felt a whole lot better had my accountant and physician been present to testify. Juries are more apt to give credence and credibility to professional testimony over the testimony of friends and relatives of a defendant. At least it is always good to be corroborated by the testimony of a professional person or disinterested party. My defense, however, had been predicated largely on the testimony of friends, associates, and relatives, with the exclusion of the bartender, the manager of ADT, and the manager of the sign company.

The trial had taken over a week to complete hearing the evidence. Now the most agonizing and anxious part of the ordeal was to take place—awaiting the jury's verdict. And little did I realize at the time when Judge Brown gave the jury its final instructions that it would take then) so long to deliberate my fate.

Hours passed into days as I sat outside the courtroom in the corridor of the Justice Center—sometimes I anxiously paced up and down aimlessly like a caged beast. It was a lonely wait, and I had to be present each day in case the jury reached a verdict. Tolliver too had to be in the courthouse, but he went about his other legal business, always leaving word with Judge Brown's bailiff where he could be reached if needed.

My only break in the monotony of waiting came when the bailiff would take the jury to lunch. Then he would advise me what time I could expect them back in the jury room. This would afford me an opportunity to also go to lunch and spend some time walking aimlessly about the downtown section of the city until it was time to return to the Justice Center.

The jury was not sequestered. But the jury was admonished by Judge Brown not to discuss the case with anyone after they left the courtroom to go home each evening about five o'clock.

On the third day of deliberation, I was seated in the corridor reading a newspaper when Mr. Freeman, Judge Brown's bailiff, came out of the courtroom. He was a portly, brown-skinned, congenial person, very courteous and always ready to be of service. "Mr. Jennings," he called to me in a quiet manner. "The jury will be coming in shortly. Have you seen Mr. Tolliver about?"

I stood up, outwardly calm. But all hell was breaking out inside my mind and body. I had the inner shakes. "Why no. I haven't seen him today anywhere around here," I replied a little apprehensively.

"He was down in one of the courtrooms on the third level not too long ago. But when I just called down there, he had evidently left. I'm sure he's still in the building. I'll make a few more calls. Please stand by, Mr. Jennings," he concluded before returning inside the courtroom.

I paced up and down excitedly. "Well, this is it," I whispered to myself. My mind was electrified with thoughts of acquittal and conviction intermingled with the great anxiety that pervaded my brain. Peering into the courtroom I saw Mr. Freeman enter through one of the rear entrances followed by the jury. Judge Brown emerged from another entrance and ascended to the bench cloaked in his black robe.

I stepped quietly into the courtroom and took my position at the defense table as I glanced at the faces of the jurors, trying to read some sign of hope; but their faces were expressionless.

Mr. Sullivan, the prosecutor, appeared out of nowhere. My heart was racing. I held my lips so close together that I could feel the pressure; it was almost painful.

Suddenly, Tolliver appeared at my side, and we were all permitted to be seated. No sooner had my bottom touched the chair than Tolliver leaned over and whispered. "Don't get yourself worked up. The jury only wants to get some additional instructions from the court, this is not a verdict."

At that precise moment, I envisioned myself as a huge balloon being suddenly deflated. The letdown was almost unbearable!

The jury wanted to know the difference between *arson* and *aggravated arson*. It only took the judge a few minutes to inform the jury of the difference. Judge Brown explained that if the jury found that people were occupying any parts of the structure when the fire occurred, that would be *aggravated arson*. But if they found from the evidence that no one was in the structure when the fire occurred, it would only be *arson*. With that out of the way, the jury was sent back to the jury room to deliberate some more while everyone else went about his own business.

Finding myself back in the corridor pacing up and down, my nerves shattered by the recent turn of events, I exclaimed, "Holy shit! I need a drink!" Without further thought of the consequences of taking a drink, I hurried out of the court building and purchased a pint of vodka at a nearby liquor store.

When I reached level twenty of the Justice Center where Judge Brown's courtroom was located, I went straight into the men's rest room just off the corridor. Going into one of the stalls, I consumed a good portion of the vodka before concealing the bag containing the bottle in a receptacle for used paper towels. Thereafter whenever I felt the urge to take another drink that day I would return to my stash.

This was the first liquor I had drank in months. It did not take long before I was feeling no qualms. In fact, the whole world suddenly lit up as one big beautiful globe! The euphoria brought on by the alcohol stimulated my optimism to the point that when I arrived home that evening. I was in a very happy mood, so happy in fact that my wife thought that I had been acquitted.

The jury deliberated seven days before notifying the court that it could not reach a verdict. Being fortified with vodka, I took it all in good stride. At least the suspense had been lifted.

"Next time I would win," I told Tolliver. "Next time. I'll be better prepared. Next time I'll make certain that all of my witnesses are present."

Tolliver found out that the jurors were deadlocked ten for conviction and two for acquittal. It was two of the four blacks on the jury that had held out for my acquittal.

Needless to say, I was extremely grateful for the second chance to establish my innocence. What a disaster it would have been had

I been found guilty on the trumped-up charges leveled against me. Something I had witnessed for years happening to other falsely accused and convicted persons almost happened to me. And I was still not out of the woods.

A few months before my trial, the prosecutor's office had almost succeeded in railroading three innocent young men to prison for the robbery and murder of a Cleveland vice detective that they did not commit. This was the *Sherry* murder Case.

The vice detective, Desmond Sherry, was robbed and killed on July 3, 1980, on Cleveland's East Side. Two brothers, Nathaniel and Roger Wilson, and another suspect, Gerald Edwards, were arrested and charged with the robbery along with two other suspects. The three were arraigned in court on the same date that I was arraigned, July 30, 1980. All five of the suspects had police records and were suspected of committing a rash of robberies and other thefts; but they did not rob and kill Detective Sherry.

The Wilson brothers and Edwards were tried together and acquitted by a jury after the prosecution in sheer desperation had tried in vain to obtain these defendants' convictions on the testimony of a lying pervert, a lying county jail inmate seeking leniency, and other highly unsavory evidence which the jury rightfully refused to believe.

Following the jury's verdict of "not guilty," the police and prosecution screamed to the high heavens over what they deemed to be a great miscarriage of justice. A few days later, however, two teenagers were apprehended, and they confessed to the robbery and slaying of Detective Sherry. These suspects were later tried and convicted.

Prior to being placed on trial, the Wilson brothers and Edwards had all successfully passed lie detector tests. But that did not mean a damn thing to the police or the prosecutor who were all hell-bent on railroading the three suspects on some of the most despicable evidence that this writer has ever known to be used in a criminal trial proceeding.

The *Sherry* case did not endear me to the methods used by the county prosecutor's office—especially after I was almost convicted on lies and manufactured evidence at my trial. But I was by no means a tyro to such questionable methods of prosecuting defendants with tainted evidence. After all, I was a seasoned veteran who had fought injustice in Illinois——- then one of the most notorious states in the union, north of the Mason-Dixon line, for violating the rights of the accused. And if I learned one lesson well as a jailhouse lawyer, it was that most policemen and prosecuting attorneys are far more interested in obtaining convictions than in obtaining justice.

Chapter 23

WITH THE FIRST TRIAL, WHICH settled nothing, behind me, I immediately started making preparations for the retrial that the prosecution was proceeding with. And the biggest problem I had to contend with at this time was a total lack of funds with which to apply toward my second defense. The first trial had left me cash broke and back on the bottle for over six months before I had to check in the hospital to be dried out and regain my sobriety.

A recession was creeping into the nation's economy, and most of the people I knew were holding on to their savings if they had any. Li'l Arthur, being well-heeled, had advanced me some money toward my defense, which came in handy when I really needed it the most. He had moved to Detroit, Michigan, and had gone into the taxicab business. But he died from natural causes in January of 1982, a few months before my second trial. His death cut off any further possibility of obtaining another loan from him.

In desperation, Juanita and I had put our Gold Coast condominium apartment up for sale that we had been leasing out. But this was a time when mortgage interest rates were extraordinarily high and the national economy was sinking lower and lower because of the high inflation plaguing the country during this period. We therefore found it extremely difficult to find a buyer for the condo as the date for my second trial drew nigh.

My situation became even more desperate when I was laid off from my job for lack of work due to the rising recession in the automotive industry. Being without access to funds made me an indigent in the sense that I could not hire counsel of my own choice. And Attorney Tolliver, feeling that he could not put off waiting any longer for me to raise a defense fund, found it necessary to withdraw from the case when the prosecution started pressing harder for a retrial date.

When we appeared before Judge Lloyd Brown, Tolliver moved the court to withdraw from the case as my attorney of record, and he asked the judge to appoint one of his law associates to represent me at the retrial.

I certainly did not relish losing Tolliver as my attorney. He had represented me quite well under the circumstances, and he now possessed a keen knowledge of my case with all of its many problems gleaned from the first trial. I was, however, reluctant to have Tolliver's law associate appointed to represent me, but not because I deemed him incompetent in any respect whatsoever. For he was in fact a very good lawyer. But drawing on my past experience and wisdom in such matters, I still held fast to my old belief that if I had to fight my case as an indigent person, I would prefer to be represented by the public defender's office and take an active part in my defense.

What I really wanted to do more than anything else was to orchestrate my defense and direct it personally. I knew that I was not being egotistical in wanting to aid my own cause. But for practical reasons I realized that without Tolliver, there might be a risk in turning my complete defense over to a newcomer—only to find out too late that we could not work harmoniously together in planning and executing my defense. So, I devised a plan to test Tolliver's associate for compatibility right from the start.

When we appeared before Judge Brown, Tolliver, his associate, the prosecutor, and myself all were present before the bench. Tolliver made his motion to withdraw from the case and the court asked me, "Do you have any objections to the appointment of Tolliver's associate as your court-appointed counsel, Mr. Jennings?"

"I have no objection, Your Honor," I replied, "but I do wish to state that I plan to take an active part in my defense even to the point of cross-examining witnesses and perhaps addressing the jury." Out of the corner of my eye, I could see Tolliver's associate shaking his head negatively, and it was difficult for me to keep from smiling.

My remark had obviously not set too well with the judge either. For he abruptly disqualified himself as the judge to preside over the retrial before he appointed the public defender's office to represent me. My only regret was that Judge Brown would not be presiding over my new trial because I had a profound respect for him as a judge.

Tolliver escorted me down to the public defender's office where we shook hands as I thanked him sincerely for all that he had done in my behalf. He in turn wished me luck before departing. I was now on my own again with the personal legal talent and the wisdom to shape my own destiny.

Mr. Hyman Friedman was the public defender of Cuyahoga County. He had an impressive large complex of offices in the Justice Center for himself and his staff. Some of the assistant public defenders were very talented and others showed great promise of becoming fine defense attorneys.

One of Friedman's brilliant assistants, Donald Tittle, won the acquittal for Gerald Edwards and the Wilson brothers in the *Sherry* murder case. And the PD's office had a good track record for being dependable, fair, and honest in aiding its indigent clients.

The office was fully equipped with all the facilities to do an excellent job. There were social workers, secretaries, and investigators available as well as good lawyers to assist indigent defendants.

A receptionist wrote down my name, address, and telephone number. I was told that I would be contacted when an attorney was selected to represent me. I left the office knowing that one of my best friend's oldest daughter was a social worker employed in the office, and she was the sister of the sales clerk that worked for us at Zodiac World up until the time of the fire. I did not approach my friend's oldest daughter directly to seek favoritism in the appointment of counsel, but I knew that she would automatically be greatly concerned as soon as she found out that I was being represented by the public defender's office.

Several days later, I was notified that Attorney Dave Borland had been appointed to represent me at the retrial, and my friend assured me that his oldest daughter had told him that Borland was one of the best lawyers in the PD's office, that he had worked both sides of the fence—having been an assistant prosecuting attorney before turning to defense work. And it was rumored that Borland wasn't too pleased with what he learned from the prosecuting side of justice and that caused him to make the switch to the defense side. Now one in my position could not ask for anything better than that as a good sign in a lawyer appearing as his defense counsel. I thought before going down to the Justice Center to meet with Borland and put him through a few tests to satisfy myself that we would be able to work together harmoniously.

Dave Borland was a tall, slender, and handsome man in his early thirties. But his youthful features and Ivy League appearance belied his actual age. He had sent me a message to meet him in Judge Harry Jaffe's courtroom for a hearing pertaining to my retrial. Judge Jaffe had been assigned to hear the case.

When I arrived in the courtroom, Borland was already there. We only had time to introduce ourselves and shake hands before the bailiff called the court to order.

Judge Jaffe, who was rather small in stature, stood up as he conducted the proceedings. He appeared to be in his seventies with no hint of senility in his alert demeanor. I later learned that the judge was hearing cases in semiretirement to help alleviate a crowded court docket in the Court of Common Pleas.

The assistant prosecuting attorney, James Columbro, was also a youthful-looking man in his early thirties. He too had that collegiate look about him, which belied his maturity and experience.

The proceedings were brief. The judge wanted to clear the way for a pretrial hearing so that he could set the case down for a trial date. And I thought that this would be as good a time as any to test the attitude of the court as well as the attitudes of Borland and Columbro with respect to my taking an active part in my defense.

"May I address the court, Your Honor?" I asked.

Judge Jaffe nodded. "You may."

"Your Honor, I would like to say at the outset that I plan to take an active part in my defense, cross-examining witnesses and addressing the jury. But I promise not to make a circus out of your courtroom."

There was a moment of thoughtful silence with no audible or visible protest from Borland or Columbro. Finally, Judge Jaffe spoke out in a stern voice, "No one will make a circus of my courtroom, I assure you! But you are within your right to engage in your defense."

"Thank you," I uttered quietly and remained silent as Borland and Columbro agreed to meet at the Maple Heights Fire Department to go over the evidence, since most of the state's evidence was being held at the fire station.

Columbro would arrange to have Scharfenberg and Petronis present one evening, and Borland and I would meet with them at the fire station for the discovery proceedings, i.e., revealing the evidence that each side intended to use at the trial.

I leaned over close to Borland and whispered to him that we be furnished with the same copies of the transcript of evidence introduced at the first trial that the prosecution might obtain for use at the retrial. Because it was a foregone conclusion that the prosecution would want transcripts of what was said by all the key witnesses to refresh their own witnesses' minds as well as to review what the defense witnesses had testified to in case any of them altered their testimony at the retrial.

The court agreed that it was only fair that we be given copies of any evidence that the prosecution had access to that was taken from the first trial.

As we left the courtroom, Borland suggested that he and I go into the privacy of a conference room to go over the case and get better acquainted. Inside the conference room, I gave Borland full details of the case as well as my legal background and past criminal record.

Borland manifested no resentment whatsoever over me taking an active part in my defense. But I knew from experience that most trial attorneys would prefer to represent a client without any interference in the courtroom from the client. The client was like a child to them—to be seen and not heard until spoken to. This of course worked well from the vantage point of the lawyer and the client in most cases, but it did not always work so well for the client under exceptional circumstances when the client was better informed about the case than the lawyer and was also capable of supplying valuable input into his own defense.

Lawyers can retain so much of the facts of a case, but an intelligent client with my experience, not wanting to suffer a conviction, could be depended upon to retain almost everything of value in a case to preserve his ass from going down the drain.

With this in mind, it was my intent to not let any facts of consequence be overlooked in trying the case. Yet I did not really want to be unreasonable. In the back of my mind wisdom dictated that I was not qualified as a trial attorney. Most of my legal experience had been gained from appellate proceedings and post-conviction actions. I had mastered those specialties of the law. Yet I only knew the rudiments of criminal and civil trial procedures and the rules of evidence. It would therefore be foolhardy of me to try to substitute my poorly equipped trial experience and knowledge for that of a highly trained and skilled defense attorney.

I certainly did not intend to end up like Caryl Chessman,** defending myself and ending up with a fool for a client. With this in mind, it was not my real intent to cross-examine any witnesses or address the jury. I just wanted to see to what degree my attorney would go in letting me involve myself in my own case. Borland had passed the test without the slightest apprehension on my part. He as good as said in substance, "I'll try the case anyway you want me to. It's your red wagon."

I was pleased with this well-poised and neat-appearing attorney. "Dave," I said, "you don't mind me calling you Dave, do you?"

"Not at all." He smiled pleasantly.

"No need to be formal, is there? And you can call me Bert,"

I told him before giving him assurance, "I think we're going to hit it off real good together. So I've decided to turn all of the active trial defense work over to you with the provision that I will orchestrate and direct my

---

** In the cause celebre *Chessman* case, Caryl Chessman defended himself against the kidnapping and rape charges before a jury. He was found guilty and sentenced to die in the gas chamber. Many distinguished criminal lawyers felt that the jury may have been more sympathetic had he trusted his defense to a skilled defense attorney and his life may have been spared.

defense. But I will not address the court or jury, nor will I cross-examine any witnesses during the trial. You in turn, however, will consult with me on all important legal decisions and just before concluding your examination of any witness. Do this just in case I have something to add—or have you add," I concluded with a grin.

"Sounds fair enough to me," Dave agreed, obviously pleased that I was leaving the active defense work up to him. But he assured me that he wanted all the help I could give him in directing my defense from my intimate knowledge of the case.

With that put to rest, we shook hands and departed.

*   *   *   *   *

The pretrial meeting at the Maple Heights Fire Station took place several weeks later. This meeting was more for Dave's benefit than for mine since he had to be familiarized with the evidence that the prosecution intended using against me at the trial. Most of the evidence had already been exposed to me during the first trial. The prosecution in the same respect had been exposed to most of the evidence I intended to use, although James Columbro had taken Sullivan's place as the prosecuting attorney at the trial coming up and he too had to familiarize himself with all of the evidence. There were, however, a few new aspects to the case that both sides shared at this meeting.

The photo slides taken by Scharfenberg were shown to Borland along with the gallon cans that contained samples of the fire debris taken from Zodiac World allegedly showing traces of gasoline. Borland and I both made notes during the meeting and displayed some photographs of the fire scene that I had taken. These photographs were to be used as evidence at the retrial along with some other photographs of the interior and exterior of the store that were taken before the fire during our grand opening.

We also displayed another piece of evidence that we intended to use as evidence. It was a diagram of the rear portion of Zodiac World showing placement of the office furniture, storage racks, electrical panel boxes, and outlets. The diagram was very professionally done by my friend Woody, who owned Pat's Lounge. Woody was an industrial arts teacher and draftsman, as well as being a real estate broker.

One of the purposes of the diagram was to show the placement of the storage racks that contained the flammable spray paint and the area where defense testimony at the prior trial had indicated where Leonard's moped was parked. Because it was in this area where the deep burn pattern actually occurred as a result of the spray paint and not gasoline as the investigators would have every one believe. I knew this for a fact because I had personally observed the scene after the fire in making my own investigation. But I was not qualified as a fire expert, and my testimony would not be permitted as such or accepted as such. The jury, however, could use its own discretion in considering all of the facts surrounding the fire.

Scharfenberg had taken photographs of the floor area but in such a way that it was virtually impossible to tell by any identifying marks, due to the almost total destruction of the store, what precise spot the photos were taken at. One would therefore have to rely on Schafenberg's word as to exactly where the photographs were taken. The investigators were therefore in a position to maneuver the deep burn photographed pattern of the floor anywhere in the rear of the store that they pleased.

I of course knew all along what Scharfenberg and Petronis were up to, but as I have said before, "It is almost impossible to convince anyone that you are being framed by public investigating authorities, simply because any such accusations by an accused person are looked upon as self-serving." I therefore kept my thoughts much to myself knowing that if I were ever to be believed that I would first have to have some damn good proof of a frame-up and not just my word for it. Yet as the events continued and unfolded, it was very difficult for me to hide my profound contempt and dislike for Scharfenberg and Petronis—dislike that bordered near hate. No matter how guilty they may have regarded me, they had no right to tamper with the evidence in such a way as to create a situation that was not the absolute truth.

Scharfenberg and Petronis had a diagram of the rear and the front of Zodiac World drawn to show that the deep burn pattern and point of origin of the fire was in the area of the store near the doorway that separated the front of the store from the rear of the store, and the diagram was marked with all of the exhibits of fire debris allegedly found in that particular area. The diagram also showed a bright-red, shaded-in outline of the alleged point of origin of the fire and the so-called trailer of flammable liquid alleged to have been put there by me. All of this evidence was diagramed to show that the point of origin of the fire was a good distance from the storage racks where the spray paint had been stored and where the moped had been parked.

Scharfenberg and Petronis, both wearing smug expressions, were cleverly trying to circumvent my theory that if they found gasoline on the carpet, it came from where the moped had been parked; and if they found deep burn patterns there in the rear of the store, it would have been in the area of the storage racks. This therefore very gravely concerned Dave Borland and me. Because what their diagram and theory purported to show was that I backed out of the rear door into the front of the store pouring gasoline on the carpet. Then I supposedly ignited the fire, used the fire extinguisher, briefly and fled from the store.

Borland remarked as we left the fire station and stood outside in the parking lot: "Bert, their theory with the diagram is very damning to our case, because the point of origin of the fire is moved a considerable distance from where you claim the moped leaking gasoline was parked."

"Yes, it does," I admitted. "And I know what they are up to, but proving it is another thing," I concluded very much concerned over how I could possibly overcome or explain their claim of having found traces of gasoline on the carpet samples taken from that particular area of the store. And the diagram they now had was positive proof that they meant to focus in on and emphasize that the fire was started by the doorway at the rear of the store exactly in the same area where I had said that I first saw flames and smoke.

"One thing is certain, we can't use our diagram of the rear of the store now. It is larger than their diagram and projects the distance where the moped was parked even farther away than their diagram designates as the point of origin of the fire," Dave commented disappointedly.

"Yes, I agree, Dave. We would only be confirming their theory, in a sense, to use our diagram under the circumstances," I responded dejectedly.

As Dave left, I continued to fret over the problem while driving home that night. Suddenly, my subconscious mind evidently released a flow of recollections into my consciousness. Leonard never testified at the first trial that he only parked the moped between the storage racks in the rear of the store. We, Juanita, Delores O'Bryant, and myself, we were the ones who testified that that is where we saw the moped parked. It was now my recollection that Leonard only testified that he had parked the moped in the rear of the store without designating any particular spot. If that were true, then it was quite possible that he had parked the moped in more than one place in the rear of the store.

I would have to review Leonard's testimony given at the first trial to ascertain if my recollection was true, and if proven to be true, we might have a surprise in store to counter the machination being employed by those two cagey and unethical fire investigators. Perhaps both sides could play at the game of maneuvering the evidence.

About a month before my second trial date, Leonard and I took his moped back to the dealer from whom it had been purchased. The moped required certain repairs and a tune-up. But while we were at the repair shop, I seized upon the opportunity to question the mechanic about the gasoline leak that they had not been able to repair satisfactorily. To my appreciative surprise, the young mechanic replied, "This moped was manufactured in Holland, and there is a defect in the type of carburetor used on the engine that is virtually impossible to prevent from leaking very small quantities of gasoline. There is also a fuel shutoff valve on the machine that must be turned off when the machine is parked or not running. Failure to shut it off will cause the gasoline to leak also," he concluded in a positive tone.

I was delighted with the information just imparted to me. I made up my mind then and there to subpoena this young mechanic as a witness and also produce the moped at the new trial. We had only used a photograph of the moped at the first trial. Without telling the mechanic of my plans, I simply thanked him for the information before we left the moped with him to be serviced.

A copy of the transcript of Leonard's testimony given at the first trial proved my recollection correct. He had only testified that he had parked the moped in the rear of the store. When I questioned my son about his parking the moped in the shop I did not make him aware of what he had testified to at the first trial. We were in the living room of our home when I brought up the subject of where he had parked the moped.

I could have asked Leonard to say he parked the moped anywhere in the store I wanted him to park it, and he probably would have done so. But that would have been asking him to lie, and he might get caught up in his prevarication under cross-examination, which, of course, could be very deleterious to my cause. Whatever he testified to, I wanted Leonard to believe it himself. In the living room, there was no prosecutor present to object to leading questions as I cautiously began to interrogate my son.

"Leonard, you parked the moped in more than one spot in the shop, didn't you?"

"Yeah. I guess I did. But most of the time I parked it between the racks."

"Yes, I know, son. But let's not guess. Let's start right when you came to open the store. And remember, son, you had to turn off the burglar alarm within forty-five seconds or it would go off after the front door was opened. Right?"

"Right. Well, now I just went in and turned it off right away, Dad."

"But you didn't leave your moped outside, did you?"

"No. I rolled it in."

"And you rolled it right up to the back door near the alarm boxes, isn't that right?"

"Yeah. Right up to the back door."

"Is that when you turned off the alarm?"

"Yeah."

"Then you would have had to park the moped there in the doorway, right? Or thereabout?"

"That's right, Dad."

"I'll bet that sometimes you forgot to turn off that fuel shutoff valve, didn't you?"

"Yeah." He grinned sheepishly. "I guess I forgot to turn it off now and then."

"It was dark back there too, wasn't it? So did you turn on the lights first before moving the moped?"

"Sure. I couldn't see too good to be movin' about back there in the dark."

"Sometimes, you leaned the moped against the wall because the kickstand was broke, didn't you?" We had just had the mechanic repair the kickstand that supported the moped when it was parked. I knew Leonard would have to truthfully answer yes to this question. But he hesitated, and I quickly reminded him by saying, "Well, you couldn't have leaned it on the kickstand because it had been broke for quite some time before we recently got it fixed. Isn't that right?"

"Yeah, Dad. I had to lean it against something when the kickstand was broke."

"And you leaned it against the wall there by the door. Right?"

"Right."

"Now just remember what you just told me if you are called upon to testify at my next trial. Just remember what you told me about the different places you parked the moped, son."

"Okay, if you say so, Dad."

"Not if I say so, son. It is you who has told me where you parked the moped, right?"

"Yeah, that's right."

After Leonard left the room, I settled back with a complacent smile on my face. I couldn't wait to see Scharfenberg's and Petronis' faces when Leonard testified at the next trial. Because Leonard's moped was going to prove to be one hell of a prop when the stage was set to dramatize how gasoline could have leaked on the carpet in the area the two investigators claimed that they found so-called traces of gasoline on the carpet—which I knew damn well was a monstrous lie!

Chapter 24

I T WAS ALMOST ONE YEAR exactly from the date of the first trial when the second trial started on April 14, 1982, in Judge Jaffe's courtroom. A jury was carefully selected by the prosecution and the defense. Columbro then made his opening statement to the jury first.

In his opening statement to the jury, my attorney set the theme for his defense theory that the evidence would show that the fire investigators were far more interested in making a case than in finding out the truth. After his opening statement, Borland returned to the defense table. The trial then proceeded with Columbro calling his first witness for the state.

Most of the same witnesses that testified at the first trial also testified at the second trial, and their testimony was substantially the same as to what they had testified to before.

But the prosecution made its greatest mistake in its anxiety to produce a preponderance of evidence by calling in additional witnesses to substantiate the state's case so as to booster its obligation to prove me guilty beyond a reasonable doubt.

Some of the new witnesses called to the witness stand by Columbro unknowingly gave aid and comfort to the defense. One such witness was an electrical expert from the state arson laboratory. He was a professor with a degree in electrical engineering. His background in his field of study was very impressive. The prosecution was using his testimony to confirm that he examined the electrical wall outlet taken from our store after the fire and that he found it not to have been defective or capable of causing the fire.

Columbro also made the mistake of pushing his luck in his eagerness to convince the jury that the fire could not have been caused by any electrical failure in Zodiac World. Evidently recalling that I had made a statement that there was sparking in the switch box when I turned on the store's outside sign, Columbro had Scharfenberg flash slide number 80 on the screen for the professor to view. The slide was a photograph of the back wall of the store. There were unmistakable deep char marks surrounding the electrical panel boxes on the wall. And Columbro asked the professor could he tell from the slide whether it might appear that the fire could have been caused by the electrical panel boxes.

The professor quickly replied that he could not tell anything from a slide or photograph. Then he went on to add that "if I had the boxes in my hand to examine them physically I could tell if they were defective and capable of starting a fire."

The professor's last remark was a big plus for the defense theory. And during his cross-examination of the professor, Borland had him reiterate that by failure of the fire investigators to submit the electrical boxes to him, as they did the electrical wall outlet, they precluded the boxes from being ruled out as a possible cause of the fire. This of course scored points for Borland's opening statement before the jury that the fire investigators did not make a thorough investigation of the cause of the fire.

Another witness that backfired when the prosecution put him on the stand had not been called to testify at the first trial. He was Captain Norman Hoprich, commander of the Maple Heights Dunham Road Station. Under direct examination by Columbro, the captain testified that he and his men were the second fire truck to arrive on the scene of the fire, that the Maple Heights Fire chief had not arrived and that he was acting chief whenever the regular chief was absent.

When Hoprich was asked what he did after arriving on the scene of the fire, he very frankly replied that he was short of manpower and also discovered that the fireman already on the scene had a problem with the water pressure; they were unable to effectively fight the fire.

I almost jumped out of my chair with delight! At last a vestige of the truth was beginning to seep out into the open to expose the lies that the firemen and investigators had been telling. I could see the look of disappointment on Scharfenberg's usually calm expression, because at the first trial, and during the foregoing proceedings of the present trial, all the firemen who had testified that arrived on the scene first had said that they began to fight the fire almost immediately upon their arrival. I knew that they were lying because I was also on the scene at the time they first arrived. But here and now, a captain, acting as fire chief, was truthfully contradicting his fellow fire fighters' testimony.

On cross-examination of Captain Hoprich, Borland brought out the additional testimony from him that it was at least fifteen minutes before the firemen could effectively fight the fire with water after he arrived. Add another three minutes to that for the truck that arrived before Hoprich and you have approximately eighteen minutes that firemen were on the scene of the fire but could not effectively fight it with water, and all during that period of incapacitation, the stores were burning like hell because the firemen could not effectively use their fire hoses.

Score more points for the defense. It was not a flammable liquid that caused the fire to burn out of control. To the contrary, it was the lack of water pressure that caused it to burn so rapidly.

Borland and I were both elated over the sudden turn of events. Some more of the truth had trickled out of the cesspool of subterfuge that Scharfenberg, Petronis, and their fellow firemen had created by deceptive and evasive testimony. But now, these new state's witnesses were bringing into question the credibility of the other witnesses that testified before them.

Petronis, the deputy fire marshal, was allowed to remain in the back of the courtroom after having given his testimony earlier. He had a glum look on his face as Captain Hoprich stepped down from the witness stand. Columbro and Scharfenberg did not look too happy either.

During a recess in the trial, Dave and I stretched our legs pacing the corridor. "Well, Counselor," I said, "the truth is beginning to gradually seep out. You're doing a great job!"

"I think we made some damn good points in there, Bert," Dave commented. "But we've got a long ways to go yet. I just hope that the prosecution continues to make mistakes like they did in there with the professor and the captain and that we don't make any such blunders. The state was going for overkill in there, and it very well could turn out to be suicidal."

"Things are looking a hell of lot better now than they did at this stage of the first trial. I can sure tell you that!" I told Dave before adding, "And this time, we are better prepared in our defense. I sure don't want to be overly optimistic, but I must say that I have a pretty good feeling about the case at this time," I concluded before we returned into the courtroom where the trial proceedings were resumed.

When Scharfenberg testified, he followed the pattern of his previous testimony with the exception that Columbro endeavored to bring out that Scharfenberg had very carefully examined the electrical panel boxes and could find nothing wrong with them.

Borland repeatedly objected that Scharfenberg was not an electrical expert and that he should not be permitted to state any opinion about the electrical panel boxes.

The court perhaps allowed a bit more leeway in Scharfenberg's testimony about the electrical panel boxes than should have been permitted, and this angered Borland until he was almost flush with indignation. He got permission to approach the bench where he, Columbro, and Judge Jaffe had a long, heated whispering discussion about Scharfenberg being given too much latitude in expressing opinions about the electrical system in Zodiac World when he was not an electrical expert.

Before the trial, Dave, in reviewing the facts and evidence of the case, had developed a theory that if there was an electrical defect in the panel box containing the switch for the sign, it was possible that a short circuit could have started a fire inside the wall that smoldered until it was fed sufficient oxygen from the air space between the roof and the false ceilings in Zodiac World and its adjacent stores. The fire would have naturally spread upward into the area between the roof and the false ceiling then on into the two adjoining stores which shared the same common roof.

The fact that I first saw smoke coming out of the empty store next door, according to Borland's theory, could possibly be explained by the additional fact that there was no wall separating the front and rear portions of the empty store, as everything in there had been cleared away to make way for the remodeling that was in progress. Also, there were no airtight windows to contain the smoke in the empty store, because the front of that store had been boarded up with loosely fitting plywood panels, which made it easy for smoke to seep through the cracks. Under the circumstances of Borland's theory, which was sound in principle, he was not about to let Scharfenberg, who failed to thoroughly investigate the panel boxes by having them examined by an electrical expert, set himself up as an electrical expert on the witness stand to try and undo what should have been done in the first place by a qualified expert.

Judge Jaffe had been commendably fair in allowing Borland's request for portions of the transcript transcribed from the prior trial to help him with my defense. The judge had also, upon Borland's motion, made an allowance for us to retain, at the state's expense, an expert witness with a learned background in fire prevention and arson investigation to testify in behalf of the defense to substantiate with expert authority some of the theories and facts that Dave wished to have presented to the court and jury concerning his theories of how the fire could have got started.

Try as we did, however, we were unable to find a suitable expert witness. Most of the experts that Dave approached refused to deal with us. And one expert very candidly admitted that he would be committing professional suicide if he appeared for us as an expert witness because like most of the other experts in his field, he made his living testifying for insurance companies that would take a dim view of him if he testified for a suspected arsonist.

The only expert that we found who would have been willing to aid us was a fire prevention official for a large steel company that Dave located. This expert had only recently appeared at the jury trial of a defendant in another case charged with setting a fire in a shopping center. It was through his testimony that credit was given for helping to free the defendant. This expert on fires had extraordinary credentials and was highly respected in his profession for being honest and forthright. Unfortunate for me, however, he was committed out of state on a fire investigation at the same time my trial started, and it was impossible for this expert to assist my defense. Therefore Borland and I had to get along without an expert fire witness.

When direct examination of Scharfenberg resumed, the court appeared to keep the matter more in hand by upholding most of Borland's objections whenever Scharfenberg tried to express an opinion with the certainty of an electrical expert—which he was not.

Scharfenberg's overzealousness in his desire to prove his theory that I started the fire in the same area where I had discovered the fire in my store turned out to be his undoing under Dave's cross-examination, and that also turned out to be the biggest break to come my way up until that time.

The prosecution introduced the fire extinguisher into evidence that I had used upon discovering the fire in the rear of the store. Scharfenberg then testified that upon his examination of the fire extinguisher on the day of the fire, he discovered that only about one pound of the chemical had been expelled from the extinguisher and that the normal capacity of the extinguisher was ten pounds. Therefore, nine pounds of the chemical remained in the extinguisher.

Scharfenberg, on cross-examination, went on to testify further that the extinguisher was not damaged by the fire in any way, that it looked the same as new, that the fire was too hot in the area (the alleged point of origin of the fire) where the extinguisher was affixed to the wall for it not to have shown some signs of fire damage before I was able to use it.

Scharfenberg's testimony was obvious in its inference that I took possession of the fire extinguisher before setting fire to the rear section of the store then I expelled a small amount of the chemical from the extinguisher and fled from the store. This is what Scharfenberg wanted to make the jury believe.

Upon hearing Scharfenberg's testimony, I was at first stunned with surprise and simultaneously overwhelmed with elation. In vain, I tried to get Borland's attention at first as he continued his diligent cross-examination of the fire investigator. He drew forth from Scharfenberg that he did not arrive on the scene of the fire until well over an hour after it started and therefore questioned his ability to determine how hot the fire was in the area of the fire extinguisher.

Scharfenberg, undaunted, maintained that his investigation with Petronis established that the area by the rear door of the shop near the fire extinguisher was the point of origin of the fire where gasoline was found and that it would have to have been the hottest part of the fire in that section of the shop. He went on to further testify that an flammable trailer was discovered there and that by my own admission, fire was already in that area when I claimed to have used the fire extinguisher. It would therefore follow, Scharfenberg pointed out, that if fire was already in that area there would have been some scorching or damage to the paint on the fire extinguisher before I got my hands on it.

I was almost frantic with delight! Scharfenberg's testimony was leading him into an entrapment, and I wanted now so much to get my attorney's attention to pass on some valuable information to him that would spring the trap shut on Scharfenberg. But Borland, with his back to me, was focusing all his attention on the big fire investigator as he continued his persistent cross-examination.

Finally, Borland turned away to pick up the fire extinguisher from a table containing the state's evidentiary exhibits. Before he could carefully examine the fire extinguisher, I managed to catch his eye. I motioned him back to the defense table. He leaned over close to me where by I revealed the scorched periodic maintenance inspection tag bearing the name *Sentry*, the trade name on the fire extinguisher being used as an exhibit at the trial. "Dave, this is the tag that came off the fire extinguisher," I whispered.

Borland could not completely mask the surprise on his face as he stared at the scorched tag with part of its right section missing, apparently from fire damage. A portion of the string that had attached the tag to the fire extinguisher was still intact on the tag that was now encased in a plastic envelope to preserve its scorched and brittle surface. Quickly, Dave covered the tag with his palm and slid it under some papers on the table so no one else could see it. Then he returned to his position several feet from the witness stand to resume his cross-examination of Scharfenberg, some of whose testimony is quoted in substance only.

Borland cleverly diverted his questions away from the fire extinguisher to other areas of Scharfenberga's testimony given under direct examination. He examined him for several minutes about other things before picking up the fire extinguisher again. Pointing to a piece of string still attached to the extinguisher, Borland inquired, "What is this little piece of string here?"

"That probably held an inspection tag," Scharfenberg replied.

"Well, could it have possibly been burned off during the fire?" Borland asked.

"I don't think so. The string on the extinguisher shows no signs of being burned."

"But if there were a scorched or burned tag that came off of there, that would be evidence that when Jennings used the fire extinguisher there was some fire back there, wouldn't it?" Borland inquired matter-of-factly.

"Yes. But there is no tag showing that," Scharfenberg replied.

"But you do agree that if there were a scorched tag, it would prove that Jennings used that extinguisher after it had been exposed to the fire, is that not correct?"

"Yes. But there is no tag," Scharfenberg insisted again, probably taken off guard because the tag was not used at the first trial, and it was now over two years since the fire occurred.

Dave nodded thoughtfully before continuing his cross-examination on other subject matter. I was now more than pleased with the crucial way in which he had set Scharfenberg up for the self-contradiction that would be evident when we introduced the tag into evidence. Still, I was not quite satisfied. I wanted Dave to milk Scharfenberg for even greater admissions concerning the fire extinguisher and about other subject matter to try and draw out additional contradictions in his testimony. But during another whispered conversation, Borland said, "I don't want to beat a dead horse. I'm going to let him off the stand."

Before Dave let Scharfenberg off the stand, I insisted that he elicit testimony from him that he personally transported the samples of the fire debris evidence to the state arson laboratory. Because this seemed unusual to me since Petronis was a deputy state fire marshal and Scharfenberg only a suburban fire prevention official of the city of Maple Heights. Why then did Scharfenberg take over the duty normally belonging to Petronis to submit the evidence to the arson laboratory by acting as his courier? Could it be possible that Scharfenberg tampered with the samples and tainted the material with a flammable liquid before the samples were tested at the state arson laboratory? All these things crossed my mind because I knew that there was no gasoline present where Scharfenberg had said that he and Petronis took samples of the carpeting and woodwork. It just did not make sense that they could have found any significant traces of gasoline in that particular area, notwithstanding the fact that Leonard's moped had been in the shop several days before the fire.

At the end of the day, when court was adjourned and we were gathering up our papers to go home, Borland stopped Columbro, Scharfenberg, and Petronis before they could leave the courtroom. "Gentlemen, a moment or two more of your time, please. Mr. Jennings has some evidence that we intend to use during his defense. At this time, we would like to share this evidence with you." Motioning to me with a nod of his head, Dave added, "Bert, please show these gentlemen the tag that came off the fire extinguisher."

I wish I had had a camera to record the stunned expression on Scharfenberg's face when I displayed the scorched tag. Columbro and Petronis looked far from pleased also. And there was a moment of icy silence before I took the opportunity to break the lull in conversation with a hint of cynicism. "By all means, Dave. This is a good time to show them the tag, because I wouldn't want them to think that I manufactured this evidence after I left the courtroom this evening."

Dave appeared a little displeased with my cynical remark, but his happiness over our most recent *coup* de theatre showed all over his youthful visage as we rode down on the elevator and walked into his office.

"Wow!" I exclaimed happily. "Boy! Did you see that look on Scharfenberg's face when I showed them that tag? Now that has surely taken some of the wind out of his sails. He just about scuttled his own ship with the holes you made him lay open in his theory of how I was supposed to have set fire to the place. Just wait until we introduce this tag into evidence before the jury. It's bound to make a profound impression on them."

"The whole case isn't riding on this one question of the tag and the fire extinguisher," Dave cautioned before adding, "Although I must agree that Scharfenberg's theory is in jeopardy, and when we introduce the tag into evidence, it will afford me some excellent ammunition for my closing arguments to the jury." Dave paused, shaking his head incredulously. "Now tell me, Bert, how did you happen to come by this tag and keep it so long?"

"I guess I tore it off when I activated the fire extinguisher and unconsciously put the tag in the pocket of the sweater I was wearing the day of the fire. I really don't remember exactly. All I know is that before I took the sweater to the dry cleaners, a few days after the fire, I found the tag in one of the pockets. I almost threw the tag in a wastebasket, but on second thought, I decided to keep it. So I placed it in an envelope and filed it away with some other papers pertaining to the business. I don't want to sound overly religious, but there must have been some divine guidance involved in helping me to preserve this tag because I never had an occasion to really think of using it in any way. In fact, I didn't know what had happened to the fire extinguisher until the prosecution used it as an exhibit at the first trial.

"But you didn't have occasion to use the tag at the first trial, did you?" Dave inquired.

No. Because Scharfenberg did not raise the question at the first trial of whether I removed the extinguisher before there was fire in the rear of the store. This is something new he has brought up at this second trial. Why, you saw what he was trying to do up there in the courtroom this afternoon—but it backfired on him."

Dave was noncommittal. "Let's get out of here and go home. We've got another big day tomorrow, Bert."

"Oh, but things are looking up perceptibly!" I exclaimed, thrusting my thumbs up in a gesture of encouragement.

The next day during the trial proceedings, I was introduced to another pleasant surprise. Having taken a beating on the testimony given by the two new witnesses, the professor and Captain Hoprich, I didn't expect Columbro to produce the president of the shopping center to testify—especially since he was not called to testify at the first trial. But in his endeavor to establish that I was behind in my rent and about to be evicted from the store, Columbro put Jerry Zahler, the president of the Southgate Management Company, on the witness stand.

Jerry, a middle-aged, swarthy-faced, and pleasant individual, had gained my respect and admiration during my negotiations with him to lease a store at Southgate. And during the period that I was a tenant at the shopping center, I enjoyed good rapport with Jerry even though he was the one who had apprised me that my first application for a leasing agreement had been denied. It was also Jerry Zahler to whom I responded to with my belief that it was because of my race that I was denied the lease. Still, I couldn't help but believe Jerry when he called me and said that he personally had advocated my cause but was overruled by other members on the board of management. It was the consensus of the negative members that my business venture was too novel, untested, and impractical as a retail merchandising enterprise.

The decision of the board was at best based on a lame excuse. I knew all too well the real reason that I was denied a lease the first time I applied. I therefore advised Jerry during our telephone conversation that I would call the matter to the attention of the National Association for Advancement of Colored People and to the *Call and Post*, a black weekly newspaper. "If thousands of blacks could spend thousands of dollars at Southgate, then there ought to be some black merchants out there too." This was my message for whomever Jerry proposed to carry the message to. Because I did not accuse him directly of racial prejudice, and to this day I do not believe that the man harbors racial prejudice against blacks or any other race.

As Dave Borland cross-examined Jerry, he unwaveringly admitted from the witness stand everything I had said to him during our negotiations. He even conceded that the four months advance rent deposit that I paid was more stringent than what was customarily exacted from the other white tenants at Southgate. Nothing in his testimony, however, was of any great detriment to my cause. To the contrary, much of his testimony was helpful as the white and black jurors strained forward not to miss a single word of what was said concerning the racial issue projected into the case whereby I was treated differently from the white tenants at Southgate.

Jerry readily admitted that he accepted the exorbitant rent deposits against past due rent, and he acknowledged that he was aware of the tentative agreement that I had with Delores O'Bryant to buy Zodiac World. All in all, Jerry was one of the most honest and truthful witnesses that the state produced during the entire trial proceedings.

I feel certain that if some of Jerry's colleagues harbored racial prejudice that it did not rub off on him and that he did not share their views, even if discretion kept Jerry silent about his true feelings while in the presence of racial bigots.

I prefer to believe that Jerry Zahler is the kind of person who would work from the inside to make the situation better for blacks rather than jeopardize his personal security and position by creating public waves. Based on the first law of nature, I cannot therefore condemn Jerry for such an attitude.

When Jerry walked off the witness stand and out of the courtroom, he walked away still in possession of my admiration and respect for the honest manner in which he gave his testimony. I do not know what Jerry thinks of me today. But that is not nearly as important as to what I think of him for being the only white person in management that I met at Southgate of whom I could really say that I had a good, complete, and intuitive feeling about from the very beginning.

With Jerry's testimony in the record, I was hoping for the final miracle that Columbro would continue his pattern of calling in witnesses who had not testified at the first trial, because these new witnesses were boomeranging on him something terrible! And the state's case was beginning to suffer because of these new witnesses who had not testified at the first trial. I am almost sure that Scharfenberg and Petronis prompted Columbro in calling these new witnesses and therefore they were jointly responsible for their unanticipated inept performances.

I especially wanted the prosecution to call the chief of the Maple Heights Fire Department with the hope that perhaps on cross-examination that Dave could get him to corroborate my statement that the first signs of fire came from the empty store next door to Zodiac World.

Fire Chief Vincent Jacobs had told a newspaper reporter who published his remarks that "it was first thought that the fire started in the vacant store." This was something that the prosecution had suppressed and denied all during the first trial and the second trial.

Without Chief Jacobs on the witness stand, Borland could not cross-examine him about his remarks made to the reporter, and when the prosecution rested its case, it appeared that we would not get a valuable piece of evidence into the trial record.

Chapter 25

DAVE BORLAND AND I GIRDED ourselves for the task of putting on our defense. In doing so, I at first left the subpoenaing of my defense witnesses up to the public defender's office. In doing so, I planned on making a personal follow-up on the return of the subpoenas to make certain that all of the defense witnesses had been properly served. My attitude was no reflection on the PD's office or the office of the county sheriff. It was just that my determination was to see to it personally that all necessary witnesses would be present at this second trial to prevent a recurrence of what had happened at the first trial. Therefore, in order to accomplish having all my witnesses present in court to testify, I was not going to be totally dependent on anyone but myself for seeing to it that the witnesses would be present. After all, it was my ass facing time in the penitentiary; and at this particular time, I could not foresee anyone caring more about my ass than myself.

Our defense ran smoothly at first. We called my wife, Delores O'Bryant, Dick Howell, the bartender, the manager of the ADT alarm company, and the manager of the sign company. They all testified essentially to the same things that they testified to at the first trial.

The manager of the sign company, however, could not recall what defect if any was found wrong with the sign when it was transported back to his company a few months after the fire. But he did confirm his testimony given at the first trial that his company had replaced a defective ballast in the sign several weeks before the fire.

Bill White appeared and testified that he had been the salesman who had placed the Monroe calculator in our store on a trial basis and that I had returned the calculator to him the evening before the fire because it had stopped working. It was later determined that the calculator had blown a fuse in its mechanism, and it was possible that the fuse could have been blown by a short circuit in the shop's electrical system.

The young mechanic who serviced the moped turned out to be a brilliant and impressive witness for my defense. The moped was rolled into the courtroom by my son, Leonard, and parked in front of the jury. It was then introduced into evidence as a defense exhibit.

The jury showed unusual interest in the shiny vehicle as the mechanic, guided by Dave Borland's direct examination, described the manufacturer's defective carburetor to them and how it was virtually impossible to prevent the machine from leaking small quantities of fuel. He also described the shutoff valve, telling the court and the jury that failure to close the valve when parking the vehicle would cause additional leakage. As he testified standing over the moped, he designated by pointing his finger to the different parts of the machine that he described so that the jury could get a clear picture of just what he was talking about. This was very impressive. And here, again, I have my attorney to thank for his meticulous adherence to the most minute detail in having the mechanic bring out the most pertinent factors in convincing the jury, especially how and why the moped leaked gasoline. The mechanic guided by proper questioning from Borland went on to testify and describe the shutoff valve—telling the court and jury that failure to close the valve when the vehicle was parked would cause additional leakage; and if that wasn't enough in our favor, he went on to further testify that when Leonard and I came to pick up the moped after it was serviced, my son made a trial ride to test the machine. When he returned and parked it in front of the mechanic's shop, Leonard inadvertently failed to cut off the fuel valve. The mechanic went on to state that he cautioned Leonard at that time about shutting off the fuel valve. When Borland wanted to know did the mechanic notice many other moped owners, with machines like Leonard's, neglect to shut off the fuel valve, the mechanic acknowledged that it was something of a common oversight among many of his customers.

Try as he may, Columbro could not make any dint in the young mechanic's testimony on cross-examination. And when the young man stepped down from the witness stand, I would have given him a standing ovation were I not in a courtroom. For he had clearly confirmed the possibility of how gasoline could have gotten on the carpet in the store, leaving its detectable chemical residue long after its flammability had evaporated.

The first snag in the orderly presentation of my defense came about when once again, to my great dismay, I discovered that my personal physician was unavailable to appear at my trial. He was away from the city on vacation. This time, however, I had an ace in the hole. During a court recess, I personally went down to the court clerk's office and made out a subpoena for my psychiatrist, Dr. Bush. I had been referred to him by my physician, and Dr. Bush had treated me for alcoholism on three different occasions. The most recent occasion was when he had me hospitalized for detoxification several months after the first trial.

When the psychiatrist testified at my trial, he left no doubt concerning my chronic alcoholism caused by periods of depression, and he went on to describe how drinking affected my memory and induced hallucinations.

When my son took the witness stand, he testified under Borland's skillful questioning that he parked the moped in several different places in the rear of the store; that he always parked it near the doorway leading into the rear of the store, because he had to turn off the burglar alarm on the wall by the doorway leading into the rear of the store that if he did not turn off the burglar alarm on the wall by the doorway within forty-five seconds after entering the store, the alarm would go off.

As Leonard, testified I overheard Scharfenberg's audible whisper to Columbro, "That kid is parking that moped right on our hot spot." Both their faces registered indignation, and I had to choke up to keep from laughing out loud.

When it came time for Columbro to cross-examine Leonard, the lad showed his true mettle. Usually, a lad of quick temper and unbridled aggressiveness, Leonard remained calm when the prosecuting attorney attacked his credibility. But in doing so, Columbro miscalculated Leonard's anticipation of the question concerning where he had parked the moped in the rear of the store.

Columbro, with Leonard's prior testimony in hand, made the mistake of trying to pin the lad down that he testified at the first trial that he always parked the moped in the same spot between the racks in the rear of the store. Leonard, however, denied positively that he had ever made such a statement.

Columbro, waving a copy of Leonard's prior testimony, insisted that Leonard had made such a statement. But Leonard, knowing better, continued to insist that he had never made such a statement.

Borland also was aware from the copy of Leonard's prior testimony that he had in front of him that Leonard never made the statement that Columbro was trying to force the boy to admit to.

At the first trial, Leonard had only testified that he "parked the moped in the rear of the store"—period! Therefore Borland rose indignantly from his chair and objected to Columbro browbeating the witness. The attorney insisted that any evidence the prosecution had showing that Leonard made any contradictory statement be read before the court and jury.

Judge Jaffe, getting a little agitated too, ordered Columbro to read from Leonard's prior testimony any discrepancies, if any did in fact exist.

Columbro perused the transcript of Leonard's prior testimony. Slowly, the confidence drained into a hesitant look of disappointment when he did not find what he was looking for. The courtroom was very quiet. The jury and spectators were electrified with anticipation of something of a damning nature about to be revealed. But nothing happened. Yet Leonard, Borland, and I all knew that Columbro had somehow jumped the gun either on Scharfenberg's ill advisement or over Columbro's confusion as to where my wife and Delores O'Bryant had testified to having seen the moped parked. In any event, Columbro now had egg on his face, and he tried to salvage what composure he could by quickly dropping the matter and going on to another subject with his cross-examination. Shortly thereafter, he allowed Leonard to leave the witness stand. The lad's testimony was unimpeachable.

Columbro found himself in another similarly embarrassing situation when he cross-examined me. My testimony on direct examination had been about the same as that given at the first trial. Columbro, however, attempted to impeach my testimony in one particular respect by showing that I carried my fire insurance policy in my attaché case and that it was locked up in the trunk of my car on the day of the fire. The implication he tried to convey was that I did not want the insurance policy to be destroyed when I set fire to the store.

Apparently, Columbro got his wires crossed again when he reviewed my previous testimony given at the first trial and at the deposition hearing in the office of the Nationwide Insurance Company's lawyer. His helpers, Petronis and Scharfenberg, in particular, in their anxiety to see me convicted, probably aided in confusing Columbro during the whispered conferences that they held.

When queried by Mr. Reader at the deposition hearing, he had asked me the following questions and I made the following answers:

Q: When had you taken the insurance policy home?
A: It never left home.
Q: You kept it there at all times?
A: Yes. I have a little office on the third floor.

During the first trial, the prosecuting attorney, Mr. Sullivan, had also asked me relatively the same questions and got the same replies. Then he had followed with the question:

Q: Where was your attaché case on the day of the fire?
A: In the trunk of my car.

Columbro somehow evidently got confused and insisted before the court and jury that I had said that I kept the insurance policy in my attaché case in the trunk of my car. He became so adamant in his insistence that I cried out, "Show me anywhere in the record of my prior testimony that I ever said that I kept my insurance policy in the trunk of my car. You must think that you're Edgar Bergman and that I'm Charly McCarthy to try and put words in my mouth." This drew laughter from some of the jurors.

Columbro asked the court to stop me from arguing with him from the witness stand. Upon hearing this, old Judge Jaffe leaned over the bench and replied a little irritably, "Maybe if you stop arguing with him, he will stop arguing with you," After that, order was restored. Dave Borland slowly drew his tall frame erect as he stood up, and he asked the court to have Columbro read from the record any such contradiction in my testimony so that we could get on with the trial.

Borland later told me that he of course knew from the copies of the transcripts in his possession that there was no contradiction in my testimony concerning where I kept the fire insurance policy, that he did not object or attempt to intervene earlier to Columbro's browbeating method of interrogation because he wanted him to take all the rope he needed to hang himself with. Very good point indeed!

When the transcript of my prior testimony was finally read with respect to the insurance policy, it certainly did not reflect Columbro's view of the situation. Once again, he came away with egg on his face in his frustrated anxiety to discredit a defense witness.

Apparently, the prosecution had not done its homework on the case with the same diligence and intensity as we had done ours, or perhaps Columbro was getting a lot of confused and erroneous input from his calculating helper, Joe Scharfenberg, while Borland was getting more precise and accurate information from me. Because not once can I recall during the entire trial when Borland had an occasion to wipe egg from his face.

We were into the second week of the trial, and both Dave and I were becoming very apprehensive because my accountant had not responded to the subpoena that was reportedly left at his home by a process server. During the weekend, when the trial was adjourned, I tried unsuccessfully to contact my accountant by telephone. Apparently, the prosecution had anticipated that we might call the accountant as a defense witness, because Columbro suddenly acquired an assistant to help him oppose our defense strategy. His assistant was well-versed in accounting and tax law.

Borland suggested to me that it might be feasible to get the news story admitted into evidence quoting the Maple Heights fire chief's remark that "it was first thought that the fire started in the vacant store" if we could subpoena the newspaper reporter who had interviewed the chief. I therefore spent my weekend also trying to locate the newspaper reporter.

Checking with the *Southeast Sun* newspaper that had printed the story, I was informed that the reporter was a young lady who was no longer working for the newspaper. I was aware of the reporter's name because the story appeared under her byline, but no one at the newspaper would give me her last known address or telephone number. Not to be discouraged, I relied on my own legal investigative knowledge and training in locating witnesses. It turned out to be a simple task. Rule one worked. I looked her up in the telephone directory. Not finding her listed, I started calling the several listings under her last name to make inquiries. On the second call, I luckily hit pay dirt.

"May I speak to Rosemary please?"

Without asking me any questions, the reply came back, "She's away at college. This is her mother speaking."

"College?" I repeated.

"Yes. Kent State."

"Oh, she's no longer with the *Southeast Sun*?" I asked to confirm that I had reached the right Rosemary's home.

"No. She's away at school."

"Thank you, ma'am," I said, quickly hanging up before her mother asked me any questions.

The next task proved equally as simple. I called Kent State University and stated in an authoritative manner that we had a subpoena to serve and would like the address of the young lady so we wouldn't have to serve her in one of the classrooms. Without hesitation, I was given her address.

At 8:30 a.m. the following Monday, I appeared at the court clerk's office and had a subpoena issued for the reporter to appear and testify at my trial. I also had another subpoena issued for my accountant. This time, I personally took possession of the subpoena for the accountant and gave it to a friend who had accompanied me to the courthouse. He had my instructions to personally serve the subpoena on my accountant and have him sign a copy showing receipt of the document.

I was aware that my accountant made it a practice to pick up his son at a parochial school about 3:00 p.m. each day and that he could be conveniently served with the subpoena either leaving his office or his home. My friend had already been pointed out the office, residence, and the accountant's car. He simply had to determine which place the car was parked. Then he would wait until the accountant started to his car about 2:30 p.m. At about that time, he could accost him and serve the subpoena.

Regular process servers are usually not very patient in making a personal service if they can leave a subpoena either at a person's home or place of employment. A person-to-person service of a subpoena, however, makes it virtually impossible for a person to deny knowledge of receiving a subpoena.

It was inexplicable to me why we were having so much difficulty in getting my accountant to testify at my trial. But one thing was certain, I could not rely on the sheriff's process server any longer because time was now of the greatest essence. I had to make certain that under the threat of a contempt of court citation that my accountant would comply with the mandate of the subpoena. And my friend was ideally suited to instill the necessary fear of going to jail if the accountant did not comply.

After trial adjourned Monday evening, I called my friend's home, and he assured me that the mission had been accomplished. That same evening, my accountant called my home and advised me that he would be in court the next morning without fail. He apologized for not being able to appear at the first trial and denied receiving the first subpoena to appear at the second trial. He admitted, however, that my trials were always colliding with his schedule during the busiest period of the income tax season.

Perhaps that gave him the justification to put his livelihood above my freedom. In any event, the accountant was in court the next morning and so was the newspaper reporter.

Dave Borland put the reporter on the witness stand first since he only had a few questions for her. She admitted to interviewing the Chief of the Maple Heights Fire Department and that she obtained from him the facts that her news story was predicated upon. The court allowed her to read the news story into the trial record that quoted the chief as saying, "It was first thought that the fire started in the vacant store."

At last! My statement was corroborated by the chief himself in an indirect manner that the first signs of fire did, indeed, emanate from the vacant store. The prosecution's suppression of this important fact by the deceptive state witnesses who had testified to the contrary was now out in the open for the court, the jury, and all to be aware of. Once again, we outwitted the prosecution that tried its damndest to keep the chief's own testimony out of the trial record.

The state could not now claim hearsay evidence was being used, because the news reporter got the details for her story directly from the chief himself. The only thing the prosecution could do now was call the chief as a rebuttal witness and have him deny the reporter's testimony—something, for fear of opening a Pandora's box, Columbro would not dare contemplate doing.

The big moment had finally arrived. The prosecution had used two large portable blackboards with diagrams of their evidence showing the locations of certain parts of the fire scene. Now Borland obtained permission from the court to bring in another blackboard for his personal use in questioning the accountant. The moment of real truth was about to begin!

Borland, who possessed a scholastic background in accountancy himself, put my accountant on the witness stand. He was a short brown-skinned man in his early forties who was very meticulous in his answers to all questions. My attorney briefly brought out the accountants educational and professional background and also his association with me as my accountant.

The accountant identified the tax return for Zodiac World that he had prepared as well as the personal federal tax returns filed by my wife and me that he had also prepared. These tax returns were admitted into evidence.

Borland then had the accountant step down from the witness stand and write on the blackboard what the total assets showed on the Zodiac World tax return. The accountant wrote $26,000. Next, he was asked to write down what our business net worth was that showed on the tax return after he deducted $3,208 listed as liabilities. The accountant wrote $22,792 on the blackboard. And all this information was based on the tax return filed two months before the fire, which represented only a small change in our business assets from that time until the day of the fire.

The accountant, under further questioning, testified that Zodiac World had no outstanding business loans and that in his opinion, our business was on a sound financial footing even though we had suffered some paper losses, which was normal for a comparatively new business.

It was plain to see what Borland was driving at. If our store was insured for $20,000 with a net worth of almost $23,000, then why would I destroy the business and take almost a $3,000 loss—especially since we did not carry any business interruption insurance?

When the accountant was done testifying under direct examination, Columbro and his assistant tried in vain on cross-examination to shake the accountant's accurate and brilliant testimony, only to have it brought out that my wife and I had a combined income from our places of employment of over $32,000 annually and that we did not rely on any money from Zodiac World for our livelihood.

Our accountant may have been reluctant to testify at first. But once under oath, he turned out to be one of the most impressive defense witnesses we had against the state's claim that I burned the store to collect the insurance money.

When the accountant left the witness stand, the defense was nearing its climax. Borland, however, had one last surprise for the prosecution before the final cause.

The manager of the sign company was put back on the witness stand. I had called him that afternoon at lunchtime to inquire whether he had examined the Zodiac World sign to determine if it was defective. Now back on the witness stand, the court and jury got a second look at the manager as he testified to examining the sign. He stated that he discovered that the ballast had been blown out and that that was the second time in less than a year that this had happened. He went on to state further that it could not be denied that I was having some type of electrical problems in the shop even though he could not say whether the electrical problems had anything to do with the cause of the fire.

The state's case appeared to have disintegrated right before our very eyes. The serious expressions on the faces of Scharfenberg, Petronis, and the prosecuting attorneys reflected very little if any confidence now that the nadir of their spirits hit rock bottom.

Borland rested our case. He had been terrific! He was thorough, cautious, and never overconfident to the very end. But this young attorney's true greatness showed unmistakably during the closing argument he made to the jury.

After Columbro had concluded his argument to the jury in which he employed every skill at his command in trying to convince the jury of my guilt, Dave Borland drew his slender frame erect. His handsome and youthful face somehow took on a serious look of maturity and wisdom far beyond its usual mien.

His eyes were intense with the dramatical sobriety of the occasion as he thanked the jurors for their patient and dutiful attention to the details of the case all during the somewhat protracted trial. Then in a casual manner, he walked over to the defense table and picked up the plastic envelope containing the scorched tag marked "Defense Exhibit V."

All eyes in the silent courtroom followed Borland's movement. Holding the tag in one hand, he began his closing argument, not mentioning at first anything about the tag. But as he talked to the jurors, he would occasionally slap the tag in the palm of his other hand while making a point. The jurors' eyes constantly focused on the tag, perhaps they were now wondering what Borland was going to say about it. But he said nothing as he analyzed much of the other state's evidence as being totally insufficient to sustain a conviction of guilt beyond a reasonable doubt.

Borland accused the fire investigators of wanting so badly to please and appease their demanding superiors that they were determined to find an explanation for the cause of the fire at any cost— even to abandoning the principles manifested in the motto of their profession to be "truth seekers and not case makers."

Borland went on to review the evidence of how Scharfenberg and Petronis had botched their investigation by failure to consider fully all elements that may have caused the fire. He especially criticized them for, as he put it, "sending one lousy electrical outlet to the arson laboratory when they were aware of the sparking in the electrical sign panel box" and also the trouble I had had with the store's sign on a prior occasion.

Their negligence in the investigation is indefensible. Borland argued vehemently above the normal tone of his quiet but very audible manner of speaking. Next, he pointed out that not long after the fire had occurred, the wall holding the electrical panel boxes was knocked down and the debris carted away, destroying forever any chance of determining whether the sign box switch could have been a contributing cause of the fire.

Not letting up on his attack, Borland castigated the credibility of the state's witnesses who had suppressed the truth about where the first signs of fire showed, the fact that there was insufficient water available to promptly extinguish the flames when the firemen first arrived on the scene, the denial of a workable fire alarm system in our store, the failure to investigate the leaking moped even though Scharfenberg painstakingly investigated the purchase of the coffee. Each time Borland made one of these points to the jurors, he slapped the tag audibly against his left palm and the eyes of the jurors followed every movement of the tag.

Finally, Borland said, while shaking the tag before the jury, "Now let's talk about this piece of evidence for a few moments." The jurors became tense with expectation. Even Judge Jaffe leaned forward while Scharfenberg's bald pate blushed as his huge frame seemed to shrink and go tense.

"You all heard how the witness, Mr. Scharfenberg, tried to convince you of his implied theory that the defendant apparently play-acted with the fire extinguisher after once setting fire to the store because he could not have reached the fire extinguisher after he poured and ignited gasoline on the carpet." Holding the tag aloft, Borland went on, "Well, we know better than that now, don't we?" Still holding the tag, he picked up the fire extinguisher with his free hand and held it too, aloft. "This scorched tag, ladies and gentlemen of the jury, is living proof that the defendant did in fact reach this fire extinguisher while there was fire back there in the store, and we know now that he did use this extinguisher against that fire until he was overcome by smoke and had to withdraw from the building. We know that now to be a fact, don't we?" Some jurors' heads moved slightly as though in acknowledgement. Borland had made his master point.

Now he slowly returned the tag and fire extinguisher to the table with a dramatic pause, allowing his last remarks to sink in before continuing to review other evidence showing that I had no motive for burning the store.

Columbro's assistant made the state's final argument and tried his best to cast doubt on our financial solvency. But his remarks tended to be anticlimactic more or less in a desperate attempt to snatch victory from imminent defeat, I thought, feeling somewhat confident that the trial was going favorably in my direction.

After Judge Jaffe instructed the jury and sent the jurors off to deliberate, Dave Borland appeared to be very reserved. He was noncommittal in predicting any outcome of the trial in spite of his fine performance before the court and jury. Perhaps experience had taught him that sometimes what appeared to be a "shoo-in" could turn out to be a "shut out."

Borland's reservation was justified when late afternoon the next day, after several hours of deliberation, the jury returned to the courtroom, unable to reach a verdict. My hopes fell to the pit of my stomach. There was a terrible feeling of disappointment! "Oh no! Not another mistrial!" I ejaculated in a soft whisper.

Judge Jaffe, noting the lateness of the day, nevertheless, sent the jurors back to the jury room to deliberate for another hour or two before making a decision on whether to declare a mistrial.

Disappointment showed on everyone's face as each of us filed out into the corridor and the judge returned to his chambers.

"What could have gone wrong? I felt almost certain that I would be acquitted this time. I don't understand it," I complained to Borland.

"It's difficult to say. Juries can be very unpredictable," he replied a little irritably.

"I sure hate going through all of this a third time. My God! What do we have to do to convince a jury of my innocence?" I said in a hopeless tone.

"I wish I knew," was all Dave said; then he walked away after first cautioning me to stand by. He apparently went down to his office to await the next call to return to the courtroom.

I paced the corridor like a jungle cat that had missed his quarry in the hunt, restless, disappointed, and very much chagrined over not being acquitted. This time, however, I resisted any temptation to make a beeline to the liquor store. For I realized what a disaster that would be.

Time passed so slowly. It seemed like hours, when in reality, it was only a little over a half hour before we were all summoned back into the courtroom.

The jurors were standing as they awaited the entrance of Judge Jaffe. Borland and I stood nervously at the defense table. Across from us stood Columbro and his assistant with fixed expressions as anxious as those on our faces.

The jury had reached a verdict.

Judge Jaffe ordered everyone in the courtroom to be seated. Then he had his bailiff take the verdict from the foreman of the jury. The bailiff handed the slips of paper to the judge. Adjusting his glasses slowly over his eyes, Judge Jaffe took what seemed to be hours perusing the contents of the verdict. He shuffled the papers one under the other a couple times as he silently read them again. All the while I was twisting inside until my guts seemed to ball up in a knot. "Holy shit! Why don't he read the verdict and get it over with?" I mumbled to myself. Then I tried to detect a hint of what the verdict might be by quickly scanning the faces of the jurors. It seemed that my eyes caught the faint trace of a drawn smile on the face of the juror in the first seat of the jury box. He was a black man in his late sixties. The other jurors all wore stony expressions on their faces as they stared vacantly ahead.

Finally, Judge Jaffe read aloud, "We, the jury, find the defendant not guilty of aggravated arson . . . We, the jury, find the defendant not guilty of arson . . . We, the jury, find the defendant not guilty of attempted grand theft."

Suddenly all the jurors were beaming smiles in my direction. "Thank you! Thank all of you!" I called out to them, extremely elated and happy with the results.

Borland thanked them too. Then we both embraced in a victory hug as I thanked my attorney for defending me in such a victorious manner. Juanita, Leonard, and my other friends were not there to enjoy this moment of supreme joy with me, and I could hardly wait to bring them the good news.

Columbro and his assistant sat in stunned silence. And I wished that Scharfenberg and Petronis were present to join them in defeat so I could have relished the looks of disappointment on their faces also.[‡]

It was over! We had emerged victorious at last! I was exonerated! What a beautiful word, I thought—*exonerated!*

[‡] CLEVELAND PLAIN DEALER, Magazine section, page 2, September 17, 1995. Jim Columbro swears his journey down Cocaine Lane is over. He swears he will never take that path again. He is so convinced of his newfound health that he wants his license to practice law back again. Columbro was an assistant Cuyahoga County prosecutor when he started to steal cocaine from the evidence locker of the Cleveland Police Department. After years of abuse, he had lost 30 pounds, could barely concentrate and had left his family so confused and angry that he had almost lost them, too. Then he got busted. He pleaded guilty to 36 counts of drug abuse and theft in office. He went to prison, serving 11 months of an 18 month sentence. And his license to practice law was indefinitely suspended.

The sound of it cleansed me of all wrongdoing of the charges.

A great weight had been lifted from my shoulders after two years of doubt and anxiety. Justice had finally triumphed!

Judge Jaffe rapped his gavel lightly for order. Then he thanked and dismissed the jurors. Next, he summoned the attorneys and me before the bench where he formally discharged me. I in turn thanked the judge for presiding over what I sincerely believed to have been a fair trial, and he acknowledged my gratitude with a little smile. Had the verdict gone against me, I still would have felt that Judge Jaffe had made a sincere endeavor to preside over the proceedings in a fair and impartial manner even if he had made some inadvertent errors in his rulings.

It was nearing five o'clock as several of the jurors came back through the rear entrance of the courtroom. Immediately, they were surrounded by the attorneys and a newspaper reporter asking them questions about the trial and the verdict. Judge Jaffe, still clad in his black robe, came down from the bench to talk with them also.

I went about shaking hands with the jurors and thanking them individually before singling out the number one juror for a bit of conversation. He was standing next to a younger black juror who was lavish in his praise for the way my attorney had defended me.

I asked the number one juror what caused the indecision in the jury room concerning my innocence. He told me that at the very beginning of their deliberation, a straw vote was taken, and the great majority of the jurors were in favor of my acquittal. A few were undecided at that time, and they proceeded to review all the evidence until it boiled down to just two jurors having doubts. One was the foreman who was a vice president of one of Cleveland's largest banks! And he also was a certified public accountant. The foreman had some reservations concerning what he thought to be too large an inventory for a small business such as Zodiac World. That at the time of the fire, we had an inventory valued at $16,000, and the foreman, joined by one other male juror, speculated that we may have encountered difficulty in selling the bulk of the inventory to establish the necessary cash flow required to run the business. If this were true, then it was possible that we were stuck with the inventory, thereby tying up our capital, which may have motivated me to set fire to the store to collect on our insurance.

The number one juror went on to tell me that one of the other male jurors recalled that during the course of my testimony, I had stated that we carried a line of Masonic gift items and books that did not sell well and that we returned those items to the vendor we purchased them from for a refund less ten percent for handling charges. At that time, I had also testified that the same held true with just about all the merchandise we stocked, that with permission from the vendors, it could be returned for credit less the usual 10 percent handling charge. Therefore when the jurors returned to the jury room to deliberate, after their initial deadlock, the foreman and the other holdout juror were reminded of my prior testimony, they then realized that we were not stuck with the inventory, and they readily joined in with the other jurors in rendering a verdict of not guilty on all of the charges in the indictment.

The number one juror pointed out to me one of the white jurors and said, "There is the man who broke the deadlock. He fought for you in that jury room almost as hard as your lawyer fought for you in the courtroom."

I immediately hurried over to the juror and grabbed his hand and thanked him again. Then I asked him, "What made you have so much confidence in my innocence, sir?"

"Many things, Mr. Jennings. But most of all, it was the manner in which those two fire investigators went about investigating the fire. It was hard for me to believe that with their backgrounds and experience that those two investigators could have been so negligent in investigating all of the electrical problems that you had in the shop. Then too they were not truthful in many instances during the trial, nor were many of the other witnesses produced by the state completely believable. There was just too many conflicting statements about that fire, and you were not treated fairly in the investigation or as a tenant at the shopping center."

Once again, I thanked this juror before he wished me luck in getting a settlement from my insurance company now that I had been acquitted. Then I joined Dave Borland and left the courtroom.

Once again, the truth had made me free.

*   *   *   *   *

A reporter for the *Cleveland Plain Dealer*, in the following excerpts of his story, aptly reported my elation the next day in the May 1, 1982 newspaper:

> "I am glad it is over," Jennings said as he left the courtroom "It's been two years, two trials. I am broke . . ."
>
> In the hall, he spread his arms like wings, took a few running steps and called to some bystanders.
>
> "Here I am—free like a bird, like a bird."

Chapter 26

AFTER THE JUBILATION OF MY legal victory died down, I focused my attention on recovering my insurance claim for the loss of our business. My two trials had consumed most of my attention during the past two years, and I had relied heavily on the Alex N. Sill Adjustment Company to adjust my insurance claim. But this, to my great dismay, turned out to be my own undoing.

Although the Nationwide Insurance Company denied any liability to my claim on August 7, 1980, as a result of the fire which occurred on March 16, 1980, the adjuster, Mr. Gerald J. Curran, assigned by the Sill Company to adjust my claim, did not promptly notify me of the denial or what recourse I could pursue to protect my rights to an appeal.

On March 18, 1981, about one year after our fire loss, I wrote a letter to Mr. Curran advising him that on advice of my attorney, I was terminating my agreement with the Alex N. Sill Adjustment Company because the Nationwide Insurance Company had denied liability for the fire that occurred on March 16, 1980. I also asked Mr. Curran to return all my papers, including my insurance policy.

To my great consternation, Mr. Curran called me and expressed surprise that I had not already filed an appeal against the denial of my claim as he had advised me to do in a notice he had mailed to me, stating that "a suit must be filed no later than one year from the date of loss. This means you must file before March 16, 1981."

Recovering from my initial shock, I told Mr. Curran that I had never received his so-called notification. I also asked him why he had not telephoned me on so important a matter since he had both numbers where I could be reached at home or at my place of employment. He gave me some lame excuse that he had tried calling me but was unable to reach me. I immediately became suspicious of collusion to circumvent my efforts to collect on my insurance policy with Nationwide because I worked from 8:00 a.m. to 5:00 p.m. every day and was very easy to reach during those hours. I demanded to see some evidence of the notice that Curran purportedly had mailed to me. It did indeed seem strange that I perhaps received every piece of junk mail that was ever mailed to me, but one of the most important letters in my lifetime had failed to reach me.

Enclosed with the return of my insurance policy and other papers was a copy of the notice that Curran purportedly had mailed to me. One thing in the notice, however, that perplexed me even more was the date—November 11, 1980. If the Nationwide Insurance Company denied liability to me on August 7, 1980, why did it take Curran over three months to notify me? This mystery has never been satisfactorily explained.

Of course, had I received the notice in November 1980 advising me to appeal the insurance company's decision within one year from the date of our loss, I would have beat a path to my attorney's office posthaste. But I never received any word at all from Curran or the Alex N. Sill Adjustment Company until I contacted Curran almost a year after my loss.

Being preoccupied with my pending trial did not leave me much time to think about my insurance claim. I thought I had placed the claim in good hands, much to my later chagrin and sorrow for having trusted the Alex N. Sill Company to represent my interest in the fire loss.

An attorney was recommended to me following my acquittal who was a specialist in recovering insurance claims. I retained him to represent me, and he set right to work on trying to recover my loss. The first thing he did was review all the facts of the claim and the papers pertaining to the fire loss to ascertain whether we had grounds for a lawsuit.

The attorney later pointed out to me a paragraph in my insurance policy which stated that "no suit shall be brought on this policy unless the insured has complied with all the policy provisions and has too commenced the suit within one year after the loss occurs."

The attorney went on to further advise me that the validity of the one-year suit provision had been recently upheld by the Ohio Supreme Court in a case entitled *Broadview Savings vs. Buckeye Union Insurance COT*. And the attorney who had successfully represented the insurance company in this appeal was none other than Harold Reader, the same attorney who represented Nationwide in my claim.

This dismal news of course was the worst news I could receive after losing the store's contents to the fire and having spent a considerable amount of time and money fighting the charges brought against me. To say I was "bitter" would be a euphemism for what I really felt. My mind immediately turned to thoughts of reprisals. There were ways to recoup my losses and then some if I put my mind to it—a mind that had been taught a great many angles during my days of incarceration and close association with criminal elements. I toyed with the idea only briefly before more rational thoughts entered my mind. But for those brief moments of stress and outrage, the criminal element dormant in all of mankind was awakened within me.

My attorney and I discussed the possibility of filing a lawsuit against the Alex N. Sill Adjustment Company for negligence. But after due consideration, we decided that such a suit would be futile because I did have prior knowledge of Nationwide's decision to deny me liability even though Sill had my insurance policy and other papers in their possession, which prevented me from reviewing the documents had I a mind to do so.

My attorney thought that it was shameful the way the Sill Company showed a lack of interest in making certain that I was notified of my right to appeal, and he considered the three months delay in notifying me, if in fact Mr. Curran did mail the notice, an unforgivable dereliction of duty. Still, the attorney could not come up with valid grounds for a lawsuit against Curran and the Sill Company.

Before parting, my attorney made the observation that if there was one thing more than anything else in my case that convinced him of my innocence, it was the fact that I failed to show more motivation in pursuing my insurance claim with the usual greed and diligence of a malefactor intent upon defrauding an insurance company. His confidence in my innocence made me feel good morally, but it was no balm for the painful experience that I had suffered as a result of my fire loss and the personal deprivation of additional funds spent to defend against ensuing trumped-up charges, not to mention the two years of agony and waiting to be exonerated of any wrongdoing.

I had to call upon all my courage to resist taking a drink and wreaking vengeance against those responsible for all that I had suffered. For my many years spent in prison, in association with hardened criminals, had indelibly left its mark of "the law of the jungle" on me. No matter how hard an ex-convict endeavors to redeem himself, he will always be an outcast in the eyes of society, and "the law of the jungle" lies dormant within a person for a lifetime who has been exposed to the ugliness of incarceration for long periods.

A prisoner is never completely rehabilitated. His criminal instincts can be arrested with proper guidance and training, but once he has been exposed to a life of crime and prison, he will never be free of criminal tendencies. But under normal circumstances, an ex-convict can function as trustworthily as any other citizen. It is therefore equally important that an ex-convict be treated with the same fairness and consideration as other members of society if he is to have any chance of leading a normal life once he is released from prison. Because once he feels uncontrollably frustrated and threatened by those who would do him harm, the law of the jungle will be invoked within him from its dormant state; and he will revert to basic elements and become an animal to live and act not by the law of man but by the "law of the jungle."

I had triumphed over setbacks before in prison and on the outside by channeling my resentment and frustration into constructive thoughts and action, which enabled me to accomplish almost the seemingly impossible. If I did not blow my cool now, it was possible that I could still salvage something from my recent ordeal. Some of the monetary loss could be taken off our personal income tax, and as long as I remained sober of mind with good health, I could count my blessings that I was still free to enjoy life and look to the future with optimism.

*   *   *   *   *

A funny thing happened on December 22, 1981, during the time I was making preparations for my second trial; and I don't mean funny in the amusing sense of the word.

The funny thing that happened was during the morning hours, a few blocks from the Southgate Shopping Center where Zodiac World used to be. And the funny thing was a fire almost similar to the fire that destroyed Zodiac World and the two other stores on March 16, 1980.

The fire on December 22 occurred on Northfield Road, a busy thoroughfare running through Maple Heights; and the fire, like the one that occurred at Southgate, destroyed three businesses. One was the French Quarter Restaurant and the other two were the Dial Finance Company and the Trexler Photography shop. It too apparently had smoldered for some time before erupting.

The manager of the Dial Finance Company told fire officials that he saw smoke coming through the heating register and that when he checked the back room of his place of business. he found the ceiling on fire.

The Maple Heights Fire Chief Vince Jacobs said that "the fire, which caused about a half million dollars damage, was shooting from the roof and windows at about 9:45 a.m. when the firemen arrived on the scene."[§†]

The chief was unsure about where the fire started, although the employees at the Dial Finance Company were first to spot the fire in their place and called the fire department.

The three places of business that were destroyed by the fire were joined by a false ceiling much the same as Zodiac World, Jo Ann Fabrics, and the vacant store were joined; and the flames were funneled from store to store with a chimney-like effect.

It took about sixty firefighters from Maple Heights and adjoining suburbs and over two hours to bring the fire under control and was in almost every respect reminiscent of the fire that had destroyed Zodiac World and the other stores about twenty-one months earlier. But the similarities did not end there. Because when a friend of mine

---

[§§] Source of information: *Cleveland Plain Dealer* Dec. 23, 1981.

introduced me to the owner of the French Quarter Restaurant that had been destroyed by the fire, a revelation of additional similarities unfolded that were astounding in several details.

It was reported in the press that fire Chief Jacobs at first said, "Arson is not suspected and that the Dial Finance Company was the only store occupied at the time of the fire."

The chief went on to say that "originally, the fire was thought to have started in a furnace on the roof of the finance company. Now we're not sure. Burn patterns indicate it may have started in that office."

This was the same Chief Jacobs who said almost the same thing about the fire that destroyed Zodiac World when he stated to the press that "it was first thought that the fire started in the vacant store next door to Zodiac World."¶‡

Following his same pattern of giving the press confusing information, Chief Jacobs, in another issue of the same newspaper, stated that "the fire started in the lounge of the French Quarter Restaurant near the wall next to the Dial Finance Company. From there it spread to the finance company and to Trexler's Photography Shop."***§

The circumstances here, too, were strongly similar and familiar, whereby a fire is discovered in one store only to be claimed later, after an investigation, that it started in another store. And the principal investigator at both fires was the Fire Prevention Officer of Maple Heights, Joseph Scharfenberg.

In another weekly suburban newspaper, it was printed that "fire department investigators have determined the origin but not the cause of a fire which swept through a building on Northfield Road, near Southgate Shopping Center, during the pre-noon hours last Tuesday, December 22. According to Maple Heights Fire Chief Vince Jacobs, the fire started in the French Quarter Restaurant, 5246

¶‡ Taken from a weekly suburban newspaper, the *Garfield Heights Maple Heights*, Sun., Dec. 24, 1981 issue.

**** Same Source, Dec. 31, 1981 issue.

Northfield Road. Jacobs estimated the monetary loss from the fire at $615,000."***

The pattern of similarity got further involved when I was introduced to Willy Austin, the owner of the French Quarter Restaurant. And as a result of this experience, I discovered the following facts:

- Mr. Austin had been in business only a short time—about eight months before the fire tragedy put him out of business. (I had been in business about eleven months.)
- Although the manager and his employees, as eyewitnesses to the fire, practically conceded that the fire started in the Dial Finance Company, Scharfenberg came along later and, pursuant to his investigation, determined that the fire started in the French Quarter Restaurant.
- That, like me, the owner of the restaurant was a man, and he was the first black man to ever lease a store in that particular area in Maple Heights. Like me, also, Mr. Austin had been given the impression by a white businessman that he would not be a welcomed businessman in the previously all-white business area.
- As a result of Scharfenberg's investigation, he advised Mr. Austin that he had detected a flammable liquid on the carpet in the restaurant where Scharfenberg claimed he had located the point of origin of the fire.

Fortunately for Mr. Austin, a very personable and intelligent man who enjoyed a background with no criminal past record, he was evidently spared an indictment and a trial on the flimsy evidence that Scharfenberg apparently tried to amass against him.

Mr. Austin did, however, encounter difficulty in collecting all of his fire insurance coverage. And at this writing litigation is pending to try to force collection on the "business interruption" clause in his insurance policy. Consequently, he has suffered a great financial loss

---

*** Taken from Maple Heights Press, Dec. 31, 1981 issue.

in not being able to promptly recover all of his losses or to reopen his business in Maple Heights or elsewhere.

Maybe lightning does not always strike twice in the same place. But sometimes, it can strike too close to the same place for comfort.

Epilogue

THE PEN IS TRULY MIGHTIER than the sword! If not so, how could one little seemingly insignificant nobody locked in a prison cell with no money, no political contacts and no influential or affluent friends become such a power to be reckoned with by the powerful forces in the Illinois and federal judicial systems? It would seem to be almost unbelievable, and most certainly impossible, for one to do what I did if we forget to consider the inherent fair structure and strong fiber of "justice for all" woven into the fabric of our great Constitution, which gives one citizen, no matter how insignificant and poor, the right to protest deprivation of due process of law and the equal protection of the law; and also, that one lowly, lonely citizen is licensed by that very same Constitution with a right, a duty, and an obligation to scream out to the holy high heavens his indignation in his quest for justice as guaranteed and protected by the Constitution of the United States of America.

Like a far cry in the cold, lonely, darkened wilderness, I screamed out, loud and long, until ears high in our judicial system heard and listened to my deafening, plaintive cries for justice—and the United States Supreme Court redressed my grievances not once . . . not twice . . . but thrice!

And the record of my accomplishments will stand as an example for many, many years to come as evidence that one lonely, lowly, and seemingly insignificant person can defeat the ends of tyranny and injustice no matter how high and mighty his opponents may reign in the establishment so long as the Constitution of the United States acts as a safeguard for every citizen in America.

As Alan Dershowitz pointed out in his book *The Best Defense*, "There are those who argue that on occasion illegal methods must

427

be employed to preserve the rule of law" (to prevent the guilty from going free). But in negating such a notion Dershowitz goes on to quote Justice Brandeis, "Our government is the potent, the omnipresent teacher. For good or for ill, it teaches the whole people by its example. Crime is contagious. If the government becomes a lawbreaker, it breeds contempt for the law; it invites every man to become a law unto himself". The corollary to this, of course, is that man will live by the law of the jungle if his security goes unprotected by a government ruled by law.

Quoting Dershowitz again from his book *The Best Defense*, "Here the witness Parola's testimony was shot through with lies. Yet Judge Bauman elected to believe the witness because he was a police officer."

Dershowitz went on to very correctly state in his book that "nothing could demonstrate more graphically, and more distressingly, the virtual impossibility of persuading some judges that any policeman is ever lying. Police perjury, and the way some segments of the American judiciary encourage it, is simply a fact of life that most criminal lawyers cynically accept as readily as they accept the inevitability that most defendants will also lie but will not be believed."

This reminded me of Judge Ashcraft and police officer Edward Piotter. Even after we proved conclusively that Piotter had lied, the judge called his lie a "mistake" in giving his testimony even though he was compelled to grant me a new trial.

I appreciate a man of Dershowitz's intellect, courage, and professional background—Harvard law professor, criminal lawyer, author, and appeals expert—for pointing all these things out in his praiseworthy book *The Best Defense*. So many people turn a deaf ear when a convict or ex-convict says these same things. Because they think that such statements from men of ill repute carry no weight and are self-serving in some way or another. But when men like Dershowitz state these same facts, people are more apt to sit up and listen.

I wish there were more Alan Dershowitzes in the nation. Maybe then the point would sink in that one of the greatest barriers that stands in the way of justice in this country is not the criminals but the men trusted to uphold law and order and administrate justice in accordance with the law and constitution.

Because if these men keep stepping on the law and constitution and bending it all to hell to meet their own standard of justice, and for their own immunity against wrongdoing instead of upholding the letter and spirit of the law intended, then the judicial system in this country will never work properly.

The people can insulate and protect themselves from criminals in many ways if they follow sensible precautionary rules. For people know that criminals are waiting to rob, burglarize, rape, defraud and commit other sundry crimes against society. There are alarm systems, security guards and many other methods to foil criminal activities. These methods do not always work one hundred percent – but in most cases they do work. But what if any defense do the people have to protect against the crooked cop, politician, judge or other public officials who place their hand on a Bible and swear to Almighty God to uphold the laws and constitution? None! Why? Because these officials start off gaining the people's trust and confidence. You expect them to do what they have sworn to do. They are supposed to be your friendly servants. On the other hand, a criminal in the street does not swear not to rob you, hurt you or kill you, nor does he swear to uphold the law and constitution. Now you tell me, which is the greater menace? And which is the bigger crook?

With that, dear readers, I rest my case.

Finis.

Index

(Case Law)

Brown v. Allen, 344 U.S. 443

Carter v. Illinois, 329 U. S. 173

Eaton v. Bibb, et al, 217 F.2d 446

Foster v. Illinois, 332 U. S. 134

Griffin v. Illinois, 351 U. S. 12

Jennings v. Illinois. 342 U. S. 101

Jennings v. Nester, et al, 349 U.S. 958

Johnson v. Avery, 393 U.S. 483

Loftus v. Illinois, 334 U.S. 804 & 337 U.S. 935

Marino v. Ragen, 332 U.S. 561

People v. Jennings, 144 N.E. 2d 612

People v. Griffin, 137 N.E. 2d 487

People v. Crenshaw, 155 N.E. 2d 599

People v. LaBostrie, 153 N.E. 2d 570

Rogers v. Richmond, 357 U.Sw 220

U. S. ex rel Jennings v. Ragen, 358 U.S. 276

U. S. ex rel Bongiorno v. Ragen 24 F.Supp. 973

White v. Ragen, 324 U.S. 760

Woods v. Nierstheimer, 328 U.S. 211

Young v. Ragen, 337 U.S. 235

CPSIA information can be obtained
at www.ICGtesting.com
Printed in the USA
JSHW020758010620
5983JS00001B/7